Autobiography of Values

Books by

Charles A. Lindbergh

"We"

The Culture of Organs
(*with Alexis Carrel*)

Of Flight and Life

The Spirit of St. Louis

The Wartime Journals

Boyhood on the Upper Mississippi

Autobiography of Values

Charles A.

Autc

of

Editor: William Jovanovich
Coeditor: Judith A. Schiff

Lindbergh

Biography

Values

 Harcourt Brace Jovanovich

New York and London

Printed in the United States of America

Library of Congress Cataloging in Publication Data
Lindbergh, Charles Augustus, 1902-1974.
Autobiography of values.
Bibliography: p.
Includes index.
1. Lindbergh, Charles Augustus, 1902-1974.
2. Air-pilots—United States—Biography. I. Title.
TL540.L5A27   1978   629.13′092′4 [B]   77-7873
ISBN 0-15-110202-3

First edition

B C D E

Contents

CONTENTS

Illustrations

All the pictures are from the Lindbergh Papers, Yale University Library, except those otherwise credited below.

Between pages 74 and 75

Evangeline Lodge Land
Charles August Lindbergh
Charles Augustus Lindbergh
With Fluff
On a hunting expedition
At age six, with his mother
At age eleven, with his father
With his dog Dingo
Grandfather Charles H. Land
The Lindbergh farm home
At White House Easter egg rolling
The old Ford
With his motorcycle
With ROTC pistol team
Commission in U.S. Army Air Service
During flying-cadet days
With Bud Gurney

Between pages 138 and 139

Taking off on a test flight
After bailing out
The vital parachute
Flying the mail
Transferring the mail
Relaxing in Panama
Wing of *Spirit of St. Louis*
Posing for the press
Mrs. Lindbergh visiting her son
On return from Latin-American tour

ILLUSTRATIONS

With Ambassador Herrick in Paris
In ticker-tape parade up Broadway
With the Coolidges and his mother
Raymond Orteig awarding the Orteig Prize
In 1927

Between pages 202 and 203

Christmas at the Morrows' home
During Missouri National Guard maneuvers
    Department of the Air Force
On first trip to Mexico
At National Air Races
    Department of the Air Force
Charles and Anne after their marriage
About to join search for missing plane
Exploring cliff dwellings
With Juan Trippe in British Guiana
Ready for flight tests
In Japan
On floodwaters by Nanking's wall
Arriving at Nanking
Leaving Shetland Islands
At Karachi
Greeting Russian fliers in Moscow

Between pages 266 and 267

Working with Alexis Carrel
At rocket test with Guggenheim **and Goddard**
Visiting Igor Sikorsky
In Germany with Truman Smith
Testing effects of altitude at Mayo Clinic
After going on active duty as a colonel
With MacDonald and McGuire in the South Pacific
On round-the-world inspection tour
Conferring with Boeing staff
Receiving the Guggenheim medal
At Glenn L. Martin Company
With Juan Salcedo, Jr., in the Philippines
With Juan Trippe and Harold Gray
Agta huts on Luzon
With Elizalde and Fox on Mindanao
With drawing of perfusion pump
In a Taboli hut

ILLUSTRATIONS

Maps

Foreword

When he telephoned the morning of August fourteenth, a Wednesday, Charles Lindbergh said, "It is time we talked. Can you come to Columbia Presbyterian?" It was 1974. He was seventy-two years old. Several months earlier at my office on Third Avenue, he met in passing another friend of mine, a surgeon who is writing his memoirs. The surgeon was surprised that I did not know Charles was dying; he observed the signs of the cancer Lymphoma immediately.

He sought no assistance and was made uncomfortable by sympathy, and he would not credit physical disability in himself. All his life he had been lean, agile, graceful; he never drank coffee or alcohol or smoked tobacco, and, despite his quick and restless intellect, was not anxious and slept soundly. At seventy he looked almost as he did at thirty except for balding: his physical presence was assuring, as if he bore promises for all others.

At the hospital he spoke of his memoirs and asked that I read about four hundred pages of manuscript in various drafts to determine "whether it is any good and if it should be published." That evening I began and stayed the whole night reading and rereading, and when I returned I told him the book remarkably conjoined the events of his life with reflections and speculations. Like *The Spirit of St. Louis,* it was written surely and with distinction: Charles Lindbergh was a superb writer. He accepted my comments as a warrant to proceed but described the difficulty in publishing caused by his present situation.

Altogether there were more than two thousand pages of manuscript: several drafts of some chapters; sections of two or three pages or a few paragraphs; and notes that he called "sketches." About one half of the work was in the hospital room inside the brown bag he used as his sole piece of luggage as he traveled around the world over the past thirty years; the remainder was at his house in Darien or in locked files at Yale University, where a good part of the Lindbergh archives are kept. Anne Morrow Lindbergh, who was constantly at the hospital but withdrew occasionally as we talked during the last four days, told me that she had read little of the memoirs because her husband was waiting to complete it. Charles put the question plainly: how was the manuscript to be made whole if he could not continue?

He reached an answer after two days of intermittent discussion during which I drew up an author's contract and drafted a letter to the Trustees of Yale. His instructions were these: I should act as editor as well as publisher; in the event of my death one of my sons should complete the editing; I should use variously the several drafts without being bound by the dates of their composition and thus establish a sequence; finally, I must inform the reader that while the work was his own, parts of the text were subject to editing consistent with his purpose. This request I seek to fulfill here.

He did not live to redact the account of his life in relation to the values he held as an aviator, scientist, adviser to enterprise and government, soldier, conservationist, and writer. The editing of the manuscript was intricate and worrying and I spent about six hundred hours on it over a period of two years, carrying hundreds of pages on trips to Hawaii, where I saw his grave, to Quebec and London and Majorca and Florida. The cutting of the manuscript and the insertion of words and phrases and punctuation to make bridges between certain sections are my sole responsibility. I was greatly aided by my coeditor, Judith Schiff, and by a tireless and skilled colleague, Roberta Leighton, and by Margaret Mary McQuillan and Susan Weinstock.

On Friday, two days before he flew to Hawaii, where he died

eight days later, Charles Lindbergh said suddenly: "Do you think I am dying well?" "Yes," I replied. "That's good," he said. "You would know." The next morning I came to the hospital at six-thirty and met in the corridor a physician, who said in distress that there was a chance his patient could die in the air. Of course Charles Lindbergh knew that and knew, too, that death chooses its venue. In the ambulance he apologized for the early hour and explained he must catch the flight to Honolulu while there was time. His wife and sons Jon and Scott met him at Idlewild on his firm insistence—he opposed waste in logistics—that they could easier proceed to the plane from Connecticut. His family waited in the closed-off first-class section while he was brought aboard by two stretcher-bearers. As they made ready to swing him from a stretcher to the bed made up over two seats, Charles said, "I know you are strong fellows but let my friend here hold my middle: I am pretty tall." After that I bent over and kissed him twice and never saw him again.

He has been called the last American hero. He disliked such soubriquets. Yet one can only conclude that Charles Lindbergh was a leader without followers. His life, told in this book, is altogether singular but profoundly characteristic. There cannot be another like it.

WILLIAM JOVANOVICH

A few weeks after the death of Charles A. Lindbergh, I first learned of the existence of the *Autobiography of Values*. His previous books described mainly his early life and World War II activities, but his collected papers in the Yale University Library included myriad notes and chapter drafts, some written as early as 1938, which promised a work of much greater scope. The fascinating and sometimes perplexing array constituted an unfinished legacy. As archivist of historical manuscripts at Yale, I first met General Lindbergh in 1963 and had assisted him and Mrs. Lindbergh in special projects involving their papers. Few persons were granted permission to consult the restricted collection. It was a great privilege to delve into the letters, documents, and photographs that provide a detailed record of the Lindbergh family experience and document many aspects of modern American history. Consequently, I was delighted to learn that the promise had been fulfilled, and to be asked to take part in a final project on General Lindbergh's behalf by helping to prepare the autobiography for publication.

When I received a complete photocopy of the contents of the twenty-four thick envelopes containing the autobiography and related notes from William Jovanovich, I began by assembling them according to Lindbergh's most recent outline. There were nearly one thousand typed pages of text and perhaps twice that number of pages of handwritten and typed notes. The date and place headings on most notes provide in themselves an interesting record of the odyssey during which the autobiography evolved: from "May 13 '56. PPA Clipper—DC-6B, Dakar-Lisbon" to "April 5, 1974 (PA-1; Los Angeles-Honolulu)." The reason for the long time span of its writing is given in a note from about 1960: "Life is like a landscape. You live in the midst of it, but can describe it only from the vantage point of distance."

The manuscript was nearly complete, but included a number of repetitious accounts and the author's queries to himself. After reading the notes, many of which were organized in a dated series of over two hundred pages titled "Incidents of Memory and for Further Thought," I realized that the repetitions were deliberate reworkings of an event in various contexts. In 1964, Lindbergh drew up the following list, headed "on writing autobiography":

> The need of living and experiencing the incident again
> Collection & listing of scattered incidents (largely from memory)
> Boiling down in thought
> Importance of subconscious
> Memory clarifying, like spinning a web—one event clarifies
>   & brings out others
> Time essential for correlation and mellowing.

For him, "thinking by writing and by the necessary redrafts" was perhaps not only a stage in the completion of the composition but also a guide to the conduct of his life.

> Writing through time—letting life grow into the chapters—watching the underlying character unfold, like an embryo whose characteristics can be discovered only by allowing them to unfold.

Lindbergh's final stage of composition would be to select and condense, for "History is as limitless as space. To be interesting it must be selected and condensed—like a planet."

His papers began to come to Yale in 1940, just thirteen years after the flight to Paris. On October 3, 1940, at the invitation of the Yale Chapter of the America First Committee, Lindbergh explained his anti-interventionist stand to an overflow audience at the university's largest hall. After acquiring the signed manuscript of his speech for the library, the University Librarian asked if related correspondence might also be deposited. Lindbergh agreed and began to send to the library his mail from the public and his writings. In July 1941, Colonel and Mrs. Lindbergh formally placed all of the collected personal papers in their possession in the custody of Yale. During the next twenty-three years, Lindbergh continued to add substantial groups of papers, usually carrying them into the library in large wicker suitcases and personally filing them away. By 1974, the collection had grown to over six hundred linear feet of letters, business papers, family records, photographs, memorabilia, and special subject files.

A smaller, but highly important, collection of Lindbergh papers had earlier been deposited in the Missouri Historical Society. To verify the sequence of events concerning Lindbergh's vain efforts to convince the Du Pont Corporation of the potential value of rocket research in 1929 (probably the most active year of his life), it was necessary to consult those papers. In St. Louis, with the help of Frances Stadler, Archivist of the Society, I examined the core of Lindbergh's papers covering the period 1927–1933. These papers complement the large collection of awards, gifts, and memorabilia that Lindbergh presented to the people of St. Louis in appreciation of their sponsoring the construction and the flight of the *Spirit of St. Louis*. (In the Lindbergh exhibition hall are the flying suit and his grandfather's watch that he wore on the flight.)

In Minnesota, where my research was thoughtfully aided by Russell Fridley, Director of the Minnesota Historical Society, I examined the papers of Lindbergh's father, Charles A. Lindbergh, Sr., and his grandfather August Lindbergh, a Swedish political reformer who settled on the Minnesota frontier in 1859. I spent one golden early fall day at the Lindbergh State Park and Interpretive Center in Little Falls, where stands the restored boyhood home of Charles Lindbergh. I gained new insight into the formation of Lindbergh's character as I viewed the reconstructed suspension bridge built by him as a boy, the tame chipmunks at the kitchen door, and the countless acorns underfoot which for Lindbergh came to symbolize life's mystery and selectivity. I was fortunate to dine with Mrs. Eva Lindbergh Christie Spaeth, the elder half-sister of Charles Lindbergh, who graciously shared with me many family stories.

I wish to acknowledge the gracious assistance of Mrs. Anne Morrow Lindbergh. She provided photographs from her personal collection for illustrations here. Above all, I wish to express my deep appreciation to my coeditor, William Jovanovich, for inviting me to join him in the project, and thereby opening a door to a new realm of experience for me as an archivist and editor. I have enjoyed and learned much from our co-operative enterprise and from his wide knowledge of history and his editorial expertise, matched by a deep sense of purpose, as well as a sense of humor. Mr. Jovanovich's friendship and loyalty to the memory of Charles Lindbergh inspired his determination to produce a work that would match the standards of accuracy and completeness and candor Lindbergh set for himself.

JUDITH ANN SCHIFF
Yale University Library

Chronology

1859   Father, Charles A. Lindbergh, Sr., is born in Sweden; family emigrates to the United States

1883   Father graduates from University of Michigan Law School; settles in Little Falls, Minnesota

1887   Father marries Mary LaFond

1898   Mary Lindbergh dies

1901   Father marries Evangeline Land

1902   Charles A. Lindbergh, Jr. is born, on Feb. 4

1906   Father is elected to U.S. Congress

1912   Attends his first air meet

1916   Drives to California with his mother

1917   Father leaves office to oppose U.S. entry into World War I

1918   Is excused from senior year of high school to operate family farm for war effort

1920   Enrolls in University of Wisconsin as engineering student

1922   Leaves college in February to become flying student at Nebraska Standard Aircraft Corporation; makes first flight, Apr. 9

1923   Buys first plane, a war-surplus Curtiss Jenny; goes barnstorming

1924   Enlists as U.S. Army flying cadet; father dies in May

1925   Graduates first in class from U.S. Air Service Flying School, Kelly Field, San Antonio; is commissioned second lieutenant in Air Service Reserve Corps; becomes Chief Pilot, Robertson Aircraft Co., St. Louis

1926   Makes first Chicago–to–St. Louis airmail flight

1927   Establishes transcontinental air record, San Diego to New York, May 10–12; May 20–21 flies from New York to Paris and wins Orteig Prize for first nonstop transatlantic flight between these cities; is awarded first Distinguished Flying Cross; tours U.S. with *Spirit of St. Louis,* making 82 stops in 48 states; makes first nonstop flight from Washington to Mexico City; is awarded Medal of Honor by act of Congress

1928   Completes air tour of Latin America; begins service as consultant to Transcontinental Air Transport and to Pan American Airways

1929   Marries Anne Morrow; inaugurates first transcontinental air passenger service; meets Robert Goddard and works to fund rocket research

1930–34   Develops perfusion pump with Dr. Alexis Carrel

1931   Makes flight across North Pacific to China with Anne

1932   First son is kidnapped

1933   Makes Atlantic survey flight and trip to Russia with Anne

1935   Richard Hauptmann is tried, and convicted, for kidnapping; in December moves, with family, to England

1936   Makes first of five trips to Germany to investigate and evaluate air power

1937   Flies to India with Anne

1938   Moves to Illiec Island, off the coast of France

1939   Returns with family to U.S.

1939–41   Speaks against U.S. intervention in war in Europe

1942   Becomes technical consultant for bomber production to Ford Motor Company.

1942–43   Serves as test pilot and aviation consultant

1944   Flies fifty combat missions in South Pacific while serving with Navy and Marines as adviser on fighter planes

1945   Is member of naval technical mission to study Germany's missile and aircraft developments

1946   Is consultant for University of Chicago Ordnance Research Project (CHORE)

1947–54   Serves as special adviser to Air Force

1949   Is awarded Wright Brothers Memorial Trophy

1954   Is appointed to rank of brigadier general; is awarded Pulitzer Prize for *The Spirit of St. Louis*

1954–74   Goes on conservation and wildlife preservation expeditions

1965   Redesigns perfusion pump for Naval Medical Research Institute

1966–72   Serves on World Wildlife Board of Trustees

1968   Addresses Alaska Legislature, first public speech in twenty-seven years

1969   Is awarded Baruch Conservation Prize for 1968

1969–72   Is member of Citizens Advisory Committee on Environmental Quality

1974   Dies on Maui, Hawaii, on August 26. Buried at Kipahulu.

Autobiography of Values

ONE

Life Stream

The age of seventy gives one a vantage point from which to look back on the values of a lifetime. With health, one is still close enough to life to feel its surgings and close enough to death to see beyond one's passions.

I find myself at a vantage point in human evolution as well as my personal life. Born at the beginning of the exponentially advancing twentieth century A.D., I have experienced more change in the environment of man than took place during all previous centuries since civilization began—as though the impact of thousands of years had been upon a single individual.

Many men and women now living have of course experienced this change, but the circumstances of my life gave me an extraordinary opportunity both to watch it and to take part in it. Can I pass on ideas and define values that are of benefit to others? In contemplating and writing, I can at least for myself clarify them.

Life's values originate in circumstances over which the individual has no control. I was born a child of man, in the city of Detroit, on February 4, 1902, of Swedish, English, Irish, and Scottish ancestry. The great forces of science and technology had already been loosed, but horses still dominated the streets and Orville Wright had not yet made the first power-sustained airplane flight.

My mother's home was in Detroit before she went to Minnesota to teach chemistry and there met and married my father, a lawyer, and settled down on a farm on the west bank of the Mississippi River near the town of Little Falls. Her father, Charles Henry Land, was a dentist and inventor. Her mother came from the Lodge family, several of whose members were doctors. Dr. Edwin Lodge presided at my birth. A few weeks afterward, my mother and I returned to our Minnesota farm.

The first values of my memory naturally centered on food, on seeking attention, and on toys. My toys particularly manifested the history and adventure of the period. I had both horse-drawn vehicles and automobiles, leaden Indians with bows and arrows and soldiers with rifles. These toys merged almost daily with the reality of life. One of my steam engines whistled and powered a tiny saw. When the wind was right, the whistle of a sawmill up the river reached my ears. I used to sit beside my mother in our buggy while she drove Crook back and forth to town, and I remember excited adult voices calling me to a front north window to watch an automobile pass by.

There were neither Indians nor soldiers in the area of Little Falls. The one had been confined to reservations, and the other was therefore no longer needed to maintain security. I learned that I was living one generation beyond the Minnesota frontier, but my father's stories brought it vividly to my mind and entered into the clashes I staged between leaden Indians and soldiers.

My father grew up on the frontier. His parents had brought him there from Sweden when he was six months old. They staked out a homestead and from it axed a clearing and plowed a field. His early boyhood had been spent in constant fear of Indians and reliance upon soldiers. On one occasion when the Sioux had taken the warpath, my grandfather abandoned his homestead and with his family fled by oxcart to the fort at Saint Cloud. A massacre of settlers took place in a village to the south, and reasonable security was not regained until soldiers came with their rifles.

Guns played a big part in the values of my boyhood. The soldiers' guns had saved my grandfather's homestead farm. On that farm, my father's guns had kept the family supplied with deer meat and game birds, for he had been appointed the hunter, while his younger brother split wood and did other household chores and his older half-brother helped with haying and heavy work. At the age of six, I was given a twenty-two-caliber rifle. I owned a twelve-gauge shotgun before I was old and strong enough to hold it steadily to my shoulder. I often hunted with my father, although game in that part of Minnesota was getting scarce; we usually brought back a few ducks or partridges or prairie chickens, but we never saw a deer or a bear.

During early years of my life, I lived under the influence of three environments: our farm and town, my grandfather's Detroit laboratory, and the city of Washington, D.C., where my father served for ten years in the Congress and where I attended school. My interests were divided between the farm and the laboratory, for I disliked school and had little curiosity about the politics of Washington.

I loved the farm, with its wooded river and creek banks, its tillage and crops, and its cattle and horses. I was fascinated by the laboratory's magic: the intangible power found in electrified wires, the liquids that could dissolve either metal or stone, the lenses through which one could see the unseeable. Instinctively I was drawn to the farm, intellectually to the laboratory. Here began a conflict between values of instinct and intellect that was carried through my entire life, and that I eventually recognized as inherent in my civilization.

In any child's environment, and perhaps regardless of it, there comes a time when questions first arise about values of death, religion, and God. I do not recall how the concept of God formed in my mind, any more than I recall learning to speak and understand the English language. When God first appeared in my memory, he was linked with death. When you died, you went to God and he took care of you. He was good, all-powerful. He had created life and the earth, the sun, and the stars. He should therefore be worshiped. When I was old enough to understand the Bible, I would understand more about God.

But, I wondered, if God is so good, why did he make you die? Why should he not let you live forever? There was nothing good about death; it was terrible. I thought of chickens whose heads I saw chopped off—the spurting blood, the body's violent kicking and flapping. Of course that did not happen to people. People got sick or old and went to bed and then life just left them—but they

5

were as dead as the chickens. Their bodies were taken to church, where the minister talked about God, and then buried in a cemetery. Something called "the Spirit" went on living. That was the way God wanted it to be.

Hanging on a wall of my grandfather's operating room was a framed drawing of an apelike man who lived more than a hundred thousand years ago. He represented a step in human evolution, for scientific discoveries showed that in past epochs we had been four-legged animals, my grandfather said. Of course if that was true, the Bible story about how God created Adam and Eve was wrong. Maybe all our ideas about God were wrong.

As I lost confidence in the Bible, I gained confidence in science. Each year new discoveries were made, new miracles were produced —as my own grandfather invented porcelain teeth. Man knew much more than he had ever known in the past and his knowledge was increasing rapidly. He saw farther out to the stars and farther into the atom. With his radiotelegraphy he communicated all over the world in an instant. With his medicine and surgery he cured diseases of the body that had been fatal in previous generations. Was it not possible that through science he could achieve eternal life? If man could do that, he would not need God.

In 1912, my father bought a Ford Model T automobile, which my mother christened with the undignified name "Maria" (pronounced like rye). For me, Maria brought modern science to our farm, and nothing else attracted me as much, or was as challenging or as symbolic of the future.

I learned to drive the next summer, at the age of eleven. It was before the time of licenses and age requirements. Tearing over roads at many times the speed of horses, I explored areas of Minnesota that before had been beyond my range. Fixing tire punctures, adjusting the carburetor and coil points, watching garage mechanics disassemble the engine to replace a connecting rod or to chip out carbon and grind valves, confirmed my growing desire to become an engineer and take part in the world's unprecedented progress.

Maria's engine was hard to start because at eleven, and even twelve, I did not have enough weight to spin the hand crank. In cold weather, I would bring boiling water from our wood stove to fill the radiator—often two or three times, before the cylinders sputtered enough to keep their pistons pumping. But advancing science soon produced electric batteries and self-starters for automobiles. In 1915, my father sold my beloved Maria and bought a Saxon-Six, with full electrical equipment. I no longer needed to spin a hand crank or adjust the brilliance of calcium-carbide headlights by the rate of dripping water.

With the Saxon came the greatest adventure of my life up to that time. In 1916, after I had chauffeured my father on some of his political campaign trips, my mother and I decided to drive to California for the winter. I could complete my junior year of high school there before we returned the next summer. It would be a wonderful experience, my mother said, and add importantly to my education.

We reached California that year, but did so far behind schedule. The trip took more than a month. There were rainy days in Missouri when mud collected on the Saxon's wheels until we could not move. Frozen ruts in New Mexico slowed us down to a speed of less than ten miles an hour, as did Arizona desert sand. Frequent trouble with our car's semicantilever springs delayed us for hours that added up to days. When we finally arrived and rented a cottage on the beach at Redondo, I was weeks late for school. I had always been late for the start of school. Maybe that was why my marks averaged so low.

During our winter in California, our values were affected by the war raging in Europe. The United States's position of neutrality in the beginning months of the war soon shifted rapidly to intervention. Hundreds of thousands, maybe millions, of American soldiers would be sent abroad to fight. It was a staggering concept to a people who had felt itself immune to wars beyond the oceans. In our family, one of my uncles became subject to the draft; in a few years, I would be.

Another crisis hastened our return to Minnesota. A letter arrived saying that my grandmother Land was hopelessly ill. I did not wait for classes to end. We started eastward as soon as the roads were dry enough for automobile travel. Again, the trip took us more than a month.

In the fall of 1917, at Little Falls, I began my senior year of high school. For me, graduation was doubtful because as usual my marks averaged low and the distractions of automobile and farm made studying difficult. The war came to my rescue. Even as farm hands of draft age were being called to service, the cows had to be milked and crops planted and harvested. One day in general assembly our principal announced that any boy who wanted to work on a farm would be excused from his studies and graduated without having to take examinations. I was among the first to leave school.

My father felt it a patriotic duty to use our farm for the wartime production of foods. I could take charge of running it, he said, and he had an old Norwegian friend, a former lumberjack, who would help me. To start out, my father bought a carload of cattle and sheep—hogs, chickens, ducks, and geese would come later. With my father, I laid plans to mechanize the farm. I ordered a tractor and a gang plow and finally a milking machine; all such "contraptions" were novelties to neighboring farmers. My intention was to farm until I reached the age of eighteen and then enlist in the Army Air Service to become a scout pilot. I knew that flying a scout in war was extremely dangerous, but I had become so fascinated by airplanes that danger seemed a secondary consideration.

America's entry into Europe proved decisive. The end of the war, in November 1918, brought an end to my war plans. My mind was forced to consider the dreary prospects of college. I would farm for one more year, I decided, and then begin the study of mechanical engineering. The farm, I realized with concern, attracted me much more than a university degree.

The record of my satisfactory graduation at Little Falls's high school was accepted by the University of Wisconsin, where I entered as a freshman engineering student in the fall of 1920. It did not take my instructors long to discover my deficiencies in knowledge and my inability to concentrate on studying. They put me on academic probation. Even so, at Wisconsin I had my first experience with the values of military life, as an ROTC Field Artillery cadet. I enjoyed the ROTC course, partly because I was immediately accepted as a member of both rifle and pistol teams. The amount of time I spent in the rifle gallery did not benefit my academic marks, but our teams won first place for Wisconsin in the national university ROTC competition; and in an individual shooting match, I won first place on the team.

Soon after the start of my sophomore year I realized that I would be dropped from the university. My chemistry notebook was far behind; I had not kept up in mathematics; my English papers were returned with such professorial notations as "A for composition, reduced to C— for punctuation and spelling." I decided to leave before I received notification of dismissal. My greatest regret lay in leaving the ROTC.

What would I do now that school life was over? The time had come when I must enter a profession and support myself. Aviation attracted me above all else. For months, I had been assembling flying-school catalogs. One of them offered training at Lincoln, Nebraska, for five hundred dollars. It was a price my father and mother could afford, and to me the name "Nebraska" was full of romance. I enrolled with the Nebraska Standard Aircraft Corporation for flying instruction in the spring of 1922.

My early flying seemed an experience beyond mortality. There was the earth spreading out below me, a planet where I had lived but from which I had astonishingly risen. It had been the home of my body. I felt strangely apart from my body in the plane. I was never more aware of all existence, never less aware of myself. Mine was a god's-eye view. But as my hours in the air increased in number, I lost the keenness of that early vision. With piloting expertness, I looked vertically down on people and trees and houses as I had looked at them levelly before, and I felt as connected to my body in an airplane as in a motorcar.

In the spring of 1923, in Georgia, I bought a salvaged World War I training plane, a Curtiss Jenny, and began barnstorming the countryside. In the Jenny I could carry only one passenger; still, I managed to make a living and even put away a little money each month. Its OX-5 engine was underpowered for the average farm pasture I landed on, but that fact developed in me piloting skills I could not have otherwise achieved. The Jenny's lack of power also prompted my return to Army life.

On a barnstorming expedition in southern Minnesota, I learned that the Army was accepting flying cadets at schools near San

Antonio, Texas. The Hispano-Suiza engines in postwar Army training planes had twice the power of my OX-5, and the Liberty engines in observation planes were four times stronger. Cadets flew both types. I disliked the idea of enlisting as a cadet when I was already a competent pilot, but the thought of climbing into the sky with a four-hundred-horsepower Liberty attached to the throttle overcame my reluctance. I was also impressed that at the end of a year flying cadets were graduated as second lieutenants in reserve. Because I believed that a country's security depended on its army, I would proudly wear a commissioned officer's uniform, and welcome the call to duty in case of war. I applied for and received the appointment, flew to Texas, and enlisted as a cadet in March of 1924.

I had expected to spend most of my time piloting and working with airplanes. It shocked me to learn that every weekday afternoon would be spent in "ground school," that more than seventy subjects were to be taught before graduation, and that the examinations were stiff—to fail more than two subjects caused you to be "washed out" of the school. My shock was greater when my first two examination papers were returned with barely passing marks.

Of course low marks were not new to me, but marks had not meant much before. I had not felt it important to graduate from high school or college. Now, the value of flying Army aircraft and receiving an officer's commission seemed greater than anything else in my life. Obviously, I would have to develop a different attitude about studying, or else I would be washed out. I concluded that the surest way of passing all seventy-plus examinations would be to strive for the highest marks I could get. I began studying as I had never studied before—evenings, weekends, sometimes in the washroom after bed check far into the night. When I graduated in March 1925, I had the highest standing in my class. The Army schools had taught me how to study. In the latter months of the cadet course, I achieved my ambition to become a scout pilot, for I was assigned to the branch of military aviation called "pursuit." That allowed me to fly the single-cockpit SE-5s and MB-3s in sham combat and fire their guns on tow targets.

On graduating I applied for a commission in the Regular Army, but before obtaining one I accepted the position of chief pilot on the airmail route between St. Louis and Chicago that was soon to be inaugurated. Responsibility for the airmail brought a halt to my itinerant flying and gave me what appeared to be a permanent home. With this in mind, I enlisted in the 110th Observation Squadron of the Missouri National Guard, which was stationed on Lambert Field, near St. Louis. I received a first lieutenant's commission immediately, and a few months later, a captain's.

While piloting the night mail in the fall of 1926, I envisioned a nonstop flight between New York and Paris across the Atlantic. I believed that airplanes and engines had advanced to a point where such a flight was practicable, and I was convinced that the broad experience I had gained as a civil and military pilot put me in a good position to organize and execute it. It would be an extraordinary adventure and, if successful, help to advance the cause of aviation, to which I was devoted.

On May 20, 1927, after months of concentrated effort, frustration, and the threat of probable failure, I flew from New York to Paris in a single-cockpit, single-engine monoplane christened *Spirit of St. Louis*. I had spent twenty-three hours without sleep when I took off, and obviously there would be no opportunity to sleep before I landed. My lack of sleep turned out to be the most difficult and dangerous factor of the flight, but it resulted in an inner experience that, like the experience of my first ascents in Nebraska, seemed to penetrate beyond mortality.

There comes a point when the body's demand for sleep is harder to endure than any other pain I have encountered, when it results in a state of semiconsciousness in which an awareness exists that is less acute but apparently more universal than that of the normal mind. Before my flight was halfway finished, I found that I could not force myself to stay awake through will power. The rational mind I had previously known and relied upon had less and less effect on my body's responses. There were lengthening periods when it even lost the knowledge of its own existence, when an intelligence without the need for reason had replaced it.

Over and over again on the second day of my flight, I would return to mental alertness sufficiently to realize that I had been flying while I was neither asleep nor awake. My eyes had been open. I had responded to my instruments' indications and held generally to compass course, but I had lost sense of circumstance and time. During immeasurable periods, I seemed to extend outside my plane and body, independent of worldly values, appreciative of beauty, form, and color without depending upon my eyes. It was an experience in which both the intellectual and sensate were replaced by what might be termed a matterless awareness. It was the only occasion in my life when I saw and conversed with ghosts.

They appeared suddenly in the tail of the fuselage while I was flying through fog. I saw them clearly although my eyes were staring straight ahead. Transparent, mistlike, with semihuman form, they moved in and out through the fabric walls at will. One or two of them would come forward to converse with me and then rejoin the group behind. I can still see those phantoms clearly in memory, but after I landed at Paris I could not remember a single word they said.

Hallucinations can result from extreme fatigue and subconscious ravings from a sleepless brain. My visions are easily explained away through reason, but the longer I live, the more limited I believe rationality to be. I have found that the irrational gives man insight he cannot otherwise attain.

Certainly my visions in the *Spirit of St. Louis* entered into the reality of my life, for they stimulated thought along new lines: thought enters into both the creation and the definition of reality. Had not my vision in a mail plane resulted in the reality of my New York–to–Paris flight, just as the flight itself resulted in further visions? I recognized that vision and reality interchange, like energy and matter.

My desire to sleep had vanished when I reached the Irish coast, almost directly on course and well ahead of my estimated landfall. Tail winds increased the cruising speed of the *Spirit of St. Louis* and brought me to Paris only thirty-three and a half hours after take-off. I had broken the world's record for an airplane's nonstop flight. I had, in fact, enough fuel in my tanks to fly another thousand miles.

I was unprepared for the world acclaim that followed my landing at Le Bourget Aerodrome. Since my arrival was after ten o'clock at night and few people had thought I would succeed in reaching Paris, I expected to be welcomed by French aviators, perhaps talk to a small group of reporters, and, after my plane had been put in a hangar, inquire about a hotel. I had concentrated so intensely on the preparation and execution of the flight that I had thought little about what I would do after landing. I had no way of knowing that thousands of men and women were at the field waiting for me, and that approaching roads were blocked with automobiles bringing thousands more.

I awoke in a room in the American Embassy the next morning to a new environment. When I went to bed I had not noticed the pillows' lacy edges or the furniture's tapestry. A glass of fresh orange juice stood within arm's reach, and a warm bath had been drawn by the valet. My breakfast would arrive on a tray in a few minutes, he said. Ambassador Herrick wanted to see me, and a crowd demanding my appearance had assembled on the street.

The following days were filled with parades, lunches, dinners, and other ceremonies. I was greeted by the President of France, Gaston Doumergue, by Marshal Ferdinand Foch, and by the famed French flier Louis Blériot. Invitations from American states and from European countries poured in. I accepted one from Belgium, and another from England. At Brussels, King Albert came to the airdrome and asked me to show him the *Spirit of St. Louis*. In London, at Buckingham Palace, I talked to King George about my flight.

I had hoped to visit Sweden and Germany, to spend several weeks in Europe, and then to return to the United States either by crossing the Atlantic Ocean westward or by flying on around the world. But while I was in London, the American Ambassador informed me that President Coolidge had ordered a warship to carry me back home.

The success of my New York–to–Paris flight forced a reconsideration of my most fundamental values. Previously, I had been following the career of a professional civilian pilot who held National Guard and Army Reserve commissions. I expected to devote my life to flying and aeronautical activities, for I was making a good living and no other occupation attracted me as much. Now, tens of thousands of telegrams, letters, and verbally conveyed messages included business propositions by which I could make huge sums of money. I was offered fifty thousand dollars to endorse publicly a cigarette, half a million dollars plus ten percent of gross to star in a motion picture. Lecture bureaus would guarantee me an income for a single lecture of many times what I could make annually as a mail pilot. I was advised that if I would enter a political career, there was a good chance I could eventually become president.

What really meant most to me—the development of aviation, or the millions I could make? When I considered the question carefully, I realized that money would always be minor to the other terms of the life I led. I decided to continue concentrating on the development of aviation.

After receptions in Washington, New York, St. Louis, and Ottawa, I spent three months touring the United States with the *Spirit of St. Louis,* landing and speaking at least once in every state in the union. I talked about the tremendous development of aviation I believed was coming, advocated the construction of airports and the inauguration of air routes. In December of 1927, I flew nonstop from Washington to Mexico City, and then around the Gulf of Mexico and the Caribbean Sea, studying the requirements for scheduled air services to Central and South America and through the West Indian islands.

In the spring of 1928, at Washington, I turned the *Spirit of St. Louis* over to the Smithsonian Institution for permanent exhibition. Thereafter, as a consultant to the Transcontinental Air Transport Corporation and to Pan American Airways, I began concentrating on the development of commercial aviation. It seemed obvious to me that the development of air routes would take place in three major steps: transcontinental routes, intercontinental routes, and transoceanic routes. My consulting positions let me proceed along all three.

The establishment of air routes required a great deal of survey flying. The low cruising speeds of that period gave me plenty of time for contemplation between points of take-off and destination. My mind would wander without limit through fields of memory and fantasy, returning at intervals to meet problems of the moment—thereby causing the present, past, and future to converge. Emerging from my contemplation were two areas of extraordinary interest. One related to aviation's progress, the other to the quality and mystery of life.

I tried to foresee the airplane's development through years to come. Since its speed was limited by the propeller's grip on air, a way might be found to transform fuel into thrust without using a propeller. The only possibility I could think of lay in rockets, like those I had shot skyward in boyhood on the Fourth of July. Thinking of rockets extended my vision from air into space. Through the centuries, man had developed the wheel to travel over land, the hull to sail across water, and the wing to fly through air. Only space remained unconquered. Might the rocket make it possible for him to travel through space? My decision to look into the potentialities of rockets brought me eventually to know a professor of physics named Robert Goddard.

Before I met Goddard, no scientist or engineer I talked to believed rockets would be practical either for aircraft or for flights into space. Goddard said a rocket could be built that would reach the moon, and that jet propulsion could be used advantageously to power airplanes. The thought of sending a rocket to the moon set my mind spinning. If man could reach to the moon, then why not thence to the planets, even to the stars? My interest in Goddard's accomplishments and ideas began a collaboration and friendship that continued until his death. Throughout, I was able to help him obtain essential funds for his experiments.

Imagining a trip through the stars was fascinating, but it raised problems that seemed beyond human ability to solve. At maximum foreseeable rocket speeds, a man's life would be over before he could get much more than started on his way to the nearest star. What might be done to postpone the stroke of death? Might men learn to hibernate through years, as animals do over winter? How long could one live in a state of hibernation? Could a way be found to freeze the body without killing it? These questions penetrated the second area of my interest: the quality and mystery of life.

The concern I felt as a child over death and God had remained in the background during my early flying career. Now, it pressed forward in more mature and implemented thought. Why could not aging be prevented or at least postponed through the use of chemicals and special foods? If the arteries and veins of an old man and a youth were so connected that the blood flowing through them was both old and young, what would be the result? Scientists had already learned to control elements of life and death that in the past had been considered subject only to God's will. Surely still greater control would come in the future. I began studying textbooks in biology, cytology, organic chemistry, and surgery. I bought a binocular microscope and planned to set up a laboratory.

On May 27, 1929, I married Anne Spencer Morrow. From the standpoint of both individual and species, mating involves the most important choice of life, for it shapes our future as the past has shaped us. It impacts upon all values obviously and subtly in an infinite number of ways. One mates not only with an individual but also with that individual's environment and ancestry. These were concepts I comprehended before I was married and confirmed in my observations over the years that followed.

My wife's father, Dwight Morrow, was ambassador to Mexico. I had met her in his embassy a year and a half before, when I flew the *Spirit of St. Louis* to Mexico City from Washington. After our wedding, we spent a fortnight trying to avoid the press in a small motor launch cruising off Long Island and New England coasts. Then she took part in my aviation activities—in the inauguration of TAT's transcontinental passenger service, in carrying the first airmail to Paramaribo in a Pan American amphibian. We searched the jungles of Quintana Roo for ancient Mayan cities and photographed archaeological sites in New Mexico and Arizona. In the spring of 1930, in a new plane I had specially designed for survey flying, Anne and I broke the transcontinental speed record. With this plane, in 1931, we surveyed a northern route from New York to Tokyo.

Between these flights, I visited laboratories and studied textbooks of biological science. Then an illness of my wife's older sister converted my interests into action. She had a cardiac disease, which, her doctor said, was incurable because the heart could not be stopped long enough for an operation to be performed. When I asked why an artificial heart could not be used to circulate blood during an operation, the doctor replied that he did not know. Thereafter, I asked the question of every doctor I met. To my amazement, none could answer it. Finally an anaesthetist told me that he had a friend who could give a satisfactory answer. This brought me to the great French surgeon Alexis Carrel, at the Rockefeller Institute for Medical Research.

Carrel knew and explained the problems involved in constructing an artificial heart. He had been trying unsuccessfully for years to develop a somewhat similar apparatus, one in which isolated organs could be perfused without infection. I could have the use of his laboratories, he said, if I wanted to work along such lines. I accepted with delight. A successful perfusion apparatus would be a first step toward creating an artificial heart.

At the Rockefeller Institute research facilities were available that I could not have duplicated in a laboratory of my own. Still more, I had opportunities to talk to Carrel. His experience as a physician, combined with his experiments in surgery and tissue culture, gave him extraordinary contact with basic elements of life and death. In Carrel, spiritual and material values were met and blended as in no other man I knew.

On March 1, 1932, for my wife and me all material values were shattered by the kidnapping of our infant son. He was taken at night from his nursery room in our Sourland Mountain home near Hopewell, New Jersey. A few weeks later, his body was found at the edge of a nearby woods. I curtailed my aviation activities and began working with federal, state, and city police hunting for the kidnapper. Months passed while clues were developed and followed unsuccessfully. Newspaper publicity continued to be so intense, so inaccurate and sensational, that it resulted in our suffering threats, extortion letters, and the presence of sight-seers in such numbers that I had to arrange for an armed guard to protect our second son, who was born in August of the same year.

The following year, attempting to rebuild a somewhat normal life, I undertook a survey of potential transatlantic air routes. On July 9, 1933, using the same plane with which we had surveyed the route to Tokyo two years before, my wife and I departed from Long Island. She again acted as radio operator and relief pilot. We spent nearly half a year on the trip, flying to Denmark by way of Newfoundland, Greenland, and Iceland, visiting various European countries, inspecting possible bases in Norway, Scotland, Ireland, Portugal, and the Azores, and returning home by way of Africa and South America. Thereafter, I continued working on specifications for long-range flying boats and base requirements for their regular operation.

In the fall of 1934, while I was in California, I received a message from the New Jersey State Police saying they thought the kidnapper had been apprehended. I flew back to the East Coast and for months became involved in investigations and testimony related to the court trial. Newspaper publicity intensified and continued after the conviction of the kidnapper. Life for my family became so difficult, disagreeable, and dangerous that I decided to take up residence abroad until such time as we could live in our own country with reasonable assurance. On December 22, 1935, we sailed for England.

Living in England forced me to make a fresh start. Our first task was to establish a home. After months of searching, my wife and I rented a fifteenth-century house in the weald of Kent, called "Long Barn"—a mellow, rambling structure, with time-sagged roofs and slanted floors.* Here I was, of course, cut off from my airline activities, from the Rockefeller Institute laboratories, from contact with Robert Goddard and his rocket-launching tower.

Before leaving America, I had completed the construction of a successful organ-perfusion apparatus. At Long Barn, I spent many hours designing—on paper—some improvements in it, and I began to consider the problems involved in the construction of an artificial heart. I also resumed flying. I drew up specifications and placed an order for a small airplane. I intended to visit countries in Europe, Africa, the Middle East, and Asia, and I wanted especially to fly to India and study the mystical phenomena so frequently reported as

* The house was owned by Harold Nicolson, diplomat, historian, and author of the biography of Dwight Morrow published in 1935. He and his wife, author V. Sackville-West, occupied the house from 1915 to 1930.

lying beyond conventionally accepted fields of science. In this connection, I obtained permission to use the library of the Royal College of Physicians, in London, where I read reports on fakir and yogi practices.

I had been in Europe only a short while before I felt the mounting threat of war. Germany and Italy were arming rapidly and making demands that could not be satisfied in peaceful ways. The plans I laid, and all values I held, became shadowed by the danger of a major conflict. Inevitably, my mind turned more and more from thoughts of peace to those of war.

In the early part of June 1936, I received a letter from the American Military Attaché in Berlin, Major Truman Smith, asking me to fly to Germany to help him evaluate developments he had been watching in the Luftwaffe. Major Smith also transmitted an invitation from General Hermann Göring. As I learned later, the U.S. State Department approved this mission. I accepted. I had for many years looked forward to visiting Germany; doing so, I could better evaluate the trends under way in Europe. As a Reserve officer, I wanted to assist the War Department in any way I could.*

My background in civil and military aviation had placed me in a unique position from which to survey the air forces of European nations. I had friends in aeronautical professions in England, Germany, and France. Through State and War department officers, I could arrange for a trip to Russia. American military attachés were restricted to the country of their station, while I could travel with relative freedom throughout Europe. I worked unofficially with

* Truman Smith (1893–1970) served as military attaché for air with the U.S. Embassy in Berlin, 1935–39. In the mid-1950's he prepared a report on Lindbergh's five visits to Germany entitled "Air Intelligence Activities: Office of the Military Attaché, American Embassy, Berlin, Germany, August 1935–April 1939, with Special Reference to the Services of Colonel Charles A. Lindbergh, Air Corps (Res.)." He deposited the 163-page report in the library of Yale University, his alma mater, in 1957, with no restrictions upon its use. In the Foreword, Smith states: "Air Intelligence . . . was then in its early infancy," and "the gathering of air intelligence concerning the very rapid expansion of Goering's Luftwaffe posed difficult problems." The full text of his letter of invitation to Lindbergh dated May 25, 1936 (pages 22–24) includes this persuasive paragraph: "From a purely American point of view, I consider that your visit here would be of high patriotic benefit. I am certain that they will go out of their way to show you even more than they will show us."

American embassies at London, Berlin, Paris, Moscow, took part in conferences with Ambassadors Kennedy, Bullitt, Wilson, and their staffs, attended meetings of French Intelligence, and carried out some open and some secret missions.

The Germans placed no restrictions on the aviation establishments I chose to visit. Obviously, they felt they were making extraordinary progress and that it would be advantageous to have this known abroad. I was deeply impressed by the number and efficiency of German factories and laboratories, but the unparalleled destructive power that the Luftwaffe was building alarmed me. I realized that in a few more years it would be possible for bombers to wipe out hundreds of thousands in the great cities of Europe. I had always thought of aviation as symbolizing the advance of civilization. Here, in an extremely disturbing contradiction, I saw aviation advancing the destruction of civilization.

I had considered my civilization as everlasting. It was too extensive, too scientific, too intelligent, I believed, to break down as earlier civilizations had. Now, suddenly, conflicting ideologies and powers were rising that could easily cause a breakdown. The countries of Europe reminded me of the city-states of ancient Greece— in their democracies, in their tyrannies, in the fragility of their cultures.

A flight to India, on which my wife and I took off from England in February of 1937, emphasized civilization's vulnerability. Our first landings were in Italy. There, after driving along Roman streets dotted with the uniforms of Mussolini's soldiers, we walked through the crumbling Forum. Here had been a civilization that must once have seemed to its citizens as invulnerable as mine seemed to me. A few days later, in Egypt, we visited the Pyramids, the monuments of another civilization that had disappeared. Flying eastward, we circled the ruined walls of Babylon. In India, abandoned temples and palaces marked a power vanished. Would human eyes look on broken vestiges of my Western civilization in another thousand years? Many historians assumed that all civilizations break down eventually. Why should my own be an exception?

Engine trouble in Nagpur forced us to cancel the trip to Himalayan areas we had planned. I regretted this change in plans, for there was so much I wanted to learn there. Was it true that ascetics in those mountains lowered their body temperatures by rhythmic breathing in the rarefied air? What were the conscious and subconscious effects? Did they have any relationship to the longevity ascetics sometimes claimed? No one I met in lower altitudes of India could answer such questions or seemed to have much interest in them.

Back at Long Barn, I began experimenting with the effect of altitude and oxygen on animals. I found that within a few hours I could reduce the body temperatures of mice and guinea pigs in a partly evacuated bell jar. What effect did such temperatures have on the mind's perception and vision? Adequate answers could be obtained only through the experiences of men. I hoped someday to fly to India again and study mystical phenomena in the Himalayan mountains.

In June of 1938, my wife and I changed our residence from England to France—to Illiec, a small, bouldered island we had bought off Brittany's northern coast. There, storms raged with a fury that tossed head-size stones upon the shore. Clouds, light, and sea wove patterns of kaleidoscopic variety while the tide rose and fell through a span of forty feet. When the tide was out, we could walk across sea bottom to the mainland or to the nearby island of Saint-Gildas, where Dr. and Mme Carrel maintained their summer home.

Walking from island to island through mists and shadows on a moonlit night, now between weed-covered reefs, now skirting high boulders in a field of gorse, I often felt that ghosts were walking with me, that Illiec and Saint-Gildas were mystical islands where life and spirit could communicate. At the Carrels' stone-walled, Napoleonic-period home, mysticism was a major subject of our conversation. What lay beyond the mind's perception? How much significance should be accorded to visions, to intuition, to clairvoyance, to prayer? Were subconscious powers manifest through pendulums, divining rods, and trances? Could the miracles of Lourdes be scientifically explained or duplicated?

Such discussions alternated with talk about practical experiments to be made with my perfusion apparatus, about the deplorable condition of French politics and the imminence of war. By the summer of 1938, no day passed without thoughts and talk of war.

Nothing seemed of much importance, after a time, in contrast to the holocaust that would result from a conflict between modern powers.

The situation became so critical that I pushed other interests aside and concentrated my efforts on a survey of military aviation in Europe. A considerable part of my activities in the valuation of foreign nations' air power, not only their present status but also their future capacity, I undertook at the request of United States Army Intelligence. Major Truman Smith, later a lieutenant colonel, asked me in 1937 and 1938, as he had in 1936, to use my access to German aviators to keep the United States informed. My wife and I flew to Russia, to Czechoslovakia, and to Germany again. I also received a telegram from Ambassador Joseph P. Kennedy asking me to come to London to talk to British statesmen. Another telegram, from Ambassador William C. Bullitt, asked me to take part in conferences in Paris. A letter from Ambassador Hugh R. Wilson said it would be advantageous to him if I would attend a dinner in Berlin at which Marshal Göring would be a guest.

Working with the French Premier and Minister for Air, I carried out a secret mission to Germany during which I obtained an offer from the Germans to sell military aircraft engines to France. I felt this could be a major step toward lowering the tensions that existed. In view of the military weakness of England and France, I believed their best policy would be to rearm behind the British fleet and the Maginot Line of forts and let the totalitarian forces of Germany and Russia clash.

Early in 1939, when political conditions were continuing to deteriorate in Europe, I returned to the United States. At the request of General Henry H. Arnold, Chief of the Air Corps, I went on active duty as a colonel. My objective was to help increase the number and improve the quality of our aeronautical research facilities, and to lay down specifications for military aircraft that could outperform those produced in Europe. To achieve this objective, I took the chairmanship of a committee composed of General Arnold, Admiral John Towers, Chief of the Bureau of Aeronautics, and Robert Hinckley, head of the Civil Aeronautics Authority.

For several months I flew back and forth across the United States to attend conferences and visit factories and laboratories. Then, when Germany invaded Poland, leading England and France to declare war, I asked to be relieved of my Air Corps assignment so that I could act as a private citizen in opposing participation in the war by the United States. I believed that a second world-wide conflict within a quarter-century would result in the decline, if not in the destruction, of our Western civilization. I held that from the standpoint of America, as well as for the future of mankind, it would be wisest for us to keep out of Europe's ceaseless internecine battles.

I spoke over radio networks and at antiwar meetings, wrote magazine articles, testified before committees of the House and Senate in opposition to American intervention. I advocated that we build our military strength, and at the same time use our influence to bring about a negotiated peace in Europe. In these activities, I spent two years—unsuccessfully. The prowar forces were too great and influential. Step by step, the United States was maneuvered into a position that inevitably brought war. When Japan attacked Pearl Harbor on December 7, 1941, we had no practical alternative but to enter the fighting.

I immediately offered my services to the Air Corps, though months before, in deep disagreement with the President, I had resigned my colonel's commission. My offer was declined on orders from the Roosevelt administration. It soon became clear that whatever part I played in the war would have to be that of a civilian. Accordingly, I accepted an invitation from Henry Ford to act as aviation consultant to his company, especially in relation to the bomber factory being built at Willow Run, in Michigan, to mass-produce four-engine Liberators (B-24s).

I had never before worked as a member of a big manufacturing organization. Nor had I known a man combining such extremes of genius and eccentricity as Henry Ford. I had met Ford in 1927, when I landed at Detroit with the *Spirit of St. Louis*. On that occasion, I took him up for his first airplane flight. He sat, with obvious delight, on one arm of my pilot's seat, hunched into the low and narrow cockpit that had been designed for me alone. Previously, he had refused to fly with anyone, even in the trimotor passenger planes his own company was building.

At Willow Run, I often walked through the factory with Ford

and his guests, through long lines of machinery, jigs, and bombers undergoing assembly. Sometimes he would come to my office, sit on my desk in his favorite leg-swinging position, and talk about creating a Parliament of Man to prevent war in the future. His vice president Harry H. Bennett and I would head it. There were days when he invited me to accompany him on an inspection trip through his vast industrial empire. It usually started at "The Rouge," where there were the blast furnaces, rolling mill, and automobile production line, and ended at one of his small "decentralized" factories in the nearby countryside.

Ford seemed always torn between his fascination with the modern colossal and his love of old-time simplicity. He was proud that his factories produced millions of automobiles each year. He was disturbed by the dullness that the production lines induced and by the city life the workers led. He tried to find a solution in a decentralization where every workman would own enough land to have a garden of his own. "But it's not practical for everybody," a Ford Motor Company vice president told me. "The costs would run too high."

After months at Willow Run, I understood Ford's apprehension. On the one hand, I was impressed by increasing organizational efficiency and power; on the other, I felt revolted by the regimentation of life that resulted. Looking down from an airplane when the shifts changed, I saw the thousands of men and women streaming through the entrances; they made the factory appear a giant anthill. What contrast to the Lincoln Standard factory in Nebraska, where I had learned to fly, where there were not more than a dozen workmen, and where every man knew every other. I remained at Willow Run and with the Ford Motor Company only because of my friendship with Henry Ford. It was a significant place where I could help my country at war.

As a consultant to Ford, I found one opportunity to advance my experiments with the effect of lowering body temperatures. In connection with shakedown flights of bombers—and a special high-altitude ignition-breakdown project I had taken charge of—I spent two weeks in 1942 at the Mayo Clinic at Rochester, Minnesota. The clinic had established an Aeromedical Unit for Research in

Aviation Medicine. They had two altitude chambers for training personnel in high flying. The big altitude chamber was too intensively programed, and its operation too costly, to permit running long experiments on body temperature and accompanying reactions. But a smaller steel tank, a one-man altitude chamber, stood vertically nearby, abandoned in the mass-production methods of the war. I obtained permission to use it. How rapidly could I reduce my own temperature, and by how many degrees? What would the mental and physical sensations be? Might I gain some insight into the values Indian mystics found through their techniques? On one occasion, I spent over three hours in this chamber at simulated low atmospheric pressures, trying various methods of pulsating breathing. My temperature dropped two degrees Fahrenheit rather quickly, but then began to rise, and I ended up with two degrees of fever. Clearly, a more complicated procedure would be required to overcome the human body's regulating mechanism. I noticed no change whatever in mental acuity within a spread of four degrees. On a number of occasions, I remained at simulated altitudes of as much as forty-five thousand feet, breathing pure oxygen through an unpressurized mask. Although my mind functioned reasonably well under these conditions, I noticed that its acuity decreased. I experienced no indication of unusual sensory phenomena. I wanted to test the effects of low atmospheric pressure impinging on rhythmic breathing, mental disciplines, and controlled temperatures, and to put some habitually hibernating animals under a bell jar; but tight military schedules made experimental hours scarce. When your country was at war, you had to concentrate on programs that would shorten life, not lengthen it.

In 1943, in addition to my work with Ford, I took a consulting position with the United Aircraft Corporation, in Connecticut. There, I specialized in fighters, my originally chosen branch of aviation. At its Stratford factory, United produced the Chance Vought Corsair, a single-seat fighter-bomber equipped with six fifty-caliber machine guns. The Corsair or F4U was used by Navy and Marine squadrons, especially in the Pacific Ocean areas.

The next year, as a United Aircraft representative, I flew to various Marine bases in the United States and on Pacific islands to study Corsair operation and the requirements for designing a still more advanced fighter. This study took me also to Army Air Force bases where twin-engine Lightning (P-38) fighter squadrons were stationed. I flew a total of fifty combat missions with Corsair and Lightning squadrons, sometimes bombing, sometimes strafing, shooting down one enemy plane, and, once, almost being shot down myself. I stayed with the Army squadrons longer than I had planned in order to instruct their pilots in long-range-cruise techniques which I developed and which proved successful in combat.

War in the Pacific gave me contact with values of life and death unlike any I had experienced before—both the highest ecstasy of life and the most degrading depths of death. Flying with combat squadrons, you never knew when death would come. Survival depended as much on chance as on skill, on the position of a ground gun or the trajectory of an ack-ack fragment. The uncertainty of living caused an intensity of life. Thought flashed, awareness deepened, one had a greater appreciation of the moment because it might be one's last. The man you laughed with tonight might exist only in memory tomorrow—as might yourself.

On battlegrounds of the Pacific, death appeared to lose its dignity. There were the ripped fragments that had once been men, severed heads lying like coconuts on the ground, slit trenches full to the brim with swollen bodies, bomb craters where a mixture of garbage and uniformed enemy corpses had been dumped. But did these sights—could such circumstances—degrade the dignity of death? Death, I came to feel, was beyond man's ability to degrade. It was only life that man could compromise. Mixing human bodies with his garbage degraded the quality of the living, not the dead.

Wartime transitions—instantaneous, flesh-obliterating—from life to death intrigued me. On a special mission with a Corsair over Wotje Island in the Marshalls, I dropped a two-thousand-pound bomb that wiped out the crew shelter at the edge of a Japanese naval-gun emplacement. I was watching when it struck. One moment the earth below me lay motionless; the next, a column of earth and dust appeared like magic in the air. On the razor-edge of time, an unknown number of human lives and bodies vanished by my pressing the red button on a control stick.

When the debris settled and the dust drifted away, I saw only a crater where the shelter had been. The bodies of the crew had become a part of the debris and dust. But did the intangible, unique element of life in those bodies vanish completely? Surely, theology's acceptance of a spirit surviving death was more plausible than the nonentity that one infers from science.

Several times during my tour of Pacific combat areas, I had myself touched the edge of death, once during a head-on pass at the end of a bomber-escort mission while I was piloting a Lightning. On that pass, elements of chance and skill interwove as in no other incident of my life. When it began I had an advantage in altitude, and I was slightly diving, my enemy slightly climbing, when we opened fire. As we were flying directly at each other, there was no deflection to my aim or to his. Bullets streamed through the air like hail. I watched his wingspan widen in my gun sight as flashes rose from the bullet hits. When I could see the engine's cylinders, I released my gun trigger and pulled back on the control stick. The enemy plane pulled upward, too, to collide. I yanked back on the stick with all my strength, braced for the crash, felt a bump as we passed, but it was only air. I banked steeply in gaining altitude and saw below me the Japanese plane, out of control in a spiral dive toward the sea, twisting as it gathered speed. There was a splash and spray drifting. I felt I had approached so close to death that I could almost penetrate its mystery, that every time I saw life disappear I came closer to an essence that remained.

In mid-September of 1944, I returned to the United States and attended conferences relating to fighter design and maintenance. After my experience in combat, I felt in my bones what I had known in my brain before—the value of having the most modern weapons. Probably I was still alive because American fighting planes were faster than Japanese, because we had greater fire power, because our gun sights were more accurate. I was determined that these advantages be maintained in laying out designs for future warplanes.

On May 13, 1945, six days after Germany's surrender, I landed at Paris, attached to Naval Technical Mission Europe. My assignment was to study enemy developments in military aircraft and missiles. I spent weeks flying over and driving through devastated countries. The great cities of Germany had been bombed into piles of rubble, under which lay the bodies of thousands of men, women, and children. Refugees lined both sides of the highways I drove along, pulling handcarts, pushing baby carriages, carrying huge bundles on their backs. Many of them were fleeing westward from the Russian occupation forces. Dirty and ragged, they hoped to reach some place with shelter and food where life could be sustained. In the center of Nuremberg, where I spent a night in the bomb-cracked telephone exchange, shattered and roofless walls bordered the streets in every direction as far as I could see. In Frankfurt, the entire ancient city had been wiped out by strings of high-explosive bombs. At Dessau, at the aeronautical museum I had visited before the war, the exhibits were broken and scattered, its irreplaceable documents and photographs trampled.

In Europe, the culture of centuries had been destroyed. Still worse, both Allied and Axis countries had lost vast numbers of their finest men, causing a possible decline in genetic qualities of the human race. This was the outcome of modern power, of science and technology, of the aviation to which I had devoted so much of my life. I felt revolted by some of the values I had held in the past and by the martial and material developments of science. I considered renouncing my profession and living far away from modern technology, some place where I would be in touch with nature and the earth.

But could a nation survive without modern weapons? We won the war because of the modern weapons we produced, because of the aviation I had helped develop. Without them, the United States would be as vulnerable to conquest as France had been, or as the American Indians had been when our forebears took their lands away from them. Nations are always faced with the menace of conquest. Nazi Germany had no sooner been defeated than the menace of Soviet Russia took her place, and Russia was hiring or shanghaiing German scientists and engineers to modernize her weapons.

The menace of Russia kept me working in military fields for many years after World War II ended. With the American atomic bombing of Hiroshima on August 6, 1945, we entered a radically new era of warfare. The threat was too clear: a single bomber had already destroyed a city; a hundred bombers could lay waste all the major cities in the United States. It was obvious that attacking forces would have always the advantage of surprise, both in weapons development and in timing their attack. Defensive forces had never been able to keep enemy bombers from reaching their targets. I concluded that American security lay less in defense than in establishing so great a retaliatory strength that an enemy would know we could absorb a surprise attack and still strike back with a greater blow.

I began working with Army Ordnance at the University of Chicago to help develop more effective weapons. As a consultant to the Secretary of the Air Force, I took part in reorganizing the Strategic Air Command. The technical development of weapons, as always, fascinated me. Like the officers, scientists, and engineers I worked with, I was hypnotized by the effects of titanic powers and meteoric speeds. Sitting in a SAC briefing room, I felt myself a demonic god as I watched plastic discs being laid down on maps of target cities to show the area that one bomb of the latest kilotonnage could destroy.

Flying in a bomber on a simulated mission, I realized the sense of easefulness and irresponsibility that can precede an act of atomic destruction. I had no sense of the earth below me. There was no window at my station through which I could see out; in any event we were miles above a solid cloud layer. The only signs of movement came from the engines' drone, the fuselage's vibration, and the weirdly changing green patterns on the radar screen. A city was emerging in that pattern—a river, a bay, a mass of buildings, vague but definite. On a wartime mission, that city would have been wiped out by nothing more than pressure on a button.

The pressing of a button always seemed to me so absurdly trivial in relation to the dropping of a bomb. I thought of my dive-bombing of the Japanese-occupied city of Rabaul during World War II. My target was a building that our Intelligence thought to be an officers' quarters. All seemed quiet on the ground as I approached. Fighters did not take off from the airstrips below to intercept me; nor did antiaircraft guns fire. I banked into position, lowered my dive brakes, and lined up on the building far below. When I pressed the red button on my stick, it was hard to believe I had released a high-explosive bomb. But there it was, deadly and irretrievable, apparently floating in the air. I saw it clearly for a moment as I climbed, and within seconds a pinhead puff of smoke appeared behind me in the city of Rabaul, a puff so small and far away that I could not connect it to the button on my stick, or realize the writhing hell it covered on the ground. I had carried out my mission, and felt little responsibility for what I had done.

The bombardier who wiped out Hiroshima must have had a similar experience. I flew over the ash-gray disc of Hiroshima some months after the bomb was dropped. A future atomic war, a pressing of buttons in sequence, I realized, would probably turn all American cities into ash-gray discs.

Although I could find no wise alternative, each year that I worked on weapons development left me more concerned about our future. It appeared to me that our civilization involved a negative evolution for life, and that the security we were building for today and tomorrow led toward eventual catastrophe. I felt this most keenly when I flew on missions with the Strategic Air Command.

On arriving at a SAC air base, I would be surrounded by highly selected groups of men. Both officers and airmen had passed rigorous physical examinations; most of the officers had achieved college and university degrees. Yet they would be among the first to die in war. Through epochs past, nature had used the killing of individuals in a selection that advanced life's species, but no selection resulted from man's atomizing of his cities or by the downwind fallout that ensued.

SAC briefings on bomber attrition rates and the destruction of cities, and the effects of lethal fallout downwind, were alarming. The ease with which we flew our simulated missions over Omaha, San Francisco, Alaska, Greenland, or the north magnetic pole showed me how vulnerable our planet was. Of course the primary purpose of the Strategic Air Command was to prevent a major war, but mass hysteria, an accident, or a dictator's insanity could always launch war.

The advent of intercontinental ballistic missiles with megaton nuclear warheads seemed to bring the ultimate in destructive power. In position and targeted, they could devastate our entire civilization within hours.

I served for six years on scientific committees charged with development of ballistic missiles, especially those of intercontinental range. (How often, at committee meetings, I thought of Robert Goddard's pioneering with his toylike rockets!) Then, with Atlases and Titans in position, and Minutemen and Polarises under way, my mind turned from the value of immediate security to the darkening long-range problems of mankind.

What fools men were, I among them, when they found security by keeping lethal weapons pointed toward each other! But what was the alternative? Mutual limitation of arms seemed an answer, but adequate inspection of Russian or Chinese or other countries' activities would be extremely difficult. If nuclear weapons could be outlawed effectively, then our security would depend on maintaining factories in which such weapons could be constructed more quickly than in the factories of an enemy.

I came to accept that even a catastrophic war was probably not the greatest danger confronting modern man. Civil technology vied with the military in breaking down human heredity and the natural environment. Every day, increasing numbers of bulldozers and trucks tore into mountains, slashed through forests, leaving greater scars on the earth's surface than those created by bombs. Gases from civil vehicles polluted our atmosphere. Wastes from civil factories poisoned our rivers, lakes, and seas. Civil aircraft laid every spot on earth open to the ravages of commerce. Paradoxically, civil technology diminished the hereditary quality of man not by killing people but by preserving their lives and proliferating their offspring. The resulting increases in population made unsupportable demands on our planet's natural resources. What was the prospect for mankind?

As a young aviator, I had concluded that the best way to cope with danger is to keep in contact with it. I believed this so thoroughly that I found myself, in encounters, unconsciously moving toward dangers rather than away from them. Since I felt my civilization threatened, I spent more time reading about fallen civilizations of the past. I decided to travel more widely so I could better understand various peoples, their interests and ideologies, and their habits. To do this, I returned to my prewar consulting position with Pan American Airways. Pan American's extensive routes gave me frequent and easy access to most areas of the world.

In the decades I spent flying civil and military aircraft, I saw tremendous changes take place on the earth's surface. Trees disappeared from mountains and valleys. Erosion turned clear rivers yellow. Power lines and highways stretched out beyond horizons. To me, the most spectacular change came in the sprinkling of myriad lights that I saw when flying over the United States on a clear night. Huge areas that once lay black when I was a young pilot now glowed with electrification. Almost everywhere I landed, I heard stories of disappearing wilderness, wildlife, and natural resources. Many species of animals that had taken epochs to evolve were, within decades, on the verge of extermination. I became so alarmed that I decided to take some personal action.

I began working with the World Wildlife Fund, with the International Union for the Conservation of Nature, with the Nature Conservancy, with the President's Citizens Committee on Environmental Quality, with governments and organizations in the United States, in Europe, Africa, South America, Mexico, the Pacific islands. I spoke to the legislature of Alaska, to the Constitutional Committee of Montana, to chief government officers of Indonesia and Taiwan, to the President of Peru about selective bans on whale killing, to the President of Brazil about Amazon parks and reserves, to President and Mrs. Ferdinand Marcos of the Philippines about saving the country's tamarau and monkey-eating eagle, to governors, businessmen, and philanthropic organizations about the critical importance of preserving our planet's environment and wildlife.

Preserving the environment is inseparable from maintaining our heredity itself. Where our environment declines, both human and animal decline with it. I am amazed at how little this is generally understood. Governments, philanthropies, and individuals still pour tremendous attention, thought, and funds into social welfare, education, art, science, technology, and superhighways, without realizing that none of these activities will have much value if the quality of individuals breaks down. I do not want to be a member of the generation that through blindness and indifference destroys the quality of life on our planet.

Flying Pan American routes, I was struck by the expansion of cities. At the high altitudes where our airliners cruised, I saw little detail on the earth's surface even when it was not cloud covered. But at each end of a flight, I had intimate contact with a city, usually a great city. I always felt that I escaped from a city into the expanses of the sky, and then sank back to submersion in degenerating human life.

Los Angeles, more than any other city, impressed me with its rapidity of growth. On my first visit, as a boy in 1916, after driving from Minnesota to California, it seemed a lovely place, basking in clear air and sunlight, surrounded by orchards and little farms, framed by the ocean and a distant semicircle of mountains. When I flew over it in a Pan American jet transport fifty years later, the orchards and farms had vanished. The city itself had expanded to the distant mountains and spilled over them into valleys beyond. Smoky haze screened off the sunlight that once bathed farms, yards, and streets.

I soon found that what had happened to Los Angeles was happening to all great cities. High-rise buildings ruined the harbor's beauty at Hong Kong and flat-toothed the ancient grace of background ridges. Looking down on Tokyo and its subcenters, I likened their spread to a gigantic protoplasmic mass. The widening ring of gray concrete structures around old Rome was like a devil's halo. Yet a great city, I realized, was more than indicative of our civilization: it *was* our civilization.

What caused modern cities to grow uncontrollably? As in the uncontrollable growth of military power, the answer lay in technology. Technology reduced the need for farm labor, caused shifts in population, resulted in high urban wages, and made it difficult for the small farmer to survive. As a youth in Minnesota, I had experienced the impact of technology when I replaced horses with a tractor. Working our fields was much easier than before, but the tracts were too small to keep the tractor busy. Farmers with large fields could use tractors more efficiently and produce their crops at lower cost than I. Improved agricultural implements soon made small farms impractical. Their owners sold out, moved to cities, helped man the factories that produced still more efficient machinery that would take still more farmers from their farms.

Year after year, I watched the cities of the world enlarge and become more standardized. Their streets filled with similar vehicles and with people in Westernized clothes. New buildings in Beirut, Rio, and Chicago looked the same. Riots and crime in Washington were not unlike riots and crime in Manila. I became alarmed by the exponentially mounting complication, luxury, and cost of cities—not by the cost in money, but by the cost in irreplaceable resources of the earth.

I think of flights to the Philippine Islands. My first was on a military mission not long after World War II. I was enthralled by the beauty of the islands—the sea-dashed coasts, the horizon-pushing jungles. More than a decade passed before I returned, this time on a Pan American Airways route inspection. There was no change in my memory's picture of the dashing seas, the most spectacular I know. But I was shocked by the slashes in the jungle I looked down on, caused by lumber companies. I saw mountains denuded, their stream beds dry, their rice paddies parched and useless. Many tribal peoples had been brought to a state of desperation by the invasion of road-construction gangs and loggers. Some of their once proud hunters begged for food and coins. Many of their women became penny prostitutes.

Once, I rented a light plane at Manila and flew to an abandoned logging strip on the isolated northeastern coast of Luzon. There, the Pacific Ocean foams white against black lava reefs and cliffs; and there, on sand beaches and at streamsides, the black-skinned Agta people erect their shelters. The women lace big leaves on flat frameworks of poles; when an owner wishes to change location, he simply carries his home on his back, like a big turtle crawling over the sand.

I wish I could always leave my civilization behind at night, to sleep under an Agta shelter on a Luzon beach. At times, I feel like abandoning modern life. No going-to-bed procedure is required—no washing dishes, locking doors, opening windows, turning down sheets, not even undressing. You walk to your shelter, lie down on a grass mat, and look upward at the stars. The glow of campfire embers warms your face. You hear rippling surf, rustling leaves. Smoke from driftwood chips traces through the weedy smell of ocean. Your body's usual movements contour the sand to fit your bones. You have time to think, to become aware of your awareness.

I have only once reached a people who lived beyond the tangles of civilization. I had been working as a director of Panamin, which is a combined Philippine government and private organization headed by Manuel Elizalde that is charged with administering the welfare of national minorities. A cave-dwelling, stone-age-culture tribe called the "Tasaday" had been discovered in mountainous rain forests of southern Mindanao. They knew nothing about the outside world, and had long ago lost contact with neighboring tribes. No trails extended through the forest beyond their foraging grounds.

With Elizalde and his staff, I took part in organizing the first expedition to the Tasaday caves. Looking up at the brown-skinned, black-haired Tasaday, squatting and standing in the openings to their caves, I felt that a time machine had moved me back through ages. It was incredible that such a people could be living in the twentieth-century world.

The Tasaday were deeply interested in us and our civilization, but they loved their caves and wished to live in them always, as their ancestors had lived since time began, they told us. They had no enemies to fight, and the jungle supplied them bountifully with food. What could they gain by exchanging their way for the miraculous life we represented and described to them?

I lay in my tropical sleeping bag at night, the earth pressing against my body, big drops of water from the rain forest pattering on the tent, and the boom of primitive voices rolling down from the cave above. Was not this a twentieth-century Garden of Eden? I had never seen a happier people. My instinct drew me toward the Tasaday; my intellect toward civilization.

Discovering the Tasaday raised practical and ethical questions as to how they should be treated by the Philippine government. Now that they had been discovered, irresponsible expeditions would come in to see them, photograph them, and exploit them. Newspaper and television publicity about a cave-dwelling, stone-age tribe had created world-wide interest. Even if the Panamin expedition had not gone in by helicopter, logging roads would have one day reached the Tasaday area—in a few more years at the most—bringing theft and rape and degradation.

Primitive man is unable to withstand either the force or the temptation of civilization. "Civilization is like a weed that grows on our trees," a Samoan chief told me. "You cannot get it off, once started, and it always kills the tree in the end." The destructiveness of civilization is obvious, whether seen in the rubble of Nuremberg, in the atomized hell of Hiroshima, or in the end of the Tasaday paradise.

I have never seen my civilization as clearly as on the plains and in the jungles of East Africa. There, in a few remaining wilderness areas, life exists in evolutionary balance much as it did millions of years ago. The values of traveling to the wildness first appear in a mounting awareness of the senses. I notice that especially when I select my campsite. Sweating, I search for shade from the sun. Wanting a night's sleep, I look for drainage in a rain. Hungry, I need deadwood for a fire for cooking. How fresh are tracks on the animal trails? Is a water source nearby?

Gradually, my mind and body seem to merge until there are moments when I cannot distinguish between the thought of my senses and the sensations of my mind. I am part of the earth that dusts my knees while my hands drive down the tent stakes. I know this without need for rationality. The line of elephants watching from the river bed fifty yards away—suppose they charge? In their stance, I sense curiosity, not aggression; therefore I have no fear.

When I watch wild animals on an African plain, my civilized values of security, and of measuring time, give way to a timeless vision in which life embraces the necessity of death in a miraculous plan of existence. I see individual animals as mortal manifestations of immortal life streams; and so I begin to see myself. I am not only one, I am also many, a man and his species. In death, then, is the eternal life for which men during centuries have sought so blindly, not realizing that they had it as a birthright. Only by dying can we continue living.

Of our planet's myriad beings, man alone has become aware of his life stream, and even his awareness was not achieved until recent generations. It is one of the greatest and least implemented discoveries of science. In a miraculous plan of existence, we can only partially describe the life stream that regularly splits off and makes conscious individuals who both manifest the present form of human development and, by their environmental successes and failures, direct its future. We are tangible only temporarily. Our intangibility continues at least as long as there is a human species. According to our wish, we can correctly claim to be either years old or epochs old.

The giraffe's head staring at me from a neck higher than the acacia trees between us—I know that a body of awkward grace is hidden from my sight. The long forelegs, the spotted hide, the slanting back, the tasseled tail, are clear in imagination. But now I also visualize its body trailing a life stream of phantom forms that extend back through the epochs. Millions of ancestors died in stretching that neck to achieve its survival value—ghosts of the past, forever reincarnated in each new generation's shape, ghosts with shorter necks, with lower bodies, with lizard legs, with fins.

When I watch species other than my own, their instinct's wisdom is what most impresses and disturbs me. I am impressed because of the achievements of animal species in survival and perfection. I am disturbed because their methods so greatly challenge human ideals. Instinct procreates freely, competes constantly, and selects inevitably. When life is defective, weak, or old, instinct destroys it without compassion. The individual animal has no value beyond its contribution to the species, and its final contribution to the life stream is likely to consist of being killed and eaten. The wilderness evolved successfully for billions of years. Our Western civilization is quaking after a millennium. It is threatened by intellectual ways that are far more bestial and much less compassionate than the ways of wildness.

After my visits to East Africa, I returned to civilization's apex in New York. My business activities centered in the city, and my home lay in its suburbs. New York brings out the intellectual as the jungle does the sensate. It emphasizes life's accomplishments rather than life itself. Time becomes tempo, death is quickly hidden in morgues and cemeteries, and the cosmos exists unnoticed above the tops of skyscrapers and beyond the walls of streets. Here there was prolificacy and competition, but of a different order from the animal life in Africa.

I had visited New York with my mother as a boy, but my close contacts began in 1927 when I landed the *Spirit of St. Louis* on its outskirts after flying from St. Louis and San Diego. When I was in the city, I looked forward to air-route surveys that would take me back to open spaces. Ideas I formed during those surveys invariably drew me to New York again—the organization of airlines, the financing of Goddard's rocket experiments, collaboration with Alexis Carrel at the Rockefeller Institute for Medical Research. A project was best started in New York, even though its execution might take me to the far side of the earth. Men and women on the crowded streets were like corpuscles of a blood stream nourishing a gigantic body that was essential to the advance of my own ideas and those of Western civilization. The city was even more prolific and in its own way more competitive than the jungle; the city was jammed with struggling, multiplying life. I saw competition, economic, social, academic, but not biologic. Civilization's ideal is to preserve, not to select.

From the flaked-stone edge of a primitive weapon to the ballistic missile, man's intellectual progress has gone hand in hand with his development of weapons—affecting negatively his biological evolution. Both the value and the ominous impact of weapons on our planet's life were emphasized for me during the days I spent with the seminomadic Masai of East Africa.

I once spent three days and nights at a Masai *boma* a few miles south of the Kenya-Tanzania border. No one at the *boma* spoke English, and I had declined the services of an interpreter. One of the tall, spear-carrying headmen was my host, and, according to tribal custom, I slept in the hut of the oldest woman. The next day, I accompanied one of the cowherds, and several of the men and boys accompanied me, carrying long-bladed spears, dark-red blankets swinging over their otherwise naked bodies.

No raid was undertaken during my visit at the *boma,* but the night after I departed, a nearby *boma* was attacked. Cattle raids had been an accepted part of Masai life for generations. In the past, they had included the capture of women, and thereby contributed to the tribe's genetic evolution. Civilization in the form of a Christian, well-armed colonial government put a stop to that, but the "old times" were looked back on with nostalgia by both Africans and Europeans. "You know, if I could be reincarnated," a British game warden said as we sat at an evening campfire, "I'd like to be a Masai *moran,* a warrior, a hundred years ago. Just think of going off on one of those raiding parties and bringing back all the cattle you could steal, and a lot of squealing little Kikuyu girls for wives!"

"We have known freedom far greater than yours," a Masai told me. It disturbed me to have my freedom challenged. I had grown up and lived with the belief that I possessed great freedom, that mine was "the land of the free," where every man could carry on according to his wish. I had the freedom of farm life in Minnesota, the freedom to choose the occupation I wanted to follow, and then the freedom to fly over the world as man had never flown over it before. Of course I had no opportunity to take part in cattle raids or raids to capture women. That would have been unrespectable, illegal, and uncivilized.

But the wilderness experiences now impinged on my thoughts. Was it not necessary to reconsider our civilized values in the light of long-term survival and of the human life stream? How much freedom did civilized man really have? After all, he was constantly conforming, both obviously and subtly, to laws, customs, religions, and ideals invented by his own intellect over thousands of years. He conforms to an intricately codified system.

Real freedom lies in wildness, not in civilization. Possibly that is why civilized man views the earth's remaining wildernesses with increasing nostalgia. As we lose our wild freedoms, we recognize their value in opposition to the tyranny of intellect. In nature, the freedom of individual life requires only food and shelter, and often no more shelter than one's own skin. A deer is born in the forest, dropped easily from its mother's womb onto leaves and moss. In minutes it sucks milk. In days it nibbles grass. The earth is a bed; the sky, a sufficient cover. It is free to compete in its environment and return directly or indirectly to its life stream.

Man has more and more separated himself from his life stream and natural environment. I have spent many years living in city suburbs of New York, of Los Angeles, of Detroit, of London. Even so, I did not realize sufficiently the rate at which human life and environment were changing. Even though I had lived through the revolutionary change from horses to motor vehicles for power and transport, had seen the logs stop floating down the Mississippi River, and had listened to my grandfather speak with amazement about the growth of my birthplace, Detroit, I did not sense in my bones that civilization was moving exponentially, not by means of a simple progression.

Within a fraction of my lifetime, I saw New York parking space disappear, the waters of Long Island Sound become polluted, and the coasts of Maine and Florida packed to the shoreline with houses and motels. The distant howl of a superhighway and the thunder of jet aircraft in the sky broke into the tranquillity of my New England home. Rampant pressures of improved technology and increasing population were rapidly destroying what my Masai friend and I considered freedom.

Obviously, freedom was incompatible with regimentation, standardization, and maybe with population density. I began to wonder if it was compatible with the development of arms and communication. Certainly arms and communication destroyed the freedom of wildness; but did they not eventually also destroy the freedom of those who developed these tools? Thinking along these lines shook fundamental concepts I had formed during my earlier life, of the freedom that weapons had given my grandparents on the frontier, of the freedom that aircraft had given me in my global travels.

A country had to have arms to keep its freedom. Both contemporary experience and a study of history showed that. Had I believed otherwise, I would not have spent so many years in military activities. In the past, my ability to shoot and fly was a part of my sense of freedom. During World War II, my combat missions in the Pacific helped to protect the freedom of my country as the quality of my arms helped to protect me. I felt great freedom of action during those missions, in a combination of individuality and teamwork. There was freedom even in the duel of life and death—his bullets and my bullets, the freedom of life if they passed, the freedom of death if they struck.

But working with the ballistic missiles of modern warfare gave me no sense of freedom. There was no individual judgment required, once the computerized figures guided our missiles to their targets; there was no sense of human choice in the knowledge that among their objectives was the obliteration of cities full of millions of men, women, and children. It used to be that when you finished fighting you stacked your gun away, though you kept it close at hand. Now, to maintain national security you have to serve your weapons day and night—keep missile guidance systems spinning, keep strategic bombers flying, early-warning radars turning, atomic submarines and carriers constantly cruising at sea. All of these activities consume a fantastic amount of energy, and enslave us to the supply of oil, coal, and other irreplaceable natural resources of the earth.

The development of transport aircraft once seemed to me a wonderful way to increase human freedom and to bring the peoples of the world together in understanding and peace. What could advance civilized progress more rapidly than fast communication? Years passed before I began to realize that bringing peoples together does not necessarily increase understanding and peace. I saw also the deadly standardization that fast communication brings.

When I began surveying air routes of the world, every place I landed had its character and beauty. Paris, London, New York, St. Louis, San Francisco, Quebec, and Mexico City were as different as the costumes of European peasants in the Middle Ages. To an American, Tokyo, Shanghai, Calcutta, and Cairo were as fascinating and contrasting as the growths of a tropical sea. Even smaller places had their individual qualities—Belize, Cartagena, Saint Thomas, Port-au-Prince. And flying overhead, I never tired of studying the varieties of tribal cultures in wildernesses below me.

A few decades later, the communication I helped to bring with my airplane is rapidly standardizing all cities, towns, villages, and even remote tribes—so much so that there is no longer a city in the world I have a desire to visit. A city's degeneration is seen at its roots, in its basements, subways, and those half-abandoned areas where people gather who must live as cheaply as they can—usually on a dole, often through crime. This degeneration is not apparent to the visitor who stops in modern hotels. He is isolated from it by the conventions and other ceremonies of the economic system. He seldom sees even the effect of riots, arson, and looting.

I will never forget the shock of seeing a riot zone in our nation's capital. My wife and I had gone to Washington for a White House dinner. After the dinner, we were told it was dangerous for us to walk to our hotel, a block and a half away, because of the many muggings that took place in the area. The next day, driving back to our Connecticut home, we detoured through the riot zone—block after block with window-shattered and fire-gutted buildings, like a bombed city. I could hardly believe my eyes. I had spent many boyhood winters in Washington when my father was serving in Congress. I had walked by day and by night through the streets, wherever I felt like walking. Now, to see the city crime-ridden, locked tight at night, and partially destroyed was beyond my understanding.

There are but two measures of life's basic progress: heredity and environment, and these interweave generation after generation. It is no longer possible to escape the fact that the tyranny developed by the human intellect has been seriously destructive to both. The genetic defects that affect each individual are obvious in our dependence on surgery and therapy and medication. And the planet's surface environment is breaking down.

Twentieth-century man has had the mysterious fortune to bear the historically unprecedented development of science and technology. In this century we are suddenly confronted with problems that have been accumulating gradually over thousands of years. They can be condensed into a single question: Can the intellect select among life's fundamental values? On the one hand, man is bound by his intellect. On the other, he inhabits his body. Even the intellect must have a body to exist in, and its body is the product of biological selection. The intellect must accept its place in the community of life, its place with the senses and the emotions, for all are members of the body. This, I think, can only be accomplished by combining the knowledge of science with the wisdom of wildness.

Wildness created man, his intellect and his awareness together, in the first place. The principles that created him have not changed.

Man has simply turned his back on his birthright. The primary lesson taught by wildness is selection of individuals within the life stream. The wisdom of the wildness does not submerge individual character; rather, it brings it out. A sound individual is produced by a sound life stream.

Apple
of Knowledge

In the late 1950's, on a trip westward from Connecticut, I stopped in Chicago to visit one of my father's sisters. She had then reached an age of ninety-six. Sitting in her straight-backed wooden chair in a parlor on South Princeton Street, she talked both of her girlhood on the frontier and of her life in the great city as she approached her hundredth year.

Aunt Linda was born in a stockade fort at Saint Cloud, Minnesota, to which my grandfather had fled with his family when Sioux Indians, under Little Crow, went on the warpath in 1862. It had been a forty-mile oxcart trip from their homestead to the fort, a hard ride for my grandmother, who was then "big with child." A man on horseback had arrived at the homestead, warning that all settlers should flee for their lives. My grandparents turned loose cows, pigs, sheep, and chickens, loaded a few belongings and supplies into the cart, and started eastward with their oxen.

All farmers in my grandfather's area reached the fort safely; but more than three hundred and fifty Minnesota Valley settlers lost their lives. At the village of New Ulm, to the south, there had been a massacre of whites. Men were shot, women were tomahawked, and children were shoved into stove ovens and the fires lit—according to stories that reached the fort. Weeks later, after Governor Henry Sibley's soldiers pushed the Sioux westward into the Dakotas, my grandparents drove back to their homestead and found that no damage had been done. They collected most of the animals they had let go and went on with their farming.

Aunt Linda said she remembered Indians coming to the family's log cabin door, near the present city of Melrose. But that was several years after the uprising, and these were friendly Chippewa, themselves enemies of the warlike Sioux. She had watched them erect their pointed birch-bark teepees on the banks of the Sauk River, where they liked to hunt and fish.

By that time, waves of European immigrants were breaking westward, and new neighbors laid claim to homesteads on surrounding land. To own a farm it was only necessary for a man to stake out a quarter section and work it for five years. Soon a community built up. Frontier life had never been monotonous, Aunt Linda told me. There were enough chores to keep everyone busy: cooking, milking, washing, feeding pigs and chickens, trimming oil lamps, hoeing the garden, making hay, mending clothes. She and her sister June helped with the housework. Perry, an older half-brother, worked the fields with my grandfather.

Charles, my father, hunted and fished to keep the family supplied with food. Frank, the youngest of the children, fetched water from the spring and carried in firewood. My grandmother, in addition to cooking, cleaning, tending children, also washed, carded, and spun wool, from which she knitted clothes. There wasn't any farm machinery. Mowing was done with a scythe; threshing, by hand; women made butter by pushing a plunger up and down through cream inside a tall wooden cask.

My aunt felt well, she said, in answer to my question, really in excellent health, although her legs had been bothering her a bit since she broke a hip two or three years before. She did not go out walking as much as she used to. And she did use glasses for reading because they made it so much easier for her eyes, but she could still get through a letter without them, she insisted, if the light was good. Television gave her great enjoyment. She nodded toward a big set in a corner of the room. Was it last night or the night before she had watched the launching of a satellite down in Florida? She could not understand "all this business about space." Was it really as important as they made it out to be?

I looked at my aunt sitting there, heavy black shawl across her knees, recalling the savages and oxcarts of her youth, discussing the televised space ventures of her old age. Airplanes droned overhead. Parked automobiles lined both sides of the street outside her window. Two pink-flesh grapefruit I had ordered shipped from Texas looked ripe and fresh upon a table; and beside them was a dial telephone through which one could speak to almost any section of the world. Into my aunt's lifetime, I realized, had been compressed more change in man's environment than five thousand years of previous civilization had caused. In experiences of my own family in America, the cycle from manual to mechanized in the human species was manifest.

My father died years before this visit with my aunt in Chicago. Born in 1859 in Stockholm, he was the oldest of the children my grandfather conceived by his second wife. The family sailed from Sweden in 1859 to America and settled on the banks of the Sauk River in central Minnesota. My grandfather was then fifty years of age, and my grandmother, twenty. The journey had been long, weeks under ocean winds and more weeks spent in overland travel between the Atlantic coast and the Mississippi Valley.*

My grandfather had been a very influential man in Sweden, one of the leaders of the Riksdag and a close friend of the King. A combination of political intrigue and financial troubles caused him to emigrate. He was a self-educated reformer who had led the movement to abolish corporal punishment, which in Sweden took the form of public whipping. He was strongly opposed by the Riksdag conservatives, who were said to have trumped up a financial scandal in an effort to disgrace him. He traveled westward to Minnesota because the frontier had then reached that far, and possibly because he knew the country was much like that he had

---

* Charles Lindbergh's grandfather Ola Månsson took the name August Lindbergh at the time of his emigration from Sweden. With the growing population, the customary usage of patronyms had become a problem, and the government encouraged the adoption of permanent surnames. The combination of two nature terms was recommended. Lindbergh (linden tree/mountain) had already been selected by Månsson's two oldest sons; it was therefore a natural choice, so that his infant son would bear the same name. Among the many reforms advocated by August Lindbergh in the Swedish parliament were increased rights for women, full citizenship for Jews, and reduced trade restrictions.

left behind in his native state of Skåne. Many Swedes were choosing Minnesota as their New World home.

I recall vividly my father's stories of frontier days. I used to lie beside him in bed or on a patch of grass and listen to them—how my grandfather traded a gold medal he had been awarded back in the "Old Country" for a breaking plow because he did not have enough money to buy one; how the family had first built a sod hut on their claim of land and then replaced it by a house and barn built with the barked logs of trees chopped down to make a clearing; how half-brother Perry burned charcoal to sell; how my grandmother chased some Indians who had stolen an axe; how they hunted duck and deer for meat and trapped mink and muskrat for their furs. Unless he was near home, my father told me, he would keep only the saddle of a deer he shot, because a larger part of the carcass made a load too heavy for his back.

The Lindbergh family was poor in those days, but their log cabin did not take much furnishing—it measured about twelve by sixteen feet—and they did not have a great deal to buy—a little salt, shoes, a few tools, things like that. The rest could be obtained from the forests, the river, and the farm. They boiled down maple sap for sugar, syrup, and vinegar. There were plenty of blackberries and blueberries in season, and the woods were full of wild grapes. Seven children were born to my grandfather by his second wife, but Louise, Victor, and Lillian died in childhood. Infant mortality was high in frontier life, before the time when doctors could reach people by automobile and when they knew more about surgery and medicine.

On occasion, my father and I drove our 1912 Ford touring car to the site of the old family homestead. It was about forty miles from my own boyhood farm near Little Falls. We wandered along the Sauk River, where he had laid his lines of traps, and he showed me a nettle-filled depression in the ground where the log cabin used to stand. A few foundation stones were still in place.

Tracks of the Great Northern Railroad ran through the old homestead. My grandfather had welcomed its first construction crews, and told his children that good transportation was essential to the community's development. Less than a five-minute walk beyond the tracks, and paralleling them, were deep grass-covered ruts that had been cut by "Red River" oxcarts as they carried settlers westward before the rails were laid. You could hear the axles squeaking miles away, my father said. There were forests full of game then, instead of the fields of wheat and oats around us. He had hunted with a muzzle-loading gun, and carried a powder horn and pellets. "No trespassing" signs and barbed-wire fences did not exist.

My grandfather had started the community's first school in his farm granary, then joined with his neighbors to build a one-room schoolhouse and to hire and board a teacher named Jennie Stabler. The teacher "boarded around" with various families, starting on the Lindbergh farm. By that time a local lumber mill was cutting logs into beams and boards for building. Lindbergh children walked a mile between home and classes, and helped carry wood for the school's single stove. Winters were so cold that sometimes the thermometer dropped to forty degrees below zero. Studying was often dull for sons of those pioneers. They looked forward to the wild freedom of summer. But birds and deer outside the windows lightened school drudgery.

The frontier had its own social life, even though transportation was slow. Settlers moving westward often stopped at the Lindbergh farm, and there always found a brace of partridge or a few pounds of deer meat and maybe a pail of milk for the younger children. On a Sunday there might be visiting between the nearer neighbors. The Lindberghs and the Wheelers used to trade about for entertainment. Each could see the other's house across an area of prairie between forests. In late morning, my father said, he and his brother and sisters would watch the Wheeler farm. When Mr. Wheeler began harnessing up the oxen, Mother Lindbergh would put her dinner on the stove, so that it would be ready for serving when the visitors arrived.

After lunch men and women talked while the children played together—games of one-o'cat, tag, and hide-and-seek. Frontier jokes would be told. A favorite was about a boy whose mother told him he must make some polite remark to his hostess during his visit. "This is pretty good butter, Mrs. Foote, what there is of it," the boy

said. Then, realizing his mistake, he added: "And there's plenty of it, too, such as it is." Laughter always followed the frontier: it was the frontiersman's relief.

Children of those days lived in constant fear of Indians, though the Chippewa were friendly and even if, as grownups told them quite truthfully, there was no longer any danger from the Sioux. Now and then, when parents were out of hearing, boys would hide in bushes and whoop like savages to frighten sisters and their friends.

As community population increased, the village of Melrose was formed and named, according to family legend, by my grandfather. Here, a two-room schoolhouse was built. My grandfather became town clerk and was appointed postmaster. It had been difficult on the frontier, my father told me, to get the education required for entrance to a university. But my grandfather had helped by insisting that his children speak only English in the home, and by encouraging them to read good books in addition to their routine schooling.

My father saved some of the money he made hunting and selling furs and, later, working on the railroad to pay for his tuition at Grove Lake Academy and the University of Michigan, where he took a two-year course in law. He graduated in 1883 and thereafter he returned to Minnesota, where more farmers were moving in, borrowing money, buying plows, building houses and barns. He found plenty of legal work to keep him busy.

Eastern interests had money to invest in the West, where wild land was cheap. My father worked first as an assistant lawyer in Saint Cloud, and then set up an office in the town of Little Falls, where he combined a real-estate business with his rapidly growing law practice. He pleaded cases in the yellow-brick county courthouse, constructed thirty-five houses and business buildings, bought and operated several farms through tenants. He represented Eastern financial interests, and soon became active in state politics. He turned down an opportunity to go to New York as lawyer for a large store with the assertion that he would not then be his "own man."

My father married twice. His first wife was Mary LaFond,

daughter of a pioneer Little Falls merchant. By her he had three daughters, Lillian, Edith, and Eva. She died in 1898 of complications following surgery for the removal of an abdominal tumor. In 1901 my father married his second wife, Evangeline Lodge Land. She had been teaching chemistry at the Little Falls high school. Her age was twenty-five; my father was forty-two. I was their only child.

The frontier was gone by the time I was born, in 1902. Indians had been assigned to reservations. Horses replaced oxen. Forests were disappearing. Men hunted with breech-loading guns. Houses were built of lumber, not of logs. Towns and villages dotted the map of Minnesota. More than four thousand people lived in the village of Little Falls, mostly Swedes, Norwegians, Germans, and Poles. My father hired men to run the farm we lived on, and my mother kept a cook, a nurse, and a maid.

My parents belonged to a social circle that included the lumber-mill Weyerhausers and the paper-mill Tanners. There was a lot of entertaining, of trotting back and forth to town in black horse-drawn carriages over two miles of sandy road. I do not remember much about the house we lived in, because it burned down when I was only three and a half years old. It was middle-sized, squarish, three-story, built of wood, painted light gray, and sat on a bank overlooking the Mississippi River. A red-brick chimney stuck up through the center of the roof.

To furnish the house, my mother had bought highly polished mahogany and oak pieces from factories at Grand Rapids, Michigan. She and my father went to Grand Rapids to pick them out. There were straight chairs and rocking chairs, an extendible dining-room table, a curved-glass-front cabinet for dishes and silver, an upholstered settee, several sectional bookcases. My father gave my mother an upright piano, at which she played and sang for me: "A Spanish Cavalier," "Ninety-Nine Blue Bottles," or maybe some song from the Civil War, probably "When We Go Marching Through Georgia." A set of dishes from China and wedding-present silver occupied most of the shelves in the curved-glass cabinet. Daintily colored figures of little men were painted on the dishes. My father had bought them for my mother in San Francisco's Chinatown when they were on their honeymoon. Whenever the silver and china were placed on the dining-room table, I knew it meant a party, probably with parlor acting and card playing into late night.

Our farm comprised about a hundred and twenty acres of field, pasture, and woodland. The county road running through it, north and south, cut off twenty acres next to the river, on which our house was located. Pike Creek, named after Zebulon Pike, who explored the area in 1805, wound across the western portion and saved us the problems of watering our stock. The woods contained a tangle of brush when my father bought the property, but he cleared it out in a year or two with the help of goats. Then you could walk everywhere easily, under branches of oak and ash, birch and poplar, linden, ironwood, and pine. There were four buildings in addition to our house: a barn, the tenant's house, a chicken coop, and an ice shed—all made of wood. Three dogs lived on the place: Breeze, Shep, and Sweet Snider—a Dalmatian, a shepherd, and a great Dane. Sweet Snider sometimes knocked me over with his tail.

I recall a day of sudden excitement. People began shouting and running through our house. Someone grabbed me up and carried me away to the barn, where I escaped long enough to peek around a corner to see a great column of black smoke billowing skyward from the roof of my home.

Our second and new house was built on the granite foundations of the first. It was also of wood and painted light gray, but it was smaller, only a story and a half high, with fewer porches. It was finished in 1906, the same year my father, a Republican, was elected to Congress as representative from the Sixth District of Minnesota. I was then almost five. For the next decade, my summers were spent on the farm and most of my winters in Washington. My mother and I traveled back and forth by train, and broke our journey always at Detroit to visit my maternal grandparents.

I was born in Detroit because three of my great-uncles were Michigan doctors, and my mother wanted one of them, Great-Uncle Edwin, to attend my birth. Detroit was a progressive city, one of the largest in the United States, and it was growing fast; by 1927 it was fourth largest. Its citizens understood the use of man's scientific knowledge. New factories were being built, electricity was replacing the old gas lighting, and Henry Ford was soon to perfect techniques of mass production. Grandfather Land thought Detroit had a brilliant future. Someday, he prophesied, the nearby firehouse would have no stable and need no hay.

Among the wonders that appeared in my grandfather's home was a telephone, with which you could talk to distant people through miles of wire stretched on poles. (Main 3172 was his number.) Another was a radio set my uncle had constructed. When conditions were just right and you moved the "tickler" to the right point on a crystal, you could pluck voices and music from the air! The city outside my grandfather's door was full of wonders, too: a theater with a big white screen on which people and vehicles moved about as they moved about on the streets. The movement on the screen was more interesting than that on the streets, because a story always accompanied the incidents.

Grandfather Land was Canadian, born at Simcoe, Norfolk County, Ontario, in 1847. He had descended from English and Scottish peoples. His branch of our family had been Tories in the Revolutionary War. There is a record of a John Land, who fought with the King's forces, barely escaping to Canada with his life after his powder horn had stopped a well-aimed rebel bullet. In Canada he received word that his wife and children had been killed during an Indian raid that had been encouraged by the revolutionists. He therefore built a cabin in Ontario, on the west bank of the Niagara River, so close to the falls that he complained of the constant roaring. In 1779, he exchanged his Niagara grant for another at Head of the Lake, now the city of Hamilton.

But it was all a consequence of error. Actually, his wife had been warned of the raid in time to escape with the children, but they in turn were told that John had been killed in the war. Later, Mrs. Land heard mention of a man by the name of Land living in Canada. On investigation, she found him to be her "dead" husband. After reuniting, a willow tree was planted in commemoration of the end of their separation. For more than a century, it guarded the several residences that succeeded the original cabin, and in fact "Landholm," as it was called, was lived in until the early part of the twentieth century. My mother named the Little Falls house "Lindholm."

The English Land family genes mixed with Scottish Chisholms;

then with English Haydens. Thereafter my grandfather, Charles, was born, one of six children. His father, John Scott Land, moved from Hamilton in the 1850's and lived with his family in New York City and in Keokuk, Iowa. About 1861 he abandoned his family. It was reported that he joined the Union Army and was killed in the Civil War. Others said that he went to Pikes Peak and was lost. In any event, his family never heard from him again.

His son Charles Land was fourteen when the Civil War began. One of his brothers became a Union soldier. Charles apprenticed in dentistry, first at Simcoe, then at Chicago, where he was burned out by the fire of 1871. Eventually, he hung out his shingle in Detroit and married the English-Irish daughter of Lodges and Kissanes. From this union were born a son, Charles Land, Jr., and a daughter, Evangeline, my mother.

My mother attended Miss Liggetts Private School for Girls in Detroit, then the University of Michigan at Ann Arbor, where she was graduated with a Bachelor of Science degree. In 1900, she accepted a position teaching chemistry in the high school at Little Falls, Minnesota. There she met my father, and there followed the sequence of events that took our family to Washington, D.C.*

In Washington I found aspects of America I had not experienced before. My mother rented rooms in a big apartment house and I started school, most unwillingly. The Greek-columned government buildings were impressive to a boy, especially since his father's office was in one of them, and the sidewalks and asphalt pavements were wonderful for roller skating. But there were no woods or streams within walking distance of my new home. Children played in vacant lots and in parks guarded by policemen.

I felt the restrictions of city life. I could not go hunting with a gun. The pruned trees were not for climbing. Once, when I was eight years old, a watchman ordered me to stop walking along the

---

* About this time, Lindbergh's parents became estranged. Mrs. Lindbergh and Charles lived in Washington from fall through spring when Lindbergh, Sr., served in Congress, however, and were visited at the farm each summer by him. The parents continued to be in frequent communication with each other in regard to their son's welfare, attended social functions together, such as the inauguration of President Wilson, and enabled young Charles to maintain a close relationship with both of them.

top of a stone wall in the Capitol grounds, and relented only when I informed him that I was a Congressman's son. Although I enjoyed the prestige accorded my position, I thought Congressmen lived unenviable lives—sitting all day at desks either in their offices or in the House of Representatives. Most of them were pale-faced and paunchy. They even had a tunnel dug so they would not have to go outdoors for the five-minute walk to the Capitol when they attended roll calls. My father did not like that tunnel, but I would coax him to take me through it now and then. It reminded him of how much he missed Minnesota's outdoor life, he said.

I realized that my father must be greatly interested in politics, else he would not have let re-elections take him back to Washington. He thought laws should be passed to keep "Big Business" from exploiting the common citizen, that the government allowed banks too much leeway in manipulating money, and that our system of taxation needed readjustment. He voted for Theodore Roosevelt for President, and supported Senator Robert La Follette's progressive movement. Conservative politicians, like cigar-smoking Speaker Joseph Cannon of the House, considered him a radical.

I was deeply impressed by speeches my father made on the House floor. Sometimes I sat beside him when he made them. I was still more impressed by the fact that everything Congressmen said was put down in a printed record, of which thousands of copies were distributed in pamphlets and clothbound books. My father wrote several books himself. These included *Banking and Currency and the Money Trust* and *The Economic Pinch*. He had his own portable typewriter, on which he hammered out letters and manuscripts with one finger from each hand.

In Washington, at the age of five, I had my first contact with the rivalry of races. I had slipped outside our apartment house soon after my mother and I arrived from Minnesota, to find an adjoining lot occupied by two or three dozen boys of about my age. They were throwing stones and chunks of brick at one another. Not understanding the seriousness of the situation, I joined in the fight, flinging the first fragment that came to my hand quite ineffectively. In the excitement of the moment I had not noticed that the boys on my side of the lot were all black, while those on the other side were white. I had no sooner flung my stone than I heard an angry shout from the far side of the lot: "Look at the white kid fightin' with the niggers." And a hail of missiles landed around me. Since our apartment house was close by, I got back through its door before my pursuers could catch me. Afterward, my mother explained some of the conventions followed in Washington.

Just outside Washington, I attended my first air meet. My mother and I traveled by streetcar to Fort Myer, Virginia, for an occasion that she thought not only would be interesting but also would let us witness an important event in American history. There I saw an airplane race an automobile around an oval track. I watched the pilot of another airplane bomb the chalked outlines of a battleship with oranges tossed out by hand. Two or three airplanes were having engine trouble on the ground, and one glided down to a forced landing behind trees shortly after take-off. The experience was so intense and fascinating that I wanted to fly myself.

Living in the nation's capital gave me a sense of the history and greatness of the United States of America, for I was in touch with the entire span of my country's history: Congress's latest legislation, a suffragette parade, a delegation of Indians asking for consideration of their rights, and, all around us, the monuments, the museums, and the libraries. On occasion, in poor weather, I would go to the Smithsonian Institution and wander through its rooms and halls looking at whatever roused my interest. There were stone implements and pottery from the pre-Columbian past as well as blunderbusses that early white settlers carried. Among items that attracted my attention most were the buckskin clothes, war feathers, and tomahawks of the Sioux, who had so fiercely woven in and out of my father's stories.

Not far from the cases of Indian relics were others containing uniforms, swords, and medals that belonged to generals who fought in various wars. Many of these generals were themselves buried in Arlington Cemetery, a short distance up and across the Potomac River. In good weather, my mother and I might go for a Sunday walk past graves and arches marking the memory of Sheridan and other heroes. At Arlington, I felt surrounded by ghosts of my country's past, just as at the Fort Myer air meet I had an insight into its future.

There were sometimes trips to places of interest within a day's train or streetcar trip of Washington, like Fort McHenry and Mount Vernon. I recall that as we walked through the very house and grounds where General Washington had lived, it was a disturbing thought to me that the father of our country, who had led Revolutionary Americans in their successful fight for freedom, found it possible to run his home and farm with slaves. "The Star-Spangled Banner," which I had so often sung mechanically with other children, took on significance after I visited Fort McHenry and slid backward into the muzzle of one of its old cannon.

The forty-eight stars on the flag that flew from poles all about Washington turned into a roll call of the states when I walked through House Office Building corridors and read the name plates on high mahogany doors: Mr. Evans of Montana; Mr. Underwood of Alabama; Mr. Curley of Massachusetts; Mr. Furgusson of New Mexico. The United States was growing. Arizona and New Mexico had just been admitted to the union, and people prophesied that the huge territory of Alaska would someday be divided into additional states. Only a hundred and thirty years had passed since the thirteen colonies won their independence, yet America might soon be greater than Great Britain was!

The very name "America" made one think of miracles. We had conquered a continent. We had abolished slavery. We had developed the automobile. We had invented the airplane. We were showing that peoples of all races could live in harmony together. And now we were building the Panama Canal. My father was on the Congressional committee for the canal. The Panama Canal would show what doctrines of freedom and equality could do for men. France had tried to build it years before, and failed. Now, the young United States of America was succeeding. We were cutting two continents apart. We would carry ocean liners through jungles and over hills, between Atlantic and Pacific oceans. After the canal was finished, our government would not have to keep two separate navies. The old countries of Europe were watching us with awe.

I stood beside my father on the floor of the House when he voted for a bill to provide money for the Panama Canal's construction. He and some other Congressmen voyaged there by ship to inspect the progress being made. His account of the ocean, jungle, and machinery was so interesting that my mother and I decided to go to Panama, too, in spite of the cost and at the risk of my missing days at school. We sailed from New York on January 4, 1913, on the U.S.S. *Colon,* over the Atlantic, between green-mountain islands of the West Indies, past an old square-rigger under sail on the deep-blue Caribbean Sea. Finally we steamed between strong fortifications of the Canal Zone. It took us seven days to reach Panama. We watched barges working in the Culebra Cut, steam shovels chewing through a mountain. We walked over the concrete bottom of the still-empty Miraflores locks, stared at the rusting hulks of machines French engineers had abandoned to the jungle. We shopped in native cities and hired a horse and buggy to take us to Pirate Morgan's castle.

"You are living in an extraordinary time," my father told me back in Washington. "Great changes are coming. Great things are going to happen. I may not live to see them, but you will." He was fascinated by the future and apprehensive of it.

It is a Congressman's duty to keep circulating between the grass roots of his constituency and the branches of his nation's capital. As a member of a Congressman's family, I was, of course, affected by it. In springtime, weeks before the close of school, my mother and I would pack our trunks and suitcases and board a night train bound westward. After the usual visit at Detroit, we would continue on to Little Falls, walk the two miles from railroad station to farm, and open our house for the summer. On the way, we stopped to get my dog from his winter boarding home.

My father had sold his livestock and rented the farm when he entered Congress. He kept for his own use the twenty-acre strip of woodland between the road and the river on which our house stood. We encountered the problems that usually arise between owners and tenant farmers. One tenant after another came, stayed a few months or a couple of years, and left. Manure accumulated in the barnyard; fences deteriorated. Tenants said the proportion of woodland to field and pasture was too high, and complained about the distance of the barn and well from their house. They were glad to sell us fresh milk and eggs, but now we did not have any more meat of our own, and bought from a butcher, and if we wanted a horse and buggy we had to rent one from a livery stable in the town. Each spring, my mother and I planted a small vegetable garden.

Aside from routine chores about the house, summer days were vacation days for me. I spent them swimming in river and creek, running over log jams, climbing trees, and playing with neighbors' children. Swimming was the most fun. Sewage from Little Falls polluted the river, but that did not bother me too much. I used to walk upriver to play with friends, and then swim downriver through rapids, fully clothed, to reach home in time for supper.

Twice each summer, the "river pigs" came through, with their wanigans and bateaus, to break log jams. That was a wonderful time for boys. We would walk along the Mississippi's banks watching skillful use of peavey and pickpole. Now and then pigs would treat us to a contest demonstration to see which one of them could stay longest on a log rolling freely in the water. The lumber companies followed a policy of giving free food at mealtime to anyone who lined up at the cook's wanigan. Children from nearby farms were always there. The food was plain, but limitless.

If I grew tired of being outdoors, our house had lots of room for playing, either upstairs or in the cooler basement. Since we now lived there only in summer, my father had not finished the top floor. My mother let me leave its rough boards littered with collections of stones, toys, and tools; and there were tunnels running through the eaves big enough for me to crawl through. In these I secreted my more important possessions.

While playing on the upper floor I had my first experience with human flight. It was sometime before the Fort Myer air meet. I heard the noise of an engine in the distance. Something about it made me stop and listen. An automobile on the road? No, too loud and different. I rushed to a window and climbed out on the roof. About two hundred yards away, and not much higher than our house, I saw an airplane flying up the river. It had two wings, one above the other, and a man sat in between them wearing his visored cap backward. Except in photographs, I had never seen an airplane before. The aviator, my mother told me, had come to Little Falls to give exhibitions and to carry up into the air anyone who dared to ride with him. But it was very dangerous and very expensive, she said.

In 1912, my father bought the Model T automobile. It seated five people when three crowded into the back. He did not like very much to drive it at first because the engine had to be cranked by hand and was often hard to start. Also, he had had an experience of pressing the wrong foot pedal and going backward instead of forward. Before he got the car under control again, two or three lengths of sheep wire had been torn off posts of our fence. I was on the back seat when it happened and thought it awfully funny, but I did not dare laugh.

My mother also encountered problems driving the car. Speed frightened her so much the first summer that she would never let the clutch pedal out of low gear. With a Model T, that meant she had to keep pressing down hard with one foot on the pedal as long as she wanted the car to keep moving. This was a severe strain on her leg muscles during the two-mile trip to town. Moreover, the engine got hot and the water in the radiator boiled. It was a sight for the townspeople to see us chugging along so slowly past churches, saloons, and pool halls, engine racing and steam snorting from the radiator cap.

The next summer, at the age of eleven, I learned to drive. My eyes could barely see over the steering wheel, but if I sat on a cushion, my feet would not reach brake and clutch pedals. That summer my father did most of the driving. When I went with him, I usually rode outside, standing on one of the wide running boards and hanging onto a top brace with one hand. Then I could practice picking leaves off branches along the roadside or catching up pebbles from the ground on turns. I would jump off to open and close the bars of farm gates, or to help hold a team of startled horses while my father drove past. By the second summer I had learned to drive with reasonable skill. After that, my parents seldom took the wheel when I was with them. Several years elapsed before my father became accustomed to driving, and my mother remained a rather timid driver.

I chauffeured my father on several of his campaigns through the Congressional Sixth. He could get about much more easily by car than by train, especially when political meetings were held on someone's farm. Driving let him set his own schedule and go directly from one place to another; he could stop and talk to farmers and village storekeepers whenever he wanted to.

Automobile speeds were not great in those days. The state limit was twenty-five miles an hour for open roads; but the condition of the roads was such that we seldom had a desire to go faster. Asphalt or concrete paving did not extend far outside cities. Village streets were almost always just graded dirt and they were often pocked with holes; many became impassable for automobiles in wet weather. I took routine care of the car myself, cleaning spark plugs, adjusting coil points, filling grease cups and screwing them down after every long drive. For major repairs I drove it to one of the livery-stable garages that had sprung up all over the state in anticipation of the rapid acceptance of the automobile.

In the fall my father and I used our car to go on hunting trips through the country around Little Falls. Game was not as plentiful as it had been when he was a boy my age. Deer were scarce, and bear had disappeared entirely. But we seldom came back without a few partridges, prairie chickens, or ducks. He hunted with a double-barreled shotgun. I carried a twelve-gauge automatic he had given me. It had a heavy kick which I hardly noticed in the excitement of shooting birds. Occasionally I would find a carnelian arrowhead, a reminder of hunting in generations past. Once I picked up a spearhead on the road outside our house.

My father served ten years in Congress, from 1907 to 1917. During that time the growth of the United States was rapid, but our hometown of Little Falls did not change very much. The most noticeable change I saw was on the river. Fewer logs were drifting down because forests were disappearing farther north.

Little Falls may not have changed much during those years, but there was no question about the progress of Detroit. There you saw steel frameworks under construction in almost every direction you looked. A big garage had been built across the street from my grandfather's old house; fire engines had become motorized; electric streetlights had entirely replaced gas lamps. But Detroit's progress was not all beneficial. Noises increased. Varieties of bird life dwindled. Air and water were polluted. My grandmother's white curtains grayed with smog until my grandfather invented an air-filtering system for the house consisting of muslin screens and an electric fan.

My father's last year in Congress coincided with the declaration of war against the German and Austrian empires. My father had opposed the United States's entering World War I. He thought it in the best interest of our country to stay neutral.* I was not old enough to understand the war's basic issues, yet I felt pride in the realization that my country was now powerful and influential enough to take a major part in world crises. We would fight for good and right, and for freedom of the seas. After it was won, peace-loving nations of the world would get together and never fight again. Such an objective justified the sacrifice of life required to destroy the German Hun.

I remember World War I from the viewpoint of a farmer, a very young one. I was fifteen, and a high-school student, when my father decided to put me in charge of our hundred and twenty acres. He would buy a carload of bred Western heifers and of sheep, he said. Daniel Thompson, a slender ex-lumberjack friend of his, would help me. Thompson had spent many of his seventy years on farms and in forests of northern Minnesota. Born in Norway, he spoke English fluently, but with an Old Country accent, like so many of the neighbors around us.

The tenant who had been running our farm "on shares" was leaving. Otherwise I would not have had this chance to take part in winning the great war. Farmers were just as important as soldiers, government officials in Washington were saying. Our European allies needed food, and the United States had to produce more than

* Charles A. Lindbergh, Sr., was a leading member of a group of Republican Congressmen known as insurgents who banded together to limit the power of Speaker of the House Joseph G. Cannon during the 61st Session, from late 1908 to 1910. The insurgents demanded railroad regulation, conservation, more direct democracy, and various economic reforms. In the nearly three-year period of American neutrality, 1914–17, Lindbergh opposed entry into the war. His last opportunity to express his antiwar stand came on March 1, 1917, when he cast one of fourteen votes against the armed ships bill. A detailed analysis of Congressman Lindbergh's career is provided in Bruce Larson's *Lindbergh of Minnesota: A Political Biography* (Harcourt Brace Jovanovich, 1973).

ever in the past. My father could not be on the farm very much himself, because of politics and business; but he gave me the authority to buy whatever machinery I needed for plowing the fields and reaping the harvest.

I was fascinated with the idea of farming. Of course I would institute modern methods. I ordered a tractor, a gang plow, a disc harrow, and a seeder, and started repairing our cedar-post fences, which had been strung nearly fifteen years before. We built a new paper-roofed chicken house, and bought some ducks and geese. I studied pamphlets on agriculture more than schoolbooks. Would I need a team of horses or could I mechanize the land entirely? Daniel Thompson thought it would be impractical to farm without horses. But he had not had any experience with tractors. When ours finally came, three-wheeled, steel-tired, and orange-painted, he stared at it as though he were looking at a strange animal in a circus.

Farm work enabled me to combine my love of earth and animals with my interest in machinery. Each day was an adventure: taming cattle fresh from the range, breaking pasture for more cropland, dynamiting stone islands out of older fields. After the heifers began calving, I installed a milking machine—one of the first in Morrison County. I built a wire suspension bridge across Pike Creek, repainted the barn, decided to breed stock. Finally, I bought a team of horses, much to Daniel Thompson's satisfaction.

It was great fun and extraordinarily interesting, this taking food from the earth as I interwove my life with sun, rain, and season. I loved the smell of share-turned sod and fork-tossed hay. I slept as only men who work with the soil can sleep, and tasted bread and meat as no city dweller can. But as months passed I began thinking about my future. If war continued, I would soon become of military age, and soon afterward I would probably be in the Army. If peace came first, I would be faced with problems of college and examinations far more difficult than those I had avoided by farming in the war emergency. Under either circumstance, an unhappy day lay ahead when I would have to turn over the farm with its animals and machinery to another family of tenants.

I tried to study during evenings by the light of a kerosene lamp, but my efforts were not very successful. I was too sleepy after a day's work for much academic information to penetrate my mind. I found it easy to convince myself that study was unimportant when compared to the farm and war—or to a desire that was growing in me to become the pilot of an airplane. I dreamed often of having a plane of my own. After war started, I searched newspapers for reports of aerial combats—articles about Fonck, Mannock, Bishop, Richthofen, and Rickenbacker. In one of the monthly magazines we subscribed to, I followed the fictional account of "Tam o' the Scoots," a British pilot who displayed new feats of heroism with each issue. Attacking enemy fighters, bombers, and balloons in mortal combat, he represented chivalry and daring in my own day as did King Arthur's knights in childhood stories. If I joined the Army, I decided, I would apply for the branch of aviation and, if possible, learn to be the pilot of a scout.

I was attending a farm auction sale when the first announcement of the armistice was made, on November 11, 1918. Word came by telephone. The auctioneer broke off his chant to tell us. Time was allowed for celebration before the sale continued. Men cheered, slapped each other on the back, and then, with nothing else to do, they simply stood about.

I farmed for another year; then enrolled as a student in the College of Engineering of the University of Wisconsin at Madison. I had hoped to graduate with the class of 1924 with a degree in mechanical engineering. Instead, that year found me enlisted in the United States Army as a flying cadet. My interest in science and mechanics had not been sufficient to carry me through the long hours of study required for a university diploma. I was put on academic probation as a freshman owing to low marks. In my sophomore year, faced by almost certain expulsion, I left the university and entered a civil flying school in Nebraska. There, I learned to wing-walk, to parachute-jump, and eventually to pilot an airplane.

The life of an aviator seemed to me ideal. It involved skill. It commanded adventure. It made use of the latest developments of science. I was glad I had failed my college courses. Mechanical engineers were fettered to factories and drafting boards, while pilots had the freedom of wind in the expanse of sky. I could spiral the desolation of a mountain peak, explore caverns of a cloud, or land on a city flying field and there convince others of aviation's future. There were times in an airplane when it seemed I had partially escaped mortality, to look down on earth like a god.

I felt a little guilty on occasion, to gain such joy from exploiting products of the toil of others—from flying planes designed and built by hard-working engineers and craftsmen. It was as though I had been rewarded instead of penalized for shirking school. But to my amazement I discovered that most other men were contented not to fly, that few scientists or engineers had even the wish to be a pilot! The speeds and altitudes of flying were disturbing to them. The hazards were too great. They were delighted to have professional pilots hired for trying out their concepts and designs.

It was true that aviation was dangerous. Talks of pilots and airplanes almost always included accounts of fatal crashes. I saw two "washouts" during my first weeks as a flying student. In one, two men were killed when a wing broke off in a loop. In the other, pilot and stunt man escaped with minor injuries—through chance, not through caution or skill. It was commonly said that anyone entering aviation did not place much value on his life.

But how was one to measure the preciousness of life? Some men lived but found no joy in their carnality; they really did not care to live at all. Was it not better to enjoy living even though life might be cut short as a result? I believed the value of life related to its quality as well as to its duration. I took chances on occasion, but I never experienced an hour so difficult, dull, or tragic that there was no worth-while quality in it. Of course I would like to become a centenarian, but I decided that ten years spent as the pilot of an airplane was in value worth more than an ordinary lifetime.

After two years of barnstorming, first with older pilots, then with planes of my own, through the Mississippi Valley and Rocky Mountain and Southern states, I joined the United States Army and became a flying cadet. Aside from my love of flying, I had made a reasonable profit from my passenger-carrying and flying-circus ventures, but the Army Air Service offered opportunities to pilot high-performance aircraft, types of airplanes no barnstormer could afford to buy and operate. Such opportunities were more desirable than money.

At training fields in Texas, in 1924 and 1925, I flew the airplanes I had read about while farming, the bombers as well as the scouts, but even then I had little sense of war, although there was around some of the instructors an aura of past fighting. We cadets waged sham combats, dropped bombs, and fired guns, but we felt no bullets flying past us. There was no living enemy to kill.

The American attitude toward military development during the decade following the war was typified by our cadet training in gunnery. The ranges were outside Ellington Field, on the Gulf of Mexico, near Galveston. Our class was ordered to Ellington in February, though the field had been deactivated after the war. Mechanics went ahead with trucks. We cadets flew cross-country from Kelly Field during a spell of cold weather, in DHs, SE-5s, and MB-3s. The MB-3s were postwar fighters, the most modern in Texas. They had a speed of more than one hundred and twenty miles an hour in level flight. Frost had whitened the grass we landed on. Ice had glazed the top of pools. The men who took our wings as we taxied to the line had put on heavy flying suits, with fur beneath the outer khaki cloth. Ground crews drained the water from our radiators, roped our struts to iron stakes screwed into the earth, and fastened canvas covers over our cockpits.

The temperature was below freezing in the barracks to which we were assigned. Stoves they once contained had disappeared. But chimneys were still in working order. We discovered lengths of pipe, scrounged tin canisters, and constructed half a dozen fireboxes of individual design. Stacks of rotting crates outside furnished plenty of fuel.

In early morning, mechanics would pour hot water into our radiators to get the engines warm enough to start. Even then it took a chain of three men to pull a propeller through compression. That required experience, because a blade could easily smash several fingers or an arm—there were too many such instances on the Army Air Service record. There was a long wait while the oil warmed, and our open cockpits had no heat. Fur-lined helmets, gauntlets, boots, and flying suits had to conserve the calories our bodies manufactured.

We experienced little reality of battle when we shot our synchronized Lewis guns at a fluttering cloth-sleeve tow target, or our turreted Brownings at an observation plane's shadow on waters of the gulf. We tried for high scores to beat each other, without regard for the usefulness in real combat of the tactics we developed.

The Army Air Service graduated two classes a year from its advanced flying school at Kelly Field. Nineteen cadets out of the hundred and four carefully selected men who started, twelve months before, were commissioned second lieutenants, Reserve. That was in March of 1925. Since the active squadrons needed few additional pilots, most of us began looking for jobs in civilian life. I dressed in my old blue-serge business suit, packed my officer's uniform in my foot locker, and boarded a northbound train.

For the next several months, I established my home in a boardinghouse near Lambert Field, St. Louis. I instructed students, barnstormed, took part in flying circuses, and joined the Missouri National Guard. Then the Robertson Aircraft Corporation appointed me chief pilot, at a salary of three hundred dollars a month. My job was to select two other pilots and supervise flying operations of the contract airmail route between St. Louis and Chicago, C.A.M. No. 2, which was soon to be established. We were to use De Havilland observation planes that had been purchased from Army salvage and rebuilt. The mail pilot would sit in the wartime observer's cockpit, and the mail would be carried forward, where the military pilot used to be. The DH-4 was a fabric-wing, plywood-fuselage biplane with a four-hundred-horsepower, twelve-cylinder Liberty engine in its nose. It cruised at about ninety miles an hour.

The U.S. Post Office Department planned to improve its service; doing so, it could help develop commercial aviation and maintain the American system of business by contracting with private companies to operate federal airmail routes. These were to connect, at various strategic cities, with the government-operated transcontinental route. Eventually the transcontinental route itself, which had begun as an experiment at public expense, was turned over to private enterprise. The first contract airmail routes had been awarded. The Robertson Aircraft Corporation was a successful bidder. Just as my father worked on one of the early railroads in Minnesota, I began working on one of the early air routes in Missouri and Illinois. By that time railroads connected practically every city and village in the United States and their regular operation was taken for granted. I believed that airplanes, on a smaller scale but with greater speed, would someday render a similar service.

When the torn wings and broken fuselages of the DH-4s with which we were to fly the mail arrived at Lambert Field, I had serious misgivings. The planes had been considered unfit for any kind of military use. To make sure they would not be flown again, an axe had been applied to the longerons and plywood fuselages. The result looked more like a pile of refuse than potential airmail planes. At best, DHs had the reputation of being "flying coffins." Many had crashed with their Army pilots, often breaking into flames. But the Robertson Aircraft Corporation had long experience in rebuilding salvaged Army airplanes—Standards, Jennies, and Canucks. Why not DHs?

I knew that Robertson did not have enough money to buy new airplanes at five or ten thousand dollars apiece. We had to fly the rebuilt Army DHs or not fly the mail at all. I stipulated that each pilot must be equipped with a new seat-type silk parachute for emergency, and that no penalty would be laid against him if he used it.

I piloted the first southbound airmail from Maywood, outside Chicago, on April 15, 1926. It took me two and three-quarters hours to reach St. Louis, including stops at Peoria and Springfield, Illinois. Hurtling through the air at ninety miles an hour behind my mail sacks, I thought of the two-mile-an-hour oxcart travel of my father's boyhood. Our St. Louis planes, together with planes from Texas, Minnesota, and Michigan, connected at Chicago with the government's eastbound transcontinental route. That put our mail into New York for delivery the next morning, and thus saved one business day.

Philip Love and Thomas Nelson were the other pilots on our line. Flying over the level terrain of Missouri and Illinois, we were able to complete ninety-eight percent of scheduled flights. But the Chicago–New York plane was often grounded by Appalachian Mountains weather. Night after night, in winter, telegraphed messages came in: DOWN AT CLEVELAND. DOWN AT BELLFONTE. WAITING FOR DAYBREAK. MAIL ENTRAINED. It was a discouraging record for men who had cast their lot with commercial aviation's future.

Airmail pilots in 1926 flew in visual contact with the ground. Some of the best aviators had been killed trying to wedge under a low cloud layer or to push on through heavy haze. Weather reports were unreliable. No radio aids had been installed. From take-off to landing a pilot's only communication with earth came directly through his eyes. Mail planes carried a gyroscopic turn indicator on their instrument boards, but the pilot seldom used it because he had no way of knowing whether any clear air lay beneath him when he wanted to get down out of the cloud he was flying in.

When we started operating the St. Louis–Chicago route, the only light installed in our mailplanes was a dim one for the compass. Electric current for this feeble glow passed through a button on the control stick, so it could be switched on and off easily and not reduce the pilot's vision on a black night. Each pilot carried a good pocket flashlight of his own, but during the first weeks of our night flying there were no red and green navigating lights on our wings and no other lights, aside from those on the ground, to help in landing. My own policy was to take off when the visibility was good enough to let me fly, and to land or turn back when I could not see enough on the earth to go farther. If a pilot went down because of mechanical trouble or lasting weather, he telephoned the nearest post office and put his mail on a train.

Our loads were light. Often the sacks weighed more than the mail they carried. Contract routes were losing money, for the service we gave was not good enough to attract a large number of letters at the added cost of postage. To give efficient service, we needed better airplanes and radio communication with the ground. The chances we took flying "contact" to get through on schedule with our DHs inevitably added to the cost of operation. Love had a forced landing in a cornfield where he had to stall in so steeply to keep from overshooting that it loosened all the mailplane's landing wires. In addition to several forced landings I made during daytime, I abandoned two planes caught in weather at night. They were piles of tangled wreckage after crashing, but I had waited until all fuel was consumed before I jumped; since they did not burn, the mail I carried eventually reached its destination.

Early aviators had faith in their profession's future, possibly more intuitively than logically. Ranges, carrying capacities, speeds, and safety of aircraft would increase. Someday light and reliable radios would help pilots through the weather. Then we could fly St. Louis mail directly to New York, without dog-legging it through Chicago; and we could take a few passengers along to help pay our cost of operation. We would take off from Lambert Field in evening instead of afternoon, and thereby give a vastly better service.

The United States government had a program under way for improving ground facilities along contract airmail routes. Within the next year we would have revolving beacons and lighted emergency fields, just as pilots of the transcontinental route had. Radio stations would be installed when developed sufficiently to be of value. But the government would not furnish airplanes to an airline operator. Their purchase had to be financed by private capital. Where could an operator get enough money to buy planes? These cost from five to fifty thousand dollars each, depending on the number of engines and on the number of passengers they could carry. Businessmen and financiers did not share aviators' enthusiasm about transportation through the sky. They did not foresee "heavens filled with commerce." To get financing we had to demonstrate the airplane's capabilities, but to build capable airplanes we had first to get financing.

THREE

No Man
Before Me

The problems of establishing aviation as a common means of transport ran through my mind during solitary hours of mail flying. They entered into my decision to compete for the Orteig Prize. Raymond Orteig had offered a twenty-five-thousand-dollar prize for the first nonstop flight between the cities of New York and Paris. I read about it in an aviation-magazine article describing the failure of an attempt to make the flight. René Fonck, a great French ace of World War I, had crashed his overloaded plane at the end of a runway on Long Island. Two members of the four-man crew lost their lives in the resulting fire.

I was fascinated by the idea of flying nonstop between America and Europe across the Atlantic Ocean. Think of being able to leap over the earth at will, touching a continent, skipping an ocean, landing on this hemisphere or that! Twenty-five thousand dollars would be enough to pay for such a flight—to buy the plane, the fuel, and all necessary equipment—if a pilot flew behind a single engine.

I thought it was a mistake to build a multiengine plane, such as Fonck's, for a nonstop distance-record-breaking flight, especially when the route lay across an ocean. A single-engine plane would have greater range, and it seemed to me it would offer its pilot greater safety. An engine in the nose of the fuselage could be better streamlined than engines strung out along wings. The chance of engine failure with a multiengine plane increased proportionately with the number of engines used. When people talked about the safety gained by having more than one engine for the transatlantic flight, they did not stop to realize that a plane, in those days, could not fly many hundred miles after one of its engines stopped.

With reconditioned wartime engines, such as we used barnstorming and flying airmail DHs, failures in the air were frequent. I had experienced many as a pilot behind OX-5s, Hispano-Suizas, and Liberties. But in 1926 the Wright Aeronautical Corporation, in New Jersey, was producing an engine of postwar design, a model named the "Whirlwind," developing about two hundred horsepower. It had demonstrated a reliability that would remove much of the hazard from long-distance over-water flying.

As far as hazard was concerned, I concluded that a nonstop flight between New York and Paris would be less hazardous than flying mail for a single winter with our Liberty-powered DHs. And in addition to its sheer adventure, the reward of a successful flight would be much greater than that of a winter spent on the mail line. It would demonstrate the airplane's capabilities and show financiers that investments in aviation now might return big profits later. After landing at Paris, I would still have a plane and engine almost new, with which passengers could be carried and still other records broken.

But I could not buy a long-range plane with a prize I had not won. I faced the same problem of financing that contract-airmail operators were faced with. I decided to put two thousand dollars of my own money into the project, and somehow to raise the rest. Since I would try to get financial support in St. Louis, I decided to talk about, and actually make, a St. Louis–to–Paris flight—stopping at New York to qualify for the Orteig Prize. I would need at least ten thousand dollars, I estimated. For me that was a tremendous amount of money. Even so, the cost might run higher. My plane would have to be equipped with special instruments and oversize fuel tanks; and I would have traveling and hotel expenses, and bills for gasoline and oil to pay.

Weeks of planning and frustrating effort passed, during which I had obtained only a single pledge of one thousand dollars. Then, two St. Louis businessmen took the problem of finance from my shoulders. Harry Knight, a broker by profession, and Harold Bixby, a banker, were fliers who had a vision of aviation's future. Bixby had been influential in persuading city bankers to help the Robertson Aircraft Corporation finance its mail line. My idea of a one-stop flight from St. Louis to Paris appealed to them. "You concentrate on the plane and getting ready for the flight," they said. "Leave the financial end to us."

At Bixby's suggestion we decided to name our plane *Spirit of St. Louis*. Seven men besides Bixby took part in its financing: Harry F. Knight, Albert Bond Lambert, J. D. Wooster Lambert, E. Lansing Ray, Frank H. Robertson, William B. Robertson, and Earl C. Thompson. We raised a total of fifteen thousand dollars, which turned out to be about fifteen hundred dollars more than the cost of the plane, its equipment, and all expenses incurred up to the time I landed at Paris.

To my amazement, I found buying the plane as difficult as it had been to get my project financed. For the first time I encountered aeronautical organizations that were more interested in their reputation than in selling their product. Manufacturers were shocked by my insistence on a single engine, given the hazards of a trans-oceanic flight. Finally, in February 1927, I signed a contract with Ryan Airlines, Inc., at San Diego, California, to construct a single-engine monoplane capable of flying nonstop from New York to Paris. It would be powered by a Wright Whirlwind. The fuselage would be tubular steel; the wings and ribs, wood; and the entire machine, fabric covered.

The control of Ryan Airlines had been purchased by Benjamin Franklin Mahoney, a young man of Irish lineage. A few days before I arrived in San Diego, he had hired a young engineer named Donald Hall. Hall felt sure he could design a plane capable of the New York–Paris flight, and Mahoney was willing to build it at a price of six thousand dollars without engine and instruments. They estimated that the plane would be ready for its test flights within sixty days of the time I placed my order. The recently formed federal Bureau of Aeronautics, in Washington, had published regulations stating that civil airplanes must be licensed, and that before a license would be given certain minimum specifications regarding performance and structural safety must be met. These specifications worried us at first, but a Department of Commerce representative said licensing would be no problem on a non-passenger-carrying flight. Pilots, too, were required to carry licenses, but I had already received mine: Number C-69.

Dedication, skill, and many hours of overtime on the part of engineers and craftsmen kept the construction of my *Spirit of St. Louis* on schedule. I ran the first test flight on April 28, exactly sixty days after placing the formal order. On May 11 I landed at St. Louis, completing a nonstop overnight flight from San Diego, the first nonstop or overnight flight to be made between those cities. Originally I had planned on remaining in St. Louis for several days with my plane. After all, it had been named for the city, the saint, and the citizens. St. Louis men were supporting my adventure. I was to make a St. Louis–New York–Paris flight. A dinner with speeches, followed by a dedication ceremony at Lambert Field, would be only appropriate. Thereafter I would fly to New York, an intermediate base on a one-stop flight connecting Missouri with France.

Originally, too, I had not considered the possibility that competition for the Orteig Prize might turn into a race. Possibly the fact that Fonck had no contender when he attempted the New York–Paris flight threw me off guard. But before I landed at St. Louis with my plane, four other contestants had arisen, two of them with multiengine and two with single-engine planes. There was a time when it appeared that all four of them would be able to take off for the flight before the Ryan factory could roll my *Spirit of St. Louis* out its door. Then one of the multiengine planes crashed in a swamp on a test flight, killing its crew. The other nosed over on a landing, with structural damage and crew injuries resulting. One of the single-engine planes took off from France for New York, crossed the Atlantic coast of Europe, and was never heard from again. The other had a minor accident in addition to becoming involved in legal complications.

When I reached St. Louis on my eastward crossing of the North American continent, two planes had been tragically eliminated from the Orteig Prize contest, but the remaining two had been repaired and were at the take-off point on Long Island, apparently ready to start for Paris as soon as weather conditions were satisfactory. If I delayed long enough for a dinner and dedication in St. Louis, the prize might be won before I reached New York. In a conference with my partners we decided to have no ceremonies whatever so that I could continue eastward the following day.

I landed at Curtiss Field, Long Island, on May 12, 1927, to be confronted by new and unexpected problems. The first was created by newspaper reporters and photographers and motion-picture men. There were several times as many as I had seen at one place before. A dozen or more ran out into the area where I wanted to land. They apparently had neither consideration for a pilot nor respect for airport regulations. I shifted my approach and touched down a safe distance away; but as I taxied to the hangar line they crowded around the *Spirit of St. Louis* until I feared somebody would be struck by the propeller.

As soon as I stepped down from my cockpit I was accosted by requests for interviews and camera poses, with the result that a large part of the time I usually devoted to my plane, after landing, was devoted to the press. But I wanted publicity for the St. Louis–New York–Paris flight. It was part of my project. It would draw public attention to aviation. It would increase my personal influence and earning capacity. I found it exhilarating to see my name in print on the front pages of America's greatest newspapers, and I enjoyed reading the words of praise about my transcontinental flight. I did not begrudge the time I spent with the press—at first. I answered all the questions I could about my airplane and flight, and tried to laugh off questions that seemed too silly or too personal. But I was shocked by the inaccuracy and sensationalism of many of the articles resulting from my interviews. I had encountered nothing like it in San Diego or St. Louis. I found myself quoted as saying things I had neither said nor thought. Much the papers printed seemed not only baseless but also useless.

In some cases the careful explanations I had given appeared to have no effect at all on the reporters, as when they wrote that I had to take off and land the *Spirit of St. Louis* while looking through a periscope. I had told them I intended to use the periscope only in

Evangeline Lodge Land, 1899   Charles August Lindbergh, 1901

LINDBERGH'S PARENTS

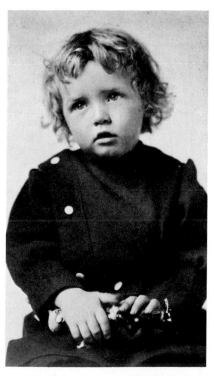

Charles Augustus Lindbergh

With Fluff, the Lands' cat

On a hunting expedition

At age six,
with his mother

At age eleven,
with his father

With his dog Dingo, 1913

Grandfather
Charles H. Land
firing porcelain for
dental use

The rebuilt Lindbergh farm home in Little Falls, Minnesota

Charles at White House Easter egg rolling, 1913

The old Ford, Maria

With his Excelsior motorcycle, 1921

With University of Wisconsin ROTC pistol team, 1921
(on left, back row)

Lindbergh's commission as second lieutenant
in the U.S. Army Air Service

UNITED STATES AIR SERVICE
This is to certify that

Chas. Augustus Lindbergh has been

appointed Second Lieutenant in the

AIR SERVICE
OFFICERS RESERVE CORPS
(INACTIVE STATUS)
of the

ARMY OF THE UNITED STATES
for period of five years commencing

March 14, 1925

received the rating of Air Plt.

O.73-7. OCAS. 3/28/25. 19

F. Fravel, Lt. Col., A.S.

Chief, Personnel Division.

Age 23   Wt. 165

Hgt. 6 ft. 3 in.

Color Hair Light

Color Eyes Blue

Date of issue April 15, 1925.
(Card not official without Air Service Seal.)

Signature

Chas. Augustus Lindbergh
Name Typed

Rank Second Lieutenant

Organization   Air Service

Officers Reserve Corps

Rating Airplane Pilot

During flying-cadet days in Texas, 1924

With friend and fellow barnstormer Bud Gurney, 1925

cruising flight when I was heavily overloaded and flying very low. By glancing into it I would have warning of high obstacles ahead, like factory chimneys, without having to lean from one side to the other of my cockpit to look out. It would have been impossible to take off and land looking through that periscope. But the idea made a better story, I was told; and better stories helped sell newspapers.

Contacts with the press became increasingly distasteful to me. I felt that interviews and photographs tended to confuse and cheapen life, especially those printed in the "tabloid" papers. Most of all I disliked what I learned were called "composite photos." These were made by having models take whatever poses the photographer desired, and then substituting the heads of the newsworthy. The trick required no more than the skillful use of scissors and a little glue. You had to look carefully to realize the photographs were faked.

I was furious about the first composite photograph I saw in which I had a part. My mother had come to New York to be with me for a few hours before I started out for Paris. We had posed together for the photographers, but refused to take the maudlin positions some of them had asked for. The next day I was startled to see newspaper photographs showing us in exactly those positions. I thought it cheaply sentimental and thoroughly dishonest on the part of the papers. At New York I began to realize how much irresponsibility and license can lurk behind the shining mask called "freedom of the press."

A second, and far more serious, problem consisted of the fact that I had not yet become eligible for the Orteig Prize. One of the rules connected with the prize stated that sixty days must elapse between the prize committee's acceptance of entry papers and the contestant's take-off for the flight. Entry papers could not be filled out until certain specifications of the plane were known. For me, sixty days had not elapsed. If I waited until I was eligible under prize rules, either Commander Richard E. Byrd with his Fokker or Clarence Chamberlin with his Bellanca would probably reach Paris ahead of me.

I felt that making the first nonstop airplane flight between the continents of North America and Europe was more important than any amount of money. But I had used the twenty-five-thousand-dollar Orteig Prize as an argument to finance my flight. I had said that if my flight was successful it would not cost anybody anything. Therefore I could not give up my chance to win the prize without consulting my partners. I telephoned St. Louis. The answer was what I expected it to be. It came clearly over the thousand miles of wire: "To hell with the money. When you're ready to take off, go ahead."

Other problems turned out to be relatively minor. When I landed on Long Island, I did not know where I would find a field long enough for my overloaded take-off. Commander Byrd generously solved that for me by offering the use of the runway that had been prepared for his trimotor Fokker. It was the one René Fonck had used for the take-off on which he crashed; and it was on Roosevelt Field, adjoining Curtiss. I could taxi my plane from one field to the other by climbing a slight rise in ground. The runway was close to a mile in length—more than I required.

I had again been a little worried by the government's new regulations because, to save weight, I had not installed navigating lights on my plane. The Assistant Secretary of Commerce for Aeronautics, William P. MacCracken, Jr., relieved me of this worry when he came to see the *Spirit of St. Louis*. "You probably won't encounter much night traffic up where you're going," he said, smiling. "I think we can give you a special dispensation." I had not been at Curtiss Field very long before I discovered that my flight was considered "unscientific." "Why aren't you carrying a radio?" reporters asked. "Because a radio is too heavy," I replied, "and because I haven't been able to find an airplane radio set that's reliable. When the weather is bad you can't make contact with the ground. When the weather isn't bad a pilot doesn't need a radio." My reply was not convincing to the reporters. "Byrd and Chamberlin are going to carry radios," they said. "Why aren't you carrying a sextant? Byrd and Chamberlin have sextants."

Much emphasis was being placed on what the New York–to–Paris flight would do for the benefit of science. I had never thought about making a "scientific flight," although I realized I was using scientific developments whenever I flew a plane. My objective was to get into the air and reach a goal across three thousand six hundred miles of land and ocean. I had made everything else secondary to it. I bought the best available instruments for my plane, including an expensive earth-inductor compass. But when I found I could not obtain a reliable radio, I saved the weight of a radio. When I calculated the weight of a navigator and his cockpit to be equal to several hundred miles of range, and that, allowing for the greatest possible errors in navigation, I could not miss striking Europe's coastline somewhere, I decided to do my own navigating. Since I could not take a sextant sighting at the same time I was flying my unstable *Spirit of St. Louis,* I saw nothing to be gained by buying and carrying a sextant.

But newspapers were measuring the scientific character of a flight less by the practicability of instruments carried than by the fact that instruments were put on board the airplane. Reporters had little understanding of factors I considered most important for a successful flight—an excess of fuel, lightness of weight, and the freedom of action that came from having no worry over a crew's welfare.

Mechanics rushed the servicing of my plane. Engineers reinspected critical items. In a few days I had completed final test flights. Only weather delayed my taking off for Paris. Areas of fog and storm lay across the coast of North America and covered the Atlantic. On May 19, a week after I landed on Long Island, the afternoon weather forecast predicted four more days of fog. I wanted to break away from the press and crowds at Curtiss Field, and accordingly I accepted an invitation to attend a theater in New York that night and watch the show from backstage. I thought it would be an interesting experience.

When I reached the city in the evening, I took the precaution of phoning for a final check on weather. To my amazement, a report came back to the effect that weather along the North American coast was clearing! I returned immediately to Curtiss Field and ordered my plane made ready for a daybreak take-off. I had hoped to get some sleep that night, if only for two or three hours; but too many incidents arose requiring my attention. When I climbed into my cockpit, I had been awake for twenty-three hours. Ahead was a thirty-six-hundred-mile solo flight.

The runway was soft and muddy. A light tail wind was blowing. For seconds after I opened the throttle it seemed doubtful that my plane would take to the air. But I had an excess of speed at the runway's end, and enough altitude to clear telephone wires beyond.

At 7:54, local time, on the morning of May 20, 1927, I was in the air with my *Spirit of St. Louis* holding four thousand miles of fuel in my tanks. The two-hundred-twenty-three-horsepower Whirlwind had lifted a gross weight of more than five thousand pounds off the ground. I carried instruments by which I could keep my plane upright and on its proper heading through any amount of cloud and fog.

No man before me had commanded such freedom of movement over earth. I had enough gasoline to fly northward to the Pole, or southward to the Amazon, or to Africa, if I wished to change my course. For me the *Spirit of St. Louis* was a lens focused on the future, a forerunner of mechanisms that would conquer time and space. Wherever I could fly my plane, then someday mail or passengers or bombs could be delivered. In peace and in war a third dimension was opening to man's travel.

A great storm area over the ocean almost turned me back. Its icy clouds were a formidable danger. For a time during the night my compasses swung so erratically that I held my course by stars, instead of instruments. But the great hazard on my New York-to-Paris flight turned out to be my lack of sleep. It brought me closest to disaster. To combat it I was forced to draw on reserves beyond my conscious mind's command, and at times it seemed that they were insufficient. I saw mirages as real as reality had been; I conversed with ghostly forms riding with me in the fuselage; I understood the visions described in ancient myths and sensed elements of man's existence unknown to me before.

The wish for sleep had left by the time I crossed green Ireland's coast, within three miles of my plotted route. I was too exhilarated by my landfall to continue being sleepy, too grateful for my return to earth from the fantastic stage of dream and vision on which I had found myself an actor. Europe was strange, intriguing. I had never been there before I flew across the ocean. School geographies left me unprepared for the compactness of the countries I flew over— Ireland, not as big as Maine; England and Scotland together about the size of Minnesota; France, with an area that could not match a Texan's boast.

With my background of the Mississippi Valley and its quarter-section farms, I did not see how European peasants lived from the pittances of land they cultivated—plots often the size of city lots, separated by stone walls, ditches, and hedgerows. Looking down on Europe I felt my world compressed. Miles and hours were disjointed after my transatlantic flight: New York and Paris, less than a day and a half apart! New York and London, closer still! Man's concepts of world geography must change as he took to his airplane's wings.

My course lay over Plymouth, from which the *Mayflower* had sailed three hundred and seven years before. The Pilgrims took two months to reach the coast of Massachusetts. My voyage back had taken less than thirty hours. I struck France at Cap de la Hague, with the sun about to set. The Seine wound in from the north, before nightfall, to guide me on to Paris. The sky was clear; the stars came bright; I circled Eiffel's tower and landed at the airdrome of Le Bourget thirty-three and a half hours after my take-off on Long Island. I had broken the world's record for an airplane's range, and averaged over one hundred miles an hour. Contrary to newspaper reports, when I landed I had enough fuel remaining in my tanks to have continued on to Rome.

Even the eight days on Curtiss Field, in New York, had not prepared me for the world-wide interest and tremendous publicity my successful landing at Paris caused. I had planned to spend the night in some hotel. Instead, I slept in the American Embassy as guest of Ambassador Myron T. Herrick. I thought most of my days in France would be passed on flying fields with French pilots. Instead, I received such an extraordinary welcome that its lunches, dinners, and ceremonies left hardly any time to be with my plane. Hundreds of cables and telegrams arrived, filled with congratulations, with invitations and business proposals. I met the great French general Ferdinand Foch, the famous aviator Louis Blériot, and the President of the Republic, Gaston Doumergue. Everyone made speeches emphasizing good will between the United States and France, prophesying that aviation would help unite nations of the world in peace.

My short visit to Europe—I spent only two weeks in the Eastern

Hemisphere in 1927—strengthened my belief that the United States of America offered the greatest opportunity for developing aviation. Our combination of industry and technical skills and our vast space was unequaled by any other country: forty-eight states teaching the same language without a customs border between them; two and a half thousand miles from east to west, more than a thousand miles north to south, under the regulation of a single national government; around a hundred and twenty million people working together in a political system that was also an economic system.

President Calvin Coolidge ordered a Navy flagship, the cruiser *Memphis,* to bring me back to the United States. I was officially welcomed at Washington, where I stayed at the temporary White House as his guest. There was a big celebration on my arrival at New York, and another at St. Louis. Wherever I landed, crowds came to see my plane, and to hear me talk about aviation and its future. From St. Louis I flew to Ottawa at the invitation of Canada's government; then back to New York to have my plane and engine serviced and to complete plans for a tour through all of the forty-eight states.

My successful New York–to–Paris flight had put me in a position from which, I realized, I could be of great assistance in developing aviation. Airplanes and flying had suddenly gripped the imagination of Americans as though the quarter-century of effort following the Wright brothers' Kitty Hawk ascent, contributed to by thousands of men and women, had been crystallized by my flight across the ocean. I found myself symbolizing aviation. What I said and did was printed in newspapers all over the country, in addition to much I did not say and did not do. Invitations to visit came from dozens of cities.

While I was at Curtiss Field before taking off for Paris, many influential people had come to see my plane. Among them were Harry Guggenheim and his wife, Carol. He was president of the Daniel Guggenheim Fund for the Promotion of Aeronautics, about which I had read in aviation magazines. After I showed them the *Spirit of St. Louis,* Guggenheim said, "When you get back from your flight, look me up." Later, he told me he had not thought there was much chance of my getting back from such a flight. I had considered his invitation a gesture of politeness and dismissed it from my mind; but events thereafter brought us together often, first in the development of aviation, later in personal friendship.

Harry Guggenheim had been a Navy aviator in World War I. He was a son of one of America's richest families. His grandfather Meyer Guggenheim emigrated to the United States from a Swiss ghetto in the mid-nineteenth century, started out as a peddler in Pennsylvania, and thereafter made his fortune in the mining business. Meyer's sons had augmented that fortune and they had strong feelings of gratitude to the country that had given them a freedom of action Jewish peoples were denied in Europe. As a result, the Guggenheims established various philanthropic foundations, endowed with tens of millions of dollars. When I returned to New York after my Paris flight, I was advised by various people to talk to Harry Guggenheim about my desire to help develop aviation. He and I together decided on a three-month flying tour with the *Spirit of St. Louis,* which the Daniel Guggenheim Fund would finance.

That tour let me know my country as no man had ever known it before. When I returned to New York in October, the United States was represented by a new image in my mind. Instead of outlines on a paper map, I saw New England's valleys dotted by white villages, the crystal waters of Michigan's great lakes, Arizona's pastel deserts, Georgia's red cotton fields, the cascades and deep forests of the Oregon Northwest. I saw three great mountain ranges running north and south: the Appalachians, the Rockies, the Sierras—walls of a continent, holding rivers, warning off oceans. I saw waves foaming on the rocks of Maine, cloud layers pressing against Washington's Olympics. I saw California's "Golden Gate," Louisiana's delta, Florida's wide sand beaches hundreds of miles in length.

There were intimacies, too, detailed points of matter and of life: I circled a glacial lake in the high Sierras, almost inaccessible by foot, and saw its clear water like the air above, its gray rock bottom; I saw wild horses galloping over Oklahoma badlands; a skiff-filled harbor in New Hampshire, with fishermen standing at their nets and looking up; I dived into Death Valley, its hot sands ten feet below my wheels; I saw, wedged down between sun-seared mountains, a village of Indian teepees apparently deserted except

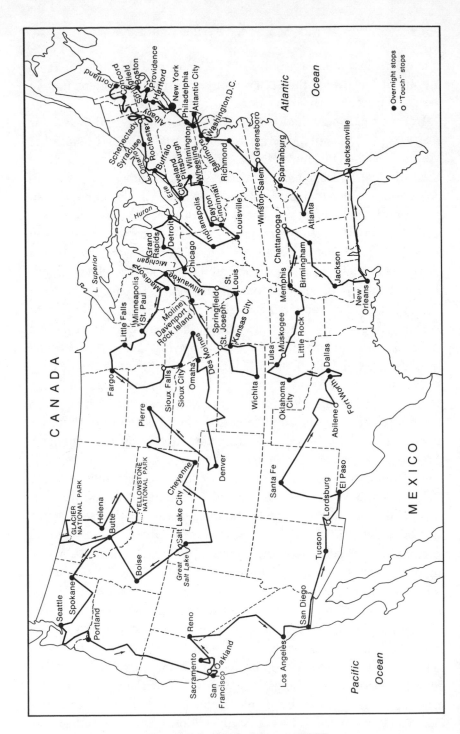

Tour of the United States, 1927

for one teepee that brought all the rest to life, for stuck in its triangular entrance was a fat squaw struggling to take cover from my wings.

I landed in every state in the union, spoke in scores of cities, dropped messages on still more. I inspected sites for airports, talked to engineers and politicians, and tried to convince everyone who would listen that aviation had a brilliant future, in which America should lead. It seemed obvious to me that the development of airlines would be made in three stages. First within the continents; then between the continents; finally across the oceans from hemisphere to hemisphere. In the fall of 1927, after my tour of the United States had been completed, I met the new ambassador to Mexico, Dwight W. Morrow. He had recently headed a board, appointed by President Coolidge, to investigate the conditions of American aviation. I had gone to his New York apartment at 4 East 66th Street for a conference, and while there, he invited me to fly the *Spirit of St. Louis* to Mexico City for a visit later in the year.

The Ambassador's invitation gave me an opportunity to accomplish several objectives on a single flight. In addition to the gesture of friendship toward Mexico he desired, I could demonstrate still more clearly the capabilities of modern aircraft. After the visit was over, I could fly on to South America, thereby helping link together the continents of our Western Hemisphere by air. I would fly nonstop to Mexico City from Washington, I decided, rather than from New York or St. Louis. Connecting the nations' capitals might give my flight greater political significance, especially in drawing the attention of Congressmen and Senators. Instead of selecting the best weather conditions, as I had done for my Paris flight—planning it for the long days of spring and waiting for favorable weather—I would fly through a long December night. I would schedule my time of arrival at Mexico City in advance, and attempt to hold to schedule regardless of wind, fog, or storm, as though I were once again on a routine mail flight between St. Louis and Chicago.

I scaled the distance from Washington to Mexico City at slightly over twenty-one hundred miles. As that was fifteen hundred miles less than the distance from New York to Paris, on such a flight the

Spirit of St. Louis would not be so heavily overloaded. I would not have to worry about the strength of my wings in any ordinary storm. I ordered the engine to be thoroughly inspected again; and I had a new instrument installed on my panel, a Kollsman supersensitive altimeter, which could be read accurately to a fraction of a hundred feet. I added a rifle, a machete, and some tropical medicines to the emergency equipment in the fuselage behind my cockpit.

Ambassador Morrow was disturbed when he learned of my plans. He had expected me to fly to Mexico in easy stages, as a sort of extension of the tour I had just made around the United States. He did not want me to undertake a hazardous flight, he said. I told him to leave flying problems to me and not to worry. We set 2:00 P.M. on December 14 as the time for my landing at Mexico City. I would take off from Bolling Field, across the Anacostia River from Washington. I had no difficulty obtaining Army permission for its use.

Bolling was a sod field with no paved runway for take-offs and landings in wet weather. Rains that fell before my day of departure left numerous shallow pools half hidden by the grass. Those pools, pushing against tires and splashing against wings, fuselage, and tail, would lengthen my take-off run considerably. The field's length was not great. Even though my plane carried a lighter fuel load than for its Paris flight, I wondered whether the elements of runway, weight, and power would let me climb fast enough.

I could not calculate an exact scientific answer to this problem. Its solution required an impingement of the senses on the mind. The morning of December 13, I walked back and forth over the section of Bolling that the wind decided I must use, kicking my heels into sod to test its firmness, hunting for a path between most of the pools, deciding on the last point at which I would either cut the throttle or commit myself to take off.

When the test came, water spewed up around my cockpit as though the plane were a speedboat getting on its step. But hundreds of feet of field still lay ahead when my wheels lifted, and I cleared treetops easily. My southwestward course lay across the state of Virginia, almost paralleling its Blue Ridge Mountains. I knew there were storms along my route, but weather reports contained little information about visibility and ceilings. During daylight hours my flying was routine by the standards of a mail pilot—nothing worse than an overcast sky and heavy rain squalls. But as twilight fell and night blackened above Georgia's hills, the line between earth and air was often undistinguishable. I wove back and forth through the squalls, flying lower to stay beneath clouds.

About halfway between sunset and the time for dawn, a band of white not quite blotted out by night appeared under my left wing— a surf line. I had reached the Gulf of Mexico. I angled slightly westward to follow that dim bank of foam, for it gave me some perspective. Mist thickened and the overcast dropped down until I found myself flying less than two hundred feet above the water. Even then wisps of cloud slipped under me, screening off the surf for periods of seconds. Then I would hold my course by compass, keeping the sensitive altimeter needle on its mark, starting to climb slowly if more than a quarter-minute passed without a glimpse of foam appearing.

I thought more than once I had given up contact with the earth, and planned to continue climbing until I saw stars—unless the overcast mounted above fifteen thousand feet. But patches of clear air mixed in with lower clouds. Each time, the surf appeared again and I glided steeply down. My cockpit was warm and humid as I flew along the gulf. In spite of the alertness that flying at such low altitude requires, I experienced the relaxation that comes to a northerner transplanted to a southern climate. It seems strange, looking back from the modern day of pressurized and air-conditioned cabins, but in planes of the 1920's the climate you flew through actually came inside the cockpits, bringing a sensual contact with the geography below.

Following the Gulf of Mexico coast that night I experienced a feeling I have often had in carrying on my profession. It is disturbing because it detracts from the joy of being a pilot. It relates to my isolation from the ground I look down on, and it is keenest when I see some spot where I would like to set my feet. Then the planetary accessibility that my airplane gives me and its very speed prevent my alighting, birdlike, on a post or branch. It is like smelling food when you are hungry, with no chance to take a bit. I felt a desire to land and swim, to let breaking foam wash the sweat from my skin and the smart from my long-opened eyes. But airplanes seldom permit such intimacies with the ground they let you see; and even if the beach had been wide and hard enough for landing, my commitment to a nonstop flight would have kept me in the air. I could imagine myself acting in a childhood fable where any touch of earth would break the spell.

Ceilings raised a little as I curved southward with the Texas coast, and visibility was good beyond the Mexican border. After daybreak it was easy to hold ground contact until I reached Tampico. There, clouds were so low, churning, that I had to climb above them. I saw a few patches of city streets and buildings as I turned westward. Then the earth became covered with a fluffy stratus layer above which hulks of clouds columned and floated. I wove through channels of clear air until I saw the earth again in a line of towering mountains that held back eastern weather. With my lightening fuel load I climbed easily up through a saddle in those mountains, to the sun-baked Valley of Mexico beyond.

The valley's sky was blue, its visibility unlimited. I thought the problems of my flight were over. I could throttle down and still reach Mexico City's Valbuena Airport on schedule. But the best maps of Mexico I had been able to obtain showed little detail. Straightish black lines, representing railroads, crossed wavy blue lines, representing rivers. I could not make them fit the railroad and the dry river beds below me. The country was sparsely populated. I saw fewer than half a dozen villages.

I followed the railroad westward, hoping it would intersect another line of rails and thereby form angles that would correspond with angles I could locate on my map. This was usually an effective way for a lost pilot to locate his exact position. When no intersection came, I tried another method I had found successful in the past. Strung out at infrequent intervals along the rails were towns and villages, each with a railroad station. Back in the United States every railroad station had a black-lettered signboard at each end, carrying the name of the town it served and offering an easy way to check navigation. I had often "shot" railroad stations successfully. Even the poorest maps printed the names of these towns and villages.

I glided the *Spirit of St. Louis* down with throttled engine, clearing roofs by less than fifty feet. Black-haired men, women, and children ran out from adobe stores and houses onto dusty dirt streets. Dogs barked noiselessly. A barefooted rider looked up from his donkey. Chickens of various colors fluttered and disappeared. A sign was on the end of the station, as I expected—smaller than ours in the United States, but easily read. The name of the village was CABALLEROS. I unfolded my map as I climbed. But I could find no Caballeros. Too small a place, I thought. I flew over cactus-bordered tracks to the next village. Its name was CABALLEROS, too! I tried a small town, with the same result. All the stations in Mexico appeared to be named alike. Slowly, after my sleepless night, I realized that "Caballeros" marked a convenient place for men.

I was completely lost, in broad daylight, with unlimited visibility and under a clear sky. The time I had scheduled for my arrival at Mexico City had already passed. The Ambassador would be on the field waiting for me, with who knew how many officials and dignitaries; surely, there was a huge crowd. I had never been in such a situation before. It was essential to do something immediately. But what? Possibly I could locate my position from the general system of river beds, observed as one great pattern. I opened my throttle and climbed to fourteen thousand feet. I could see clearly for more than fifty miles.

While I was studying the broad geographical features below, I saw in the distance what appeared to be a fairly large city, and banked toward it. Streets and buildings took form as I flew nearer and lessened my altitude. When I circled above them I saw, painted in huge letters on a windowless wall, HOTEL TOLUCA.

Toluca was marked clearly enough on my map, in much larger print than the towns and villages strung out along lonely railroad lines. It was about thirty-five miles west and south of Mexico City. If I had looked behind my left wing when I was flying high, I would have seen the city itself. At top cruising speed I could arrive in twenty minutes. But I would be two hours behind schedule—a poor way to demonstrate aviation's reliability!

Thousands were waiting at Valbuena Airport, including the President of Mexico. Soldiers and police had been standing guard in a hot sun. I was terribly embarrassed, but President Plutarco Calles greeted me as warmly as though my wheels had touched the ground on time. Accompanied also by Ambassador Morrow, who was to be my host, we drove into the city amid a clamor of horns and galloping horses. In twenty-seven hours and fifteen minutes I had flown all the way from Washington; it had taken the Morrows almost a week by train to come from New Jersey.

Many pleasant memories of the all too short time I was there flash through my mind: the floating gardens in Xochimilco; a bull-fight, where one of the matadors presented me with a beautiful cape; an exhibition of roping and riding at the famous Rancho de Charros; and Christmas at the embassy with the Morrows and my mother, who flew down from Detroit. During my visit I had the honor of taking the President of Mexico for his first flight. He was able to look down upon his palace at Chapultepec, into the patios, the gardens, and upon the walks laid out in color beneath him. It is easy to understand, from the air, why the ancients chose this site for their capital.

I had been advised against attempting a flight to South America in a landplane. There were few airfields in the Central American countries I would have to pass over, no clearings in their great areas of jungle where a plane could land without crashing. Weather was unpredictable: ground-hugging clouds were typical; tropical storms rushed in from the ocean without warning; rain beat down so heavily a pilot could neither see the ground nor hold his plane in air. There would be no way to find a downed aviator. Native huts were often miles apart. Even an uninjured man would find ground travel difficult, slow, and dangerous.

But a route to South America was an essential second stage in the development of airlines, and I had a reserve in the *Spirit of St. Louis* that pessimists overlooked. I carried enough fuel to take me back northward, in emergency, to the sunny Valley of Mexico, or even to the United States. I could fly all through a night and reach dawn with hundreds of miles of range remaining in my tanks. Besides, a trip around the gulf and the Caribbean Sea would be an adventure worth another reasonable risk of life.

On December 28, 1927, I took off from Valbuena Airport and headed southeastward with plans for landing at the capital city of

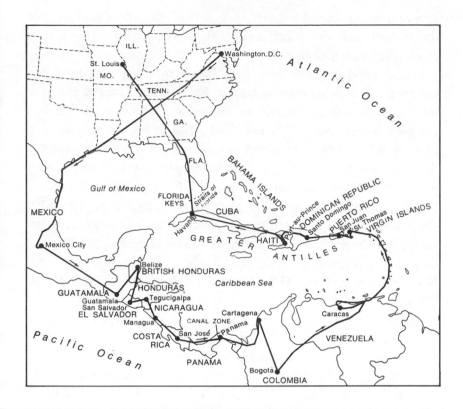

Central and South American flight, 1927–28

each of Central America's seven countries en route to the southern continent. I passed through a violent storm crossing mountains of Honduras, squeezed my plane into a polo field that was the only place for landing at Belize, and flew high over northwestern Nicaragua to avoid Sandino's bandit bullets, but the greatest danger I encountered was at the carefully guarded airport of San José, in Costa Rica.

The welcomes I received on landing at Guatemala, San Salvador, Tegucigalpa, and Managua had been so enthusiastic that police were unable to control the crowds. Thousands of men, women, and children would be standing in orderly fashion around the edges of the field as I circled overhead; but the moment my wheels touched ground they would scatter out onto the sod area in front of me, heedless of uniformed officers' frantic gestures. Hardly anyone realized that the *Spirit of St. Louis,* like other airplanes of the period, had no brakes, and that on the ground it was only awkwardly maneuverable.

I was afraid someone would be struck by my propeller. I had once seen a propeller chop a man in half; hence, I would cut ignition switches without waiting for hot valves to cool—and that was not good for my engine. At one field I had to ground-loop to stop short of the onrushing crowd. Even after I got out of my cockpit, there was danger that packed and milling people would damage my plane, as they had the year before at Le Bourget and at Croydon. Before I reached San José, the problem of airport control had become so serious that I sent word ahead saying adequate arrangements must be made to keep the field clear and protect the *Spirit of St. Louis.* Otherwise I would only circle overhead, and then continue on to one of the U.S. Army airports in the Panama Canal Zone.

On arriving at San José I was delighted to see long lines of soldiers, stationed at ten-foot intervals in front of an apparently orderly crowd of several thousand. There, I thought, I would be able to taxi up to my assigned position without endangering life and with appropriate dignity. I watched the soldiers bring bayoneted rifles to "present arms," as I glided down. Then I concentrated my attention on the field's surface and a three-point landing. A moment later I became aware of figures running toward me—on the left—on the right—closing in ahead. I cut switches, ground-looped, and jumped out onto the grass, shouting and motioning to the crowd to hold back.

I wanted to get a cordon of guards around my plane, but breathless and sweating men and boys surged under wings, surrounded the fuselage, and were crammed still closer by others catching up behind. Hands grasped me. Bodies pressed and shoved. I was lifted high on friendly shoulders to find myself half sitting, half lying, in a sea of hats and heads, and between bayonets that stuck up like huge needles all around me. The soldiers, who had been standing guard so rigidly, were now scattered among civilians in the seething crowd. Their mission of guarding the *Spirit of St. Louis* had become secondary to the immediate and essential problem of keeping their bayoneted rifles from impaling someone, and the person in greatest danger of impalement was the pilot of the plane they had been ordered to protect. Hazards of weather, snipers' bullets, and inadequate flying fields had been minor by comparison.

It was true that few places suitable for landing existed in Central America. I had often looked down on the high treetop carpet, beneath which all was mystery, and planned what to do if my engine failed. If the failure was immediate, there would be no choice. I would stall into a thick clump of foliage and hope branches would cushion the impact of fuselage and wings until I reached the ground uninjured. But if engine noise or roughness, or a drop in oil pressure, gave a few minutes' warning, I might find water to ditch in or reach a native hut. Occasionally I passed over a group of native huts on a hillside—thatch roofs with small stumpy clearings around them in which some sort of crop was growing. I seldom saw natives. Probably they were hiding from my plane. How startled they would have been to see me crash-land in their treetops! Most natives in Central America and northern South America were friendly to white men, I was told, but it would be inadvisable to get caught by some of the head-hunting tribes in Colombia.

Throughout Central America the slowness of ground travel impressed me. Much of it was by foot and donkey. Communication as we knew it in the United States did not exist. Five minutes of flight covered what would be a hard day's riding or walking for a native. The few good roads I saw never extended much beyond the cities they served. When I rode in an automobile after landing, it was usually bumping across erosions and avoiding ruts. Traffic consisted mostly of overloaded donkeys, oxcarts, and natives carrying various burdens on their heads. Naked children played in ditches and covered themselves with mud or dust, according to the weather.

I felt the great superiority of our civilization to the north. There seemed to be an unbridgeable chasm between it and Central American culture—in science, in industry, and in political organization. Even the capital cities in Central America were isolated places. Neither rail nor automobile roads connected them with Mexico to the north or Colombia to the south. A trip to the United

States or Europe required many days of travel by train and boat. No wonder the audiences I spoke to, through translators, were fascinated by my prophesies about airlines of the future.

When I reached the Panama Canal Zone with the *Spirit of St. Louis,* I experienced a different reaction from that I had after my boat trip from New York fifteen years before. Then, the zone was a strip of jungle with which American engineers were waging a hard but successful war. Now, coming from countries of Central America, the Panama Canal Zone seemed to represent civilization itself transplanted to the jungle. As I flew along the canal I saw great ships resting in locks and passing back and forth through cuts where steam shovels had been working during my boyhood visit. At France Field I landed on a modern military airport. Freshly painted hangars contained well-serviced fighters and bombers for the defense of the canal. Officers and enlisted men were neatly uniformed, alert, thoroughly trained, and disciplined. In the zone thousands of men and women from the United States lived, worked, and entertained much as though they were back in their home communities. Streets were well paved, store windows filled with latest fashions, repair shops equipped with modern tools, wharfs piled with bales and crates. Doctors and surgeons and nurses staffed modern hospitals. Luxurious hotels and restaurants flourished. I sensed the power, the wealth, the accomplishment of my United States of America.

But civilization did not extend far along my route eastward. The jungle closed in again a few minutes after I left France Field. My flights through the rest of Panama, Colombia, and Venezuela were routine except that the nearly nine-thousand-foot elevation of Madrid Field at Bogotá marked the highest elevation for a landing and take-off of the *Spirit of St. Louis,* and that a severe storm covering Venezuela's coastal mountains forced me to detour about one hundred fifty miles eastward of the route I had charted, before I reached the Caribbean Sea. As a result, I arrived at Maracay Field only a few minutes short of nightfall.

At Caracas, ceremonies of welcome ended so long after midnight that I had less than two hours' sleep before taking off on the thousand-mile flight along the Lesser Antilles to Saint Thomas. I landed on the golf course there. It made a small uphill field with mountains at the end. To overshoot meant crashing; but with the *Spirit of St. Louis* lightly loaded I stopped rolling with many yards of green to spare. Thereafter I visited San Juan, Santo Domingo, Port-au-Prince, and Havana.

The last flight of my around-the-gulf-and-Caribbean tour should also have been routine. I took off from the Havana airport about 1:35 in the morning on February 13, 1928, intending to fly nonstop to St. Louis. It should have been an easy flight—about a third the distance from New York to Paris. My take-off was quick, my cruising speed high. I felt no need to be miserly with fuel. I climbed to an altitude of four thousand feet and settled back to enjoy the night and piloting. But halfway across the Straits of Florida my magnetic compass started rotating, and the earth-inductor-compass needle jumped back and forth erratically. By that time a haze had formed, screening off horizons.

At first I thought the *Spirit of St. Louis* had dropped a wing and was banking; but the turn-indicator needle held its center, and a push with my foot on the rudder showed the gyroscope to be working properly. I had only once before seen two compasses malfunction at the same time. That was over the storm I encountered crossing the Atlantic en route to Paris. But then the magnetic compass only oscillated. Although it was through an arc of close to one hundred eighty degrees, I could get an approximate idea of direction by taking the midpoint of the card's swing, and I could hold it by the stars. Over the Straits of Florida my magnetic compass rotated without stopping, and my earth inductor was completely useless. I had no notion whether I was flying north, south, east, or west.

A few stars directly overhead were dimly visible through haze, but they formed no constellation I could recognize. I started climbing toward the clear sky that had to exist somewhere above me. If I could see Polaris, that northern point of light, I could navigate by it with reasonable accuracy. But haze thickened as my altitude increased. High thin clouds crept in to make the stars blink. Surely a storm area lay not far away—very likely above the southern states I had to pass. Should I spiral until daybreak, when I could get a general direction from the sun? That would prevent flying in the wrong direction and possibly finding myself hundreds of miles out over the Atlantic or the gulf.

While I was considering what basic policy to follow, I noticed the compass card slowing once during each rotation. I concluded this must be when its magnets were lined up with the earth's isogonic lines of force. If so, I might be able to estimate my approximate heading and set a general northwestward course toward a North American shore. If I could reach land, I could locate my exact position after sunrise, and follow railroads and rivers to St. Louis regardless of my compasses. As usual I carried a big reserve of fuel.

Clouds thickened, formed a layer, lowered. I descended to less than a thousand feet to keep contact with the sea. Even then I could barely distinguish water from the haze it joined. Turbulence increased. The compass card rotated too erratically to give any indication of direction. Dawn came slowly. Its diffused light seemed to originate in every azimuth, helping my navigation not at all. But while waves below were still half merged with night, a darker shade drew in toward me like a curtain—land, vague in early twilight, only a narrow strip with more water beyond. One of the Florida Keys? Then I had, after all, kept close to course in spite of my compasses! The hours of night were not wasted. I banked to follow the shore, flew over a gap of sea, and came to a long coastline bending right.

Nothing on my map of Florida corresponded with the earth's features I had seen. It showed plenty of keys, but no such coastline in relation to them. But if I was not flying over a Florida key, where could I be? Was it possible I had returned to Cuba, that my attempt to read the twirling compasses had put me one hundred eighty degrees off course? The coastline ended. I saw more keys ahead: low land, islands rising not many feet above the water. I unfolded my hydrographic chart—not Florida, not Cuba. Then I must be over the Bahamas. That would mean I had flown at almost a right angle to my proper heading, and it would put me close to three hundred miles off route!

Improving daylight marked the east and showed me that only the lines of ink labeled "Bahama Islands" corresponded with the land below. I banked to the approximate northwest heading I had hoped to be following before, and held it by the lighter shade of the horizon toward the sun. Somewhere along its sandy beach, I would strike the Atlantic Florida coast. The magnetic compass card stopped rotating as soon as I reached land. It continued to swing excessively, but I could hold within five or ten degrees of the course I set.

Dozens of heavy squalls lay along my route in Florida and Georgia. Rain turned to snow in Tennessee and Illinois. Ceilings were never high. Some thirty miles southeast of St. Louis clouds lowered until I was almost touching branches with my wheels. Visibility closed in to half a mile. Snowflakes streaked past my cockpit. Suddenly haze and branches merged as a hillside sloped up ahead of me. I eased the stick back, kicked left rudder, and lost contact with the ground.

Every pilot of the 1920's knew that regaining contact with a fogbound earth was dangerous. If you could not find a hole in the clouds below you, there was no way to descend in safety. You might be lucky enough to glide down into a pocket of clear air, or you might be unlucky enough to crash into a barn, a chimney, or a high-tension line immersed in fog. Flying night mail I had twice bailed out with my parachute when caught in weather that left little or no ceiling below its clouds.

Of course I knew the country around St. Louis well. North of the city and south of the Mississippi River lay a large area of level ground. I had passed over it every time I flew the mail route. That area contained no hills. Lambert Field was a southern part of it. If I could make contact with the earth there, I should be able to reach my destination. But I must be sure of clearing the high buildings of St. Louis before I descended. I climbed to fifteen hundred feet, continued on course for thirty minutes, throttled my engine, and held the air-speed needle at sixty miles an hour. The turn indicator jerked back and forth and the wings flexed in turbulence. I broke out to a three-hundred-foot ceiling and a visibility of nearly two miles. I had often flown the mail over those flats under worse conditions. I taxied my plane up to the line at Lambert Field fifteen hours and thirty-five minutes after take-off, completing my tour of Gulf of Mexico and Caribbean countries and the first nonstop flight between Havana and St. Louis.

As I look back on my flight through Central and South America and the West Indian islands, pictures form and fade in memory. I see a high waterfall, a white band of spray against green mountain cliff, connecting two levels of Guatamalan jungle. In Nicaragua, I see an extinct volcano within which a small farm nestles, shacks and fertile fields hidden by the circular lava rim except to an airman's eye. I look down at thousands of pink flamingos on the Panamanian coast, drifting above sand and water like a mist. I meet a republic's president who always arrived "punctually, fifty minutes late," so his host's guests will not be embarrassed by arriving after him. I fly over bands of peccary on wild Colombian plains, dive past a native maiden standing brown and naked in Venezuelan surf. I see Latin-American hospitality manifest itself; the lunches, dinners, speeches, and receptions in every country where I landed. Contrary to the ominous warnings I was given about gulf and Caribbean weather, it turned out to be excellent for flying. I remember blue skies far more than storm and cloud; and deep transparent waters.

I grounded the *Spirit of St. Louis* after that southern tour, although plane and engine were capable of many more years of flying. I had spent nearly a year making demonstration flights and tours. These always involved the possibility of accident no matter how careful I was, and an accident with the *Spirit of St. Louis* would have had a detrimental effect on aviation. Aside from operating hazards, a plane might be destroyed by storm winds after being staked down snugly on the ground. The last flight was between Lambert Field and Bolling, where I landed on April 30, 1928— one year and two days after the first test flight at Dutch Flats in San Diego. The Smithsonian Institution had asked to exhibit my plane permanently in Washington.

Now I wanted to concentrate my attention on the development of commercial airlines. To start a passenger airline from St. Louis to New York required huge financial backing, by aviation standards of 1928, yet now I was talking about one that would continue on to California—two and a half thousand miles from coast to coast. Planes would have to be bought, ground facilities installed, pilots, mechanics, and ticket agents hired. The figures one could put on paper did not show that a profit could be made carrying passengers in airplanes. Without a government subsidy added to the income column, the last digits were red.

To entice large capital investments—one had to think in millions of dollars, where thousands had seemed a lot before—it was necessary to convince capitalists that an airline would attract passengers, mail, and freight in quantities and at prices that would change figures from red to black. To do this, airplanes had to be faster, safer, and more reliable than the best being produced. I was, in fact, planning an airline around nonexistent aircraft. This line of reasoning took Harold Bixby, Harry Knight, Bill Robertson, and me on a trip to Michigan in the spring of 1928.

I piloted one of the latest planes built by Ryan Airlines, Inc.: a five-place high-wing monoplane, powered by a Whirlwind engine and patterned after the *Spirit of St. Louis*—a "sister ship," it was called, though it was not equal to it in performance. We picked up Major Thomas Lanphier near Mount Clemens, Michigan, and then flew to the Ford airport at Dearborn. Lanphier commanded the 1st Pursuit Group. He knew Henry Ford and had often talked to him about airplanes and their future. Months before, he had let me fly one of his pursuit planes; in return, I had let him fly my *Spirit of St. Louis*.

At Dearborn the five of us were to meet with Ford, that almost mythical character who had become one of the world's richest men by making automobiles a part of everyday American life. He could buy a railroad or order a new factory built, if the idea appealed to him, during a luncheon conversation. He was so powerful in the business world that he could make a success of almost anything he decided to support, and he had shown increased interest in commercial aviation. Several years before, he had started building all-metal single-engine airplanes under the direction of the well-known engineers William B. Stout and William B. Mayo. These planes brought the Detroit mail southwestward to Chicago at the same time we St. Louis pilots flew it northeastward in our ex-Army DHs.

The genius of Henry Ford did not depend much on logic for his business ventures. Intuition played a major part in his phenomenal success. His approach to a new project baffled engineers who worked for him. There was no telling what strange orders he would give. But when "Mr. Ford" gave an order, "something better be done about it right away." The Ford Motor Company maintained a tradition of action. Men who did not take action did not hold their jobs very long, and everybody who worked for the company was well aware of it. That was why faces had been so solemn one evening in the fall of 1926 when I landed my mailplane at Chicago. I told the story to my partners before we reached Dearborn.

I could see something was wrong as soon as I handed the wilted mail sacks down from my DH. Not a member of the Ford crew was smiling. What was the matter? Well, Mr. Ford had issued an order. It had come right from headquarters at Dearborn. There were to be no more forced landings on his airline! One of the Ford planes had been forced down in a tornado not many days before. In the crash the pilot was killed. Killing pilots did not fit in with Henry Ford's idea of doing business. Unlike the rest of us, he did not think accidents were an unavoidable part of aviation. He was not going to stand for losing his pilots, and in consequence issued an order to put an end to it.

Action had to be taken as a result of that order, but nobody could decide what to do. You could hardly stop forced landings: Ford inspection was rigid, and maintenance meticulous, but sooner or later another was bound to come. What then? The "Old Man" would be furious. Somebody would get fired. He might even decide to get out of aviation entirely.

Months later, I learned what actually had happened in the head offices at Dearborn. As soon as he heard about the crash of his mailplane, Ford called a conference of company executives and engineers. You can imagine him sitting on a table, one foot on the floor, the other dawdling in air, neatly dressed, slender, determined, keen though aging, listening impatiently to arguments and explanations. Ford had his own ideas about management, and he never placed much confidence in engineers. Such accidents had to be stopped, he said, and the Ford Company was going to build airplanes that would stop them. He had already laid down general specifications for these planes, and he repeated them. He did not hamper himself with scientific reasons. Ford planes would be monoplanes, he said, "because monoplanes are simpler." They would be made of metal "because metal's the thing of the future." And they would be powered by more than one engine "because we aren't going to have any more forced landings." It was the latter statement that went through as an order to Ford airline personnel.

Multiengine metal monoplanes! Henry Ford had laid down three of the major characteristics that resulted eventually in transport aviation equaling in stature the gigantic systems using trains and ships. He did this at a time when many leading engineers were still arguing the advantages of wood, fabric, and wire.

I had met Henry Ford about a year after this incident, when I landed the *Spirit of St. Louis* on his airport at Dearborn. He was fascinated with my plane and kept studying the arrangement of the cockpit. As a matter of politeness I asked if he would like to make a flight. I felt sure he would decline, because it was well known that Ford had never flown. Officers of the company took for granted that Ford's life was too valuable to permit the risk of flying. Most company officers had never flown in those days, including many in the field of aviation.

I was surprised, therefore, when he accepted my invitation. The Ford men standing around us looked astounded, but of course no one questioned the wisdom of Mr. Ford's decision—at least not in words. My cockpit had been designed to fit snugly around one slender man of six feet two and a half inches of height. It was possible for another person to sit hunched up on the armrest of the pilot's seat; but that was a most uncomfortable position, and it forced me to lean awkwardly to the left side of the fuselage to make room. In the *Spirit of St. Louis,* bent over, cramped, and delighted, Henry Ford made his first flight in an airplane, and looked down two thousand feet on his big gray-stone home, his famous Rouge plant, and on the cities of Dearborn and Detroit. That took place about eight months before I flew with my friends to Michigan to talk to him about a transcontinental passenger airline.

Ford greeted us warmly at Dearborn, and escorted us through the factory where his multiengine metal monoplanes were being built. We were shown the great Rouge presses, furnaces, and production lines that turned out millions of automobiles each year. Throughout the Ford empire you sensed the tremendous and growing power of American civilization. You were surrounded by organized, mechanized, and confident efficiency. Henry Ford had taught his workmen to produce more in shorter hours. That gave him bigger profits, and he gave them better pay. Employees of the Ford Motor Company had achieved standards of living and leisure of which American pioneers had never dreamed. And by their example they were raising these standards in other nations of the world.

Ford automobiles brought city dwellers to the country for a weekend picnic, took farm families to the city's stores and churches, carried people by tens of millions to new opportunities and relations with each other. Their usefulness was limited only by the availability of roads on which to travel. Certainly airplanes in their turn would bring a still greater advance to civilization by quickening its intercourse and commerce. They were not limited by the geographical barriers of ground travel, and surface vehicles could never equal them in speed.

We had lunch with Ford and some of his executives to explain our mission. Ford believed in aviation's future, but it was against his policy to take part in financing airlines. He operated the Detroit-Chicago mail route to gain experience that would aid in the development of airplanes he produced. His business was manufacture, not operation. His contribution to aviation would be through the high quality and low cost of his trimotor transports. Here, we would have his assistance, but he would not, it was certain, become a partner in our transcontinental-airline project.

We held a conference in our Detroit hotel that night, and decided to approach one of the big railroad companies for support in organizing a passenger airline. Probably Henry Ford was wise in keeping his aeronautical activities close to his own field of manufacture. On the other hand, railroad companies were in the transportation business: there were good reasons why their executives should be interested in air transportation. Airplanes were elementally much faster than trains. They were already taking some mail and, in Europe, some passenger business from railroads. How much more they would take in the future nobody could be sure, but it might be huge numbers. It would be good policy for railroads to have part ownership in paralleling airlines, and therefore a voice in their control. Many a railroad man admitted he had been too slow to realize that bus lines were serious competition. A railroad could be of tremendous assistance to an airline because they could sell tickets jointly and exchange communication facilities; a railroad could assure air passengers of continuing transportation if planes were grounded by weather or operating troubles.

Harold Bixby warned us that some railroad executives held antagonistic views toward aviation. About a year before, he had gone to see the New York Central's president to try to interest him in a passenger airline. The president was a friend of Bixby's father. He was not at all interested in the project. He was surprised, he said, that a son of his old friend was "crazy enough" to think people would travel in airplanes.

Bixby suggested we fly to New York and talk to Clement M. Keys, the chief executive of the Curtiss Airplane Company. On meeting Keys earlier, he had been impressed by Keys's ability and by his confidence in the future of aviation. Keys was a big figure in the small aviation financial world. A Canadian by birth, he had come to the United States and set up an investment business. He and his friends held controlling ownership of the Curtiss Company. When we telephoned and told him of our interests, Keys gave us an appointment immediately. In New York he told us that he had considered the organization of a transcontinental airline. Some years earlier, he said, he realized that airplanes and airways needed more development before a passenger operation would be practical and safe. Now, with public interest in aviation aroused and with more powerful engines available, it was possibly the time to start an airline. He thought capital of ten million dollars should be raised.

This was beyond any figure we had considered, but Keys said it would be wise to establish big reserves for carrying an airline through the losses it was bound to incur during early years of operation—unless, that is, we could obtain a mail contract with a government subsidy. He agreed that participation by a big railroad was desirable, and suggested we talk to William W. Atterbury, President of the Pennsylvania Railroad.

Atterbury was plainly interested in a transcontinental passenger airline that would parallel his railroad in the east, especially because the Pennsylvania system did not extend west of St. Louis. He said he would recommend to his board of directors a financial participation if we could create an organization composed of the right people. He felt sure if the great Pennsylvania took part, men of high caliber would purchase stock and go on our board of directors—and the capital be raised. He said he would talk to his business acquaintances.

A few weeks later, "Transcontinental Air Transport" was incorporated with a capital of ten million dollars. The Pennsylvania Railroad had a twenty percent participation. I was appointed chairman of the technical committee of the airline and aeronautical consultant to the railroad. Now that we were financed, the time of dreaming and talking had passed. We were faced with the practical problem of creating a safe and attractive service that would eventually make money. We estimated it would take about a year to get planes built, ground facilities organized, and operations started.

Transports had to fly east and west in daily operation. We decided to do a minimum of high flying during the first year or two of operation. We could let our passengers sleep on Pullman cars at night and still save them more than a day of travel between Atlantic and Pacific coasts. That would be one of the advantages of a combined air-rail operation. We lay out a route as close as practicable to a straight line between New York and Los Angeles, diverting slightly to touch major cities and to cross the Rocky Mountains at its passes. After considerable technical study, which I largely undertook, we decided to use big trimotor Fords with Pratt & Whitney four-hundred-horsepower Wasp engines. Wood-winged Fokkers were a little faster, but we thought they would be harder to maintain. The Boeing and Curtiss companies had designed competitive transports, but they were without experience in servicing essential to operating efficiently and safely. Also, the Boeing and Curtiss planes were biplanes. Aside from the maintenance problems, I thought biplanes overly subject to icing in flight and to wind gusts on the ground. Moreover, their light wing-loading made them wallow excessively in rough air, with a corresponding increase in passenger airsickness.

The Fords cruised at one hundred five miles an hour and carried twelve passengers in addition to pilot and copilot. If we averaged a seventy-five-percent load factor, we would have to get the equivalent of eighteen transcontinental passengers eastbound or westbound every day, or about six thousand five hundred a year, but in fact there would be far more passengers, since many people would not fly all the way across the continent. Aviators had not thought in such distances and quantities before.

Our biggest concern was about operating at night. If we flew only in good weather, our planes would be grounded so much of the time that passengers could not trust schedules and tickets would be hard to sell. But if we flew through storm and fog at night, pilots would lose contact with the ground on occasion, just as I had twice lost it flying the St. Louis–Chicago mail. What was to be done then? I had bailed out with my parachute, but of course I was alone. A transport pilot could not bail out and leave a cabinful of passengers behind him. Somewhere, somehow, he would have to land his plane before it ran out of fuel, whether or not he could see the ground. That would probably mean a crash, and a bad one.

Should every passenger be equipped with a parachute for such an emergency? There were men in aviation who advocated this. But how would passengers feel about putting on a parachute in the first place? All the women would have to wear pants to make room for the leg straps, and old people and young children would be inept handling the equipment. You could not very well turn around in your cockpit and yell to them, "Jump!" A requirement to wear parachutes would cause a real hullabaloo with passengers. I had seen that the year before, in Washington, D.C.

In 1927, on my return from Paris, I offered to carry on flights over the Capitol all Senators, Congressmen, diplomats, and high-ranking members of government who wished to go with me. I thought it an excellent way to advance aviation to acquaint politically influential people with the adventure, ease, and practical merits of flying. The Army had agreed to lend me a trimotor Fokker transport for the purpose.

Army regulations required that everyone flying in an Army

plane must wear a parachute. We did not think this would cause much problem, but we had not expected the Senators, Congressmen, diplomats, and others to turn up at the flying field with their wives, mothers, daughters, secretaries, and lady friends. Most of the women were not happy about the idea of donning some hastily borrowed Air Service mechanic's coveralls so heavy parachute straps could be snapped around their limbs. Despite protests, none of the women refused to wear a parachute. The irony was that on the low and local flights I was making, the parachutes would be useless.

All was going smoothly when the Navy, perceiving the political implications in my flights, offered me the use of a trimotor Ford with the suggestion that I could carry more passengers per hour by using two planes. Complications arose because of a difference between Army and Navy regulations. Navy regulations did not require parachutes to be worn under circumstances where they could not be of use. The result was that women who rode on the Army Fokker had to put on coveralls and parachutes, while women who rode on the Navy Ford did not. Some Senator husbands accepting the Navy's invitation wanted to know why their wives' lives were not valuable enough to rate a parachute, too.

I conferred with an Air Service officer, who advocated our carrying a parachute so large that it would let the entire airplane down, with crew and passengers secure in their seats. "We'd attach it with a long steel cable," he suggested, "so even if the plane caught fire the parachute wouldn't burn"!

Parachutes were an obsession of people who thought about commercial aviation in its beginnings. Experience with emergencies at sea had proved that in most cases some passengers panicked and did not use life belts, yet a life belt is far simpler than a parachute. Besides, only a fraction of airplane accidents were of a type where parachutes would be of value even to trained personnel. Everything considered, I concluded that equipping airplanes or passengers with parachutes would be costly and ineffective by the measure of safety.

For the next several months most of my time was spent on transcontinental survey flights, interspersed with conferences in New York and visits to the Ford airplane factory. We had ordered ten

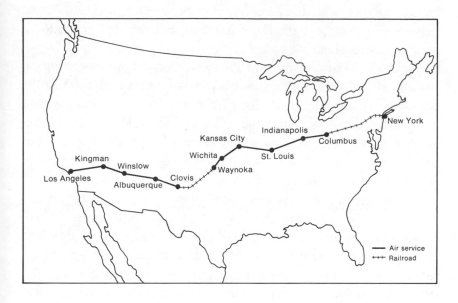

First Transcontinental Air Transport route, 1929

trimotor transports at a cost of about fifty thousand dollars each. Chief engineer Bill Mayo was supervising their construction under the watchful eye of Henry Ford himself. I talked to city officials, inspected airport sites and emergency landing fields, and worried about fog conditions at Los Angeles's Mines Field. We selected Columbus, Indianapolis, St. Louis, Kansas City, Wichita, Waynoka, Clovis, Albuquerque, Winslow, and Kingman for our points of landing en route. Unanimously, but with great regret on my part, we placed the line's major service facilities at Kansas City instead of at St. Louis. Kansas City was closer to the center of our transcontinental route and would make a better headquarters for both eastern and western divisions when we eventually stopped using trains and flew the entire route by air.

Only the government could afford to set up a weather-reporting network. Meanwhile, we would have to get along with a relatively cheap and makeshift system. We would install meteorological stations at the most critical points, but mainly we would depend on railroad agents along the air route to look outside their doors at scheduled hours and telegraph reports of the existing cloud conditions, together with temperature and barometric pressure. These reports were a step in the right direction, but they left much to be desired from a pilot's viewpoint.

When our Transcontinental Air Transport began operating on July 7, 1929, New Yorkers took a westbound train at 6:05 in the evening, and Angelenos climbed on board an eastbound plane in early-morning hours. After the official christening by Mary Pickford, I piloted the first eastbound passengers on the *City of Los Angeles* as far as Winslow, Arizona. Among them was my wife of six weeks, Anne, the second of the three Morrow daughters. At Winslow, we met the first westbound plane, which I piloted to Los Angeles on July 9. Both the Pennsylvania and the Santa Fe railroads co-operated. The one carried our passengers across treacherous Appalachian ranges, and unloaded them after daybreak at the edge of a specially constructed airport at Columbus, Ohio. The other carried them between Clovis, New Mexico, and Waynoka, Oklahoma. When weather was unflyable in the morning, air passengers stayed on board the train. Advance arrangements were made by Teletype, and each plane had a two-way radio.*

With our transcontinental passenger route in operation, I had more time to think about intercontinental airlines. After returning from my flight to Paris, two years before, I had talked to several businessmen about the practicability of a regularly scheduled airline operation between the United States and Europe. Among them were Richard F. Hoyt, of Hayden, Stone, and Co., and Franklin Mahoney, of Ryan Airlines. Hoyt had already considered such a project from a financial standpoint, and Mahoney was negotiating for the American agency of the German Rorbach flying boat.

There were three possible routes between North America and Europe: the Greenland-Iceland route in the north, the Newfoundland-Ireland route in the center, and the Bermuda-Azores route in the south. The northern route offered short overwater distances, offset by extremely severe weather conditions. The southern route

---

* The transcontinental trip took forty-eight hours, a saving of twenty-four hours over the all-rail trip. On the two daylight plane flights, which alternated with the night rail service, stops were made at Indianapolis, St. Louis, Kansas City, Wichita, Albuquerque, Winslow, and Kingman. TAT, which was known as "The Lindbergh Line," was a predecessor of TWA.

offered the best weather conditions, offset by the longest overwater distances. The central route was the shortest in distance, but aircraft following it would have a water jump of almost nineteen hundred miles of ocean, and often have to fly through fog and storm.

No one questioned the wisdom of using flying boats to start a transatlantic airline, although landplanes had better cruising speed and range. Two schools of thought contended. One said flying boats should ensure passengers the chance to land and survive in a heavy sea. The other said safety lay in airworthiness rather than seaworthiness. I believed that emphasis should be on airworthiness, because I knew transatlantic planes would have to fly through storms so violent that hulls could not be designed with sufficient strength for landing, no matter how heavy the metal put in them. I also felt that airworthiness involved a principle of flight extending beyond transoceanic operation. Someday transport planes would have to fly over all areas of the world by day and by night, through storm and over mountains. Under such circumstances the lives of passengers and crew would depend on staying in the air until a satisfactory place to land was reached.

Transoceanic airlines were still years away, yet routes to South America might be operated with existing equipment. When I had landed the *Spirit of St. Louis* in Havana, at the end of my Gulf of Mexico and Caribbean tour, I met a young man named Juan Trippe.* He had just organized a company called "Pan American Airways" with the idea of operating air routes between North and South America. In the summer of 1928 I made an appointment to talk to Trippe in New York, and joined his organization as a consultant. Trippe believed international airlines offered a great oppor-

---

* Juan Terry Trippe organized one of the first air-passenger services in the U.S., an air-taxi line to Long Island in 1923. He was born in 1899, of Anglo-American ancestry, and was named after his aunt Juanita. The son of a New York banker, he grew up in Greenwich, Connecticut, and entered the Yale Sheffield Scientific School. An athlete of note, Trippe helped to organize and direct both the collegiate and intercollegiate flying groups. After serving with the Navy in World War I as a flying instructor, he graduated from Yale in 1920. In 1925, with the backing of fellow alumni, including a Whitney and a Vanderbilt, he formed Eastern Air Transport. Two years later he realized the first step of his goal to operate an overseas line by purchasing two companies and forming them into Pan American Airways, Incorporated.

tunity for the improvement of commercial intercourse and the relationships of nations.

The first step was to fly a mail and passenger service around the Gulf of Mexico and through the Caribbean, following more or less the route I had taken with the *Spirit of St. Louis*. This was the subject of the first conference I attended with Trippe and officers and directors of his company. Agreements had to be made with various Central and South American governments, landing rights arranged, mail contracts negotiated. New airplanes had to be developed, radio stations set up, ground and water facilities installed. Where should we use flying boats? Where should we use amphibians, even with their penalty of added structural weight? Could landplanes carry passengers on long overwater flights—Havana to Panama, for instance—and should they be built of wood or metal? Some officers argued that wood planes would be buoyant and cited the fact that a Pan American Fokker had once ditched in the Florida Straits and stayed afloat until passengers could be rescued. As for navigational aids, would it be practical to anchor buoy lights at intervals across the Caribbean Sea, or would radio beacons at lighted terminals be enough? We had to consider the passengers' needs in good flying conditions and bad: how would we accommodate them at stops where no good hotels or restaurants existed? What emergency-rescue facilities should be set up?

In 1929 each flight I made through the gulf and Caribbean area combined political visits with air-route organization and surveys. Government officials liked to be called on and consulted. The resulting publicity was advantageous to them and to the company. Flying Pan American's Sikorsky S-36 amphibians, I always carried either a flight engineer or a copilot on survey trips. We studied field lengths, sea heights, harbors, anchorages. Each landing in a different country involved customs and immigration complications, especially since no rules had been established for transient aircraft. We had to clear in and out of port as ocean-going ships.

At Pan American we never forgot that flying the Caribbean was a step toward flying the Atlantic and Pacific. When you looked at a globe of the world, the Arctic routes were tantalizing, ideal for air routes. You could evade the oceans if you were willing to fly far enough north. Only fifty miles of Bering Strait separated America from Asia. It was less then seven hundred miles from Labrador to Greenland, the biggest water gap that would separate America from Europe on a northern route. These distances were within the range of planes then flying. But the foehn winds and fogs of Greenland, the fifty-below-zero temperatures of Alaskan winters, the surface transportation problems of frozen lands and seas—it was easy to forget them in a New York office when you stretched a piece of string across the surface of a globe. Still, pilots flew in Canada and Alaska through all seasons of the year.

I realized I did not know enough about the Arctic to form intelligent opinions. Therefore, in the winter of 1930–31, I began planning a flight over the great circle route between New York and Tokyo, on which my wife would be radio operator. The route I laid out would take us along the arctic coasts of Canada and Alaska, down the Kamchatka Peninsula, and over the Chishima or Kuril Islands to Japan. Since no landing fields existed along most of the route, we ordered special pontoons designed for our Lockheed Sirius monoplane. And because we needed more power to take off from water with the heavy fuel loads I wanted to carry, we arranged with Wright Aeronautical Corporation to install one of the five-hundred-seventy-five-horsepower Cyclone engines they had recently begun producing.

For the first time in a plane I owned, I had a radio set installed. Previously I had concluded that aircraft radio equipment was not only heavy but also excessively unreliable. But by 1931 the Communications Department of Pan American Airways, under Hugo Luteritz, had developed a lightweight long-range code set that was giving extraordinary results in Gulf of Mexico and Caribbean areas. We decided to try it out in the Arctic.

With streamlined smooth-skin monoplanes, six-hundred-horsepower engines under National Advisory Committee for Aeronautics cowlings, and radio communication, the right elements were assembled to make commercial aviation a success. But the performance of our survey plane, outstanding as it was, was far from meeting the operating requirements of an airline. With emergency equipment stowed on board, we were heavily overloaded,

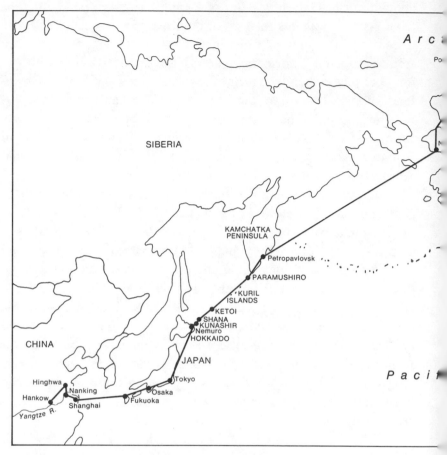

Flight to the Orient, 1931

even though my wife and I had cut our personal baggage down to sixteen pounds apiece. Our pontoons sank deeply in the water. We could not take off with fuel for a flight of much more than a thousand miles unless the wind formed a chop to help give us lift.

This was the flight that convinced me that Arctic routes to Asia would be the last ones developed. Flying boats could not operate from ice-covered water. Airports for landplanes would be expensive to construct and maintain in sub-zero temperatures. Strange electronic phenomena created new problems for radio communication.

In the early 1930's many ideas were advanced to Pan American on ocean flying. Some people believed dirigibles were preferable to

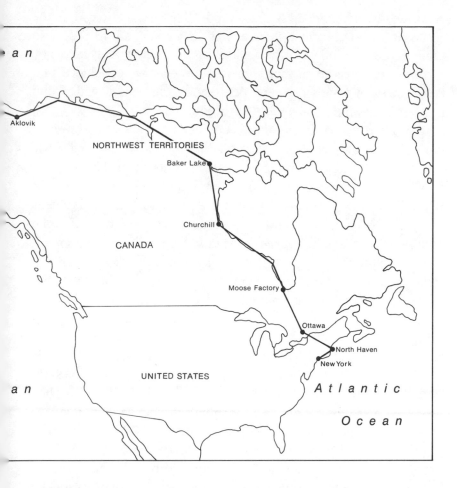

airplanes for transoceanic transport. I believed dirigibles were too awkward, too slow, too vulnerable to ground and storm gusts, even though their advocates said they could be built, with roomy quarters and little engine noise, to cruise at a hundred miles an hour, with enough range to detour storms and still equal the speed of airplanes because they would not have to stop to refuel.

Then an engineer named Armstrong said he had designed "floating islands" for installation along oceanic air routes. Each island would be long and narrow, with a runway for landings on its top supported by hollow steel pillars rooted in steel tanks. Some of the tanks were to float on the ocean's surface and some were to remain permanently submerged. A scale model had been tested, but the cost was obviously more than any airline could afford. We also studied the possibility of refueling in air, catapulted take-offs, aprons towed behind surface ships. In the end, we concluded that Pan American transoceanic services should be started with flying boats and conventional operating procedures.

Igor Sikorsky was among those convinced that the best answer to transatlantic equipment problems lay in flying boats. He had made a careful study of Pan American requirements since the company first became interested in his S-38 amphibians. Born in Kiev, in White Russia, in 1889, Sikorsky became fascinated with aviation as a boy. He had built the world's first four-engine airplanes before he came to America as a refugee from the Communist Revolution.

I had many discussions with Sikorsky about the design of flying boats, sometimes while we were traveling over Pan American routes, other times in the company offices or at his factory in Connecticut. I remember one conference in particular, in which Juan Trippe and André Priester took part. It was in 1929, in Trippe's office in the Chanin Building. We were laying down specifications for an amphibian to replace the too small and obsolescent S-38. Sikorsky unrolled several drawings on the table in front of us. They portrayed his latest design, a four-engine sesquiplane amphibian, to be designated the S-40. It looked like a scaled-up S-38, with similar struts, wires, and huge pontoons—air resistance everywhere. I objected to the awkwardness of design and said bluntly that it would be like flying a forest through the air. "I agree with you, Co-ro-nel," Sikorsky replied with his delightful Russian accent. "The resistance is high. But to remove it is still another step." I was disappointed, but I had to agree with Sikorsky that we could not afford to invest in a design that included too many radical improvements. We were in desperate need of a better plane for Caribbean routes. The Atlantic could come later.

The first S-40 was test-flown in the spring of 1931. In November of that year, I piloted one of these planes, with Igor Sikorsky among the passengers, on the first single-day flight between North and South America.

Two years later, after our son Jon was born, I undertook an

Atlantic survey flight, with my wife once again acting as radio operator. For our Lockheed Sirius seaplane, I had ordered a more powerful Cyclone engine and had a newly developed two-position Hamilton Standard propeller installed in the nose of the fuselage and a directional gyro, one of the Sperry-Gyroscope Company's latest instruments, added to our instrument board. For this flight, we would have to carry greater fuel loads than on our Orient flight, and accurate navigation would be more important.

On July 9, 1933, my wife and I took off from Flushing Bay, on a flight that was to last for five and a half months. We flew along the North American coast to Labrador, spent several weeks surveying Greenland, landed in Iceland, the Faeroes, and the Shetlands en route to the continent of Europe, visited all Atlantic countries between Norway and Portugal, with side expeditions inland to Sweden, Finland, Russia, Holland, and Switzerland.

We had planned to return to the United States by way of Portugal, the Azores, and Newfoundland, but on arrival in the Azores we found no harbor long enough for the take-off of our seaplane, which was loaded down with the fuel reserve I thought essential for the flight to Newfoundland. So we replotted our route over warm equatorial waters between Africa and South America, landed for fuel in the Canaries, and Spanish Río de Oro, shifted our route again when warnings of yellow fever kept us from the harbor at Dakar, and landed at the French flying-boat base in the Cape Verde Islands to prepare for the long overwater flight to South America. Again we were forced to change plans, because the area used by the French for their flying-boat operation (discontinued sometime before we arrived) was sheltered by the island's lee shore. Ocean rollers were too high for an overloaded take-off with our relatively small seaplane. We flew to Bathurst, back on the continent of Africa. There, on the Gambia River's glassy surface, we encountered exactly the opposite take-off problem. Without wind or wave chop, I was unable to get our pontoons up "on their steps" while carrying a transoceanic fuel load.

After several attempts, I stripped our plane of everything but the most essential emergency equipment and, using metal shears, cut an unneeded gasoline tank out of the fuselage to reduce weight by a

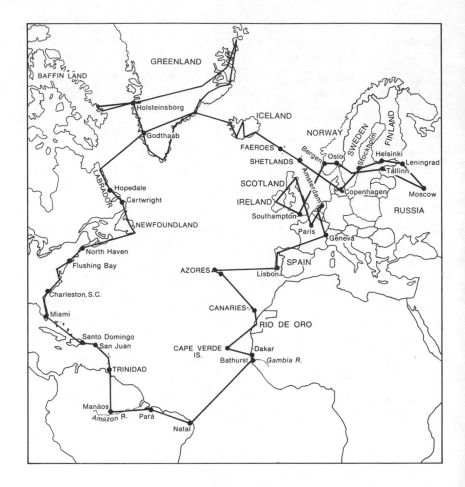

Atlantic survey flight, 1933

few more pounds. On the last night that would have enough moonlight for our take-off, a light wind sprang up to help us. After a long
run in the semidarkness, I managed to break the pontoons free
from water. Sixteen hours later we landed at Natal, Brazil. Later
we stopped for fuel at Pará, flew a thousand miles up the Amazon
to Manáos, and cut northward across wild areas of jungle to the
island of Trinidad.

Years later we learned that our flight from Manáos to Trinidad
started a myth among South American natives who had never seen
a plane before. They heard the "buzzing" of our engine high above

them, saw the outline of wings and fuselage on sky. Not knowing what our real dimensions were, they likened us to a big mosquito. Thereafter, tribal legends recalled a day when "the big mosquito" had passed above their villages.

On our landing at the U.S. Navy Yard at Charleston, South Carolina, the Commanding Admiral handed us a telegram from President Franklin D. Roosevelt. The message welcomed us home and invited us to stop for a visit at the White House on our way northward. Under other circumstances we would have accepted gladly, but we had been away from home nearly half a year and we were anxious to get back to prepare for a family Christmas.

As a reserve officer in the Army I regarded an invitation from the President as being close to a command. The situation would have been most difficult for us had not the telegram been so considerately worded. But it left open the choice of a visit to the White House then or at some unstated time after the holidays. We declined, and the next day were back in New Jersey with our family.

Our survey of the North Atlantic left no doubt in my mind about the wisdom of establishing the first air route to Europe by way of Bermuda and the Azores. Ice conditions along a more northern route would prevent winter operation with flying boats. Probably even the waters of Long Island Sound would be too cold for a midwinter terminal.

I had found work with seaplanes and flying boats more interesting than that with landplanes. A pilot was not dependent on prepared airports. He could land on lakes, harbors, and rivers, at the most out-of-the-way places. I liked the closer contact with wilderness of land and sea. Problems of hull design were fascinating. But the more I studied flying boats and their operation, the more I questioned their future on airlines of the world.

We could never give satisfactory service to transatlantic passengers if we had to move our terminal with the seasons. The addition of a third element, water, was bound to increase operating costs and slow down schedules. Also, as airlines developed, we would want many inland terminals for transoceanic routes. Paris passengers, for example, would prefer not to change planes while flying to New York. Chicagoans would object to having Baltimore or Norfolk as their air gateway to Europe. Then there was the problem of controlling landing areas for flying boats. Lights for night operation on water were difficult to install, and there was always the chance of a log or piece of wreckage drifting into the take-off or landing. Flying boats were highly subject to corrosion and barnacle formation. Spray eroded their propellers. Salt caked on windows. Water crept into bilges. Auxiliary water craft had to be maintained in addition to the trucks and cars needed for a landplane operation.

I concluded that landplanes would eventually replace flying boats wherever airports could be built within practical range of one another. I reasoned that hulls would lose their value from the standpoint of psychology as well as from that of safety. If passengers would fly in a landplane through storms and over fog-covered mountains, surely they would also be willing to fly in a landplane over water. But the first years of transoceanic airline operation would have to be with flying boats.

FOUR

Out of Eden

I had always taken for granted that someday I would marry and have a family of my own, but I had not thought much about it. In fact, I had never been enough interested in any girl to ask her to go on a date. At college I was inexperienced and shy, and I was having enough trouble in my studies without taking on the additional problem of women—you had to learn to dance, to talk their language, to escort them properly to restaurants and theaters. I preferred to ride my motorcycle. It was also a lot cheaper.

Parachute-jumping and barnstorming kept me moving from one location to another so fast that I never got to know any of the local families well. As a flying cadet, I had been too busy with my studies to visit San Antonio very often, and I had not met a single girl during the year I spent in Texas. At St. Louis I concentrated my attention on training students, organizing the mail route, and attending to my duties with the National Guard. Then I became immersed in my plans for the New York–to–Paris flight.

The ceremonies following my successful landing in France and my tours with the *Spirit of St. Louis* through America did not allow me to meet women of my age. I was surrounded most of the time by older people—officials and business executives at airports and civic ceremonies, and the wives of those officials and executives at private lunches and dinners. When daughters were present, they usually sat at the foot of the table—where I would have much preferred to be. Newspapers had reported me engaged to at least a dozen women, several of whom I had never seen. It was quite clear that any relationships I had with women would be exaggerated and complicated by the attention of the press. Nevertheless, I decided it was time to meet girls. In 1928, I was twenty-six years old.

The important thing was to meet and marry a girl you would stay in love with. I intended to pay particular attention to that. It meant not falling in love with one of the first few women you met—a question of time, patience, and intelligent selection.

Now I began observing young women more carefully, and from the weekend invitations, I tried to select those from families with daughters. Of course it was advantageous, when possible, to see the daughters before accepting the invitations. Helping to organize a transcontinental air route gave wide scope to this new activity in the various cities where I stopped regularly between New York and California.

Associating with girls, I found, required much flexibility. You had to make special effort to fit into a different way of doing things, which sometimes seemed awfully silly. One evening you might be asked to lie down on the parlor floor with a glass of water on your forehead, and then to stand up without touching the glass with your hands or spilling the water. On another, you would take part in "packing your aunt's trunk"—each person, round and round in turn, would put in another item and have to remember all the other items that had been put in before it. You spent a lot of time and seemed to accomplish almost nothing.

Girls talked about actors and actresses, tennis, golf, weddings, and "treasure hunts." They had ideas about dresses and shoes and hats, particularly, that did not make any sense at all to me. Many of them styled their hair and painted their faces until I was not sure what kind of a person I was looking at, aside from their sex. I began to ask myself what qualities I really desired in a wife. I felt intuitively that I knew what these qualities were, but it was hard for me to think them out exactly. A girl should come from a healthy family, of course. My experience in breeding animals on our farm had taught me the importance of good heredity. I knew that qualities of the father and the mother, and the ancestors before them, invariably came out in the offspring, mixed though they must be. I heard people say that environment was the most important thing, but it seemed to me they had just closed their minds to what was obvious —like the religious fanatics you met everywhere.

You did not have to be a scientist to realize the overwhelming importance of genes and chromosomes. When you saw the mothers and fathers, you could tell a lot about their offspring, and I found it interesting to try guessing the other way around. Here the relationship between heredity and environment was subtle; training, after all, had its effect on character. But you could see features of the parents in a son's or daughter's face. A nervous daughter had at least one nervous parent, often two of them.

The subtleties deepened when one parent was markedly different from the other. One sister then differed from another, although it was not always obvious. Most of the girls I met tried to bring out their good qualities and hide their defects with the clothes they wore, just as they tried to make themselves more beautiful with face grease. It seemed to me that the one attempt was about as unsuccessful as the other. There were always ways of seeing through make-up if you exerted a little effort. You could tell a great deal about a woman's body by looking at her hip line and the portion of her legs that showed beneath her skirt. And of course if you were still interested, you could get her to go swimming.

The physical characteristics I wanted in a woman were not difficult to describe—good health, good form, good sight and hearing. Such qualities could be outlined in sequence like the specifications for an airplane. I wanted to marry a girl who liked flying, because I would take her with me on the expeditions I expected to make in my plane. That ought to be great fun.

I took for granted that I would marry a girl of my own Caucasian race, but this was a matter of custom rather than of prejudice. I felt no antipathy toward red, yellow, black, or brown. If I had fallen in love with a woman of another race, I surely would have married her regardless of difficulties that might have ensued. I took for granted, too, that I would marry a girl who had no strong ties to any church, because I believed freedom of thought would be essential in my home.

The mental characteristics I desired were more difficult to list. Of course I wanted to marry a girl who had intelligence, but I did not care much about her formal education. Whether or not she was a college graduate made little difference to me. It was an attitude of mind I wanted, not a mass of knowledge. How could one describe comprehensively an attitude of mind? Such words as "honest," "just," and "truthful" were hardly adequate. She had to have a mental attractiveness that involved more than the qualities of mind. I knew what I sought, however hard it was to describe "attractiveness." What was it that attracted you to one woman, and not to another, in ways that rationality could not explain, ways that seemed only distantly related to the consciousness of mind? What did the eyes see in a face that could be translated only indirectly through the emotions to the mind? Why was a girl desirable to this man, and not to that? Mating brought out the essence of individuality.

What tremendous power the individual has compressed into his genes, and subject to his guidance—greater than governments, greater than armies, for it is the power of the past accomplishments of life. The individual is at the apex of his species' past, at the entrance to its future. Existing at a dimensionless instant called "the present," where past and future constrict to touch in time, he roots into the infinity called "origin," and emanates into the infinity called "end." I was an individual exercising evolutionary choice in a twentieth-century environment, an environment impinging on heredity with greater force than ever before in man's history because of the sudden flowering of scientific knowledge.

When I was a boy in Minnesota, playing with the neighbor children, my environment was not unlike that of country areas my forebears had known. Horses pulled plows guided by human strength; boys fetched buckets of water, and milking was done by hand. It seemed to me that farmer daughters were like all other girls, that girls existed wherever you were, and that when it eventually came to marrying you would simply try to persuade the one you fell in love with to marry you. Somehow you would find her and know her when you saw her. As of the moment, those who were good at tag and hide-and-seek were preferable. When I was on the farm, the effect of specialized environments had not occurred to me.

The girls I saw at college had become a selected group, I realized soon after I began my freshman year. They had been selected through a scholastic examination of their minds, and as a result many of the types of women I knew before were missing amongst them. Once, a junior-classman engineer instructed me in relationships with college women. It was only partly effective to approach through the intellect, he said, but if you could get your hand onto a breast, no woman could resist you. I could not understand why you should want to overcome resistance until you found a girl you really loved.

As a barnstorming aviator, my environment changed again. In moving from town to town, I found that acquaintanceships were quick and short, and the women they involved were, I felt, undesirable. Many a barnstorming pilot slept with one woman one night, another the next, and never saw them again as he followed the wind and season. A pilot I met in Nebraska was famed for his directness of approach on arriving at a new location. "Do you or don't you? That's all I want to know," he said as he canvassed a town's feminine possibilities.

A barnstormer's relationships with women were facile. There was little chance for careful selectivity, hardly any desire for permanence and children. At the end of a barnstorming season in Montana, I had bought an old rowboat and planned on drifting down the Yellowstone River for several hundred miles. "Why don't you take that girl in the tent show along with you?" a fellow aviator asked. "She'd go if you invited her. She's just the kind for a trip like that." It would hardly have occurred to me, and it certainly would not have suited me.

When I enlisted in the Army and became a flying cadet, I found that frequently a soldier's relationships with women were paid for in cash. A little board-shack village near the flying field made a few prostitutes available, and San Antonio had them on display at night, sitting at lighted windows, of various ages, at various costs. It was not an environment conducive to evolutionary progress.

Surveying airlines juxtaposed for me a feeling of omnipotence with a feeling of suppression. When I flew high in my plane and looked down on earth, it often seemed that the entire planet was mine to select from what I wished. I could swoop down and land on pasture, stubble field, or airport. Somewhere down on the surface of the earth was the girl I would marry. It was simply a case of swooping down at the right place to find her.

But after I had landed, problems of mortal men always returned to surround me. Girls were everywhere, but it was hard to get to know them. For me, the reason was unique: the fame I had gained prevented it. The mixture of awe, respect, and curiosity with which I was treated rose like a haze around me. If I talked to a girl for five minutes, gossip started as though we were beginning a courtship onstage. There was never a chance for me to take a girl quietly to a restaurant or a theater. Every newspaper in the country would have made a headline of such an act and press reporters and photographers would have followed us.

Here, the effect of my changed environment exerted its strong influence on individuality. My position in aviation in general and my work surveying airlines in particular combined with newspaper pressures to put me in contact with political and business leaders and therefore with their families. On the one hand, our interests coincided in developing aviation. On the other, their larger homes, with spacious grounds, and their influence with local authorities gave me a welcome privacy and protection from the press. Some of them had daughters about my age. There is the saying that "like tends to like," and while I did not consider this at the time, it was obviously enough taking place. The men I associated with and I were spearheading scientific and technical and material progress. Possibly, but not certainly, our genetic compositions embodied various combinations of physical and mental acuities that resulted in our being what we were and doing what we did. It was reasonable to assume that the daughter I married would have these characteristics, too, and that they would be combined and enhanced in our offspring.

After some months of carrying on my girl-meeting project rather unsuccessfully, and ostensibly as a socially polite accompaniment to my activities in aviation, I began to realize that I would like to see again a girl whom I had met before I had actively begun looking for a wife. The previous year, after my nonstop flight from Washington to Mexico City, I had stayed on in Mexico for the Christmas holidays as a guest of Ambassador and Mrs. Dwight W. Morrow. Their four children had come down from the United States for Christmas. The second daughter, Anne, was blue-eyed, dark-haired, extremely pretty, but she stood very much in the background, as though resting in a shadow thrown by the sparkling vivacity of her older sister, Elisabeth. Anne was twenty-one and midway though her final year of college. I had noticed her casually. She looked so very young, more of high-school than of college age, and she had not made a deep impression on my conscious mind. Rationally, I was surprised when I found her becoming conspicuous in memory months after I had left the hospitality of her father's embassy in Mexico. But in the fall of 1928 I began laying plans to meet her again. She was then staying at her family home at Englewood, New Jersey.

Dating a girl was seldom difficult for the pilot of an airplane if he used some discretion in his method of approach. I knew that from the experience of others. He simply asked her to accompany him on a flight around the nearby country. Aviation was romantic, adventurous, spectacular, and, except for timid creatures, the invitation seldom had to be extended twice. I had never before tried to date a girl myself. I had never met one in whom I felt sufficient interest. Of course I had invited a number of girls to fly with me, but they were all daughters or wives of friends. I decided to approach Anne with an invitation to fly and then try to extend it into a date on the ground. My visit as a guest of the family in Mexico made it proper to telephone directly to the Morrow home. Daughter Anne agreed to go with me on a flight over Long Island the following week.

Achieving my objective with the girl left me confronted with my now ever-present problem of the press. If I were seen with one of Ambassador Morrow's daughters at a New York airport, there would be a terrible hullabaloo about it. A dozen or two reporters and photographers would be rushed out to wait for us to land, and thereafter more silly stories would be published.

For the occasion, I rented a small, open-cockpit biplane with a quick take-off and a low landing speed. A friend of a friend of mine on Long Island offered me the use of a horse pasture on his estate. I had to fly under high-tension electric cables after take-off, because of the shortness of the pasture, but once past them we climbed up easily over horse jumps and mansions until we could see both shorelines of Long Island. The Atlantic Ocean lay southward, Long Island Sound behind us; New York City was in the west, shrunk small to fit the aviator's spatial vision.

Our "ground date" a few days later involved an afternoon and evening drive over roads of New Jersey in my air-cooled-engine Franklin sedan. When it was over we were engaged to be married. My fiancée was leaving for Mexico City soon, where she planned to stay for a number of weeks with her father and mother. We decided that even her parents were not to know about our engagement until we could be together to inform them. I would fly to Mexico City. That was simple enough. But what reason would I give for going there? I could say I wanted to see more of the wonderful country of Mexico than I had been able to see during my flights with the *Spirit of St. Louis* the previous year. That would probably get me by. But then I would be deluged with invitations to lunches and dinners and, moreover, have to support my statement by visiting a number of states and cities. A tour of Mexico by air might be extremely interesting, but it would hardly fit in with my desire to be with my fiancée.

My problem was solved perfectly and unexpectedly by a letter from the American military attaché in Mexico, Colonel Alexander MacNab. He invited me to accompany him on a hunting expedition. Antelope were plentiful on the Coahuilan plains, he said, and we could headquarter at the ranch house of a friend of his, Hal Mangum. An expedition on the plains of Coahuila was attractive in itself, but far more attractive was the fact that MacNab's invitation included one from Ambassador Morrow to spend several days at the embassy before I returned to the United States.

Sandy MacNab knew Mexico well, including its Army officers, government officials, and even former bandits, all of whom were helpful in connection with his hunting trips. I did not want to kill antelope—or anything else, for that matter—but I enjoyed being with Sandy and his friends. For them, the time passed too rapidly;

for me, it seemed incredibly slow. After the hunting expedition, I spent several days with the Morrow family at their Cuernavaca residence. We drove there from Mexico City in one of the embassy's big cars, the Ambassador, Mrs. Morrow, Anne, and I. Along the wilder portions of the road, I noticed rifle-bearing soldiers stationed singly and only a few hundred feet apart. There was not much danger, I was told when I asked the reason for the guards. On occasion in the past, bandits had operated in the area, and President Calles had ordered extra precautions taken to safeguard the passage of the American Ambassador's car.

Up to that time, newspapers had not circulated rumors of our engagement. But no matter how discreet we were, it was only a question of time before rumors would be started, predictably in a cheap and sensational way by the tabloid press. Even if no reporter saw us alone together, some family friend or servant would guess and talk. Because of the Ambassador's position and my own, a great deal of publicity was bound to arise sooner or later. It would be bad enough at best, but better if we could control the time and place of the announcement. I had hoped to withhold the announcement of our engagement until after my return to the United States. This would divide the attention of the press geographically, and the resulting stories would not be as sentimental and sensational as they would if my fiancée and I were together at the time.* I had found relationships with the press difficult before I had a fiancée. I found them next to impossible thereafter.

When my fiancée was at Next Day Hill, the new Morrow home at Englewood, newspapermen congregated at the gate outside and tried to follow us with their cars whenever we went on a drive together. Usually I was able to lose them by turning in and out through city traffic, and one time, driving Anne in my Franklin, I had to drive through a lot, onto a lawn, and down a six-foot hill into another street. An old couple rocking on a porch nearby stared silently.

The wide effects of newspaper, radio, and motion-picture pub-

---

* According to Anne Morrow Lindbergh's *Hour of Gold, Hour of Lead,* the engagement was announced to the public, after some delay, on February 12, 1929, before Charles arrived in Mexico.

licity caused us even more discomfort than did the nagging of re- porters and photographers. We could not walk on city streets or go into restaurants or theaters without being recognized, stared at, and approached for autographs and handshakes. Sometimes people would shout at us, slap us on the back, and poke us with their fingers. On such occasions the considerate withdrawal of men and women who respected our privacy left us to the sole and incon- siderate attentions of those who did not. As a result, we found ourselves confined much of the time to estates of family and friends, where the press and public could be effectively excluded. Even then we could seldom feel sure that a telescopic camera lens was not focused on us. When we spent a week together at the Morrow summer home in Maine, photographers and reporters hid in the woods around the house until the Ambassador hired policemen to control them. A newspaper chain bribed a workman to steal a bundle of my fiancée's letters, and servants were offered money for information about us.

We decided to have a private wedding near the end of May, at Next Day Hill, and not to announce the date in advance. Only members of the family and close friends would be asked. The invi- tation would be informal and give the impression that this was to be a prewedding party. After the guests were assembled, Anne and I would go through a simple marriage ceremony, stay on for half an hour, and leave ahead of everyone else, so there would be no chance of the press learning about it until we were out of reach. House telephones would be guarded. Only people essential to our plans would know about them.

It would be difficult to arrange for my bride and me to have peaceful days together. I had learned from experience that pleas for personal privacy addressed to the press had negligible effect. I had tried to work out "gentlemen's agreements" unsuccessfully. Several times I had offered to give interviews and pose for photographs on the condition that I be left alone for a reasonable period thereafter. My condition was always agreed to but never followed. If the men who agreed to it did not break their agreement, other reporters and photographers representing the same organizations did.

I felt quite sure the press expected me to take my bride on a honeymoon by airplane. Therefore I kept well away from flying fields and airplanes, and decided that a boat would be a good place to spend the first week or two after our wedding. I placed an order secretly, through an officer of the Elco Company, for a thirty-six-foot motor cruiser. Aside from two or three top officers of the company, no one was to know who the boat was for.

Newspapers had offered to pay workers at the airport where I kept my plane for any information relating to my activities. Here I saw an opportunity to divide the forces of the press. A day or two before our wedding was to take place, I ordered my Falcon flown to Rochester and left, fully serviced, in a hangar on the airport. As I expected, a number of reporters and photographers followed it. That alerted the press, and rumors spread to the effect that our marriage was imminent. But here the fantasies of reporters played into our hands. They had written so many stories about plans for a highly elaborate wedding that they began to believe their own concoctions. When a few dozen guests arrived at Next Day Hill in response to invitations to an afternoon reception, reporters at the gate paid only casual attention. The Morrows were noted for having many friends and for giving parties.

All went according to plan. Anne Morrow and I were married on May 27, 1929, in front of the fireplace in the big parlor at Next Day Hill. Before any of the guests left, we slipped out of the house into the back of a big car and out of the gate without being recognized by reporters standing guard there. I had arranged to have our boat, fully equipped and fueled and provisioned, left at anchor at an isolated spot off the Long Island Sound coast. My friend and lawyer, Henry Breckinridge, was waiting for us on a back street of Englewood with my Franklin car. We drove to Long Island and found our dingy tied to a tree on the bank. Meanwhile, Ambassador and Mrs. Morrow announced the fact of our wedding by telephone to the various press associations. Reporters standing at the gate were informed of it through messages from their editors. The *Daily News* came out that same afternoon with an article describing our plans for a wedding to be held soon, with fifteen hundred guests.

In peace, alone, we cruised on Long Island Sound for two days, learning the ways of our boat, the *Mouette,* and stowing our equipment in its holds and cabins. With the exception of a short voyage on the sound the previous year, I had never before navigated a vessel larger or more powerful than a rowboat with an outboard engine. But basic principles of navigation for sea and air were similar; what was more, in a boat, if you got in trouble, you had an anchor to help you. We decided to follow the New England coast northeastward to the island of North Haven, where Pulpit Harbor would offer us excellent shelter near the Morrow home.

The need for fresh food and fuel for our voyage created a problem because newspaper headlines and radio announcements certainly would have informed the entire country of our marriage. They used their old technique of writing mystery articles, and as usual they paid anyone who gave them information about us. As we proceeded northward, we were recognized while buying supplies, with the result that an airplane followed us into the darkness. At one point I had to drag anchor to get away from a reporter in a launch who circled our boat repeatedly, hoping to bring us topside out of seasickness. But we managed to escape and to enjoy our anonymity on the open water.

In a universe where galaxies sprinkle outward beyond the reach of telescopes and images of mind, where stars dust in through spirals to make single pinpricks in the night, where our earth is a minor planet orbiting a minor sun and a man or woman on it is one among billions more, the individual may logically seem of trivial importance. But such logical intellectual conclusions are challenged by other elements in man until the mind is forced to reconsider its magnitudinal directions. To a person in love, the value of the individual is intuitively known. Love needs no logic for its mission. It roots in a bare wisdom that exists in senses more than mind, a wisdom that, in primitive form, evolved the mind which so often overlooks it.

Marriage and family imply essential mutations in a man's life. I fully realized that and welcomed them, feeling I was gaining far more than I had lost. But I still expected to devote the greater part of my life that was spent apart from my family in developing fields of aviation. I felt that no activity was more interesting or held greater possibilities for advancing civilization. What wonders might not take place in a world where mountains, swamps, and shorelines were no longer barriers to travel, where the remotest wilderness was easily accessible, where men of all countries could come near in physical and intellectual contact?

I could not foresee that marriage would result indirectly in transferring aviation from a primary to a secondary interest of life. As I look back from the vantage point of time, I realize that my intuitive interest in life's mysteries was strong and fundamental in early childhood and that it increased, at least subconsciously, to the point where even my fascination with aviation was unable to hold it down. My marriage, by chance, put me in contact with Alexis Carrel, who had the most stimulating mind I ever came to know well. But it was not chance that encouraged my fascination with the basic biological qualities and mysteries of the human life stream.

I had become interested in biological phenomena when I was a child, not knowing then, of course, that my interests came under the academic heading of "biology." I was spellbound by the body of a dead horse I encountered while walking through a woods adjacent to our farm. I had seen dead things before, but never of such magnitude. The difference between life and death was so apparent in that rotting hulk, and yet it was not understandable! What stopped life from living? Later I had considered becoming a doctor, like my great-uncles, so I could study and understand such things. But I was told that in carrying on his profession, a doctor had to be able to read and write Latin. My first contact with high-school Latin convinced me that the requirements of medicine lay beyond my intellectual desires and capacities.

Thereafter, engineering studies, the war, farming, and, particularly, flying kept biology from the foreground of my mind. I did not begin again to think deeply about biological problems until the long transcontinental survey flights I undertook in 1928 gave me extra time for contemplation. Then my mind, often wandering without conscious direction, began reconsidering childhood questions about life and death. The great and rapid success of my profession of aviation played its part in rearousing my interest in biology. Aviation showed what miracles man could accomplish. If he could learn to fly on wings, which was once considered impossible, why could he not learn how to live forever? With science now at his disposal, nothing seemed beyond his grasp. The idea interested me so much that I decided to study biology seriously.

Practical problems immediately became apparent. I wanted to experiment with living material in a laboratory, yet a biological laboratory necessitates some degree of permanence. I had been leading a life of impermanence since I entered aviation, a life of stopping at hotels, barracks, boardinghouses, and staying with friends. While airlines were being organized and as long as I was making survey flights, I was not ready to settle down at a permanent location. I kept postponing action on my idea of a laboratory. I would start by buying and studying books about biology and related fields.

After our honeymoon, my wife and I first had rented rooms in an uptown New York hotel for a few weeks, then moved into a rented farmhouse near Princeton, New Jersey, while we decided where to locate our permanent home. By air and by ground we had looked over the entire country within commuting distance of New York City. We considered sites on Long Island, in Connecticut, in New Jersey, in New York State, on the west bank of the Hudson River, and finally decided to buy property and build our house on southern slopes of the Sourland Mountains, a ten-minute automobile drive from Princeton and its university.

Land in the Sourlands was cheap because it was rocky, unfertile, and wooded. Even where fields had been cleared on the property we bought, the soil was so poor that cropping had been discontinued years before. But those fields were long enough to make an airplane landing strip, with only a little labor spent in clearing. I would be able to taxi right into a small hangar that I planned to have constructed next to our garage. There were wonderful views across the valley, and endless trails for walking through the woods.

Anne and I had located the area while flying, and decided to buy when we climbed a tree on the hillside and looked down on the place where we finally built our house. We could buy groceries from the village of Hopewell at the foot of the mountains. An endless supply of deadwood for our fireplaces lay about. Rock blasted out for the basement would give more than enough material for the building of our walls. New York airports were only a few minutes' flight away. Even by road we were within a long commuting distance of New York.

I planned to put my biological laboratory in the basement after our Sourland Mountain house was built. Meanwhile, I would assemble a library for my studies. I could carry a book wherever I went, even with the weight and space restrictions of an airplane. I ordered texts on physics, chemistry, physiology, cytology, bacteriology, immunology, surgery, medical history, and various other subjects, and began to read them in whatever extra hours or minutes I could find. I bought a high-power binocular microscope as the first item of equipment for my laboratory.

While we were living in our rented farmhouse near Princeton, I visited the university's departments of physiology and cytology and watched experiments being made on animals and cells. The reactions of a decerebrate cat particularly attracted my attention, for they seemed to me to demonstrate the basically mechanistic qualities of life.

What direction were my biological experiments to take? The human body in whole interested me most, especially the reasons for its aging. But while I could consider the body intellectually, I had no way of working on it. To do so required the certification and background of a surgeon; and even a surgeon was limited in the experiments he could carry out on men. How would I begin? Thousands of biological experiments were being made in hundreds of well-equipped laboratories all over the world. What could I do that was not already being done?

My experimental interests were channeled, as so often happens, by a chance development of life—by the illness of my wife's older sister, Elisabeth. She had contracted rheumatic fever as a secondary complication of pneumonia. A lesion had developed in her heart, restricting her activities until her doctor recommended a year of complete rest in bed. Since a remedial operation on the heart was impossible, he said, her life would be limited in both activity and length. I asked him why surgery would not be effective. He said the heart could not be stopped long enough for an operation to be performed because blood had to be kept circulating through the body. I asked why a mechanical heart could not maintain the blood circulation temporarily while the heart was being operated on. He replied frankly that he did not know. He had never heard of a mechanical heart being used.

I was astounded that a leading doctor could not answer such a question. I was still more astounded when other doctors I asked were unable to give me any more information. Could it be that no one had seriously thought of designing a mechanical heart for use in surgery? The more I considered the idea, the more it intrigued me. It would be a good way to study the phenomena of aging. Why could not a part of the body be kept alive indefinitely if a mechanical heart was attached to it—an arm, or even a head? Why could not the entire body be kept alive after the heart it was born with became too old and worn to function?

At Next Day Hill, on the night the birth of our first child was expected, I waited in a room with my wife's obstetrician, Dr. E. M. Hawks, and her anaesthetist, Dr. Paluel J. Flagg. There I raised again my question: Why would not a mechanical heart be valuable for certain surgical operations? Neither doctor could give a definite answer, but Dr. Flagg said he knew a man who could tell me, and would arrange a meeting between us.

The meeting became a luncheon in New York City, at the Rockefeller Institute for Medical Research, with Dr. Flagg and Dr. Alexis Carrel. Dr. Carrel was head of the institute's Department of Experimental Surgery and a recipient of a Nobel Prize.* He could answer my questions, for the institute had entered a field in which he had been carrying on research for many years. He explained some of the problems involved in pumping blood mechanically—coagulation, hemolysis, infection, the elimination of metabolic products. He had been trying for nearly two decades, he said, to construct an apparatus that would perfuse isolated organs without infection, and had been unsuccessful. After lunch Carrel showed us his laboratories, on the building's top floor—the room where he

* Carrel received the prize in physiology and medicine in 1912 for his contributions to the surgery of blood vesels, transfusion, and transplantation of organs.

operated, the equipment used for his experiments, the cages where his animals were kept, a cabinet containing various designs of tissue-culture flasks and perfusion pumps that functioned like mechanical hearts. The perfusion pumps, he explained, were for the purpose of keeping an organ alive after it had been removed from the body. They had failed because infection invariably crept in.

I was as impressed by the perfection of Carrel's biological techniques as I was astounded by the crudeness of the apparatuses I inspected. I felt I could improve on them and that a great opportunity might be opening for me—the opportunity of working with Alexis Carrel. When I said I would like to try to design a better perfusion pump, to my delight he offered me the facilities of his laboratories. By contributing my understanding of mechanical design, I could work side by side with a man who was a philosopher, a mystic, and one of the greatest experimental surgeons in the world.

I designed a tilting-coil pump, blown in Pyrex glass, in which, in 1931, Carrel perfused a short length of chicken's carotid artery for an entire month; it survived days without infection. But the results were far from satisfactory, even as experimental work. The pressure was not high enough for the perfusion of organs, and the perfusing fluid did not pulsate as in the body. Further, the techniques required to maintain sterility while inserting the organ were too difficult. It was essential that I find some way of improving the design of my apparatus. This involved formidable problems. But I considered the problems I encountered advantageous as long as reasonable success accompanied them. They let me continue working with Carrel and the extraordinary group of men and women he had brought together in his laboratory. There, more than any other place in the world, perhaps as never before in history, man was achieving an understanding of life in its apparently essential earthly relationship to matter.

I commuted from our rented farmhouse outside Princeton to New York by automobile. It was a long drive, over New Jersey roads and through the Holland Tunnel, about two hours in each direction. I usually drove alone. That gave me time for contemplation on both conscious and subconscious levels. I could redesign a pulsation valve for my perfusion apparatus, consider the relative merits of airplanes and dirigibles for a transatlantic route, or speculate on the ability of science to solve the origins of existence, the extent of time and space, the phenomenon and rationality of death.

I became interested in the design of an apparatus for tissue culture as well as for the culture of organs. I spent hours watching experimental operations and studying living cells incubated under a microscope. Carrel was untiring in his willingness to adopt surgical techniques to the requirements of my constantly changing apparatus. No matter how often infection developed or a mechanical breakdown occurred, he was ready to schedule another operation. On my part, I studied every detail of his operating procedures in an attempt to make my designs conform to them.

It was fascinating to watch an operation by Carrel. I felt I had reached the frontier where the mystical and the scientific meet, where I would see across the indistinct border separating life from death. When I donned my gown and hood of black outside the operating room, I prepared for a supernatural experience. The moment I entered the black-walled room, I felt outside the world men ordinarily lived in. Black-gowned figures like my own stood erect, sat on stools, glided about spectrally. Eyes I learned to recognize peered through oblong slits in black, slight reassurance that a human body's expression existed. On secondary tables, sterilized instruments, bottles, flasks, and test tubes gleamed brighter in contrast with sterilized black towels underneath. All positioning, all movements marked the precision of trained efficiency. Silence, where words were not essential, emphasized the arcane ritual of the place.

Tradition associates the sight of black with death, but the animal on the operating table brought my eyes to focus on elements of life—breathing lungs, pulsing arteries, glistening skin, seeping red blood. In that room mortality was being analyzed in its ultimate physical form. Life sometimes merged with death so closely I could not tell them apart—click of scissors, cleave of scalpel, the surgeon's nimble fingers tying knots in silk—black figures manipulating flesh and organs, preserving them, fragmenting them as had never been done before, trying to learn life's limits and capabilities and to further its meanings.

In the past I had thought it easy to recognize the difference between life and death, even when separated by a razor's edge. In what degree mechanical, and chemical, and spiritual is the element we name "awareness"? Biological life could survive what seemed to be a spiritual death, as in the living body of a decerebrate cat which could eat, and see, and claw. Certainly, elements of awareness remained in the animal, and, certainly, a decerebrate human would manifest similar reactions. Then was the spirit completely separate from awareness, a quality attached to a portion of the brain? Or did it also exist in the microscopic genes of man, ready to create another generation? If not so, then when and how did it enter the embryo? At what stage of evolution does awareness begin to exist —in a biological cell, in a virus, in a molecule, in an atom, or at a minuteness not comprehensible to men, an infinitude of minuteness.

Surgical science had divided life into countless thousands of parts, each with its own genetic composition and individuality. Life was in the animal still breathing on the table, and individually it was in each of millions of leucocytes leaving that animal's body through glass cannulae. In intermediate organizations, it was in the organs exposed in the abdominal cavity I watched. If I could design a better perfusion pump, I could keep those organs alive long after the body they supported had entered the state called "death." The animal in front of me could be fragmented into an almost limitless number of major and minor parts, each one of which could live on separately in a controlled environment.

In a laboratory room nearby, Carrel kept fragments of chicken heart that had been alive for more than twenty years—much longer than the ordinary life of a chicken. I had watched the cells, still young and pulsing, under a microscope. With proper care they would live and pulse forever.

Then what was life and what was death? Could it be that the life one thought of as oneself was simply an essence created by and dependent on the organization of billions of minor living individuals? Did their communication constitute the means and qualities man referred to as his spirit, his wisdom, thought, emotion, and intelligence? Did nothing mystical exist beyond cellular relationships, no greater god than beings rounded out with flesh? Carrel believed in a mysticism that extended apart from, and beyond, science. He was fascinated by the overlapping peripheries of mystical and scientific worlds. That fascination corresponded with and intensified my own.

The men I met in connection with medical research were quite different from those I had known in fields of aviation. They were more concerned with the human body itself than with its material accomplishments, with the basic phenomena of life and the treatment of life's abnormalities. In place of Lilienthal, Wright, and Blériot, I began to think of the significance of Harvey, Bernard, and Pasteur. Often, after attending conferences and conducting activities in aviation, I would work at the Rockefeller Institute until after midnight. Sometimes I would spend several consecutive days there. I moved back and forth between groups of men in aviation and medicine, now aware of the organizational importance of the group, now conscious of my individual freedom to concentrate my attention on whichever activity interested me most. As a result, I was in a unique position to observe the juxtaposition and interdependence of individual and organizational values. At the Rockefeller Institute I felt a member of a team. I was surrounded by human organization. Almost everything I did depended on the cooperation and accomplishments of others, as much on the intelligence and dedication of generations past as on the assistance of contemporaries.

The perfusion pumps I designed had to be made of a special glass that would not crack under the heat of sterilization or dissolve to the extent ordinary glass would dissolve in perfusing fluids. Such glass was sold under the name "Pyrex." Shaping glass requires years of practice plus an artist's skill. This combination was furnished to departments of the institute by a great craftsman, Otto Hopf, whose workshop was set up in a basement room of one of the laboratory buildings. I would shape my sketches to his skill, explain the results I wanted, and often sit watching him blow his flame-tortured lengths of tubing. Glass was a new medium for me to work with. It had limitations and offered possibilities I had never thought about before.

The materials and equipment I used came from various parts of the world, from mines, from trees, from shops, from warehouses. I needed quartz sand for filters, platinum screen to restrain the sand and withstand the chemical action of sterilizing acids, rubber corks and tubes, nonabsorbent cotton, mineral oil, pressure regulators, stopcocks, electric motors, steel tanks, and many other items. These items were assembled for me by the institute's Supply Department, where their sources could be located through the indexes of thick catalogs. Further, intelligent research and development requires a study of publications concerning many related subjects. Books, pamphlets, and magazine articles by thousands of authors were available in the institute's medical library. There I could read about the early-nineteenth-century perfusion experiments by Kay or the latest techniques of cytology.

The purpose of my apparatus was to keep isolated organs functioning under conditions approximating their natural environment in the body. Placing these organs in their glass chamber required a most elaborate technique, starting at the animal house, carried on by highly trained technicians and nurses of the Department of Experimental Surgery, and culminating with the knowledge and operative skill of Carrel. The Department of Experimental Surgery, in turn, was supported by the larger organization of the institute as a whole, with its administration, hospital, and interlocking laboratories. But the institute itself had been founded by an individual, John D. Rockefeller.

It took me five years to develop a perfusion pump in which experiments could be conducted satisfactorily—five years of designing, building, testing, redesigning.* In April 1935, we cultivated a whole organ—the thyroid gland of a cat—successfully, in vitro, for the first time. At last, more than a hundred years after the first experiments in artificial circulation were recorded, we had a perfusion pump from which infection could be excluded and in which living organs could be pulsated with approximately the same pressures they had been under before they were surgically isolated from the body. This completed the first step of the program Carrel and I had discussed in connection with the perfusion of organs. The

* A book, *The Culture of Organs,* by Carrel and Lindbergh describing their work was published in 1938.

second step involved the perfection of surgical and mechanical techniques. The third and final step would be the application of organ culture to practical research.

During months that followed, Carrel and his associates perfused various organs from animals and birds—spleens, ovaries, pituitaries, and kidneys among others. Even fragments of human organs, obtained from a nearby hospital, were installed in the pumps. I had set the pumps up in batteries of three, inside individual incubators. I would sit by the hour on a high stool watching them, as I worked on improving methods and designs. There were still serious problems confronting us. Erythrocytes, the red oxygen-carrying cells of the blood, deteriorated rapidly in my perfusion pump; and without them, the organs received insufficient oxygen to maintain their normal condition. Just as serious a problem was presented by the fact that my pump had no artificial kidney. The secretions of the organs remained in the perfusing fluid, constantly increasing its acidity and necessitating frequent change.

As a sideline to my perfusion-pump project, I designed a flask through which living tissue cells could be microscopically observed and photographed while in a circulating-fluid medium. A fragment of tissue was imbedded in quartz sand between thin, converging walls of glass. Near the center of the flask's observation chamber, the layer of sand became only one grain thick. Individual cells soon migrated to this area, and there my microscope was focused. I spent many evening hours in the heat of the laboratory's big incubator watching leucocytes extend their pseudopods and studying the secretions that had formed.

We had opened a new field with the perfusion of organs. A lifetime could easily be spent developing it. But suppose we solved all problems. Suppose we could install artificial hearts and transplant limbs at will. Suppose, even, that we could learn to remove one man's head and transfer it to the body of another. How much closer would we have come to solving life's basic mysteries? Even with his fragment of chicken heart, I realized, Carrel had not achieved eternal life, for it, too, kept dividing into new individuals and generations, just as man did—and the dilution of identity was similar. The essence of life, I concluded, did not lie in the material.

Taking off on a test flight in St. Louis, June 1925

After bailing out of the plane, which went
into a left tailspin

The vital parachute

Flying the mail, 1926

Transferring mail, 1926

Relaxing in Panama during Latin-American tour, January 1928

Wing of *Spirit of St. Louis* before assembly in San Diego

Posing for the press in New York
a few days before transatlantic flight

Mrs. Lindbergh visiting her
before his take-off for Paris

(arrow points to Lindbergh)

At St. Louis
on return from
Latin-American
tour,
February 1928

With Ambassador Myron Herrick in Paris, May 1927

With Grover Whalen in ticker-tape parade up Broadway, June 1927

With President and Mrs. Calvin Coolidge and his mother on the
steps of the White House, May 1927

Raymond Orteig awarding the
$25,000 Orteig Prize,
New York, June 16, 1927

In 1927

It penetrated, but was not bound to, the physical world of science.

How are the qualities of life susceptible to mechanistic concepts? After five years at the Rockefeller Institute, I placed less and less value on the mechanistic qualities of life.

On the night of March 1, 1932, soon after my wife and I had moved into our newly built house in the Sourland Mountains, a tragedy took place that was to affect our lives forever. Our son, Charles, Jr., was kidnapped. Born on June 22, 1930, he was twenty months old, blond, blue-eyed, and just beginning to talk.

I had been sitting in the parlor with my wife. Outside, the wind blew and the night was black. Our house was long, with two stories, enclosed by walls of whitewashed stone and a gray slate roof. We had placed the house on the high edge of an old field within our four hundred acres of abandoned farm and wild woodland.

I went upstairs to the child's nursery, opened the door, and immediately noticed a lifted window. A strange-looking envelope lay on the sill. I looked at the crib. It was empty. I ran downstairs, grabbed my rifle, and went out into the night, first to the nursery end of the house. Under the lifted window I saw a ladder, and saw that it was broken. Obviously, it had collapsed as the kidnapper descended. It looked as though it had been made out of new crating boards.

I realized there was no use going into the woods or trying to follow along roads. The night was too dark and stormy to see or hear anything. I returned to the house and put in an emergency call to the State Police. To my surprise, our telephone line had not been cut. New Jersey State Police headquarters sent out a general alarm. Roadblocks were established, cars searched, neighbors awakened and questioned. Police officials assembled at our home. Carloads of reporters and photographers arrived and established their usual interference and confusion.

I arranged with my bankers, J. P. Morgan & Co., to have the ransom money ready and packaged. Their bank clerks selected gold notes and listed the number of each one as a step toward the eventual apprehension of the kidnapper. A place for delivering the ransom money was arranged through a combination of newspaper advertisements and mail, through an intermediary, an old and kindly professor in the Bronx, Dr. John F. Condon. It was to be at night, on the edge of a large cemetery. I drove the car for the professor, with just the two of us in it.

I parked across the street from the designated spot. The area was dimly lighted by city lamps. Soon a man appeared on the sidewalk next to the cemetery. His strategy was apparent: he had the spacious and unlighted area of graves and tombstones one leap away. He bowed his head as he passed, raised a handkerchief to his face, and called in a low voice, but clearly: "Hey, Doctor!"

The transfer of banknotes was made across the cemetery wall. Thereafter we waited day by day for some further contact or communication. None came with any mark of authenticity. But intricate hoaxes were attempted. A friend of mine heard from a man in Norfolk, Virginia, who said he had contact with a gang that was holding our son. I boarded a launch as part of the attempt to reach this gang, which was imaginary. While I was on that launch, the child's body was found, not far from the roadside, in a wood only a mile or two from our house. It had been taken to a morgue at Trenton. I returned to New Jersey immediately. While I was en route, newspaper photographers broke in through a window of the morgue to take pictures of the child's remains.

After the body of our son was found, my wife and I left our Sourland Mountain home, never to spend another night there. Later, we gave the house and grounds to the state of New Jersey to be used as a home for children. We moved back to the big Morrow family home at Next Day Hill. Then, on August 16, 1932, our second son, Jon, was born.

I had expected the concentration of police agencies to result in the early apprehension of the kidnapper, but clue after clue was run down without much tangible achievement. The search settled down to the tedious routine of following every rumor and reinvestigating every detail.

It was during the winter of 1932–33 that I continued my international-air-route surveys. I studied conditions along all three of the possible transatlantic routes. With my wife, I undertook the survey to examine the use of flying boats on transoceanic routes.

On February 9, 1934, President Roosevelt canceled the mail contracts of more than thirty airlines, claiming criminal conspiracy by the contract holders, and ordered the Army to take over carrying the mail. I was shocked by the President's action. He had not even accorded the companies' officers a hearing before the drastic action was taken. Its political connotation seemed obvious, for it was based on the results of an airline conference called by the Postmaster General during Hoover's administration. I knew many of the men who had taken part in that conference. They were not lawbreakers. They had been asked by a cabinet officer of the United States government to attend a meeting in Washington that was of critical importance to the organizations for which they were responsible. There had been too much duplication of routing. Airlines were losing money. Something had to be done about it. If in fact instances of collusion resulted, then they should be proven through indictment and trial. President Roosevelt's summary action seemed to me contrary to American justice.

I had not attended that Washington conference, for I was not an officer of any airline, and I had never taken part in negotiating a contract with the government. Years before, I had decided to maintain a consulting relationship with the commercial organizations I worked for, and to concentrate my attention on scientific and technical developments rather than on administration or on mail contracts. But I felt I could not remain silent in the face of action so unconsidered, drastic, and unfair. I was concerned about the detrimental effect on civil aviation of the President's action, but I was also alarmed by his order to the Army. Military aircraft were not designed to fly mail routes, and military pilots were not trained for it. They had relatively little experience in night flying, or even in operating by day through conditions of fog and storm.

I attacked President Roosevelt publicly for taking such action without trial or hearing. Within two months, twelve Army pilots were killed while flying the mail. The fatality rate was so high, and the resulting public criticism so great, that the military operation had to be discontinued. It was clear that Roosevelt had made a political blunder, and the airlines had to be returned to private operators. The routes were put up for rebidding. The President tried to save face by stipulating that no airline officer who had attended the Washington conference could hold office in an airline receiving a government contract. Again, he gave these men neither a hearing nor a trial. He also stipulated that no airline could bid on a canceled route it had flown.

Obviously new airlines could not be organized and equipped overnight. Somehow the old ones had to continue flying. A solution was found reminiscent of something to be found in *Alice in Wonderland*. The airlines simply changed their names. United Aircraft became United Airlines. Transcontinental and Western Air became Trans World Airlines. Thereafter mail was flown and passengers carried as they had been before. United brought suit. Seven years later the courts decided against the government. But by that time World War II was in progress, and the issue was not as newsworthy.

On September 19, 1934, the kidnapper of our son was apprehended. Painstaking and brilliant detective work had developed several converging clues by the time a gasoline-filling-station operator noticed that he was being paid with a ten-dollar gold certificate and wrote down on it the license number of the car he had just serviced. The bank he turned it over to found that the number on the bill corresponded to one of the numbers on the ransom list that the newspapers had been helpful in printing. An arrest followed a few days later.

The trial took place at Flemington, New Jersey, lasted six weeks, and ended in conviction, with a death sentence imposed. The evidence was overwhelming. Newspaper and radio publicity had been tremendous. It brought crackpots to our home and threatening letters in our mail. I carried a Colt thirty-eight-caliber revolver, in a chest holster, under my coat wherever I went. We kept our second son under armed guard whenever he was out of the house. A retired detective, with a sawed-off shotgun, stayed close to him. A watchman made regular rounds at Next Day Hill throughout the night. Post Office authorities made fourteen arrests during a single year in connection with threatening letters we received. Local and state police gave us all the assistance and protection they could, but alarming incidents still occurred.

One evening I was sitting in an upstairs bedroom in the big Morrow house at Next Day Hill when I heard a call outside. I opened a window and looked down. I saw a chalky face, dimly illuminated by the house lights, staring at me. The man's figure below it was barely discernible. I could not understand what the voice was saying. The words did not seem to fit together. Police arrived within minutes and escorted the man away. Investigation showed him to be harmless, an off-and-on mental-institution case. He had been excited by newspaper stories and had some vague idea of trying to help us. No one knew how he found the Morrow grounds and got inside.

On another night, I was driving my wife from New York City back to Englewood. We had turned right after crossing the Hudson River bridge and were about to swing left where the road we were following ended in a cross street. To our right the cross street was blocked by road work. All through traffic had to turn left, but a dirt-surface, unlighted alley led straight ahead. As we started to swing left, an old car carrying four men speeded up from behind and tried to force us into the alley. But they had positioned themselves badly. Startled, I put on my brakes. Their car shot ahead, and I turned sharply left behind it. My way was then clear, and the men made no further attempt to follow. It had been too dark to see faces, and too fast to read a license number. No clues remained for police to follow. We could only speculate about the motive.

As if fanatics and gangsters, stirred up by intense publicity, did not create enough problems for us to contend with, the press itself confronted us with alarming and uncontrollable acts, the most serious of which related to our second son. When he was three years old, we started sending him to a nursery school in Englewood. The school had been organized by and was under the direction of Anne's sister Elisabeth. It was several blocks from Next Day Hill. One morning, my wife received an emergency phone call from a teacher. A "suspicious-looking truck" had parked at the curb outside the school yard. It was covered with canvas, but the teachers were sure there were men moving around inside. All the children had been called in from recess, and immediately the truck left.

Police were notified. State troopers located and halted the truck not far outside the city. They found it to contain newspaper photographers, who had taken pictures, through slits in the canvas, of our child at play. The photographers had been sent by one of the New York tabloids. No arrests were made, because no clear violation of the law existed, and the press was so powerful politically that police authorities had to proceed cautiously. The arrest of a photographer or reporter invariably brought claims that freedom of the press was being suppressed. Teachers at the school and members of our family had been alarmed, with cause. The truck might as well have contained gangsters as reporters. But I could take no action that would prevent similar incidents from occurring.

Shortly thereafter, a similar incident did occur. Our son's nurse was driving him home from school one day. A car started to pass them, wedged in front, and forced them to a stop against the curb. The terrified nurse thought gangsters were stopping them. Then a man with a camera jumped out, took pictures of the sobbing child, and drove away. Again it was a tabloid photographer; again there was no effective action I could take.

The dangers of fanatics, gangsters, and newspapermen made life close to intolerable for my wife and son, and in consequence for me. I considered moving to some other section of the United States, but concluded that we would gain little more security and peace. Press publicity would certainly follow wherever we went, and no state could give us greater assistance than we were receiving from New Jersey and its police. I would have to give up most of my activities in aviation and to postpone indefinitely visits I had planned to make to Robert Goddard's rocket experimental station in New Mexico. But I could not work efficiently anyway under the circumstances that existed, and I felt uncomfortable about making any trips away from home. I decided to take my family abroad until conditions in my own country changed enough to let me establish a reasonably safe and happy home for them.

FIVE

Atlantis

My wife and I decided to go first to England, because we had been told that Englishmen respected rights of privacy and that English newspapers had more respect for law than ours at home. Kidnapping and gangsterism such as we had experienced in the United States were unknown in the British Isles. British policemen enforced the law unarmed. We knew the common language would be an advantage, and in England we had friends. Also, quite simply, we had been attracted by British tourist-bureau advertisements that described the beauties of the countryside and welcomed visitors. We left New York in December of 1935.

We passed most of the winter in Wales and London. In March, we moved into "Long Barn" at Sevenoaks Weald. Long Barn was extended and roomy. It was much bigger than any house we would have considered renting back in America, but ideas about house sizes were different in England. The rent seemed low to us, even though English friends told us we were being charged an "American price."

We started leading a peaceful life there, in the garden country of Kent. Flowers bloomed outside every window. Long twilight added to the laziness of spring. In England we were relatively undisturbed by journalists, and we had no need whatever for protection by the police. British newspapermen were a serious problem on only one occasion while we were living at Long Barn. We had declined to pose for photographs and give the interviews they wanted, so they stood outside our door and threw rocks at our dog, who barked at them through a fence enclosing the grounds we rented. They seemed delighted when our dog caught some of the stones in his bleeding mouth. Several of his teeth were broken.

Prior to 1936, most of my aviation activities related to civil life. Thereafter, for many years, they were primarily military.

One morning a letter arrived at Long Barn from an officer I had never met—Major Truman Smith, Military Attaché to the American Embassy in Berlin. Imposing developments were taking place in the German Air Force, the Major wrote, and he would like to have my opinion. That summer, my wife and I flew to Berlin in a rented monoplane, crossing the Channel near Dover, and following one of the authorized "corridors" through the Maginot Line. Within a few days I realized that Nazi Germany intended to become the greatest air power in the world. General Hermann Göring of the Luftwaffe was a dynamic political leader.

I gained the impression that Germany was looking eastward, militarily, yet it was obvious that bombing planes would not find the Maginot Line a formidable obstacle should they wish to cross it. The Germans knew that France was deficient in both defensive and retaliatory air power.

Göring invited us to his Berlin home for lunch. There we sat with German and American officers and their wives at a richly decorated table in a room lined with mirrors and carved madonnas "borrowed" from German museums. After the meal was over, Göring, white-uniformed, bemedaled, and gold-braided, escorted me to a side table, where he opened a photograph album. "Here are our first seventy," he said, turning the pages. Each page contained a picture of a military airfield. From the inspection trips I had made through German factories, I knew warplanes were being built to fill those fields.

Obviously Germany was preparing for war on a major scale with the most modern equipment. The Nazi government also obviously wanted to impress America with its rapidly growing strength. Before leaving Berlin I assisted Major Smith in preparing a special report for the War Department in Washington. Germany was forging ahead of the United States in aeronautical research and production facilities, we declared. The performance of their fighting and light-bombing types of aircraft was especially notable.

I knew theoretically what modern bombs could do to cities. At the same time, experiences in war games had convinced me that claims for the effectiveness of both ground and air defense were tremendously exaggerated. In Nazi Germany, for the first time, war became real to me. The officers I met were not preparing for a game. Their discussions gave me a sense of blood and bullets, and I realized how destructive my profession of aviation might become.

The organized vitality of Germany was what most impressed me: the unceasing activity of the people, and the convinced dictatorial direction to create the new factories, airfields, and research laboratories. Militarism was pervasive—streets were full of uniforms and banners. It was such a contrast to the complacent and tranquil life in England from which we had come. Germany had the ambitious drive of America, but that drive was headed for war.

Cruising back to England after our visit was over, I found that Nazi Germany was forcing a reorientation of my thought. For many years aviation had seemed to me primarily a way of bringing peoples of the world together in commerce and peace. The accounts of air combats I had read as a young Minnesota wartime farmer had long been pocketed away in memory. My year at cadet school, followed by service in Reserve and National Guard squadrons, was hardly more than a passing bow to the rejected god of war. I had thought and talked about aircraft overcoming surface barriers of earth for the benefit of man's relationship to man. Now I began to think about the vulnerability of men to aircraft carrying high-explosive bombs.

As we started across the Channel, I realized how concepts of military geography must change. What contrast between my viewpoint from the sky then and the earth perspective of Napoleon as he looked across the Channel! A British island opened out ahead; only a quarter-hour of water lay below. Why should the British be concerned about a battle fleet upon the surface? England was no longer a wide-moated fortress protected by majestic ships of war. Aviation had transformed her into a target for continental bombing squadrons converging from airfields with which she would be almost half encircled.

Back in the slow pace and complacency of England, I found that Germany's dynamic activity seemed veiled by attitude and distance. Great English factories produced their wares, great ships loaded and unloaded at their wharfs. Parliament deliberated problems of a great empire. Parlors heard conversation about the abdication and the coming coronation ceremonies. Appropriations were made to increase the strength of the Royal Air Force. There was a concern over the current activities in Nazi Germany, but still only a partial realization of their significance. I talked to friends in England and wrote to others in the United States about observations I had made.

Meanwhile, I watched the construction of a monoplane I was having built to my specifications by Phillips & Powis Aircraft, Ltd., at Reading.

That was the winter my wife and I flew to India. On our stops in many countries of Asia, Africa, and Europe, we observed the early symptoms of the breakup of the British Empire and of Western civilization's waning power in the East.

The city of Rome, when we arrived, was full of Mussolini's fascist soldiers. Men in uniform guarded the airport, strode the sidewalks, filed in and out through doorways of buildings boasting the fasces emblem. They contrasted with the black-robed priests. Miracles by "Il Duce" were called to our attention—the improvements to the streets we drove along, a magnificent new railroad terminus, the excavations mounted to expose the city's past greatness. The twentieth-century dictator prophesied that Italy would return for a third time to be the directing force of Western civilization. He would electrify railways, drain the Pontine Marshes, increase the birth rate, and reclaim the Italian Empire. How imitative it was! A dictatorship, conquest, and power, armies marching off for Africa and Spain, great structures rising—one might be describing ancient Rome instead of modern Italy.

We followed the coast of Italy southeast over the Bay of Naples, past Vesuvius and Pompeii, curving along mountain ranges that form the country's ankle and toes until we reached the Mediterranean island of Sicily. Far in the distance Mount Etna thrust its snowcap through a layer of clouds into a haze-blue sky. I still see clearly in my mind's eye the Grecian temple of Jupiter at Segesta, some miles from where we landed. Erected on a low hilltop, roofless to the heavens, overlooking the sea, columned and corniced, weathered by two thousand years yet perfect in its form, it seemed a place where men and gods could meet as never will be conceivable of our day. I felt that a people who had hewn such mystic beauty from the material of stone could have risen above the morbidity of war and human quarreling. Yet the Greek city-states were in constant disagreement, and the civilization they had developed gave way to the centralized power of Rome.

Our route to India took us over the ruins of Carthage, on Africa's Mediterranean coast. We refueled at Tunis, stayed overnight at Tripoli, skirted the Gulf of Sirte, crossed the barren Libyan desert to Alexandria and Cairo. We circled Bethlehem, Jerusalem, Jericho, flew low over the Dead Sea, landed in a sandstorm at the oasis of Rutba Wells, a post and watering place in the Syrian Desert. The Euphrates seemed a flat and muddy river from our plane; and Babylon but another ruined city—too far back in history to be connected to our times.

We landed in India at Gwadar, Karachi, Jodhpur, Udaipur, Bombay, Nagpur, Raipur, Calcutta, Lucknow, and Delhi. Obviously, we had planned to tour the country extensively, possibly flying south as far as Ceylon, and north into Kashmir and the Himalaya. But near Nagpur, one of the engine's push rods failed, and this kept our Mohawk on the ground for sixteen days.

While we were waiting for a new push rod, we went by train from Nagpur to Calcutta, and thereby were impressed more keenly with differences between Indian and European ways of life. We were escorted to the railroad station by new-made British friends, and to our amazement found a huge block of ice on the floor in the center of the compartment in which they had arranged for us to travel. "Without ice, the heat on these Indian trains becomes unbearable," they said. "This will keep you a little cooler. But be sure that the window stays closed."

The Indians who walked by us apparently took no notice of the ice and but little of the white-faced foreigners amongst them. Living a servile yet basically independent life, they reminded me of farm animals at times. Their interests, their existences seemed so distant from my own—we touched and still we lacked an understanding.

Calcutta struck us with the full force of the poverty of India's masses. Human life had here sunk to levels we had never seen before. Ragged, hungry people milled back and forth on filthy streets. Cripples sat on curbstones. Scabby, thin-legged children followed us with outstretched hands. At night, we stepped around stretched-out sleeping bodies on the sidewalks close to our luxurious European-style hotel. "You never know the difference," we were told, "but sometimes one of them is dead."

I could hardly believe this country once produced a civilization of art and architecture and religion—or that conditions were in fact worse before the British government took over. It was easy to accept the need for imperialist rule, but as an American, I understood the Indian wish for freedom. What people would be content with a government imposed by force, rooted in a foreign nation five thousand miles away?

Man is a mixture of desires that extend beyond his knowledge and often result in action conflicting with rationality. During the visit to India, I sat in a Calcutta auditorium listening to Sir Francis Younghusband advocate the unity of faiths under a brotherhood of man. The intense and earnest faces of his audience left no doubt that men of East and West were striving hard to break down the religious barriers between them. In spirit, they desired to bring divergent points of view to closer understanding. But a few evenings later, my wife and I had dinner at a university professor's home. "You are most welcome at our table," the Indian professor volunteered. "Being Americans, you cannot realize how little chance we have to mix with Western people."

As Americans, we were surprised to find that the relationship between Englishman and Indian had many similarities to that between white and Negro at home. At Calcutta, at New Delhi, at Karachi, Benares, and Udaipur, it was obvious that ideals of unity and brotherhood were overcome by the Englishman's desire to hold his heredity and environment intact. "For good or for evil," Toynbee wrote, "the English Protestant rulers of India have distinguished themselves from all other contemporary western rulers over non-western peoples by the rigidity with which they have held aloof from their subjects."*

Between Lucknow and Delhi, we flew over Fatehpur Sikri, the long-abandoned capital of Akbar, descendant of the Mogul khans. These were once great buildings, now a mass of ruins. Akbar had, like the British, established stable government by his conquests; and the Moguls built what was then the greatest empire on earth. Yet India remained Indian in character; and Mongolia, despite its geopolitical position, reverted to its earlier status of a vague and unimportant land.

Our return flight to England gave us no indication that our modern age was more secure than ages of the past, or that man's advance in science would improve the relationships of men. Standing amid the broken columns of the Athenian acropolis, I felt that the problems of our modern civilization deepened in perspective. In these ruins lay a timeless warning. At the same moment, one sensed the heights of Western achievement and the depths of Western failure. One realized how easily strength was perverted to decay, how human wisdom was more essential to a temple's walls than the rock on which it stood. As England faced Germany in our time, Athens had faced Sparta over two thousand years before, and the outcome brought the downfall of all Greece. War! War! What useless conflicts there had been through those intervening centuries! Yet one could see no end.

Somewhere between the extremes of Western science and Eastern mysticism, I felt, must lie a better answer than we had yet discovered. If we could not find it in time to prevent a modern struggle, our own hopes and ideals would be shattered like those Periclean temples and the civilizations of Europe would be destroyed like that of ancient Greece.

Western civilization—how I had taken it for granted before I

---

* A letter Lindbergh wrote to his mother on February 28, 1937 includes the following observations: "I believe that most Englishmen spend their years in India without realizing that it is anything more than a country to be developed; whenever I see the effect of western civilization upon eastern I feel depressed and apprehensive; I can understand the attitude of the soldier and the merchant better than I can understand the desire of the missionary and the reformer to impose Western customs upon Eastern peoples. It is like trying to make a leopard into a horse."

came to Europe! It had seemed as immortal as life does to early youth. And here I was questioning its survival after a war that was already likely to take place. I was questioning the future of the white race, which had once seemed to me secure beyond the need of questioning. We whites had become so accustomed to dominating that it was difficult to realize that we were a minority in a world of yellow, brown, and black. We had looked at other peoples and felt sure they were inferior because of our own scientific progress and because of our inability to recognize the wisdom in their viewpoints and their many subtle qualities. I had felt superiority looking at refugees in the Yangtze floods of China, at naked jungle natives in Central America, at Eskimos and their skin kayaks and their spears in Greenland, at Indians sitting in the dirt and begging at Karachi and Calcutta.

Suppose we destroyed ourselves with politics and wars, as ancient Rome had done. What would then happen to our supposed superiority of race? Would other races do to us as we had done to them? How would I feel if my white skin marked me as an inferior individual by the standards of the time? Why should anyone think a white skin superior in evaluating the qualities of human life? I did not really admire a white skin so much myself. Did I not prefer the brown that came with exposure to the sun? What "white" intellect did I admire more than I did the mind of yellow-skinned Lao Tse? And could white physique be called superior to that of the African black?

Why do men feel so strongly against the differentiation that nature has encouraged throughout the history of life—as though opposed to the very process of evolution that created their species in the first place? What causes the inner drive toward unity and similarity that makes men want to eliminate the differences of race, a drive most apparent in the youngest and least experienced of all the world's great nations, our extraordinarily powerful United States? Is this a result of our Christian ideology? Is it a passing ideal in the basic evolutionary trend of life, or is it a subtle quality emerging in the early dawn of an era of the mind? Does it arise from a basic fear of the struggle for survival, or is it grounded in a wisdom that science and education have enhanced?

"Birds of a feather flock together." It is a saying I remember from very early youth, and it was repeated by people who realized no connection between its obviousness and evolutionary principles that they denied. Its obvious meaning became clear to me in boyhood long before I understood the genetic significance behind it. Hunting with my father and watching migrations in the fall, I noticed that the wild birds never mixed. Partridge flew with partridge and mallard never crossed with teal. The birds my grandfather found when he reached the Minnesota frontier were no different in appearance from the birds I looked at in my day. Life under natural conditions maintained the most subtle differences in colors and in shapes. Change came imperceptibly, through ages.

For ages man has been less specific in his own breeding than the wild animals around him. Individuals have mated into different races by chance, by choice, and by force. Alexander ordered his generals to take Persian princesses to wife. Foreign slaves marketed in ancient Rome helped mix the modern Italian's blood. The American takes a schizophrenic pride in his genetic internationality, for while he boasts of his diversity, he can also become alarmed by the rising Negro population throughout his United States.

All over the world, in all times, war, commerce, and adventure have stirred together races and the characters of men. Notwithstanding all this mixing, and without the genetic planning that creates our various breeds of domestic animals, distinct races have managed to exist. Race is distinctive and has its character, yet a pure human race does not exist. I think of a visit in England with the archaeologist Arthur Keith when he was over ninety years of age. He showed me around Charles Darwin's nearby house and grounds, explaining some of Darwin's steps in establishing the basic laws of evolution. Keith believed in dynamic principles of race. Wherever groups of people get together, potentially a new race begins, and the longer a single group keeps intermating, the more definite are the characteristics its members manifest.

I as an individual was a gamete in the body of race, but with apparently more control over my effectiveness and destiny than that of a gamete of which an individual's body is composed. Living in a foreign country with a war about to break and human life through-

153

out the world in flux, I found it essential to consider realities surrounding the position I was in. I was faced with the old problem of competition and survival in an environment changed radically through the impact of man's science in life's new era of the mind.

The surrounding state of crisis rose above idealism's costumed stage to clarify the basic fact that survival begins with the individual and extends outward through family, group, and nation, through civilization, race, and time. I had come abroad for family survival, a combination of both chance and plan. An extraordinary sequence of events had preceded my moving from America to Europe—the attraction of the clouds in childhood, an early airplane flying past my home, my decision to enter aviation, moonlight on my mailplane's silver wings, the world impact of my nonstop flight to Paris, the ruthless irresponsibility of the twentieth-century press. The position I was in seemed so unlikely and fantastic that I could rationalize it only by the statement an English scientist once made to me in London. "Everything that happens was once infinitely improbable," he said. "Therefore nothing that happens should be surprising."

That the past is changed by time becomes obvious through man's own changing viewpoint. Instances of good and bad, right and wrong, love and hate, transpose with years for every individual. History relates to concept and concept to environment and environment to the changing qualities of men. The past changes for every man who views it, and for every memory of man.

Years before, I had adopted a policy of reconsidering my life at intervals, and of trying to do so as though I had no established principles, traditions, material assets, or obligations. I would let my mind run free completely, and then attempt to combine its fantasies with the essential realities of life. Suppose I were neither American nor Christian, that I had neither family nor friends, and within another month, say, I would have to choose a place and manner in which to live. What would I do? Would I return to America? Would I become a citizen of France? Were the political systems in those great nations of Germany and Russia as evil as they often seemed? Would I be attracted by distant white men's frontiers—Australia or New Zealand? Could I find a life of satisfaction by merging with another race, in India or China, for example? And the islands of the South Pacific—was the pull toward science and civilization as strong within me as the pull toward earth and nature?

The year and a half I spent in England left me with no desire to return for other than visits. I was impressed by the great traditions of the British and by their stability and laws and their sense of justice. The family summers at Long Barn were among the most wonderful summers of my life. I valued highly the friendships I made within a people who through commerce, Christianity, and conquest had established the greatest empire ever to exist on earth. But there was a sense of heaviness of life in England that pressed like a London fog. It was as though the Englishman's accomplishments, century after century, had become a cumulative burden on his shoulders until his traditions, his possessions, and his pride overweighed his buoyancy of spirit. I felt that England, aged, saw not the future but the past and had resigned herself to the gardens of her greatness year by year. She was satisfied with her empire and a legal status quo enforced by her warships' guns. It was as though her desires blocked out the knowledge of her mind that life is not stabilized for long by conquest, and that wings fly over land and sea and gun batteries.

The contrasting lightness of continental life was nowhere more apparent than in France. There, thought and conversation brightened like the weather. Legality was rigid of form but had less common assurance about it. I felt little sense of stability in France. The loyalty to government one found in England was replaced by a love of country in the French. The citizen was only too ready to overthrow his government while at the same time he would give his life for the preservation of his land.

Like so many other foreigners, I had fallen in love with France, but I had lived in the country long enough to be aware of its weaknesses—the terrible suspicion, the flashing hatreds, the niggardliness, the inability to unify and organize in advance of an emergency. It would be one thing, I realized, to be an American living in France with the security and resources of the United States in the background, but it would be quite another thing to merge with a people capable of the cruelties of the Revolution, the mercuriality of the Napoleonic conquests, the vindictiveness of Versailles. The brilliance of the French seemed to glitter over a lack of wisdom, and I concluded that an overemphasis on individuality could easily result in the destruction of a people. I loved France but I was highly apprehensive of her foibles.

To me, Nazi Germany was a fascinating country, but I disliked its regimentation, its appeal to mass emotions, its restriction of free thought, its fanatical attitude toward race: yet I saw there an aspect of life that was fundamental to life's evolution—the forceful challenge to a status quo. I saw a Western people preparing for aggression and developing a philosophy to justify such action—as Englishmen had justified building their empire, as Americans had justified wresting a continent from its inhabitants and then throwing out the earlier occupying forces of England, France, and Spain.

I shared the repulsion that democratic peoples felt in viewing the demagoguery of Hitler, the controlled elections, the secret police. Yet I felt that I was seeing in Germany, despite the crudeness of its form, the inevitable alternative to decline—a challenge based more on the drive to achieve success despite established "right" and law. It was a condition recorded in the past of every major nation. It seemed to me probable that it would be repeated in the future throughout time—aggression, conquest, status quo—a cycle inherent in the progressing qualities of life. Looking back through history, what nation, what civilization does not find aggression in its origin?

I was stirred by the spirit in Germany as I had been deadened by the lack of it in England and disturbed by its volatile individuality in France. But for me the ideology, the regimentation, the intolerance, and the fanaticism of Hitler's Third Reich were intolerable in comparison to alternatives that existed.

Visiting Germany after living in countries to the west, I felt the suppression of freedom under Hitler. But on returning to Germany after visiting Stalin's Russia, the freedom of the people seemed immense. I felt that Russia, of all European countries, was the last in which I would choose to make my home. The trips I had made through parts of the Soviet Union led me to observe a suppression of freedom I had never experienced before. Men and women were afraid to talk and were restricted in action and travel. You heard over and over again of individuals disappearing after secret-police calls in the night, and reports came back of prison camps far away in Siberia. The underlying greatness of the country and its people seemed to be hibernating under a minority regime that had already established a record of bloodshed and tragedy unsurpassed in history.

I thought of the smaller and more peaceful countries, Sweden, Switzerland, and Denmark; or maybe New Zealand, which seemed about as far away from war as it could be—on the other side of the earth from Europe and her quarrels—thousands of miles from any major military power. But the existence of such countries depended so much upon the whim of others. A strong enemy could invade them whenever he wished to pay the price in men and material resources, just as German forces had invaded Belgium at the start of World War I. Their influence on world events was relatively slight. Despite my interest in individual survival, I did not want to leave the major stream of life while other men exerted their influence on civilization's progress. In the great crisis that impended, I wished to take my part.

When I considered the great nations farther east, India, China, and Japan, I realized more fully the barrier of race and of the environment with which race intertwines. Of course if I had no alternative I could merge with a people of Asia, just as men of Asia had merged with peoples of European stock—my friend Lin Yutang, for instance. I could find great interest and fascination in the divergent ways of life, but my mind and instincts were so bound to my race and to its culture that I would not join another by free choice.

Regardless of how much my imagination cut my traditions and my ties, no nation drew me toward it like my own. With all the world to choose from, I would still prefer to be what I was, a citizen of the United States. I was in the fortunate position of having been born in the country I would choose after more than a third of a century's experience of life.

Now that I had considered my own position as objectively as I could, what was the position of my country and my people, and what was my relationship to be with that great organization of individuals of which I was, and desired to be, a part? The very fact that I had established a home abroad showed that life for me in America was not ideal. I had left for the safety of my family and because the daily press had made our existence so difficult and dangerous.

Living abroad, I had found great interest in contrasting peoples and countries, in admiring here, criticizing there; in studying the past, and projecting present trends into the future. England was aged and declining; her empire would surely break, probably with bloodshed. France still had vitality, but she was so individualistic and politically divided that more internal troubles seemed inevitable. Germany was in the throes of recovery from a military defeat, under a dictatorship that could bring disaster. But what of the United States, my own country, an ocean and a political philosophy away?

It was difficult to judge America on the basis of history, because such a phenomenon had never taken place before—a hemisphere discovered and opened to immigration by peoples from a group of civilized nations of a single race—independence, democracy, and unusual individual freedom established, with a continent in which to grow. And the impact of modern industry and science followed to build quickly the richest, strongest, and most influential nation in the world.

Even before moving to Europe, I had been apprehensive of trends in my country that were generally accepted as obvious virtues—the tempo, the bigness, the assumed equality of men, the rate of growth, the rising city populations, the separation of idealism from reality. I was disturbed by the realization that aviation, which I had worked so hard to advance, encouraged a regimentation and uniformity of life.

As a boy, I had often heard America called "the melting pot," but as I grew older I learned that, while life mixed, it did not melt, and that the analogy between metals and men was false. Mixing metals resulted in an alloy of complete uniformity. Mixing human beings did not, because there were different principles involved. The principle of life progressing is to differentiate, not mix. Here we encounter one of nature's paradoxes: life differentiates through mixing, and then selects through differentiation. When men and women of various nations mix, they bring forth children of various qualities with individual combinations in body, intellect, and spirit —combinations of strength and weakness relating always to survival. The process of selection involves war and peace, religion and atheism, intercourse and isolation, science and mysticism, politics, ideas, and ideals in conflict and support. The mixing of divergent peoples throws human life into flux, but this flux brings out new differences rather than a uniform alloy.

To what crises our genetics and our environment were taking us I was, of course, unsure. But it seemed obvious to me that we needed time to work them out, without the complication of a major war, and that to enter another European war would be more likely to destroy Western civilization than to solve either our problems or those of European nations. I decided to take whatever part I could in preventing a war in Europe, and to campaign against my country taking part if war broke out.

Living abroad, I missed the close contact I had maintained at home with the development of airlines and air routes, the archaeological explorations I had planned to make, the laboratories and research facilities at the Rockefeller Institute. But most of all I missed the opportunity of working closely with Robert Goddard in developing the rockets that I felt might someday carry man out into space. It was clear to me that man-carrying rockets were a long way in the future, but Goddard had shown me designs of a pulsing engine he had invented which he thought might be practical for airplanes—and now I thought of warplanes of greatly superior design. Air entered through shutters in the nose, mixed with sprayed gasoline, and exploded outward through a tailpipe, thereby creating forward thrust. No propeller was needed, and high speeds might be attained.

When the Nazis invaded Austria, on March 12, 1938, I watched for signs of British reaction. The effect of the Anschluss was noticeable primarily in mounting speculation about war—in newspaper articles, in after-dinner speeches, in club talks about the unity of

English-speaking peoples and the closeness of American cousins overseas, in discussions about the danger of Hitler's bombing fleets. But the lack of clear thinking about military aviation alarmed me.

Some Englishmen relied on the British Navy and were not overly worried about the danger of air raids. During the evening's discussion at a club in London in April 1938, the subject of bombing arose. "Of course they can't hit anything, you know," said a retired member of the Air Ministry. "Nothing is ever hit with bombs. Why, look at the last war—they never hit what they were aiming at." He turned to me among the several men standing around him. "Did you ever see anyone come down in a parachute?" he asked. I said I had. "They never land where they want to, you know," he continued. "Too many crosscurrents in the air. Now it's the same way with a bomb—" And the conversation continued in this way until dinner.

In England there were naturally men of ability and vision, the very kind who had built the greatest empire on earth, but they held too few offices of major influence. I thought of the blood loss England had experienced in the 1914–1918 war. I would have been less disturbed about the future of Great Britain if the attitude of so many men I met was not rooted in what seemed to me typical aspects of British life. Factories were inefficient by American or German standards. The quality of goods was declining. With few exceptions, mechanical designs were behind the times. I had encountered an example of industrial backwardness and bureaucratic red tape when I wanted to install parachute flares on the plane I was having built at Reading. In case I had a forced landing at night, I needed flares similar to those I had used flying airmail. To my amazement I found I could not buy parachute flares in England. British planes were still being equipped with a type of flare that had been discarded in America more than a decade before; these were attached to the wings, caused unnecessary resistance, tended to blind a pilot in a haze, and were likely to start a fire after a crash.

England's ponderousness and increasing dependence on American support were indicated in conversations I had with British officials. Before a dinner at the American Embassy in London in May 1938, Leslie Hore-Belisha, British Secretary for War, asked me if I thought Great Britain would be able to produce airplanes fast enough in the future. When I told him how worried I was about conditions then existing in fields of British aviation, he suggested that it might not be possible to compete with German aircraft production while working under the English economic system. I myself believed that the Spitfire fighter was the only plane produced in England that was not excelled by planes of its class produced abroad, and not enough of them existed to form much fighting strength at that time.

I wondered whether the temperament of the English people was compatible with the rising tempo of other Western countries' life, for it seemed more attuned to ship and sail than to wings and the speed of aircraft. Always I was struck by the paradox that the Industrial Revolution had begun in England, accelerating men's actions to a tempo that Englishmen now seemed unable to maintain. Geography, industry, ideology, and ingenuity had worked to the Englishman's advantage in the past. They now seemed to have combined against him. Instead of protecting his islands with a moat, geography had semicircled them with potential enemy bombing bases. Continental industries, grown larger than his own, were producing military aircraft for those bases. Foreign ingenuity had surpassed his own in designing machines of superior performance. Even the English ideals of political equity and Christian brotherhood were besetting themes at this time: there were increasing demands for independence by the dominions and colonies.

In the spring of 1938, my wife and I purchased the islands of Illiec, off the northern coast of France. I thought them the most beautiful islands in the world. Small, storm-scarred, and rocky, they lay on an edge of ocean where tidal waters churned their shorelines on levels varying up to forty feet. At high tide a fair-size ship could anchor between our islands and the mainland. At low tide we walked to the mainland across sandy bottoms between seaweed-covered reefs. Sea, sky, and light combined in vistas with the tides. Salt-water ponds, round stones, and rushing rapids were seen and then covered by a brimful ocean, gray in mist or sparkling in the sun.

Our house was on the highest island, a few acres of gorse and stunted trees rooting in clumps of earth on slopes of stone, and it was built of stone with a slate roof and a round turret, like a scaled-down castle. Beside it, without much space between, was a great flattish-topped rock, larger than the house and the tower, with a sheer side reaching down to the ocean. Storms dashed their spray to the top of the rock and sometimes threw head-size stones close to our kitchen door.

The house had been built many years before by Ambroise Thomas, the composer of *Mignon*. We had first seen it when we visited Alexis Carrel and his wife, Anne, on the island of Saint-Gildas. Their house was no more than a kilometer away, set among weird rocks silhouetted against a haze-blue sky. Illiec offered us the attraction of being close to the Carrels and gave us the opportunity to know the continental countries better.

We spent most of the summer of 1938 on Illiec and Saint-Gildas, furnishing the house, playing with our two sons, spending time with my mother, who visited us, as she did elsewhere regularly, working on book manuscripts, and enjoying the austere beauty of the Côtes-du-Nord. We walked and boated among the many islands, swam or clammed according to our wishes and the tide. At night we fell asleep to the sound of lapping water with a calm sea, or against the thundering waves and chattering stones when storm winds howled on the ocean. In Saint-Gildas's high-walled garden, or sitting before a fireplace at night, Carrel and I planned biological experiments and talked about his projected "Institute of Man." We timed our lives with sun and tide rather than by the clocks we wound to keep established custom. Yet even in the midst of disturbing conversation and prompted by conscious and subconscious thought, we felt the gusts of war.

SIX

Gusts of War

On August 7, 1938, with the tide's edge an hour distant, my wife and I walked over the sea bottom to start a trip that was to plunge us deeply into prewar international politics—our third flight to the Soviet Union. Obviously the future of Europe and therefore of the world was closely bound to Soviet attitudes and to Soviet capability and action. Any estimate of the European countries' competing military air strength in the face of impending war would be incomplete without a knowledge of Soviet aircraft and manufacturing facilities.

I had been amazed by the apparent lack of this knowledge in government agencies of both America and Europe. Stories about Soviet aviation I had earlier listened to were fragmentary and as conflicting as the political viewpoints of the tellers. Five years had passed since my last visit to Russia. I wanted to see for myself what developments had taken place during those years—especially in the field of aviation.

I arranged our trip to Russia with the co-operation of the American embassies in London and Moscow. For diplomatic reasons, it seemed best to make sure our application to enter the Soviet Union would be approved; as it was, it took weeks to obtain an official nod from the Kremlin. We left England on the sixteenth, landed at Warsaw for the night, and arrived at Moscow the next evening. While in Moscow we were to stay at the American Embassy as guests of the Ambassador. We were accorded extraordinary courtesy and personal attention by the Russians, but were shown so little of the Soviet aviation industry that I could make no estimate of its production capacity.

Clearly, Stalin's Russia did not wish to expose her Air Force to foreign eyes. The program laid out for me, in addition to the annual air show, included a total of seven aeronautical establishments: one of the Army experimental stations, an aviation academy, an engine factory, an engine experimental laboratory, an aircraft factory, a hydro-aerodynamic research laboratory, and a flying school. It also included two museums, a new subway, a ballet, an operetta, a trip on a canal, an ice-cream factory, a shoe factory, a collective farm, and a Young Pioneers' camp.

Russian greatness surrounded us. It was in the strength of Slavic faces, in the depth and courage of eyes, in the cautious humor. Yet we could not reach the essence. We were insulated from it as though by screens of glass. There was the careful programing of our visit, the tirelessly helpful guides and their propaganda, and the secret police, whom we never saw, but whose power every Russian we talked to feared, hoping his name would not appear on a list. Manipulation as a policy was well portrayed in a local interpreter's error during our visit to Kiev. Pointing to a large structure down the street, she said: "Here is the building of the Young Pioneers. It is here that all the best Soviet children are taken to be demonstrated."

Speaking of our flights over the world and meetings with peoples in many countries, my wife had likened individuals and nations to crystals: a small fragment indicates in some way the structure of the whole. It was from the fragments that I formed my opinion of Soviet air strength. The airplane factory I inspected was large, complete, and well equipped, but most of its machines and all of its best ones had been imported from the United States and Germany. Its average workers impressed me as being neither highly trained nor skillful. The bombers under construction were inferior in design to bombers being built in America, Germany, and England.

The engine factory was not as well laid out or as directly organized as the airplaine factory; and it was in the process of changing over from the manufacture of water-cooled to that of air-cooled engines. The water-cooled engine, of Russian design, was obviously too large and heavy for use in high-performance airplanes. The air-cooled engine was an American type, apparently a duplicate of the Wright Cyclone. Production had almost stopped, but several engines of each type were on the line and in the final assembly room. The building was full of American machine tools of high quality. There were a few German machines, but almost no Russian ones—only some dilapidated-looking lathes. I counted eighteen test stands.

My last day in Moscow included a visit to the War College and a big dinner in the evening given for my wife and me by the Cultural Relations Society for Foreign Nations and the Civil Air Fleet. Almost everyone we had met since we landed was present at the dinner—aviators, polar explorers, artists, politicians—and there was much of interest we could have talked about had Russia been a freer country. As it was, we confined ourselves to such subjects as weather, vodka, qualities of caviar, and the wonderful hospitality we had been accorded wherever we went. No unpleasant incident had arisen to mar our visit. But a newspaper correspondent had phoned the American Embassy a few hours before the dinner and said a story was being printed abroad to the effect that I had fought with a Russian policeman the day we visited the canal outside Moscow.

We said our good-byes at the embassy on Friday morning, August 26. We flew to Tula, Orel, and Kharkov, where we landed to take on fuel, then to Rostov-on-Don, throttling down to allow our official escort plane to arrive ahead of us; it was an old biplane and very slow. The collective farms we passed over were unlike any farms I had seen before—a row of twenty or so houses strung out along a road, with garden patches of an acre or so behind each one and large fields beyond. We were met at the Rostov airport by a group of men and women, including the mayor, the head of the local Intourist Bureau, and the head of the flying school we had come to see. That night the limitless Russian hospitality continued at tables piled high with rich and elaborate food.

The next morning we visited the flying school, in open country beyond the city limits—a "civil" school, according to our interpreter, but to me there seemed to be little difference between it and a military school. We were taken first to an area of the field where second-year girl students were flying. All those not already in airplanes were lined up at attention. They had alert, intelligent faces, quite different from the average we had seen elsewhere in Russia.

From the field we were taken to the school buildings. They had the run-down appearance of most buildings we saw in Russia. We walked around an oblong hole in the floor of an entrance hall, and a board I stepped on sank and seemed to almost snap under my weight. In one of the barracks for girls, it was a little startling to me to see embroidered pillows on sixty lined-up cadet bunks. Most of the girls at that school were trained to be commercial pilots. But there were a number of female pilots in the Soviet Air Force. In Moscow we had met one of them, a fine-looking young woman of about twenty-five. Women fitted into the Air Force just as men did, we were told. They commanded men and were commanded by men without regard to sex and were assigned military missions indiscriminately.

The men's barracks were not as well kept as the women's, and the male cadets seemed not as neat and snappy in appearance. Our interpreter said the boys soloed in about seven hours, the girls in from ten to eleven hours; that the boys were better at instrument flying, the girls better at night flying. No explanation of these differences was offered. We attended the examination of one of the male cadets. It was very stiff and formal, with answers to the questions shouted rather than spoken by the cadet. I felt sorry for the boy's having to take an important examination in front of visitors. But our interpreter said he did well.

We were driven back to Rostov to see the city's new theater. It was built in the form of a huge tractor. It had a seating capacity of two thousand, with a concert hall for one thousand more. The stage was large, with a revolving center. Our guide and interpreter supplied detailed information as we were escorted over each floor of the theater. Afterward, we were taken to see an ice-cream factory. We wondered why an ice-cream factory was included on our schedule, but as a fragment of the "crystal," it again verified the structure of the whole with its contrasting qualities and defects. Flies black-dotted the sticky paper laid about on rails and tables, while others buzzed in the air. The machinery was not working well. But unlike the products of the aviation factories I had inspected, this factory's products were first-class. It made a special sweet cheese, very good, quite unlike anything I had tasted before. The ice cream was better than it usually is in England or in France. The incongruities in Russia are both puzzling and revealing.

The war rumors of Western Europe had not been passed on to us by guides and interpreters in Russia. We had heard nothing about war in conversations at the lunches and dinners we attended. Yet at Rostov several hundred young men and women wearing gas masks marched with a band past our hotel.

The fragments put together let me form some conclusions about the Soviet Union's military aviation. Obviously the government was dependent on foreign sources for its machine tools, and this was a serious limitation to its production capacity. The best airplanes and engines I saw gave an inadequate performance for the conditions of modern war. The research laboratories through which I was conducted as a guest were inadequate. No advanced prototypes were flown at the Moscow air show. Reports I listened to and read indicated that what I had seen typified Soviet aviation.

I concluded that the Russian Air Force probably consisted of several thousand planes which would be effective in a modern war but were no match for the Luftwaffe in either quality or quantity.

My impression of Soviet aviation's mediocrity corresponded with my impression of the entire Soviet attempt at civilizing life, which was marked by millions of lives lost in the Revolution and in the liquidations that followed, by the Siberian prison camps and the secret trials and executions, by the queues in front of stores and the scarceness of goods, by the fear of foreign contacts, by the control of information and the suppression of free speech. The Russians were a great people, and though their living conditions seemingly had improved over five years, the system they lived under was destructive of life and incompatible with ideas of personal freedom so basic to the American mind.

That trip to Russia made me evaluate the position of Germany.

A strong Germany would be fully able to protect Europe's eastern borders against the relatively primitive union of Soviet republics. But a weak Germany would be vulnerable to the expansion of Marxist Communism westward, with the deadening effect and all the ruthless terrors this would bring. But was Germany willing to abandon her own ambitions and serve merely as a buffer for the West?

For our return flight from Russia I had charted a course across Romania, Czechoslovakia, and Germany, with refueling stops at Cluj, Prague, and Stuttgart. After leaving the first stop, a heavy storm covering the Tatra Mountains forced us to detour northward along its edge to Cracow, in Poland, where we took on more fuel. Thereafter we flew through the heavy turbulence of two narrow mountain passes, whose sides climbed steeply into cloud. The tree-merging mist of a third pass turned us back, and we landed unannounced on a Czechoslovakian military airdrome at Olmütz.

In Czechoslovakia rumors of war distorted every conversation. Press reports were printed and forgotten or denied with an irresponsibility that reminded me of our American papers. Every military unit was taut for battle. Inasmuch as German forces had rolled into Austria in March, they might roll into Czechoslovakia at any hour. The border was fortified and every frontier crossing was tank-blocked. Czech soldiers were good and skillful fighters, but they were hopelessly outnumbered.

How long could Czechoslovakian forces resist a German attack, I asked. The answer always had reference to Russia. Without Soviet support, resistance would be a gesture, a hopeless and devastating gesture, costly in life. But how could Soviet support arrive in time? And even if it did arrive, how could it hold back Hitler's modern armies? If unlikely victory could be achieved, how much independence could Czechoslovakia maintain thereafter? Men and women I talked to were as worried about having the Russians as allies as having the Germans as enemies.

I accompanied the American Military Attaché, Major Lowell M. Riley, on visits to several factories where airplanes and engines were being produced. At one of the military fields, the maneuverability of a Czech-Russian bomber was demonstrated for me, and a pilot put on an exceptionally fine stunt-flying demonstration with one of the biplane fighters. All the flying I saw at the field was skillfully accomplished. I kept thinking what a tragedy it would be if those pilots were thrown hopelessly into combat against the superior equipment and greater numbers of the German Luftwaffe.

We finally reached Paris on the afternoon of September 8. I had planned to spend the next morning in conferences with the American Embassy military staff and then fly westward to our islands. But the next day Ambassador Bullitt asked my wife and me to come to his Chantilly home for dinner and the night. There we had a conference with Guy la Chambre concerning French aviation and the French situation in general.

On September 10, we flew back to Brittany and crossed to Illiec from the mainland on a high tide. It was a wet crossing in our small *Medric*. Choppy waves covered us with spray. Alexis and Anne Carrel came over from Saint-Gildas for supper. French reserves in the area had been mobilized and were sleeping in barracks, they said.

Our stay in the islands was not long. On September 19 a telegram from Ambassador Kennedy arrived, asking me urgently to come to London. Anne and I left Illiec the following day—a cloudy morning, with frequent light showers and ceilings of less than one thousand feet. We took off at 2:21 from the field at Morlaix, where we kept our Mohawk, and reached the customs-clearing station at Saint-Inglevert without difficulty in spite of the rain and clouds. There, a broken landing-gear fitting forced us to leave our plane on the airdrome and continue to London by channel boat and train.

On the twenty-first we had lunch with Ambassador and Mrs. Kennedy at 14 Prince's Gate. Before going into the dining room, they introduced us to six of their nine children. It was a typical fall day in London, with misty rain and coal smoke in the air. The situation in Europe was extremely critical, Kennedy told me. Hitler was apparently ready to invade Czechoslovakia and had his Wehrmacht divisions on the border. He had told Prime Minister Chamberlain that in carrying out his plans he would risk a war with England if necessary. Kennedy said that England was ready to fight, even though not prepared. Chamberlain realized the disastrous effect a war with Germany would have under existing circumstances; he was making every effort to avoid one.

We discussed the military strength of European countries, the attitudes of various governments, and the part military aviation was likely to play in event of war. Since I had taken advantage of a unique opportunity, at the behest of the American military and because of my personal role in the development of aviation, to observe military-aviation developments in Europe, Kennedy said, he would like me to give him a written summary of my observations and conclusions. At another conference with Kennedy, later in the afternoon, he said that Chamberlain was to meet Hitler again, that there had already been great criticism of Chamberlain for making concessions in regard to Czechoslovakia and the Sudeten territory. He concluded that if Hitler made more demands, the feeling in London was that England would declare war.*

I now realized it was a terrible situation. The English had as usual been asleep and were in no shape for war. They did not realize what they were confronting. They had always had a fleet between themselves and their enemy, and they could not realize the change the development of aviation had brought. I was afraid that this would lead to the end of England as a great power.

On the afternoon of September 22, at a meeting in the embassy,

---

* The next day Lindbergh summarized his observations in a letter to Ambassador Joseph P. Kennedy which, according to Truman Smith, was referred to as the "Lindbergh report on German aviation." It apparently was never quoted, and "its very existence was doubted by many," wrote Smith later. His search of the State Department files in 1953 revealed a cable from Kennedy to the Secretary of State that contained verbatim the text of this report. The cable said that Lindbergh had "unusually favorable opportunities to observe the air establishments" of the countries discussed and recommended that the cable be brought to the attention of Roosevelt and the War and Navy departments. According to Wayne Cole, in *Charles A. Lindbergh and the Battle Against Intervention,* "whether that Lindbergh report, or summaries of it, reached President Roosevelt is not clear. But the President did make last-minute overtures to urge the continuing of negotiations in Europe." A key paragraph in the letter reads: "It seems to me essential to avoid a general European war in the near future at almost any cost. I believe that a war now might easily result in the loss of European civilization. I am by no means convinced that England and France could win a war against Germany at the present time, but, whether they win or lose, all of the participating countries would probably be prostrated by their efforts."

Kennedy asked me to discuss military aviation with a number of influential Englishmen, both in and out of the government. Among conferences that resulted was one the following day where I spent an hour or two talking to members of the Air Ministry. The German Luftwaffe was, of course, the subject of primary interest. An English officer told me their intelligence on German aviation was bad.

British Intelligence estimated that the Soviet production of military aircraft might have achieved a rate of five thousand planes per year at one time, but there had been a great drop in this rate, they said, without attempting to explain why. They thought the performance of Soviet planes was considerably below that claimed. The Russians had told me that the top speed of their twin-engine bomber was two hundred eighty miles an hour, and that the top speed of their low-wing fighter was three hundred ten miles an hour. British estimates placed the bomber's top speed at between two hundred forty and two hundred fifty miles an hour and the fighter's top speed at between two hundred forty and two hundred sixty miles an hour. The fighter was reported to have poor maneuverability. The British said Soviet machine guns were excellent.

We spent the night of September 26 at Cliveden, as guests of Lord and Lady Astor. War tension could not have been higher. Some people thought Hitler would announce the start of military action in a speech he was scheduled to make that night; they were relieved when he did not. On our drive to London in the morning, we saw trenches being dug for air-raid shelters in most of the parks and other open places we passed. Lines of men, women, and children stood in front of ARP centers, waiting for gas-mask fittings.

That afternoon I was driven into Surrey for a meeting with David Lloyd George, at his home, Bron-y-de Churt. The former Prime Minister greeted me at the entrance to his parlor. I saw an active man with very white, medium-long hair. He poured tea at a typically Welsh table, crammed with cake dishes. He felt war was now unavoidable and he repeated this several times. I tried to convince him that war must be postponed. He said Hitler was a strong man, not in any way bluffing, and that the same was true of Mussolini. He said President Eduard Beneš, whom I had met when flying back from Russia, was responsible for much of Czechoslovakia's trouble, that the national borders had not been drawn correctly in the first place. In fact, he said, even less justification existed for the Hungarian border than for the Sudeten boundaries. He was writing a book about this, he told me. He doubted that the "prestige of democracy" could stand another retreat after Ethiopia, Spain, and Austria.

Lloyd George said he had confidence in Eden and Churchill, but not in Chamberlain. A war with Czechoslovakia might, he thought, end in a quick victory for Germany, and in that event the English and French peoples would not be willing to fight to free Czechoslovakia. He said the Nazi system was just as bad as the Communist system, but he felt an alliance with Russia was essential to England. He did not in any way seem to share my belief that a strong Germany was of vital importance to the security of our Western civilization. What seemed to me the obvious danger of the Soviet Union's primitive and semi-Asiatic masses apparently did not concern him.

On arriving in London the following morning, I found men and women lined up in front of the American Embassy because a shipment of U.S. Army gas masks had arrived. Inside the building, I was handed two masks, and at that moment Ambassador Kennedy passed by. "You may not need them," he told me. "There's some good news coming in." But we had no time to talk; and lower echelons of the embassy did not know what the "good news" consisted of. Afternoon newspaper billboards blazoned that a meeting of Chamberlain, Daladier, Hitler, and Mussolini was to take place in Munich.

Ambassador Bullitt asked me to be in Paris the next morning and invited my wife and me to stay at the embassy. He said he wanted me to attend a conference regarding the establishment of factories in Canada for the purpose of supplying military aircraft to France. His idea was that since France could not build enough warplanes to supply her needs, she should purchase them from America. The Neutrality Act of 1935 made it impossible for a foreign country to rely on buying military aircraft in the United States; deliveries would be blocked by law in case of war. But since the United States was the only country in the world, except Germany, capable of designing and producing top-performance aircraft in large quantity, Bullitt suggested that factories be built in Canada. These factories could be supplied with machines, tools, parts, and possibly even complete subassemblies brought across the border from the United States. They would have unlimited resources and could produce aircraft of American design without hindrance from the Neutrality Act.

Bullitt had invited Air Minister la Chambre and Jean Monnet to the embassy for lunch, and we discussed how the "Canadian Plan" might be financed and organized. A production potential of ten thousand planes per year was at first suggested. Bullitt said it should be fifty thousand. I went to the Ministry of Air for a conference late in the afternoon, and again the following morning. Various government officials and military officers attended, but I was the only American.

French Intelligence had estimated that existing German factories were capable of producing twenty-four thousand planes per year, and that six thousand modern planes plus two thousand to three thousand older models were available to German air forces. Of these, about fifteen hundred fighters and two thousand bombers were "on the line." By comparison, the French situation was pathetic. There were no modern fighters in the French squadrons; and only a few light bombers could be used effectively on missions into Germany. I was informed that France was producing about forty-five military planes per month of all types, including observation aircraft. Officers present estimated that within twelve months the production could be brought up to the rate of five thousand or six thousand per year. This seemed optimistic to me in view of the country's internal conditions.

French Intelligence placed British air strength at approximately two thousand service planes, of which probably seven hundred, including all types, could be considered modern. The British had produced one hundred eighty planes in August. It was estimated that British production might achieve the rate of ten thousand planes per year in twelve months. Combining optimistic figures for France and England, the warplane production rate of the two countries would be fifteen thousand planes per year after twelve months, compared with a known German production capacity of twenty-four thousand warplanes per year—and this was quite apart from considering Italian production capacity. Also it seemed unlikely that German production capacity would remain static while the French and English increased.

I said I did not believe a production rate of ten thousand planes per year, in as-yet-unconstructed Canadian factories, could be achieved within twelve months, and that even this rate would be insufficient. Discussion turned to figures that struck me immediately as unrealistic. French Air Force officers said military plans made it essential for them to obtain at least one thousand bombers from sources outside France by the first of July 1939. Clearly, this objective would not be accomplished through the so-called Canadian Plan. French and British orders were already absorbing most of the excess production capacity of factories in the United States.

I suggested that France purchase bombers from Germany. This astounded everyone at the table. At first they took my suggestion as a joke, and laughed. Then it was discussed with more seriousness than even I expected. The French did not believe Germany would sell modern warplanes to her traditional enemy. I said Hitler might welcome the opportunity to make a gesture to protect his western frontier. But conversation soon returned to the hypothetical Canadian factories.

A French general called for me at the embassy in the afternoon. We drove to Villacoublay, where I was shown the latest types of French military aircraft. Various fighters and bombers were demonstrated for me. I flew the new Moran 406 fighter—a low-wing, full-cantilever monoplane with a top speed of three hundred miles an hour at thirteen thousand feet. Its handling characteristics were excellent, but it was a prototype and not yet in production. The performance of French airplanes was limited by the power of their engines: no engine under production in France had as much power as the Junkers and Daimler-Benz designs that German factories had been rolling out for months. English Rolls-Royce engines were excellent and had sufficient power, but the entire Rolls-Royce production was needed to supply the Royal Air Force and could not be available to the French.

What amazed me was the fact that if hostilities had started the previous week over the Czechoslovakian crisis, France did not have a single modern fighter available for defense! England was slightly better off. The Vickers Spitfire was the best interceptor-fighter in the world, but the RAF did not have many of them at the time. From the standpoint of modern war, the Royal Air Force was inadequately equipped and the French Air Force almost nonexistent.

On October 3 I again had lunch at the embassy with Bullitt, Daladier, la Chambre, and Monnet. Daladier told of his recent meeting with Chamberlain, Hitler, and Mussolini. He spoke also of Göring. Hitler had definite personal magnetism, he said, and Göring was very amusing but had ability.

The main purpose of the lunch was to discuss the Canadian Plan. By that time, as so often happens with such projects, the plan had become less ambitious. The latest draft called for a factory or factories, which were to be located in Canada, capable of producing fifteen hundred planes and four thousand engines per year on one shift. There would be an expansion potential to a rate of five thousand planes, and a corresponding number of engines, on three shifts under wartime conditions. Daladier was interested and seemed to approve of the idea. He asked why it was that France, which had produced Blériot and other famous flyers and designers, had reached such a terrible condition in her aviation that she had to consider buying military airplanes from other countries. In partial answer, la Chambre spoke about the disastrous effect of nationalizing the aviation industry and about the chaotic labor conditions. He emphasized the fact that France had considered it sufficient to build prototypes, without going into high production of any of them.

The conversation then turned to France's immediate needs. How was she to obtain modern military aircraft for service squadrons by the summer of 1939? I again offered the idea of buying planes from Germany. This did not seem to startle Daladier. He was apparently willing to consider it. I suggested that the purchase of aircraft in Germany might help in the solution of other problems. It would lead to trade and possibly to an arms-limitation agreement. I emphasized the fact that continued competition in building warplanes would probably lead to destroying Europe and to economic collapse. I said that if the French government would consider a purchase of military aircraft from Germany to be advantageous, I could fly to Berlin and inquire secretly about the possibility of negotiating a sale.

The Canadian Plan forced me to make a difficult personal decision, because I was asked to go to America to take part in the plan's execution. Aside from the personal problems involved, there were serious questions relating to loyalty to my own country and to the civilization of which it was a part. I loved France second only to America, and I had fallen in love with Europe as a whole. From the time the Canadian Plan was first outlined to me, I had reservations about the effect it would have on both America and Europe. It might have been within the law to ship airplane designs, parts, and subassemblies across the border for use in Canadian factories, but that certainly was not within the spirit of the Neutrality Act. The plan seemed a roundabout way of getting the United States again involved in Europe's wars—against the wishes of Congress and the American people. I was disturbed by this. Also, I did not see how the Canadian Plan could be effective. It was inadequate in the number of aircraft to be produced at what was already a late hour.

Still more, the Canadian Plan exemplified, I thought, the wrong approach to Europe's problems. While it was of great importance for England and France to build up their military strength, especially in the air, there were, I felt, more immediate and pressing problems. A changed attitude toward Germany was required if a disastrous war was to be avoided. Strength is necessary for character and for survival, but strength cannot be bought for gold—except temporarily, and then with the danger of bringing greater demoralization later. Strength is an inherent quality in a people. No amount of foreign aircraft could give France the security she wished.

Obviously the French and British position was hopeless without American support. But could American support, great as it might be, preserve it? Certainly no combination of opposing powers could stop German expansion initially. Aside from the overwhelming military strength Hitler controlled, the German people had a vitality the French and English lacked. Military strength was the product of their vitality, not the cause of it. The Canadian Plan would be only an inoculation of military strength; it would be no more than a "shot in the arm."

It seemed to me best to let European peoples work out for themselves the problems posed by their relative positions, and that American interference was likely to be a destructive factor in the long run—destroying the very qualities it was intended to protect. Suppose we gave France and England unlimited support, even to the extent of fighting with them in a war: Hitler's military forces could conquer all of Europe before American forces could be organized and equipped and become effective. Suppose, after years of fighting, Germany was defeated by use of America's tremendous resources: the loss of life and property would be irreparable, Europe would be prostrate, and the Soviet Union's Communist power would be enhanced—with ominous implications. Our Western civilization would be weakened, possibly fatally, and victory would be equivalent to defeat.

The period when post–World War I Germany could be controlled by military force was past. But I believed that a westward expansion by Hitler might still be prevented through a combination of diplomacy, strategic convenience, and the use of defensive power. Since it was impossible for France and England to attack effectively, it seemed to me they should not fight unless attacked; that it would be wisest for them to build their military forces behind the Maginot Line and the English Channel, and let Hitler collide with Stalin over totalitarian ideas. I was deeply concerned that the potentially gigantic power of America, guided by uninformed and impractical idealism, might crusade into Europe to destroy Hitler without realizing that Hitler's destruction would lay Europe open to the rape, loot, and barbarism of Soviet Russia's forces, causing possibly the fatal wounding of Western civilization.

Analyzing the Canadian Plan, I grew apprehensive of the amorality of science that was symbolized in aviation's power. I had taken for granted that the development of science in general, and in particular the airplane, would automatically benefit mankind. Now I realized that science and aviation were good or evil according to their use, and that their usefulness must be judged. I had spent years of my life, directly and indirectly, developing air power. Taking part in the Canadian Plan would involve me still further in that development. It was now obvious that through shortsighted leadership air power might destroy the civilization that created it.

The more I considered the Canadian Plan the more I felt it was a sidetrack from the burning issues of immediate major policy. I was far from being in accord with the philosophy, policy, and actions of the Nazi government, but it seemed to me essential to France and England, and even to America, that Germany be maintained as a bulwark against the Soviet Union. I believed that the fluxing relationships between Germany and France were critically important to Western civilization, and that I might have some effect on improving these relationships. I still hoped to negotiate the French purchase of German warplanes. Taking an active part in the Canadian Plan would almost surely prevent my doing so. My mind was clarifying the course of action I should take, but I decided to spend two or three days on Illiec before reaching a final conclusion. I told my colleagues that I would return to Paris on Sunday, October 9.

In Paris I had been staying in the same room in the American Embassy and sleeping in the same bed that Ambassador Herrick had given me the night I arrived with my *Spirit of St. Louis* in 1927. Then, my thought and talk had been of aviation bringing peace to men. Now, eleven years later, I had been thinking and talking about airplanes spreading war. On each occasion I had found the city and the embassy highly stimulating, but not conducive to clarity of thought. My mind worked best when I was not immersed in formal environments and paced by modern tempos.

I spent three days on the islands, climbing the bare rocks, following gorse-narrowed paths, edging around pools on the sea bottom. On returning to Paris I recommended men in the American aviation industry whom the French could contact confidentially in regard to implementing the Canadian Plan, wrote letters of introduction, and thereafter discontinued my own connection with it.

On October 10, my wife and I took off in our Mohawk for another visit to Germany. I had charted a course to Berlin, but weather forced us to land at Rotterdam for the night. On arriving at our hotel, I telephoned Truman Smith, who, with a number of

German officers, had earlier awaited us at the Berlin airport. He told me an urgent message had arrived from Moscow in regard to complications resulting from a story printed in London that quoted me speaking about Russia in a most uncomplimentary manner. I immediately telephoned Colonel Raymond E. Lee, our military attaché for air in London, and asked what had happened. It turned out to be a combination of political intrigue and newspaper irresponsibility. Lee said that a weekly publication, "a sort of mimeographed sheet without much standing and with a small circulation," had quoted me as saying that Russian aviation was in chaotic condition, that I had been invited to be chief of the Russian civil air fleet, and that the German air fleet could whip the Russian, French, and English air fleets combined. I was reported to have made these statements to Lloyd George, at Cliveden, and at Transport House.

This combination of fact and fiction was not unusual in a press article—there was a salting of just enough truth to give an illusory taste of reality, and the twist of phraseology to give the effect desired. But it had a serious effect on a circumstance and time that resulted in a chain reaction beginning with my journey to Nazi Germany, Communist Russia's most dangerous enemy. Moscow newspapers reprinted the story, giving it significance as though it had originated in the *Times* of London and denouncing me as a liar for saying I had been "invited to be chief of the Russian civil air fleet." It was a common habit with the press to attribute to a man a statement he had not made and then to attack him for having made it. I had come in contact with this before.

In the morning, telegrams began to arrive from various press organizations asking me to comment on the Moscow articles, which were being reprinted in the United States. Along with them, messages on weather showed the Rotterdam-Berlin route to be flyable—some low clouds and a thick haze in places, but no fog. We landed on Tempelhof airdrome at three o'clock.

That evening I accompanied Ambassador Hugh R. Wilson and Military Attachés Smith and Arthur Vanaman to dinner in a huge room lit by thousands of candles. Several of my American and French friends were there. I sat beside General Erhard Milch, now Inspector-General of the Luftwaffe, with whom I could talk of aviation in detail and with whom I now discussed the grave possibility of war.

I had come to Germany to attend meetings of the Lilienthal Society for Aeronautical Research. I used the opportunity to talk to industrialists, designers, and Luftwaffe officers, to visit factories and to fly the airplanes they produced. Göring sent word that I could visit any aeronautical establishment in the country. I visited the Heinkel factory at Oranienburg, the Junkers factories at Magdeburg and Dessau, the Messerschmitt factory at Augsburg, the Dornier factory and the Zeppelin works at Friedrichshafen, and the Luftwaffe experimental station at Rechlin. I flew various types of planes, from the four-engine Junkers JU-90 to the ME-109 single-engine fighter. At Rechlin I was shown the new ME-110 twin-engine fighter and the JU-88 light bomber, in addition to types of airplanes already in service squadrons. It was probably the first time a foreigner, with the exception of Italians, had seen the JU-88.

If any doubt had remained in my mind about Germany's current leadership in military aviation, that visit in October 1938 removed it. The slowness of France, Britain, and other farther-west countries to face the implications of the Luftwaffe's strength was to me astounding and depressing. Other foreigners in Germany shared my apprehension. At a dinner in his embassy, the British Ambassador, Sir Nevile Henderson, told me he hoped I would do all I could to make the English realize the quality and size of Germany's aviation program. He said they did not believe him when he described it.

Some days before I had left France, a letter arrived from Ambassador Wilson asking if I would attend a dinner at the American Embassy in Berlin in honor of Marshal Göring. He said he would like to take advantage of my visit to give such a dinner, for the purpose of creating a better relationship between the American Embassy and the German government. Of course I accepted. It was a "stag dinner," on the night of October 18. In addition to Göring, guests included the Italian Ambassador, the Belgian Ambassador, World War I aces Milch and Ernst Udet, Minister Adolf Baeumker, Dr. Ernst Heinkel, Dr. Willy Messerschmitt, and various other German officers. There were present also American officers and members of our embassy. There were two tables. Wilson sat at the head of one. I sat at the head of the other.

Göring was the last to arrive. I was standing at the back of the room when he came through the door, wearing a blue Luftwaffe uniform of new design. He seemed less stout than when I last saw him. Heads turned and conversation dropped as Ambassador Wilson advanced to meet his guest of honor. I noticed that Göring carried a red box and some papers in one hand. When he came to me he handed me the box and papers and spoke several sentences in German. I knew no German but I soon learned that he had presented me with the Order of the German Eagle, one of the highest decorations of the government—"by order of der Führer," he said.*

After dinner we broke up into small groups. Göring came over and suggested that we go into the next room and talk. Wilson accompanied us. We sat down in a corner, Göring in a big, cushion-stuffed armchair. His first question was about my trip to Russia. Wilson interpreted the question and my answer, and then tactfully withdrew by turning the interpretation over to a member of the embassy staff who was, he said, more fluent in German. Obviously it was not wise for the American Ambassador to take part in a discussion between Göring and me about Russia and Russian aviation.

Göring asked why I had gone to Russia, what Russian hotels were like, whether many people stayed in them, how Russian cities compared to other cities, how my wife and I were treated—seemingly endless questions. He then turned the conversation to Germany and aviation. He spoke of the performances of military planes and the numbers being produced, of retraining workers, of apprentice schools, of the ability of a man to attack any problem, regardless of his previous experience. He said there was too much

---

* The Service Cross of the German Eagle, a high civilian medal, was awarded to Lindbergh for his accomplishments in aviation, in particular the 1927 flight. He had been similarly honored by most nations of the world, but not by Germany. Both Ambassador Wilson and Truman Smith, writing in later years, agreed that Lindbergh could not have returned the decoration without personally affronting his host, the American Ambassador, and his guest of honor. The medal, which was never worn, was added to the vast collection of Lindbergh's awards and presents in the St. Louis Historical Society.

tendency to think you had to be a specialist before you could understand a problem, while in fact a specialist is often the worst man to put in charge. He referred to his own experience in solving German financial problems, and said that at one time he knew so little about finance that he could not even keep his own pocketbook filled. He said he told Hitler that he would be willing to take on any problem in Germany except religious ones.

Göring told me the new JU-88 bomber was ahead of anything else built, and that it could fly three hundred ten miles an hour —which was not a "magazine figure," but an actual top speed. He said the Germans expected to have a plane soon that could fly five hundred miles an hour. Throughout the discussion, Göring seemed highly confident of German power. I felt that he wanted to impress me with that power, and, through me, the United States. In Germany, as in France and England, the growing influence of America was apparent. Every leader in Europe realized that the destiny of his nation and government was to an important degree related to the attitude of that country deep into the heart of which my grandfather had fled by oxcart from an Indian raid.

On returning to France, I again discussed with la Chambre the notion of a French purchase of warplanes from Germany. He said he still thought it might be possible, and that his main objective was to build up an air force of two or three thousand fighting planes at the earliest possible date. Additional conferences followed. On December 16 I boarded a train for my return trip to Berlin. My mission was to find out whether or not the German government would sell her most modern and powerful warplane engines to her western neighbor. If so, Daladier and la Chambre said they were ready to buy.

France was in even more desperate need of engines than of planes, and it was felt that German engines under French cowlings would not be as conspicuous as German-built warplanes carrying the French emblem on their wings and landing on French airdromes. The purchase of engines would be less likely to stir up public anger and political opposition. This was quite openly stated by officials with whom I talked. They preferred to enter a negotiation for engines alone. The question of purchasing bombers and fighters could come later.

Once again, it seemed to me that any negotiations between France and Germany would be advantageous, and in themselves could possibly prevent a disastrous war. I laid down two conditions for my mission: first, that the French assure me they were sincere in their wish to purchase and that my inquiry would not be used simply to sound out the German attitude; second, that I bear my own expenses and receive no compensation regardless of the mission's outcome. These conditions were agreed to. It was decided that I suggest to the German government an initial purchase by France of four hundred engines. They were to be of the latest type and highest power. These final arrangements had been made between me and members of the French government. The American Ambassador had withdrawn, saying he preferred to have no further *official* knowledge of the project.

Meanwhile, the idea of building factories in Canada had faded as rapidly as it had arisen. All I learned was that a French negotiator had gone to America, and that during his trip he talked to President Roosevelt. When he arrived back in France, he told me that "as so often happens, the reason you go somewhere develops into something else before you return." Additional orders for warplanes would probably be placed with factories in the United States, he said, and a Canadian company might be set up on paper so transactions could be carried on through that dominion of the British Empire rather than directly between the United States and France. "There would be less difficulty with public opinion," he said.

Obviously, the United States was becoming more and more involved in European politics, and both American and French politicians wanted to keep the people of their countries in some ignorance concerning the transactions under way. On one side of the Atlantic, the Roosevelt administration was attempting to evade the spirit, if not the letter, of the Neutrality Act. On the other side, Daladier's government was taking the first step in an attempt to equip the French Air Force with German products. In each instance, there was danger of arousing serious criticism and opposition.

The afternoon of December 20, I met Milch and Udet, who was now chief of the Technical Bureau of the German Air Force, at the Air Ministry. The following extracts are from my journal: "Udet,

Milch, and I had a conference for about half an hour. I outlined again the possibility of selling German engines to France. Milch said it would have to be taken up with Göring and possibly with Hitler. He asked me if I thought the French were simply trying to sound out the German attitude without any interest of really purchasing. I told him I did not think so. Milch said he would try to contact Göring immediately (I had told him that I wanted to return to Paris as soon as possible) and would phone me as soon as he had done so.

"We continued talking for a time. Milch was obviously interested in the proposition. I told him I did not wish to take part in anything which would not be constructive from both the German and French standpoints, but that I felt an understanding between the two countries to be very desirable and that a war in Western Europe would be disastrous. He said he did not think there would be a war in *Western* Europe. This tended to confirm my feeling that the Germans intend to entrench themselves in the West and continue to expand their influence in the East. . . .

"Taxi back to apartment, but soon after I arrived Udet called up and asked if I could be back at the Air Ministry by 6:00. (We had agreed not to carry on any conversations over the phone and that everything would be done in the utmost confidence, so that there would be no embarrassment for anyone if a deal was not concluded.) I returned to Milch's office immediately. Milch said he called Goering, but that Goering had gone to see Hitler (apparently Hitler had called him unexpectedly) and that Goering could not be reached for a day or two and had left instructions with his secretary to avoid all new questions until after Christmas.

"Milch said he thought it would be advisable to make no attempt to press the matter until Christmas had passed and that he had phoned me (through Udet) immediately so I could return to Paris tomorrow if I wished to do so. He suggested that after Christmas he would send me an invitation for dinner or something in Berlin, with Udet and himself, and that by then he would have been able to talk to Goering and, if necessary, get a decision from Hitler."

Weather the next day was unflyable. I decided to leave my Mohawk at Berlin and to go to Paris by train. That would give me a good reason for returning to Berlin after Christmas, and so keep the press from becoming overcurious. My ground travel was slow, through a blizzard—it was a screeching, stopping, jolting night. The train arrived at Paris five and a half hours late.

French relationships with Germany and Italy had deteriorated so rapidly that I almost gave up hope of reaching any agreement on the engine-purchase project. But in mid-January I received a message that took me back to Berlin, and on January 16 I met again with Milch and Udet at the Air Ministry. Whether or not the question of engine sales to France had reached the ears of Hitler I never knew. But the answer was affirmative. I made an entry in my journal: "Milch replied that . . . Germany would be willing to sell engines to France. He said they could supply Daimler-Benz 1250-h.p. motors and that the number and price could be settled in subsequent negotiations. He said their conditions were that secrecy be maintained by both the French and German governments while negotiations were taking place. He said Germany would want pay in *Devisen* (i.e., money instead of goods). Said Germany was in a position where she had to ask for money in payment for manufactured articles such as engines, whereas she could afford to trade with raw materials such as coal, accepting something in exchange which she needed herself.

"Milch suggested that all communications in regard to the transaction should discuss the purchase of one Storch airplane and make no mention of engines. He said he would know that such communications actually referred to the purchase of engines. Milch mentioned the fact that the engine-sales question in this instance raised an important political issue."

I flew back to Paris on January 18, and the next day met with la Chambre and told him of the Germans' willingness to sell engines and the conditions they laid down. He was greatly interested; he had hardly dared to hope that the answer would be favorable. He said he felt sure Daladier would wish to carry on the negotiations. We discussed the matter of who would be the best man to send to Germany for this purpose. La Chambre suggested the French Military Attaché in Berlin, who was well liked by the Germans and spoke German fluently. He felt sure that a mission sent directly from his office would be difficult to keep secret. He also felt, as I did, that this negotiation might be used as a step toward more important things if it was intelligently handled.

La Chambre told me that the present American bomber was too slow for French needs, but a new, faster type would be out in July and France, with Roosevelt's agreement, would be given the opportunity of buying the first of these. Therefore the Canadian Plan would be unnecessary.

Later that day, la Chambre reported that Daladier was pleased and wished to go ahead with the transaction. The French Military Attaché in Berlin had been asked to come to Paris immediately.

On the morning of January 20, I met la Chambre at his home and gave him an outline of the letter to be sent to Milch. Thereafter I withdrew completely from the project. All this went on across the Maginot and Siegfried lines, and all of it turned out to be as futile as those lines of forts themselves. "What happened to the engine negotiations?" I inquired some weeks later. "Oh, everything went well until it reached the Foreign Office," was the reply, "and there it ended." By that time, in the late winter of 1938–39, relations between France and Germany had deteriorated to a point where further attempts to negotiate trade seemed hopeless.

Tensions, especially in eastern Europe, had increased to a point where the outbreak of war seemed probable. My greatest hope lay in the possibility that a war would be confined to fighting between Hitler and Stalin. It seemed probable that Germany would be victorious in such a conflict; and by that time France and England would be stronger. Under any circumstances, I believed that a victory by Germany's European peoples would be preferable to one by Russia's semi-Asiatic Soviet Union. Hitler would not live forever, and I felt sure the Germans would eventually moderate the excesses of his Nazi regime. To me it was no longer a choice between dictatorship and democracy, but, rather, between two dictators. Nothing the Nazis had done in Germany up to that time* equaled in ruthlessness and terror the record of the Communists in Russia— the assassinations, the liquidations, the prison camps and execu-

---

* The enormous extent and organized capacity to kill huge numbers of people in extermination camps were not generally known to Americans until after Pearl Harbor.

tions. "A hundred executions a day in one camp." "Forty million people killed since the Revolution began." Such were the stories told by refugees from the Soviet Union. If you cut the figures to a quarter, they were terrible enough.

In the spring of 1939, I decided to return to America, risking, possibly, gangsterism, and despite publicity and the problems involved in bringing my family home. Since the engine negotiations between France and Germany had failed, I saw no further contribution I could make to improve the relationships between European countries. If there was to be war, then my place was back in my own country. I felt I could exercise a constructive influence in America by warning people of the danger of the Soviet Union and by explaining that the destruction of Hitler, even if it could be accomplished through using American resources, would probably result in enhancing the still-greater menace of Stalin. I would argue for an American policy of strength and neutrality, one that would encourage European nations to take the responsibility for their own relationships and destinies. If they prostrated themselves once again in internecine war, then at least one strong Western nation would remain to protect Western civilization.

I was greatly concerned about the strength of America. Although I feared the combination of military strength with our idealism—it was an uneasy mixture—I believed that military strength was essential to our security. I was convinced that aviation would play a major role in future wars, and I knew we had lost our leadership in military aircraft. Germany's research and production facilities were much more extensive than ours. In addition to a huge superiority of numbers, her service fighters performed better than any our squadrons flew. Junkers and Focke-Wulf designs were challenging our position in transport and heavy-bombing fields. Back in the United States I could do something about this situation. I could help stimulate American aviation activities.

I boarded the S.S. *Aquitania* at Cherbourg on Saturday, April 8, 1939. On April 13, the day before its arrival in New York Harbor, a radio message from General Arnold was brought to my cabin. It asked me to telephone him as soon as I landed.

My disembarkation at New York involved another unpleasant experience with American newspapers. Reporters and photographers began hammering on the door to my cabin soon after the ship had docked. One photographer broke through the door to an adjoining cabin, flashed his bulb as I looked to see what had made the noise, and ran away. I was informed that close to a hundred pressmen were on the ship and dock waiting for me. I quote from my journal: "Two New York police officers came to the cabin and asked if they could be of any assistance, and suggested that they form a cordon around me as I went out of the stateroom. I replied that I would prefer to go out alone if possible. They advised against it and told me that one of the last fellows who tried that got one of his ribs broken. I told them that I would try it anyway. They said all right, shook hands, and went out.

"Both sides of the corridor and stairs were lined with cameramen and flashing, blinding lights. They started shoving and blocking the way in front of us. The police immediately formed a wedge and pushed them out of the way. There were dozens of uniformed police in addition to many plain-clothes men. All the way along the deck the photographers ran in front of us and behind us, jamming the way, being pushed aside by the police, yelling, falling over each other on the deck. There must have been over a hundred of them, and the planks were covered with the broken glass of the flashlight bulbs they threw away."

I met General Arnold at West Point on April 15. We discussed developments in European military aviation and steps that should be taken to regain American leadership and increase the Army Air Corps' strength. I spent most of the next week in Washington. I agreed to a request by Arnold that I go on active duty and make a study of American aeronautical research establishments. I discussed research programs, attended Army and Navy Intelligence meetings, and spent half an hour with Secretary of War Harry H. Woodring and fifteen minutes with President Roosevelt at the White House. It was the first time I had met and talked to the President. I left his presence with mixed feelings. As I wrote in my journal:

"I went in to see the President about 12:45. . . . He was seated at his desk at one end of a large room. There were several models of ships around the walls. He leaned forward from his chair to meet me as I entered, and it is only now that I stop to think that he is crippled. I did not notice it and had no thought of it during our meeting. He immediately asked me how Anne was and mentioned the fact that she knew his daughter in school. He is an accomplished, suave, interesting conversationalist. I liked him and feel that I could get along with him well. Acquaintanceship would be pleasant and interesting.

"But there was something about him I did not trust, something a little too suave, too pleasant, too easy. Still, he is our President, and there is no reason for any antagonism between us in the work I am now doing. The air-mail situation is past—one of the worst political maneuvers I know of, and unfair in the extreme, to say the least. But nothing constructive will be gained by bringing it up again at this time.

"Roosevelt gave me the impression of being a very tired man, but with enough energy left to carry on for a long time. I doubt that he realizes how tired he is. His face has that gray look of an over-worked businessman. And his voice has that even, routine tone that one seems to get when mind is dulled by too much and too frequent conversation. It has that dull quality that comes to any one of the senses when it is overused: taste, with too much of the same food day after day; hearing, when the music never changes; touch, when one's hand is never lifted.

"Roosevelt judges his man quickly and plays him cleverly. He is mostly politician, and I think we would never get along on many fundamentals. But there are things about him I like, and why worry about the others unless and until they necessitate consideration? It is better to work together as long as we can; yet somehow I have a feeling that it may not be for long."

That afternoon I attended a meeting of the National Advisory Committee for Aeronautics. "I brought up the question of research facilities. I asked how we expected to catch up with military developments abroad (in aviation research) with our present facilities. I pointed out that we had fallen behind while the foreign facilities were even less than they are today, that even with the full appropriation for the new Sunnyvale experimental station, we would be far behind a country like Germany in research facilities, and that we really needed the full Sunnyvale appropriation and much more besides. I made the point that while we could not expect to keep up with the production of European airplanes as long as we were on a peacetime basis, we should at least keep up in the quality of our aircraft."

A Curtiss P-36 single-seater monoplane fighter was assigned to me for the countrywide survey of aeronautical establishments I was about to make. It was the most modern of our Air Corps fighters—better finished and equipped than European planes of the type, yet not as fast as the Spitfires and Messerschmitts. During the summer of 1939 I inspected laboratories, educational facilities, factories, and airfields from Virginia to the state of Washington, and from New York to California. Obviously, the American potential was tremendous, but existing factories and research facilities were inadequate in comparison with those existing in Germany.

At General Arnold's request I sat as a member of a newly established board which was to revise the Air Corps' research-and-development program and establish advanced specifications for military aircraft. General Walter Kilner was appointed chairman; Lieutenant Colonels Carl Spaatz and Earl Naiden and Major **Alfred Lyon** were the other members. I took the chairmanship of a committee to examine existing aeronautical research facilities, to study methods of co-ordinating them, and to prepare a plan for their future extension. Arnold, Admiral John Towers, chief of the Bureau of Aeronautics, and Robert Hinckley, head of the Civil Aeronautics Administration, were the other members of the committee. I talked to Senators, Congressmen, diplomats, executives, scientists, and engineers about steps necessary for the development of American aviation and, inevitably, about the danger of war in Europe and the attitude America should take.

One crisis after another arose in Europe. On August 29 press reports stated that Russian troops were massing on the Polish border. On September 1 German forces entered Poland. World War II had begun.

Knowing the United States would be put under high pressure to enter the war, I laid plans to take an active part in opposing this step. I began writing an address, to be my first political speech on national radio. It was called "America and European Wars." In it I opposed American intervention. I decided to discontinue my tour of active duty as an Air Corps officer in order to avoid any embarrassment to the Air Corps through the political action I was about to take, and at the same time concentrate on an antiwar campaign more effectively.

On September 14 I wrote a report for our special committee, recommending that a new NACA research establishment be located at Moffett Field, Sunnyvale, south of the southern reaches of San Francisco Bay. On the morning of September 15, this recommendation was approved at a formal meeting of the NACA, and our special committee report recommending a still-greater extension of research facilities was accepted. At 9:45 that evening I gave my radio address over the Mutual, Columbia, and NBC networks.

An interesting incident relating to the address had occurred earlier in the day. Colonel Truman Smith had phoned, saying he had an important message to deliver. We met at my Washington apartment in midafternoon. I quote from my journal: "Truman and I went into the bedroom, where we could talk alone. He told me he had a message which he must deliver, although he knew in advance what my answer would be. He said the Administration was very much worried by my intention of speaking over the radio and opposing actively this country's entry into a European war. Smith said that if I would not do this, a secretaryship of air would be created in the Cabinet and given to me! Truman laughed and said, 'So you see, they're worried.'

"This offer on Roosevelt's part does not surprise me after what I have learned about his Administration. It does surprise me, though, that he still thinks I might be influenced by such an offer. It is a great mistake for him to let the Army know he deals in such a way. Apparently the offer came through Woodring to General Arnold, and through General Arnold to Truman Smith. Smith told me that Arnold, like himself, felt they must pass the message on since it came from the Secretary of War's office. Smith said he asked Arnold if he (Arnold) thought for a minute that I would accept. Arnold replied, 'Of course not.' "

Thousands of letters and telegrams arrived after my radio address, overwhelmingly in support of my talk and of nonintervention by America in the war. But I knew prowar forces were powerful, with President Roosevelt the strongest and most subtle of their leaders. I had concluded that he was lacking in a stateman's wisdom, but I did not doubt that he was one of the cleverest politicians ever born. Regardless of the fact that he had publicly advocated a policy of neutrality for the United States, it seemed to me apparent that he intended to lead our country into the war. The powers he influenced and controlled were great. Opposing them would require planning, political skill, and organization. For me, this meant entering a new framework of life.

On September 18 I finished the final draft of my article "Aviation, Geography, and Race" and mailed it to DeWitt Wallace, owner and editor of the *Reader's Digest;* it was published in the November 1939 issue. On September 20 I received a phone call from former President Herbert Hoover's office. I was asked to meet Hoover at the Waldorf-Astoria at eleven o'clock the next morning. I quote from my journal entry of September 21. "We talked for about forty minutes about the war and the policy of the United States. He is definitely opposed to the United States entering this war, but feels the question of repeal of the arms embargo is not of fundamental importance in keeping the country from war. He feels that Roosevelt definitely desires to get us into this conflict. Hoover feels, as I do, that the British Empire has been on the decline for some time—he says since the last war. He said it was inevitable that Germany would expand either peacefully, or by fighting if necessary. He said he told Halifax some time ago that the only way to avoid a European war was to permit a German economic expansion in Eastern Europe. Hoover suggested that after the embargo controversy was over, an organization should be gotten together to keep this country out of the war—nonpolitical, of course. He suggested that I take part in it."

I boarded a train for Washington that night to discuss my antiwar campaign with Democratic leaders; first, with Senator Harry Byrd, of Virginia. Byrd and I agreed almost a hundred percent on the necessity of keeping the United States out of war, and also on the best way to handle the embargo situation. A few days later I saw Byrd again. He brought the latest draft of the neutrality bill, and we discussed what authority Roosevelt could be trusted with. (We agreed it should be as little as possible.) What restrictions on shipping and credit would be advisable? I mentioned the danger to neutral shipping of an air blockade of England, because of the difficulty a plane flying in poor weather or at high altitude might have in recognizing the nationality of a ship.

Byrd and I had lunch with Senators Josiah Bailey (North Carolina), Edward Burke (Nebraska), Walter George (Georgia), Hiram Johnson (California), and Peter Gerry (Rhode Island)—all Democrats. Most of the discussion concerned the pending neutrality legislation. At that time I believed all but one of them favored our keeping out of the war regardless of who won. Burke felt that we should go to war at any cost rather than let England and France lose.

Various prowar and antiwar groups became active in ensuing months. My own role as I spoke, wrote, and took action was as an independent citizen, co-operating with antiwar groups, meeting with Congressmen and Senators, testifying before committees, writing articles, making addresses. Every poll taken showed a large majority of the American populace to be against participation in the war. Yet it was obvious that the United States was moving constantly closer to belligerency. Very cleverly, prowar organizations took advantage of the fact that Americans, although unwilling to enter an internecine war in Europe, preferred an English-French victory. A policy called "steps short of war" was therefore advocated by prowar forces—a policy that, if followed, would inevitably bring the United States into the conflict. It was a policy difficult to oppose because each step was cushioned by hypocrisy until no single one of them seemed to be of critical importance.

In speeches I gave before audiences during the spring of 1941, I repeatedly emphasized two issues relating to democracy: first, I believed that the American people had not been given a choice of voting on military intervention; second, I believed that we could not force democracy on other peoples, friends or foes. In a speech at Madison Square Garden on May 23, I said: ". . . Our country is not divided today because we fear war, or sacrifice, or because we fear anything at all. We are divided because we are asked to fight over issues that are Europe's and not ours—issues that Europe created by her own short-sightedness. We are divided because many of us do not wish to fight again for England's balance of power, or for her domination of India, Mesopotamia, or Egypt, or for the Polish Corridor, or for another treaty like Versailles. We are divided because we do not want to cross an ocean to fight on foreign continents, for foreign causes, against an entire world combined against us. Many of us do not think we can impose our way of life, at the point of a machine gun, on the peoples of Germany, Russia, Italy, France, and Japan. Many of us do not believe democracy can be spread in such a manner. We believe that we are more likely to lose it at home than to spread it abroad by prolonging this war and sending millions of our soldiers to their deaths in Europe and Asia.

"Democracy is not a quality that can be imposed by war. The attempt to do so has always met with failure. Democracy can spring only from within a nation itself, only from the hearts and minds of the people. It can be spread abroad by example, but never by force. The strength of a democracy lies in the satisfaction of its own people. Its influence lies in making others *wish* to copy it. If we cannot make other nations *wish* to copy our American system of government, we cannot force them to copy it by going to war. . . ."

SEVEN

The Reefs of Biak

We come into consciousness on a sphere called "Earth," a cooling planet bound by invisible force to a tremendous ball of fire. Spinning through endless time in limitless space, we are born the sons and daughters of man amid myriad forms of life. After inheriting the qualities of our ancestors and the conditions they created for us, we achieve various degrees of skill, knowledge, and wisdom, yet we sense intuitively beyond our understanding. In a framework of nature which is prolific, competitive, and selective, we sometimes accumulate and sometimes lose certain rights, powers, and possessions. Our future depends to an extent upon ourselves, upon our ability and our ideas.

There are occasions when incidents combine to outline basic laws of life and nature with extraordinary clearness—incidents of birth and death, of peace and war, of beauty and hardship. I think of a day I spent in 1944 with other combat pilots on South Pacific reefs. We were pushing westward over equatorial islands, surrounded by enemy positions as we advanced. When we camped beside newly captured airstrips, our Air Force squadrons often lacked fresh food. Dehydrated vegetables, powdered eggs, and K rations grew flatter to the tongue each week, but most of our camps were close to ocean reefs and every reef had schools of fish that made excellent eating for hungry airmen.

In July 1944, the three squadrons of the 475th Fighter Group,

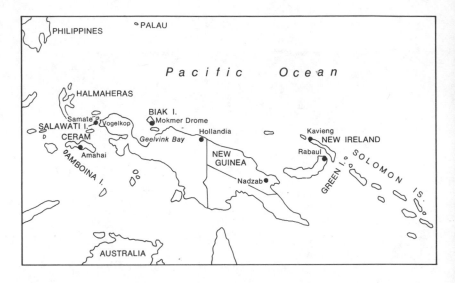

An area where Lindbergh flew in World War II

Clover, Hades, and Possum, were stationed at the edge of Mokmer Drome on a beachhead of Biak Island off the north New Guinea coast. I was flying with these squadrons temporarily as I studied their requirements for fighting aircraft and helped to develop procedures for long-range cruise. Our tents were within walking distance of the coast, where a coral shelf ran out level for a hundred yards or so before dropping into black fathoms of the Pacific. At certain places, short of the steep drop, were ledges and reefs at ideal diving depth.

Sometimes on a day off—or after an early combat mission—we would organize a fishing expedition to the reefs. On July 25, when a strike was canceled because of weather, Colonel Charles H. Mac-Donald, commander of the 475th Fighter Group, and his deputy, Major Meryl M. Smith, and I decided to forage the Biak reefs for food. Our face masks, knives, a rubber boat, and sacks containing fuses, caps, matches, and a few pounds of TNT made up all the equipment we required. The sharp coral forced us to walk in heavy-soled shoes, but clothing was optional; if you did not tend to sunburn, you did not need any.

When you swim with a face mask through crystalline waters of a tropical reef, you slip off a coral ledge and pass through the frontiers of death: you could hardly be reincarnated to a more extraordinary existence. When you leave the familiar, you take on new powers and feel new rhythms. Heat and sweat, gravity and balance disappear; lungs stop pulsing; the earth no longer presses your feet. Time enters into relationships to space while you dive, roll with weightless buoyancy, and turn through four dimensions. The world that once possessed you is curtained off, just as this marine world had before been covered by a texture of waves. You lose consciousness of land-borne existence. You sway back and forth like fronds with the sea's heave.

Having become a marine creature, you feel foam against your skin, not spray, as breakers dash against the nearby reef. You move through gardens of sea plant and forests of fern coral flowering in purples, reds, and yellows. Dozens of beak-mouthed parrot fish glide between their branches as zebras, angels, and rainbows hover nearby peacefully. In the pockets and loops of coral infinite numbers of gaudy smaller fry take shelter. You drift over starfish and cucumber, past black porcupines with fragile lances waving, over sponges, mouths open for microscopic food. Life is everywhere.

Before many minutes pass, instinct draws your mind in apprehension to slender, shadowy forms well out beyond the reef. Shark! Now merging with the depths below them, now reappearing to your view, they show a doubting interest in your entrance to their sea. You hug the reef more closely, keep a sharper watch, realizing that your present incarnation makes of you a prey for fish! Swimming that day off Biak Island, I resented the intrusion of the shark. I was tired of conflict, of bombs and machine guns, of the booming artillery a few miles inland from our camp. I had found an hour of peace. Why should it be shattered by a lurking fish? Soon, I was alert to danger and began seeing death and terror throughout the beauty of the sea—the angel swallowing the minnow, the starfish opening the clam, the crab's armored claws breaking through the porcupine's protection. Life is lived by devouring other life at one moment and, at the next, escaping from being devoured. The individual's existence depends on varying combinations of alertness, judgment, and luck.

In the sea, as on the land and in the air, one escaped from conflict only by closing shutters of the mind to the presence of physical extinction. Why must this be so? Answers lay about the reef: life is hungry and life is prolific. Where there is hunger and prolificacy, competition must exist. Every individual on earth, bacterium and man, takes part in it: the foliage of the jungle—each stem and leaf competing for sunlight, with thousands dying while one lives; the wild pigs that tripped our booby traps at strange hours of the night; the line of black-limbed natives with their knives and pointed spears; my fishing partners, bent on taking back fresh food.

We were part of it by intention. Our artillery's guns, inland, were directed at Japanese positions, while at night we ourselves were bombed by enemy aircraft. We were surrounded by enemies. The Biak beachhead was the most advanced position of our Air Force. A hundred thousand Japanese troops were in positions behind us. Millions more were ahead. They and we were competing to survive.

Lying on a rubber raft to cushion my body from the shock, I tossed a fuse-sizzling charge of TNT into the center of a coral-edged pool. There was a deafening crack; a fountain of water rose. I slipped into the ocean to measure our success. Stunned fish were all around me and settled slowly toward those bodies already on the bottom. We began diving for our victims. Dozens lay about, enough fish to feed the whole squadron for a day. Those fish had no chance against our modern weapons and techniques.

Less than a week before, I had watched men bombed from aircraft in the way we bombed those fish from a rubber boat. I was visiting Bomber Command Headquarters on Owi Island. About three miles away, across the water, among sharp coral ridges and interlocking caves that lay close to Biak's shore, a few hundred Japanese were stubbornly holding out against our infantry's attack. They were in an area about a thousand yards long and three hundred yards wide. Strips of jungle growth had been torn away on the ridges by intense artillery fire, exposing areas of brown coral accentuated by surrounding green. At times shells were bursting while I looked.

For weeks American cannon had been firing day and night at

irregular intervals in the hope of catching the Japanese outside their caves after a quiet period. The enemy had suffered a terrific loss of life, but their machine-gun fire still met our soldiers whenever we attempted to advance over the rugged and difficult terrain. Nearly a hundred casualties had already been inflicted.

The Air Force was ordered to bomb that area. Bombs would drop into crevices that projectiles could not reach, and the effect of concussion would be greater. The strike was scheduled for 0900. It was to be executed by eight Liberators. Since the Japanese forces had no antiaircraft guns, bombing runs would be made from the low altitude of six thousand feet. Bomber Command Headquarters had been placed on a coral cliff facing Biak Island. Standing there, well out of range of enemy guns, was like watching a magnificent and terrible drama. We stood in groups on the cliff's edge. The "heavies" flew in close formation—slowly, it seemed from our distance. They flew through a sky blue and clear above a land green and still. There was not a sound of gunfire, only the droning of the bombers' engines. Americans were silent, waiting for the show. Japanese were silent, resting from long siege and unaware of the impending strike—like the fish when I had looked at them a few seconds before our TNT exploded.

The bombs dropped gracefully, fluttering the sky like distant birds, gliding forward, curving downward. As they penetrated the quilt of the jungle, great concussion waves flashed from ridge to ridge. Black smoke, pierced by splintered wood and coral, burst through tufts of green. First, two, then three and three, the bombers passed. Later, our infantry went in "without firing a shot," it was said. An officer told me he saw about forty dead in one cave and "parts of quite a few more" scattered there. The few survivors sat or lay dazed, making no move as they saw our soldiers enter. At first it was rumored that one prisoner was taken; but later an infantry colonel denied it. "Our boys just don't take prisoners," he said. Survivors were found dead and dying, the official report stated— just as we found our blasted fish.

Soon after landing at the Mokmer airstrip on Biak, Major Claude Stubbs and several other officers and I drove a jeep over to the west caves. The rough military road passed a number of Japanese supply dumps, stinking with the smell of souring rice and unburied bodies. To reach the caves we had to climb two steep hills, which had been heavily bombed and shelled. Stumbling over fallen trees and the rough coral ground, we passed bits of Japanese equipment—a shoe, a canteen, a rice cup, a steel helmet. Alongside were American K-ration boxes, American shells, and rain-soaked American magazines. Ten or twelve dead Japanese soldiers lay sprawled in gruesome positions. Since the battle had taken place several weeks earlier, the heat and ants of the tropics had done their work. Little flesh was left to cover the skeletons. One of the officers said, "I see that the infantry has been up to their favorite occupation"—knocking out all the teeth that contained gold fillings, for souvenirs.

In the hollow beyond the second hill we came to a great pit in the coral, probably fifty feet wide, one hundred feet long, and thirty feet deep. A ladder of poles lashed together led to the bottom. We climbed down and picked our way past more bodies. Postcards with inked Oriental characters, slipping from a dead soldier's pocket, made me think of home. A series of caves burrowing deeply into coral led off the far wall of the pit. Sooty marks around their entrances showed where American flame throwers had struck; seared flesh testified to the efficiency of our military science.

Inside the Biak caves I saw how human life adapts itself to strange environments. Down the mud-slippery rungs of a ladder, I descended another twenty feet into the dark wet interior. I swept my flashlight back and forth over a huge stalactite-ornamented room, from which there were numerous dark-mouthed side passages. Drops of fresh water from the ceiling splashed into stagnant water on the floor, a filthy mire. Yet the Japanese had built small huts inside the cave as shelters from its climate—frameworks of poles, raised floors of plank, roofs of big jungle leaves—much as primitive natives would have built them on swampland in a rainy country.

Most of the huts had been tumbled down and partly burned by our grenades and flame throwers. The cave was strewn with uniformed bodies wherever my light beam fell, some half submerged in water, some sprawled on wooden floors. Near the bodies were cases of food and ammunition and articles of clothing, all hurriedly assembled for a final stand and all soaked by water dripping from stalactites on the dome. In one cave one of the huts had been converted to a hospital. It held a man in uniform lying on a stretcher, still partly covered by his blanket, as though waiting for attention that could no longer have effect.

Two days later, Major Thomas McGuire and I drove to one of the cliff caves. We climbed the steep shell-pocked approach to the mouth and stepped over a ledge to find ourselves confronted by a small mortar and several abandoned machine guns. Abandoned? No. Behind them was the erect but headless body of a Japanese soldier in uniform, roped tightly to a post set in the ground, facing us, opposed to his enemy even beyond the point of death.

Exploring that cave was like swimming into crevices of coral. You never knew what lay around a corner—moray, shark, or a living or dead soldier. The main portion of the cave, behind its gruesome sentry, contained the usual boxes of ammunition, bags of souring rice, and damp, mud-covered articles of clothing. There were several side passages, supply-stacked and dripping, but these we did not enter. When we had penetrated about twenty-five yards from the mouth, we could see the reflection of daylight some distance ahead of us. But it was late evening and we were half a mile from the nearest American troops, in a sort of no man's land between the American positions and enemy-occupied territory. We decided to return to camp and continue exploration at a safer time. It was like running out of breath near the bottom of the ocean.

We had gone to the shore that day and bathed in the clear cool water of a spring-fed pool—where enemy soldiers from the caves had probably bathed not many days before. Those soldiers had been killed as we had killed the fish in the sea, by using our superiority of weapons. We had competed and we had survived. But with the soldiers our competition was on a different plane. We were not separated by millions of generations of evolutionary life, and our advantage in combat was by no means genetically established, nor was it definite. We fought with humans like ourselves, against minds that also had studied the strategy of war and developed modern weapons.

The Japanese, too, had guns and bombs and factories that built military aircraft. On the average, their products were inferior to ours, but they were still formidable to meet in combat. The Pacific war cost both sides heavily in life, yet we were not killing each other for flesh to satisfy our hunger—or were we? Our enemies said that they had become a food-restricted people, seventy million of them crowded on their islands.

Man has risen so far above all other species that he competes in ways unique in nature. He fights by means of complicated weapons; he fights for ends remote in time. Yet problems of feeding a prolific life still influence the reasons for his battles. It takes some unusual experience, such as diving into shark-infested waters from a South Pacific reef in wartime, for modern man to sense the relationship of prolificacy to the availability and cultivation of food, to comprehend the incidence of strife and evolutionary progress.

Modern man was created by millions of centuries of life in competition, through time stretching back past history and myth, past rocks of the Cambrian era. Time is a measure. Time is an abstraction which, on earth, exists only for the human brain it has evolved. Time. Space. Matter. There is a growing sense of awareness scaled against magnitudes: the span of life compresses to an instant, while spirit and mind expand through superworldly frames. Time. I walk between the Stonehenge rocks of Wiltshire, and, flying, look down on Egypt's pyramids or glide between eroded temples of the Colorado's canyon. There, more than any other place on earth, time compresses for me.

When we were laying out the air route between New York and southern California in 1928 and 1929, I made many flights across the continent in my survey plane. Sometimes I took a northward detour to follow the Colorado River through its barren wilderness of rock and desert, mile after mile above varicolored buttes and plateaus, without a road or dwelling underneath my wings.

Contrary to pilots' yarns of that early period, the air below the rim of the Grand Canyon is usually less turbulent than that above. After my first cautious tests I confirmed this fact frequently and in different weathers. I would weave in and out around sharp-shadowed cliffs, now less than a wingspan above ledges no man's foot had trod, now nosing down into the granite-bouldered gorge of the swirling river.

Christmas at the Morrows' home in New Jersey

With old friends
Thomas Nelson
and Philip Love
during
Missouri
National Guard
maneuvers, 1928

On first trip to Mexico, 1928

At National Air Races, Los Angeles, September 1928

Charles and Anne
a few weeks
after their marriage
in May 1929

With borrowed Lockheed,
about to join the search for
a T.A.T. plane
that crashed
in the Southwest, 1929

Exploring cliff dwellings in New Mexico, 1929

With Juan Trippe, on early Pan American clipper, British Guiana, 1929

Ready
for flight tests
prior to
1930 Pacific
survey flight

In Japan, 1931

In the Lockheed Sirius on floodwaters by Nanking's wall, 1931

Arriving at Nanking, 1931

Leaving Shetland Islands, on Atlantic survey flight, 1933

At Karachi, on trip through India, 1937

Greeting Russian fliers at Moscow's airport, 1938

From the pine-green rim of the Kaibab Plateau to its present gray granite and schist bed, the Colorado has cut through more than a mile of the earth's crust, opening great chapters of world history. In pages of limestone, sandstone, and shale, records of millions of years lay stacked in a terrestrial library, the story of a rising continent and a disappearing ocean, layer after layer; chapters of mammals, reptiles, fish, invertebrates, all resting on a table of Archean schist. Here was the account of life's developing sensitivity. In stories of turmoil and conflict, courage and terror, tragedy and success, the survival and extinction of trillions, was told the never-ending struggle toward a higher type of being that today culminates in man.

Man has only begun to scratch his record on the stone pages of geology. Marks of more than a hundred thousand years ago are scarce—bits of chipped flint, a few fragments of bone. We have found none in the Western Hemisphere. At the Grand Canyon the only human marks I saw lay on the surface of the earth, waiting to be covered by sediments of time: a surfaced road, a sheep corral, a big hotel on the canyon rim. I once stayed in that hotel. It was prosperous, well kept, its parlors and corridors open with hospitality. I watched the waiters serving food at silver-garnished tables, listened to chattering guests and strains of music in the background. I amused myself by speculating on whether the hotel itself would eventually be buried under layers of rock, and if so, what fragments would be left to communicate life to an archaeologist's eye. A few hours earlier I had flown over an abandoned Indian dwelling, its stones already merging with the drifted sand. Who could reconstruct the life once housed in those roofless walls?

There was the "now" of the hotel. There was the "past" of the Indian dwelling, so distant to aviation's era, so recent in geological time. There were the fossils in the rocks beneath me, reaching back to ages beyond human memory. The effects of prolificacy, competition, survival, and progressively advancing weapons were evident, even in the fragments that remained. Prolificacy, strife, survival— these three basic elements of life I encountered wherever I combined archaeology with aviation.

In the summer of 1929 my wife and I explored areas of New

Mexico and Arizona for signs of ancient men. We were working with the archaeological division of the Carnegie Institution of Washington, flying an open-cockpit Curtiss Falcon biplane.*

Under certain angles of light, old ruins can be seen from an airplane, but you might walk across them on the ground without knowing they existed. Walls, rain-washed to the level of the earth, may appear as crisscross lines to the aviator's eye, and changed shades of vegetation show where people dug their pits and dumped their refuse thousands of years ago. Our mission was to photograph ancient ruins, and to map their exact position so that ground expeditions could then locate and explore them. We flew back and forth over mountains, plains, plateaus, and desert edges, sometimes climbing high to select an interesting valley, sometimes flying below a cliff rim while we watched for caves and piled-up rocks. From our altitude we saw the earth's great contours, an entire desert, the branching sources of a river, a rounding ridge of mountains that looked like a huge volcano's rim. Close to the ground we could see details that helped us separate natural formations from those of men.

Approaching a line of cliffs in Arizona, with sheer walls rising from the ground below, I opened my throttle to clear the plateau on top. Cliff edges contrasted with their valley somewhat as land contrasts with sea. To the left a peninsula jutted out like the state of Florida on a chart, long, narrow-necked before bulging. Our eyes caught, vaguely, but definitely etched upon its surface, the familiar lines that mark a ruined Pueblo city. It was not listed in archaeological records, but it was by far the largest we had seen. As we banked to take photographs I wondered what enemies had forced those ancient people to a place so high and far from water. How could attacking warriors have advanced through a neck so narrow, or scaled walls so sheer? What had caused the abandonment of a large, well-fortified city? Was it disease? Starvation? A battle line that did not hold? All three? My mind skipped across centuries to imagine a thriving culture: square adobe houses, with wooden

* In addition to working with the archaeologist Dr. Alfred Vincent Kidder, in the U.S. Southwest, Lindbergh explored and photographed Indian ruins in Mexico and Central America. After he filmed a lost Mayan site in July 1929, a *New York Times* editorial praised him as a "pioneer of aerial archaeology."

rafters, built in several tiers; men and women with their brown-skinned, black-haired children. We knew what they had looked like, and the kind of dwellings they lived in, because we had spent a night in Canyon de Chelly, in northeastern Arizona. We had even come in contact with these people's problems of survival.

On a previous exploration we had flown down the Canyon de Chelly, searching for cliff houses hidden under shelves and behind ledges in the walls. Some distance from the mouth of the canyon, near what are called the "White House" ruins, an archaeological expedition was encamped. Since we could not land on the stony river bed, we had settled for merely waving to its staff as we passed. But about a quarter of a mile upstream from the camp we saw an Indian trail, with ladders and notches, threading down the precipitous left wall. The tableland above the canyon was fairly level. It was only lightly spotted with prairie-dog holes, cactus, and brush. Why not pay the archaeologists a visit? We selected a clear stretch of ground that lay into the wind and landed—bumping over fist-size stones and hummocks.

It was taking a chance to leave our plane on that mesa all night, but the sky showed no indication of a storm and we eagerly wanted to see at close range some of the ruins we were photographing—to touch the earth, pick up the shards, and talk to scientists who worked with screen and shovel. We dug holes for the Falcon's wheels and tail skid, roped its wings to sturdy bushes, and started out for the camp. There was no sign of recent travel on the footpath that angled steeply over a cliff edge, yet it was not difficult to follow. It took us along rock ledges and through narrow crevices toward the canyon floor. The weathered wood of the pole ladders, though broken in places, was still firm enough to hold our weight.

"You landed on the mesa? But how did you get down?" Members of the archaeological expedition did not know a trail existed, although they had walked back and forth past its lower entrance for many weeks. Under the White House, isolated by the canyon's red and perpendicular walls, and somehow set in a professorial atmosphere of centuries past, we described our flights and observations. We realized that in our generation the airplane had given the eyes of birds to the minds of men.

"You must see our new-found friend," one of our hosts said as he led us to a corner of the ruins. She turned out to be the mummy of a "basket maker" unearthed a week or two before. As we were introduced, she squatted comfortably, with her back against the cave's wall and her head resting on her knees. Her hair was long and black. Her features were sharply chiseled by tight-drawn skin. Bits of clothing still clung to her figure. Her body had been so well preserved by the dry desert earth that I felt I could recognize her in life if some miracle were to close the two thousand years between us. For an instant it seemed she might arise and guide us through the tiers of dwellings.

Why had the cave been abandoned? Its natural roof gave protection from the weather, its length and narrow width let in plenty of daylight, and the canyon walls sheltered it from strong winds. Built on a ledge about twenty feet above the river bed, the White House was in an excellent position for defense. The archaeologists had some answers. A battle was fought at the White House. Most of the skulls they found had been bashed by instruments of war. Apparently an enemy discovered the location of the cave and attacked successfully. Had warriors come in overwhelming force? Had they developed superior weapons and tactics? Had they caught the defenders sick, or unaware?

Looking down from my airplane at other times, I had seen remnants of southwestern Pecos cities, animal-shaped earthworks on Mississippi Valley farms, jungle-covered temples next to Caribbean shores—all formed memorials to life's prolificacy, competition, selection, and increasingly sophisticated weapons, memorials outlined sharply by the white man's culture which survives them. The native peoples of America were unable to compete with Europe's onslaught. How could men limited to spear and bow stand firm against attacking guns? When Cortés's army shot a cannon, Aztec soldiers fled; they were terrified of the thunder and thought the Spaniards gods.

From the beginning, aviation kept me in close touch with man's competition and his advancing weaponry. I had trained for combat as a cadet, took part in maneuvers as a National Guardsman, watched the impact of military aviation on the more primitive and effusive countries to our south. At Mexico City's airport in the spring of 1929, I received an excellent lesson in the importance of superior weapons and tactics. A rebellion had broken out in Vera-cruz, over two hundred miles away. A rebel troop train was moving westward toward the nation's capital. The loyal air squadron had been ordered to attack it.

I drove out from the American Embassy to watch the military operations start. On one side of the airport several hangars contained the country's most modern weapons, a dozen or two training and fighting planes of European manufacture left over from World War I. "Whoever controls the air controls Mexico," an officer explained to me, and such control was to be exercised that day.

I was amazed by the bombs I saw attached to the planes. They were little more than tin cans filled with dynamite. "But you can't kill many men with bombs like that," I said. "There won't be enough fragmentation. You need a lot of metal fragments to make personnel bombs effective."

A young colonel beside me laughed. "Oh, you do not understand fighting in Mexico," he said. "It is different. You see it is very hot down here. Mexican soldiers do not ride inside the cars.like yours. They ride on top, where it is cooler. We dive at a train and throw out a bomb. It scares the soldiers. They jump off the cars. Some break their legs. That stops the rebellion. It is just as good as frag-mentation. What's the difference?

"The rebels don't have any airplanes," he continued. "We keep all ours here at Mexico City so we can be sure the pilots are loyal to the government." He laughed again. "These are our modern weapons," he said, pointing to the line of aging aircraft. "As long as we have them, we have Mexico."

No one knows better than the fighter pilot of World War II the meaning of competition and the value of being equipped with better weapons. The slightest advantage over your opponent can result in saving your life. A major advantage was also sure to be de-cisive in any action. I think of a combat mission I flew in the summer of 1944. By that time Japanese losses had been so heavy that American pilots were oftentimes masters of an undefended sky. Enemy ground troops took cover at the sound of our engines. We flew over great areas of the territory they held encountering nothing more formidable than light antiaircraft fire. After a fruitless search for enemy aircraft, or an uneventful bomber-escort mission, our squadrons would divide into flights to harass the New Guinea coastline.

We usually flew in string formation, high enough to be unattractive targets for small arms, low enough to observe suspicious objects on the surface. In addition to keeping the sky free of aircraft marked by the rising sun, our mission was to cut off the trickle of food into Japanese strongholds on New Guinea. It was a follow-up to General Douglas MacArthur's strategy of leapfrogging the enemy positions. After our Navy and air forces had swept the seas of unfriendly shipping in the New Guinea area, MacArthur established beachheads many miles beyond enemy fortifications. Without means of sea transport, cut off from their supply bases, the Japanese were faced with the choice of inaction, which would lead to starvation, or of penetrating long distances through dense jungle to attack our well-equipped troops on the beachheads. In some places, they attacked; elsewhere, they starved.

A few Japanese positions could still be reached from their western supply bases by small powered barges skirting desolate coasts at night. The barges did not move at all by day, for it had become too dangerous. Their captains tried to steer before sunrise into some inlet where camouflage would be effective against a bank. But if no inlets were within reach, the barges were beached or anchored as close to shore as their draft would permit, and covered with leaves and branches. But it is impossible to camouflage completely, with only bushes, a barge fifty yards from where ocean rollers break against a beach. An "island" so formed was about as conspicuous as the naked barge would have been. We could spot one miles ahead.

Rain was falling on our Hollandia campsite when we were awakened at 0530 on Tuesday, June 27. It was a typical jungle-mountain drizzle. MacDonald, Smith, McGuire, and I took time to eat a heavy breakfast because our take-off was sure to be delayed by weather. It was 1028 when we finally left the steel strip—four Lightnings with drop-tanks full of fuel. We set course across the jungle and Geelvink Bay toward Salawati Island and the Japanese bases of Jefman and Samate. Since we were on an individually planned and voluntary raid, the code name of our flight was "Phantom Special." We expected to be in the air for six or seven hours. Weather varied from overcast to broken, with high cumulus clouds in places. We flew a combat formation above the overcast, passing close to some of the mountain ranges.

I looked down on cascading streams, white raveled threads on weave of green, deep in New Guinea, not yet charted on a map. Until this war this area was known only to natives and explorers, the objective of long, hazardous, and carefully organized expeditions, one of which I had, in fact, advised on the use of its aircraft. Now combat pilots flew through the heart of New Guinea as a matter of course, seldom thinking of the natives or explorers, oblivious to the hardships as well as the romance and solitude and beauty of surface travel. We were four fighters cruising swiftly toward enemy bases on the opposite side of the world from home, bearing violent death through the sky.

We struck the Vogelkop peninsula south of Mawi Bay and continued on course for about one more hour, until we reached the coast at Kaiboes Bay, south of Jefman. Then we turned north in order to approach from an unexpected direction. Within a few minutes, Japanese airstrips came into view. We had hoped to catch some enemy planes in the air, but had no luck. We circled the strips at nine thousand feet, weaving to confuse ground fire. Many of the black bursts around us were at almost our exact altitude—too close. We circled again to check whether there were planes in the revetments and ships in the harbor, then turned northeast along the coast on a barge hunt.

We found one barge run up on the beach only a few miles away, camouflaged with leaves and branches. We formed a strafing circle and made two passes at it with machine guns and cannon. Around the next point of mountainous coast two more barges were anchored or run aground less than a hundred yards offshore and also covered with foliage from the jungle. They were cleverly placed in a scallop of the mountains, so that an attacking pilot would have to either shoot at them from a bank or chandelle up the steep mountainside after making his pass. An error in judgment would make him crash.

I curved in over the top of a ridge at an indicated air speed of two hundred fifty miles an hour, missed trees by no more than a man's height, partially straightened out as I fired a burst into one of the barges, and pulled up the mountainside beyond in a bank that left me headed out to sea in good position to rejoin the strafing circle. On my second dive, firing with all machine guns and the cannon, I aimed just above the water line aft of midship. The barge burst into flame ahead of me. After that we made two runs on the other barge, but it was difficult to shoot accurately through the clouds of smoke that were pouring from the first.

Enemy barges seemed to be spaced only a few miles apart. We saw two more around the next bend of coast. MacDonald's dipping wing signaled an attack. I armed my guns and watched his bullets spatter as I banked into position—dive, fire, chandelle out to sea, glance at the shoreline for signs of enemy resistance, glance back at the target for appearance of smoke and flame. Barge strafing was not without its dangers, for the barges were not always as helpless as they looked. Sometimes guns were hidden in the jungle, and one of our flights would lose a pilot and a plane. The Japanese had stopped using tracer ammunition, so you could not see their streams of bullets. In making a run, it was always possible that you were trading shell for shell.

Along the New Guinea coast in the summer of 1944, our superiority of weapons was tremendous. Had the Japanese been better equipped, the cost to us for each barge destroyed would have been excessively high in pilots and airplanes. When your enemy has similar or equal modern weapons, the price tags on your targets change, and you grow more cautious in selection.

One day over the Halmaheras, Major McGuire was leading Red Flight. I was leading White. Major Smith had Blue Flight well above us in case an intercept was made. On the surface all Japanese shipping had been anchored so close to antiaircraft guns that no target we saw justified the hazard of a strafing run. McGuire and I had our flights at eight thousand feet—usually a safe altitude for fighters—when a string of antiaircraft bursts blossomed behind us. We started a climbing turn; but the ack-ack followed in its own ascending spiral until our eight planes were forced to break formation to make less attractive targets. That was not an area for barge strafing. The enemy had too many modern weapons and too much ammunition. Japanese positions west and north of New Guinea had not, obviously, been subjected to enough destruction. Our ground-attack and heavy-bomber squadrons still had a job to do—modern weapons against modern weapons, America's science and industry versus Japan's.

I recognized the essential value of modern weapons during a strike against Amboina Island, which lies southwest of Ceram and about two hundred fifty miles west of New Guinea. It was July 28. American operations had been confused by weather. A cold front lay across our route. Some of the squadrons assigned to lower altitudes had turned back. Above the interior of Ceram two mountain peaks pierced through a solid cloud layer: this was the only visible mark of land below. We cruised at ten thousand feet past those peaks, under a ceiling of blue and over a carpet of white. On each side of our flight strings of fighters from other groups, sleek and deadly, bored their way westward.

Clouds broke a little over the area of our targets, enough to permit the heavies to achieve some accuracy of bombing. Here and there we saw columns of smoke start to billow from the ground. Group Intelligence had warned us to expect enemy interception, but not a single Zero awaited our arrival. While the bombs were dropping, fighter squadrons broke into flights. Colonel MacDonald was leading our Blue Flight, with Captain Danforth Miller as Blue 2. I was flying Blue 3, and Lieutenant J. Miller Blue 4. We wove in and out through clouds, paying little attention to intermittent ack-ack. The ground guns were primarily fired at bombers.

We crossed Elpaputih Bay, then swept southwest to Haroekoe Island—no interception there, nor at Liang, nor at Amboina. Enemy airstrips were empty. The Japanese seemed to have no intention of opposing us by air. We had circled northward and turned back east when the radio, which had been filled with idle chatter, sprang to life. Captive squadron, of the 8th Fighter Group, had made contact with enemy aircraft. We pushed our throttles to "combat cruise" and searched the air with alerted eyes.

"Blue Flight, jettison drop-tanks!"

Blue 1 was calling. Eight bomb-shaped objects left our wings and tumbled earthward. We had rounded another cloud to see the air ahead, above Amahai strip, black with ack-ack bursts of heavy caliber. Below us were gray camouflaged warplanes of our enemy. A Lightning had just made an unsuccessful pass at one of them.

I tripped my gun switch, brightened the ring sight, nosed down to follow in attack. To my left a Japanese plane disappeared in haze and cloud. A second was banking sharply toward the airstrip under the protection of the ground guns. We dove toward the strip, unmindful of puffs of smoke and the invisible steel fragments that were zipping around us.

Tracers spurted from MacDonald's fighter, a beam of death that forced the Japanese pilot to reverse his bank. A thin trail of smoke informed us that one of the bullets hit, but the enemy plane showed no loss of maneuverability or power. Miller, Blue 2, fired a short deflection burst against wings that were almost vertical in air. My Lightning was next in line. I watched the red balls of the rising sun on the enemy plane grow larger, shrink from round to oval, then disappear as the wings cut toward me, knife-edged against the background of gray haze. It was to be a head-on pass. I centered the plane in my ring sight and squeezed finger against trigger. Streaks of fire leapt from my fighter's nose out of four machine guns and one cannon. Raise the tracers—creep them leftward—flashes on the target as my bullets hit—but the wingspan widened in my ring sight. The enemy's guns were firing, too. I held the trigger down, head on with no deflection. There was a rattle of machine guns and streams of tracers. Slightly climbing, slightly diving at five hundred miles an hour we approached, hurtling in an eternity of time and space. The cowling in my sight expanded. Enemy cylinders grew fins. I hauled back on my stick as I sensed our closeness. The Japanese plane jerked upward, too! Was the pilot trying to collide? I yanked back with all my strength, braced for the crash. There was a bump but it was only air.

By how much did we miss? Ten feet? Five? I was zooming steeply. I banked left and saw ack-ack bursts ahead, reversed the bank and swept my eyes over sky and earth looking for aircraft. I saw only friendly Lightnings. No one but my wingman was on my tail. I saw the plane I had just shot down. My enemy was in a wingover, out of control. I watched his nose drop. His plane twisted as it gathered speed. The rising suns diminished in size. Down. Down. Down. The sea had not seemed so far beneath us. Down. A fountain of spray, white foam on water; ripples circled outward, merged with waves. The foam subsided. No mark remained.

Life had balanced on a razor edge during that encounter. If I had been ten feet behind, my enemy would have rammed me. At the speed I was flying, ten feet was less than a tenth of a second. Bullets were ripping back and forth at the rate of thousands per minute. It took only one to kill. The slightest difference in our rates of fire might have reversed the outcome of the combat—had my controls been a mite less sensitive, my guns a shade less accurate, my bullets of slightly smaller caliber . . . I had the advantage that the most modern weapons give. My enemy did not.

Back on Biak, standing on reefs, waist deep in the ocean where life began, I could cover the entire span of evolution with an eye's sweep—a clump of greenish protoplasm in the water at my feet, the shark with its teeth, the native with his spear, the pilot beside his bomber on the airdrome, a group of Japanese prisoners, some skeleton-thin, landing under guard.

Thousands of organisms exist in a drop of water. Millions of sperm compete to fertilize one ovum. Billions of people stand on areas of earth that must be parceled. Wherever one looks, life presses on its environment. Where there is prolificacy, there must be competition. As long as there is competition, selection must result. These are laws of nature by which exist all forms of life, including man. Under these laws the superiority of weapons is of consequence. It was the need for increasingly effective weapons that turned the hand-thrown rocks of our anthropoid forebears into the nuclear warheads we hold in readiness today.

EIGHT

Inheritance
of Power

Nothing before so revolutionary had impacted on the lives of men so suddenly. The announcement in August of 1945 that the entire center of a large Japanese city had been leveled by one bomb, bursting as a secret of intellectual development, seemed too fantastic to be earthly.

Militarily, following extensive and decisive victories in World War II, the atomic bomb confirmed America's dominating power. We knew that soon we would be able, once decided, to devastate any area on earth within hours. But how were we alone to have the advantage of this stupendous power? How long could we keep secret our knowledge of the atomic bomb's construction? The day was to come, surely, when other nations would have atomic weapons at their disposal; and when opposing nations had enough atomic bombs to destroy each other, a stalemate would be reached. But suppose one of them tried for victory by taking advantage of surprise—by launching suddenly, say, a five-hundred-atom-bomber attack? When a stalemate came, would not the United States find itself at an alarming disadvantage because of the American people's idealism, because of our commitment to a policy of nonaggression? Could we absorb an atomic attack and still strike back effectively? "The use of force usually brings requital," Lao Tse wrote. Were we becoming involved in an unbreakable cycle? As our elation at hastening Japan's surrender by dropping atomic bombs gave way to our concern over the possibility of our own cities being atomized, we were at the same time setting about to design still greater bombs and still faster vehicles to carry them, thereby making more and more vulnerable our entire civilization.

Before World War II ended, the University of Chicago had become the grounds for this huge step in military weapons research. Through the work of Enrico Fermi and others, the first successful atomic pile was constructed. This pile, incongruously assembled in a secret space under Stagg Field, revolutionized concepts of power, war, and international policy.

My first contact with a University of Chicago project came after the atomic bombing of Hiroshima and Nagasaki, at the end of the war. It related to a study initiated by the Ordnance Department of the United States Army that was assigned the name CHORE (Chicago Ordnance Research). This project was so secret at its beginning that even its name was classified "secret." (Someone once called CHORE's attention to the fact that its name was printed on the guarded door to its offices.)

The University of Chicago's direction of CHORE came under Walter Bartky, Dean of the Division of Physical Sciences. Not long after I returned to the United States in 1945 from my assignment with the Naval Technical Mission Europe, Dean Bartky brought to my home at Scott Cove an invitation to become a consultant to CHORE. I accepted because I believed the United States should remain dominant in weapons development. I considered asinine the assertions that weapons were now so terrible that World War II would be the last war fought.

My first trip to Chicago as a member of CHORE emphasized the difference between the life I actually led and the life that was presumed to follow upon my press-concocted reputation. I arrived carrying a worn blue canvas bag and checked in at the hotel's reception desk. I had passed unnoticed through the door, but I no sooner registered my name at the desk than I was greeted by the assistant manager. Two bellboys grabbed my bag; and the manager himself escorted me, not to a bedroom, but to a suite containing a big parlor, two or three bedrooms with baths, and a kitchenette with a stove and an icebox furnished with liquor. Sleeping alone in that suite reminded me of my early flying career when I spent several nights as the only occupant of the barracks and buildings of an abandoned Army airfield. On later visits to Chicago I arranged for simpler quarters.

The CHORE briefing room was in a basement of one of the university's many buildings. It was windowless, neon-lighted, air conditioned, a cave in which the intellect would reign, marking its magic symbols with white chalk on blackboard-covered walls, symbols more scientific and civilized, but less mystical and beautiful, than those marked by Cro-Magnon savants on walls of somewhat similar caves some thirty thousand years before—those, too, bearing a relationship to weapons.

There, I listened to a mathematics of combat effectiveness and destruction that seemed to leave the human being devoid of his senses. I studied graphs showing the value of "scatter effect" for machine guns, and others indicating probabilities of kill for existing and for improved weapons. There, hour after hour, we discussed calibers, explosives, muzzle velocities, measures of aggression, defense, counterdefense, and counter-counterdefense.

Mathematical calculations informed us that future jet-powered warplanes would fly too fast for bullet interception, that pilots of supersonic fighters would not have time to aim and fire in a head-on pass and still avoid colliding with each other, that guns would become obsolete for airplanes and have to be replaced by "homing" missiles, that human eyes and muscles and cognition were too slow for the reaction times essential to success—concepts startling to the experience of a World War II combat pilot. In the next major conflict, electronic devices would be set loose in combat with each other. They would be maintained and monitored by men who would have no sense of wielding weapons, whose very existence would be preserved or snuffed out by the result of the competing intelligence of the synthetic brains to which the human brain would relinquish control of its destiny. In mathematical war games, men were already referred to as "bodies," and were moved like chessmen according to directions issued by analog computers.

Theoretical discussions in the CHORE briefing room often made me feel that my existence and the other existences with which it intersected were purely intellectual, that mine and theirs were only retarded and distracted by the tall and short, heavy and slender, suited and collared human figures housing them and seated around the table. With what irritating stupidity had nature tied flesh to thought!

This impression was enhanced by a tendency of mathematicians to overlook the body's emotional reactions. At intervals in our combat-effectiveness studies, theoretical steel fragments would pierce theoretical cockpits, splinter theoretical instruments, and ignite theoretical fuel in theoretical tanks without having any effect whatever on the calculated efficiency of the theoretical crew as long as, theoretically, its flesh was not penetrated. But sooner or later my own war experience—black ack-ack bursts and tracers streaking past—loomed in memory to re-establish the connection between mind and senses. Then I would argue that even military aviators are human, that when a bullet hits your airplane some emotional effect takes place, that a coefficient relating to the senses must be included in combat-effectiveness formulas.

In some calculations, extrapolated points were so persistently used as an axial basis for new extrapolations that I felt my greatest contribution to the study lay in advising airborne spot checks of the mathematical conclusions reached. But regardless of the separation between theory and practice in certain instances, I had to admit that CHORE's studies contributed in major ways to improving military aircraft and equipment and thereby keeping us ahead of enemy competition.

Some of my most interesting hours at the university were only indirectly related to my activities with CHORE. I think of a small dinner group, with Enrico Fermi present. One of the scientists told of testing at Alamogordo the first atomic bomb. Fermi, he recounted, was the man who "pressed the button," and just before doing so said: "Now when I press this button, there is a chance in ten thousand it will be the end of the world." Headshakes and smiles alternated around the table, but I could feel the tenseness of that twentieth-century occasion which marked one of the great episodes in the history of man—the pressing of the button, the blinding brilliance of the sky, the great boom.

Subjects of endless interest were discussed at University of Chicago meetings. Fermi suggested that one of the most interesting experiments open to man would consist of boring a hole as deeply as possible straight down into the earth. I wished I had additional lifetimes to acquire knowledge in fields of study essential to their understanding. I felt keenly my lack of training in advanced mathematics when Walter Bartky and I argued about the presumably unmatchable velocity of light—why no relative velocities could be greater than light's measured one-way speed of one hundred eighty-six thousand miles per second. Laughing, I used my oldest daughter's last-ditch sister-brother argument, to the effect that even if it were true, I did not believe it. He quite gallantly replied that mathematics in its outer realm, like religion, depends to a large extent on what you believe.

At the University of Chicago one looked into the fantastic future toward which our civilization was headed. The speeds and powers that scientific methods could achieve disturbed me most. Aircraft had already removed the safety of inaccessibility from even the remotest crevices of our earth. Rockets with nuclear warheads would soon make dubious the presumed remaining value of defensive arms. What men had spent centuries to build they could atomize in seconds. World War II's record, like the history preceding it, showed how recklessly nations unleash their destructive powers during the lust of battle.

In connection with military activities during ensuing years, I served as a consultant to Secretaries of the Air Force Stuart Symington and Harold Talbott, and was commissioned by President Eisenhower a brigadier general in the United States Air Force Reserve. In addition to studies carried on by CHORE, my work related to the postwar reorganization of the Strategic Air Command, extending the range of planes through air refueling, developing supersonic bombers, decreasing accident rates, improving air-base morale, evaluating research laboratories, and selecting a site for the Air Force Academy. I was for seven years a member of ballistic-missile scientific committees whose chairmen were John von Neumann and Clark Millikan; and for a shorter period I sat on the scientific committee, chaired by H. Guyford Stever, that was charged with developing a defense against ballistic missiles. Mine was a life involving guarded rooms, security clearances, passes, and documents that had to be kept in hand or in a safe. The Pentagon building furnished headquarters for all these activities, and for me it symbolized the change that was taking place in our modern civilized life. In its miles of room-encrusted corridors it housed military activities with an efficiency never before achieved. The dozens of stairways from tier to tier, the branching windowless tunnels, the duty-bound men and women streaming back and forth, made me liken it to a giant termite hill. After I entered its doors, I felt similarly insulated from physical contact with the sunlit world outside. Tucked away in one corner, a small fraction of the Pentagon's floor space, were enough stores to serve a town, from bank to grocery and shoe shops.

Military projects took me to all quarters of the United States, and beyond, around the world. Sometimes I traveled as a committee member, sometimes with other officers, sometimes alone. What "circular error probable" could be expected with our radar bombing? How effective was fighter interception at high altitude? Should the construction of tankers for refueling bombers be accelerated? Was cross-training too intensive? Were housing programs adequate? Should the B-58 supersonic-bomber program be abandoned? Should the costly Arnold Engineering Development Center at Tullahoma, Tennessee, be shut down or expanded? Did we need a second intercontinental-ballistic-missile program as a backup for the Atlas? Was it possible to create an effective defense against ballistic missiles? How much effort should be diverted from nuclear-warhead rockets in order to bring nearer the launching of a satellite?

You could not know of such projects without becoming aware of the magnitude of America's scientific, industrial, and financial resources. Once a top priority was established by the Department of Defense, as it had been for the intercontinental-ballistic-missile program, the facilities of thousands of laboratories, drafting rooms, and factories were made immediately available. If a new organization, or building, or test base was required—presto, its establishment was under way. A single project might cost more than the entire Air Force budget had been but a decade before. Costs were secondary to results when the issue of national security was invoked. Congress seldom held back in appropriating money for defense. In working with the military services, it was easy to misread the zeros between dollar sign and decimal point on paper. I remember when it was argued whether or not the development of a subsonic jet transport that would cost four hundred million dollars should be undertaken. "Only four hundred million dollars? Of course we ought to do it," a general said without hesitation.

I found difficulty adjusting my thinking to the different dimensions of finance among which I moved from day to day. At home in Connecticut I kept five separate accounts for banking my children's dimes and nickels. In budgeting expenses for family living, a hundred dollars became an important item. In affairs of my wife's New Jersey family, with its successful banking background, a thousand dollars was of about equivalent importance. In New York in my work with Pan American World Airways, a million dollars formed a unit we often used in talking about the purchase of equipment. Military activities in Washington brought me in touch with people who could speak confidently of multibillion-dollar projects. "Do you realize how much a billion dollars is?" Jerome Wiesner, of the Massachusetts Institute of Technology, once asked. "A billion dollars can be a stack of thousand-dollar bills almost as high as the Washington Monument—bills laid flat, not on end."

Work with the Strategic Air Command seemed to me one of the most important of my postwar military assignments. I believed the security of the United States depended on SAC's retaliatory ability. And I was certain that the security of Western civilization was closely bound to the security of the United States. Surely, "brushfire" wars would continue, requiring the use of relatively conventional weapons and tactics, but they would be fought under an "atomic umbrella" that the major powers held over the world.

The role of strategic bombing had, at that time, been assigned exclusively to the Air Force. I myself felt the Navy should have been included in this role, but the Defense Department had made its decision, and until that basic rule was changed, our entire strategic-bombing strength would have to be concentrated in the USAF Strategic Air Command. I believed it essential for SAC to have enough power to win an atomic war. Still more important, it should prevent one. Obviously, atomic aggression could best be prevented by making other nations realize that such aggression would result in their own atomic annihilation through the overwhelming striking power of our Strategic Air Command. This was not a great problem while we alone possessed atomic bombs. But now, with issues debated contentiously, with tensions high, with the danger of war imminent, an enemy might conclude that American retaliatory forces could be destroyed by a surprise attack. Since we could not be sure of avoiding a surprise attack through strategic or tactical warning, our forces would have to be sufficiently strong and so widely diversified in means and dispersed in area that they could absorb an attack and still retaliate effectively. Put concisely, this meant the United States would have to maintain an indestructible power to destroy: the more overwhelming our power, the greater our security.

There were scientists and military officers who believed that effective defenses against bomber and even ballistic-missile raids could be developed. But I had, as a boy when World War I began, read articles and listened to statements by ground and air defense proponents. Their claims had seldom been borne out through test in actual combat. Sometimes they had been made overoptimistic by orders of magnitude. One of the causes of error in defense estimates lay in the constantly improving efficiency of offensive weapons. By the time antiaircraft batteries were made effective against bombers flying at ten thousand feet and ninety miles an hour, new bombers were flying at thirty thousand feet and two hundred fifty miles an hour. By the time supersonic fighters with homing missiles for attack on supersonic bombers were on engineers' drafting boards, ballistic missiles with atomic warheads were being designed by other engineers.

Most scientists I talked to thought a defense system capable of intercepting a ballistic-missile attack effectively could not be established. Only a few believed that ways would be found to destroy approaching warheads regardless of their speed, quantity, and their decoy devices. These scientists did not convince me of their claims. One common argument was based on nothing more tangible than the proposition that since a defense against ballistic missiles was essential to man's security, ways must be found to achieve it. It was true that, like antibodies formed by an infection, defensive techniques were perfected only after an attack. The shield followed the spear; the trench followed the rifle; the bazooka followed the tank.

I had no confidence in the ability of ground batteries and interceptor fighters to bring down more than a fraction of the number of attacking enemy bombers, to say nothing of destroying future missiles with atomic warheads approaching at several times a rifle bullet's speed. If even a quarter of an enemy force got through, the mission would be successful. One atomic bomb dropped close to a strategic air base would wipe it out. The bull's-eye accuracy required in World War II was no longer necessary.

Because of my fighter-pilot training, and because I realized it was not a game at stake, but the whole of civilization, I concluded reluctantly that while defensive measures should be developed and maintained, they should never be relied on for national security. We should depend primarily on our retaliatory power, and that retaliatory power depended on the development of ever more efficient weapons. I was faced by the dilemma that our security today and tomorrow apparently required the production of weapons that were likely to destroy us the day after.

I visited Strategic Air Force bases from Labrador to Okinawa, lived with the officers, flew with B-29 and B-50 squadrons, listened to Air Force men and women discuss problems of the lives they led. The recommendations in my reports to Washington headquarters were general and simple. They were based on the proposition that the Strategic Air Command should be accorded exceptional priorities. I recommended that SAC be given top priority in the selection of its officers and crews, that its personnel receive improved terms of tenure, that the construction of air-refueling tankers be accelerated to increase practical bombing ranges, that monthly periods of flight training in emergency procedures be inaugurated to cut down accident rates, and that every SAC pilot fly a basic trainer on occasion in order to maintain proficiency in the ABCs of flying technique.

All of these recommendations were adopted effectively except the one related to basic training. SAC pilots did not approve of the idea of flying basic trainers, and in fact demonstrated an extraordinary inability to fly them. Walker Air Force Base, in New Mexico, had been selected as the place to try out my recommendation in this respect. Several AT-6s were sent there for the purpose. They were cracked up so fast that AT-6 instructors were included with their replacements. Even then, the accident rate with basic trainers continued so high that the project was abandoned.

My activities with the Air Force and the Department of Defense made me sensitive to American power, magnitude, and tempo, and as a result to the relative weakness of other countries. There was terrific power in the huge bombers I rode, the B-29s, the B-36s, the B-50s, in their climbs to star-encrusted altitudes and in their ability to carry enormous bomb loads over mountains and flashing storms. I sensed power, magnitude, and tempo in a SAC base increasing as my bomber approached—great scars on the earth ahead; thousands of acres devoid of crops and cattle; wide concrete runways, two straight miles or more in length; a city of buildings like an isolated suburb; the concise exchange of data in my earphones while the tower communicated with a dozen bombers in nearby air; the long, sky-piercing contrails overhead. What contrast with the fragile wings, the radioless solitude, the bucking turbulence, drenching rains, and little cow-pasture flying fields of my airmail days!

After landing, we would taxi by metal bombers lined up wing to wing, each holding the destructive power of several World War II Army divisions. Other bombers would be gliding down, taking off, and moving into position on taxi strips. SAC bases, with their drone of engines, their intensity, their repeated comings and goings, and their periodic swarmings, were like bees' nests grown to titanic size.

I felt power, magnitude, and tempo all around me at SAC headquarters in Omaha. It was in the control center, with its world-wide intelligence and ability to launch hundreds of bombers on intercontinental strikes. It was in the guarded briefing rooms, with their preassigned targets and rolled-up maps of every country stretched along the walls, It was in the red dots on a Mercator projection which marked strategic bases girdling our earth. It was inferred from the knowledge that a command issued by the President over an ever-alerted communications network could, within hours, shower death upon any nation. America's power and magnitude and its strong tempo emanated from the scores of bases, from the target-destruction briefings, from the radar antennae that swept both near and distant skies, but the profound source was a union that was to become fifty states and two hundred twenty million people organized in a social-scientific-industrial civilization that devoted only a fraction of its capabilities to the Army, Navy, and Air Force combined.

Flying in strategic bombers, I sensed a godlike power that comes of viewing the earth below. Continents and oceans were no longer barriers of distance or of substance. The Sierras, the Rockies, and the Appalachians became frozen ripples underneath my wings and the Atlantic and Pacific were glass-smooth tints. Were not Zeus's thunderbolts less awesome than the atom bombs we carried? But I also sensed a separation from earth and men that had not existed in the pioneering days of aviation.

I think of a December flight to Alaska from a southwestern Air Force base—nonstop over deserts and wastelands of my United States, over hoarfrost-covered timber of British Columbia, across white snows and glaciers of Alaska to Fairbanks, where we landed in the twenty-four-hour night and forty-below-zero cold. There I was, in the vague, fascinating, distant land I had dreamed of in boyhood, where, as Robert W. Service wrote, "the Arctic trails have their secret tales" and the icy cold "through the parka's fold . . . stabbed like a driven nail"; where on one went "though the dogs were spent and the grub was getting low." But I saw no sign of trails or dogs on the great air base. The cold had not time enough to stab through my parka's fold when I climbed down from the B-50's heated cockpit into a waiting heated automobile. In fact, I did not bother to slip my parka on. And the mess hall's grub was even more plentiful and elaborate than food had been on the Air Force base we left back in the United States.

I had reached Alaska as by magic, but I had no feeling of the magic of the land itself. The distance and the solitudes of the land, "the forests where silence has lease," the gold of the stream beds, the men who toil for it, the Eskimos, the polar bear and caribou herds—all these existed only beyond the borders, regulations, and habits of the air base. Under circumstances of my visit they remained as far away as they had been from my boyhood home.

Air Force activities impressed on me more and more how a pervasive power and magnitude and a fast tempo separate men from life's natural environment. The increasing power of engines takes us above it. The increasing size of air bases pushes it away. The increasing tempo of human organization, concomitant to power and magnitude, reduces the time available to read nature's qualities. I was always depressed by the similarity and isolation of military air bases. Of course, from a superficial viewpoint living on such bases involved incomparably closer contact between various men and nations than had ever existed before—only hours of flight separated Alaska from the rest of the United States, or from Russia or England or Japan. It required only minutes of radio transmission to accomplish the global interchange of ideas. But as regards the fundamental qualities of life—those that manage to persist because of and despite the hurly-burly of competition and survival—when I landed on a distant Air Force base, I soon felt I might as well never have left the United States.

If the creators of those bases had attempted to take all interest out of travel, a more perfect result could hardly be achieved. The same airplanes landed and took off. The officers' clubs offered the same Bingo games and "one-arm bandits" as did officers' clubs elsewhere around the world. Similar drinks and conversations were served to remove boredom from the same holidays and the routine of evenings. There was almost nothing indigenous to look at: figuratively and literally, the character of the land, wherever it was, had been bulldozed out of the way. The separation of modern man from his environment was never more obvious to me than when a reconnaissance squadron, stationed at Fairbanks, invited me to fly around the North Pole. The invitation was issued casually—"If you'd like to go, just climb on board," the commander of the squadron said—since a round-the-Pole flight was a routine matter for the pilot and his crew.

I climbed on board during the endless night, knowing there was not much to see—shapes of ice on a radarscope, still vaguer shapes when I looked down through a window onto the frigid ocean miles below. Only shifting curtains of the northern lights convinced my senses that I was actually traveling through the remote and hazardous environment described by Peary, Amundsen, and Stefansson, and that the earth's axis we circled, with a touch of stick and rudder and an easy bank of wings, had been the almost impossible goal of determined men who plodded on snow, felt frost on their cheeks, and risked freezing and falls and loss of direction through weeks of short rations. As for me, I spent hours, during that flight to the Pole, sitting on my parachute with my back against a vibrating Duralumin bulkhead, working on the manuscript for a book to be titled *The Spirit of St. Louis*.

Back again in Alaska, with my polar flight in memory midway between reality and dream, I piloted an F-80 in an interception squadron's flight at Anchorage; accompanied Colonel Bernt Balchen, in his B-17, on a trip along the Aleutian chain of islands; listened to a group of businessmen discuss the territory's mineral wealth, growing agricultural production, and tourist potential; and traversed heated tunnels running through snowbanks between heated buildings. Without putting on snowshoes or seeing a dog sled, I learned that Alaska, as a newly established bastion of American defense, with rising population, expanding economy, improving communications, and modernizing cities, would soon be accorded statehood in the union, adding a sixth more land to the United States.

At Alaska in the winter of 1948–49 I left the continent of America behind to fly on around the world—to the Orient, to Pacific islands, to Arabia, North Africa, Europe, the United Kingdom, all potential staging bases for our strategic bombers. Every country I visited re-emphasized the power of America.

My first stop was in Japan, a country still occupied by American military forces. Japan's cities had been bombed and burned, but they had a different appearance from those of Europe. Flying over Tokyo and Osaka I did not look down on the piles of rubble that marked Berlin and Düsseldorf. Instead, chimneys rose stark and stiff, like branchless tree trunks, from littered, ash-strewn ground. Because the Japanese had used wood for most construction, rather than brick and stone, there were few monuments of ruin to war. In a bomber over Japan, I sensed keenly the subjugation of the surrendered people down below, but aside from looking down on its ash-gray cities and the crowded villages around them, I had little contact with Japan during that flight around the world.

My clearest memories relate to this lack of contact. The first takes me to a fighter-littered sky above a United States Air Force base outside Tokyo. I was flying as a member of a P-51 (Mustang) reciprocating-engine flight of fighters. At medium altitude we encountered a flight of new P-80 (Shooting Star) jet fighters from another base, and immediately joined combat. Both types were single-seater, low-wing monoplanes. Since the war was over and only American aircraft were involved, no guns were firing, but the competition was intense and the maneuvering as realistic as though our lives had been at stake. I was especially interested in the engagement because I never before had met a jet fighter in combat, even sham combat. The "enemy" P-80s had a tremendous speed advantage, but our P-51s had much better maneuverability. What were the relative values of such speed and maneuverability in positioning machine guns?

The first pass was almost head on, with the P-80s approaching from higher altitude. I was astounded by the shortness of the burst I could "fire" before I had to break off to avoid collision. Our P-51 flight banked around immediately, but the P-80s were far distant. They broke formation and attacked again from superior altitude. Again it was a head-on pass for me, but when I broke off I saw a second P-80 closing in on my right. I banked steeply to meet it, and found myself so dazed by a high-gravity condition that my senses could not function clearly when the enemy plane flashed through my gun sight.

I pulled up and rolled over in an Immelmann, dove as my vision cleared, and I saw a P-80 in perfect position for my attack. But I felt gravity increasing until my mind dulled and my wings trembled in a high-speed stall. The second's pressure I simulated on the trigger would have resulted in a waste of bullets in real combat. I eased forward on the stick, swept my eyes out through the sky, and saw the other P-51s having problems akin to my own.

None of us was able to get on a P-80's tail. And their pilots did not wait for us to do so. They made their passes and flew on at speeds we could not equal. Then they turned back, each from a different quarter of the sky, to follow again the same procedure. We were always on the defensive, diving, climbing, banking under high G, trying to make of ourselves difficult targets, seldom getting a chance to squeeze our triggers with the slightest hope of a kill. Finally the P-80s broke off and quickly disappeared—easy victors of the engagement. I doubt that any of our P-51s would have survived in a wartime dogfight.

My awareness of environment assumed a different aspect with the drop in tension after the P-80s left. I looked out through air; and instead of enemy planes, I saw coned, snow-capped Fujiyama in the distance. Previously I had been unaware of features on the earth's surface, even of the mountains. My sky full of warplanes could have been at any intersection of latitude's and longitude's degrees. Fujiyama suddenly brought me to the Orient, to the country my wife and I had visited with our seaplane close to a score of years before, to the rice paddies we had driven through, to the crowded village shops and crooked streets we had walked through, to the mat-floored and paper-walled inns where we had eaten and slept, to the singular costumes, ideographs, and artistic style that had so fascinated us during weeks we spent in Japan.

I wanted to land, walk through the village streets again, smell the odors, listen to the voices, step into the shops, to immerse myself in the age and uniqueness of the Orient. But how impossible it would be for me to do so on that Air Force inspection tour! The moment I landed I would be merged into the standardized construction and equipment and procedures of an air base. Recruiting posters on sidewalks all over the United States urged, "Join the military forces and see the world," but once a man in those forces was assigned to foreign duty, how insulated he became from the foreigners he lived among! If he saw the world, it was usually through glass or at a distance. He had little sensate contact with it even under peacetime conditions unless he made an extraordinary effort. He was insulated by "off limits" signs, by commanding officers' restrictions, by the reputation his predecessors had spread among local citizens. Both for cause and for convenience, the military establishment encouraged personnel to remain on their "island of America." "The more I can keep my men on the base," a commanding general told me, "the more trouble I keep out of."

Military insulation was seldom better demonstrated than through an invitation I received, while visiting an Air Force base, "to see Japan." My host was a high-ranking general with a fine military record, a man of unusual ability, experience, and hospitality. He heard me say I wished I knew the Japanese better, and he immediately offered to arrange an occasion the following Sunday. We left his home on the base in late morning, after he had taken a few drinks "to fortify the day"—the general, his wife, and I—in a chauffeured American car. About an hour's driving over country roads brought us to a garden-surrounded building that had apparently been transformed from a well-to-do residence into a semi-American-style restaurant. American automobiles were parked at the entrance. Inside, kimono-clad Japanese waitresses served "inspected and certified" Japanese food to groups of Americans seated on American-style chairs at American-style tables. Guests could order, as most had ordered, American dishes prepared from a post exchange's American supplies. American drinks were served. When lunch was over, the general and his wife stood with several Japanese waitresses while their pictures were taken. Refreshments were again available in an adjoining room, where we could look out over the gardens. In midafternoon we returned to the base and its Sunday cocktail parties, having seen Japan.

From Japan, I accompanied General Earle E. Partridge, commander of the Fifth Air Force, on an inspection tour of bases in Okinawa and the Philippines, and I then flew on Military Air Transport planes westward to Europe, via Thailand, Burma, India, Saudi Arabia, and North Africa—to countries that were bled by war or rebellion, divided by politics, retarded by poverty, lacking in popular education, modern industry, and military strength.

The United States Air Force base at Dhahran, on the desert coast of Saudi Arabia, offered a striking contrast to the bases where I had landed in Alaska. Its air-conditioned buildings were cooled instead of heated, and as I stepped from plane to car a baking air embraced me instead of the stunning frost. At Dhahran I had neither time nor chance to mix with Arabs. Officers of the base and several Aramco Oil Company men outlined for me some of their impressions of Arabia. It was still a country of mystery, of feuding tribes, they said. The sheiks both resented and desired foreigners, both more fiercely than did leaders of most other nations. Foreigners were resented because of fear that they would upset long-established customs—the absolute rule of the sheiks, the ignorance, poverty, and compliance of the peoples and their universal respect for Moslemism. Foreigners were desired because they could find and plumb the fabulous wealth of the sheiks. Tens of millions of dollars yearly in oil royalties built palaces at home, paid for elaborate tours and residences abroad, and bought the expensive automobiles and airplanes that used the oil of the Arab rulers as they grandly toured from place to place.

This was factual information I received at the Dhahran air base, comfortably transmitted, as real and at the same time as artificial as the dish of ice cubes and the cool air in the room where we were sitting. There remained outside the legendary Arabia of scorching deserts, feuding tribes, camels, and oases, where women were bought and sold and vestiges of the slave trade remained, where penalties for crime were parallel to those of Europe's Middle Ages. "It's too bad you can't stay until Friday," a lieutenant colonel said. "You could watch the executions at the city gate. There are usually some hands and feet chopped off, and sometimes a head or two. The sheiks don't like foreigners to watch, but nobody stops you if you slip up quietly."

As I traveled in the postwar period, I saw everywhere the result of fratricidal war. Italy, France, and Germany contained American Air Force bases, and each was receiving funds from the United States to aid in reconstruction, but in none of the big European countries west of Russia was there much economic or military strength. How strong was Russia? That was an enigma, which often resulted in irrational attitudes in other countries that I now keenly realized caused the Soviet Union to assume an importance out of proportion to its accomplishments and numbers, even to its geographical size. Postwar Russia is symbolized to me, in memory, by the steel-helmeted head of a Soviet soldier with his machine gun pointing at me over piles of rubble behind the zonal border in Berlin. Several hundred miles back of that machine gun lay terror. How weak the Soviet Union had been industrially and militarily was shown by the speed with which Hitler's armies had reached Stalingrad and Moscow, and by Russia's desperate need of American supplies. How effective its political, economic, and military activities had subsequently been was established by the fact that nearly half of Europe lay under Russian domination when the war was over.

Russia was still the courageous and confused giant, primitive, muscle-bound, schizophrenic, yet it was able now to challenge, ideologically, politically, and militarily, the United States of America at the very time we had emerged as the strongest power ever known! Our democratic ideology found Communism its most formidable competitor. Our political activities collided with Soviet opposition in almost every country. Our military planning centered on the current possibility of war with Russia.

Soviet ability and our own ineptness combined to create the paradoxical situation we confronted in the aftermath of World War II. We had welcomed Russia into the war as an ally—anything to defeat Hitler and Nazi Germany. But we were strange bedfellows. After condemning her for many years, we had suddenly found Russia to be an essential friend. Thereafter her ideology became less obnoxious. We convinced ourselves that Soviet ideology had been moderating and that it even held similarities to our own. Some Americans in high governmental positions gave secret and, in consequence, traitorous support to Communism and the Soviet Union.

We shipped munitions of war to Russia by ocean convoys to Murmansk and Archangel. We sent warplanes to her via Alaska, where Soviet pilots took delivery and ferried them through Siberia to the European front. At Tehran, Roosevelt and Churchill encouraged Stalin to move Poland's border westward into Germany, thereby compensating Poland for Russian acquisition of territory in the east. We urged Russia to move her forces eastward against Japan, incurring a debt of no ultimate use to us; we held back our armies while Soviet troops occupied Berlin, and agreed to terms that made Berlin a divided island in a Communist sea. Our blindness, resulting largely from our wartime hatred of the Germans and from Roosevelt's and Churchill's popular advocacy of "unconditional surrender," helped Stalin build his extraordinary postwar power and tyranny. Had we been willing to negotiate a surrender with Germany, we could have blocked Russia's movement westward and ended World War II on terms far more advantageous to ourselves. The complete military victories we achieved may have satisfied our pride and hatred, but they cost hundreds of thousands of European lives and they left weak nations on every Soviet border.

The Red Army, which had been cut through so rapidly by German forces in early stages of the war, was within a year of Germany's surrender considered invincible on the European continent. American strength lay in the air and on the sea, and only our air strength could counter Russia's military movements on the European continent that her vast territories spanned. Our supply of atomic bombs was increasing rapidly. If Soviet armies moved beyond critical lines we established, SAC would strike with its appalling atomic power—from bases in Alaska, Japan, Okinawa, Arabia, North Africa, Italy, France, Germany, the British Isles, and Iceland. The devastation of Hiroshima and Nagasaki by our first crude bombs would be trivial compared with what would happen in the Soviet Union. We had power to hold in check Communist ambitions; Stalin fully realized it.

"But time is with Russia." This argument was often made in the late 1940's. "We're much too idealistic. Stalin knows we won't commit aggression. He can wait until he has an atomic air force, too. He thinks we won't drop atomic bombs then, no matter what he does in Europe or Asia, because we'll know he'd retaliate by atomic-bombing us in America." A complementary theme went this way: "Even if there is atomic war, Stalin knows he's bound to win in the end because Communism survives chaos. What does he care if a hundred million people are killed?"

War with Russia lay in the background of American military thinking. What capabilities did Russia have today? What would they be a year from today? In five years? In ten? Air Force discussion of these questions revolved about SAC and SUSAC—the

Soviet Union's Strategic Air Command. Our knowledge of Russia's industrial awkwardness, coupled with current Intelligence reports, left us with little doubt that American warplanes were more advanced than Russia's, that we had more of them, and that our scientific laboratories and factories put us in a position to hold the aeronautical leadership we had achieved—if we made sufficient effort. But how was that effort to be spread? Billions of dollars could be saved by laying out military programs intelligently.

The radar stations we were building in Canada and Alaska would give warning of a Soviet attack in time for us to launch a strategic counteroffensive and alert interceptor squadrons and anti-aircraft batteries—providing the Soviet attack came over land, at usual heavy-bomber altitudes. But suppose enemy pilots detoured to approach our continent from the ocean. SAC bases near the coast might not have enough warning to get their planes off before the bombs hit. We would need radar stations at sea as well as on land. Of course the current SUSAC bombers could not penetrate or detour far and still have enough gasoline in their tanks for a return trip to Russia. But they could refuel in air or fly one-way missions. Our own target plans embraced such expedients.

But after a costly radar-warning network was installed, suppose Soviet bombers came in at treetop level, under the radar screen. We would need thousands of volunteer "bird watchers," with telephones or radio transmitters at their sides. Or suppose enemy submarines crept close to American shores and fired atomic-warhead missiles. Suppose saboteurs struck SAC bases at a coded hour. What should our plan of action be in the coming long-range-missile era, when interhemispherical transit time would be reduced to minutes? Such questions interwove with Air Force speculation about the Soviet Union's menace. On scientific standards, we had far greater military power. Certainly we were more industrialized, better educated. Our democratic system offered equality and freedom to more people than ever before in history. It was highly disturbing to have our sureness, intelligence, and domination challenged by the ideology of Marx and the still relatively primitive peoples of the Soviet Union. Possibly much of our frustration arose from the fact that our tremendous scientific power was fettered.

Our belief in nonaggression and in political self-determination, together with a Christian righteousness, prevented us from using our weapons to maintain the physical domination we now instinctively felt essential—unless Russia made the unlikely move of striking first. We could not reconcile our dream of a universally prosperous and law-abiding brotherhood of man with a multipolitical world. Given the rise in human population, we did not ask ourselves how life can be prolific without being competitive, and how it can be competitive unless new opponents arise to replace defeated foes.

"We are old. You Americans are young. It is your turn to carry on." It was in England that I was impressed most clearly by America's new position of influence and power. England, that fabulous country of my boyhood, whose king was emperor of the finest empire the world has ever known, with dominions and protectorates spread over continents and oceans, was now aged and declining. In her place my United States would have to carry on! We had emerged from World War II the leader of civilization.

The breakup of the British Empire was, of course, due in large measure to the exhaustion of the British people after two incredibly wasting wars, but more because of the desire of men and nations for independence—a desire that was encouraged by the Christian-democratic ideology of British missionaries and by British statesmen and civil servants in every quarter of the earth. World War II only accelerated the empire's breakup. It had begun much earlier. Men have always, it seemed to me, divided themselves into forces of conquest and of independence. In each instance their desires tend to blind them to dangers that accompany their cause—to the vulnerability of domination on the one hand; to the risks of freedom on the other. In a fight for independence, initial success gives way to internal contention. The "rights" of conquest and of freedom have conflicted throughout history. The seeds of breakdown are sown by every imperial conquest. From America to India, from Ghana to the Fijis, England's wars planted, fertilized, and watered the desire for independence.

As both an early and a major contributor to the British Empire's breakup, the United States had encouraged and acclaimed the drive for independence on the part of colonial peoples. Then how could an Englishman say with conviction: "It is your turn to carry on"? Why should it be necessary for anyone to "carry on" in England's old position? Are not different systems best at different times? The answer is rooted in those primary factors of life to which all ideologies must eventually conform: Life is inherently prolific and its units therefore must compete, whether as individuals or as organizations. In every country, after the war, the population was rapidly growing, and every nation wished to increase its prestige and improve its living standards. This was true not only of whole nations but also of groups within them.

What had been called impossible in prewar England, the break-up of the British Empire, was called inevitable after the war was "won." In less than a decade such phrases as "England's wealth is too great" and "Her influence is too widespread" had changed to "How else could it have been?" or "It was always only a matter of time." "I have not become the King's First Minister to preside over the liquidation of the British Empire," Churchill had said. He then proceeded to do so. Still, we Americans could not believe this to be an inevitable cycle. For peaceful, well-meaning, honest, and intelligent men, there must be some way of emerging from the exercise of power into a universally secure and prosperous future. We had learned from the British Empire's disintegration. We had studied errors of the past.

Idealism, rationality, and intuition churned and soon hardened into the conclusion that America must maintain its own security to safeguard its civilization. Surely we would be able to maintain order and security as we exercised world leadership. We emerged victorious from two world wars with a population approaching two hundred million. Our standards of education were high. We had organized the resources of a virgin continent to support our industry and agriculture so that our advancing systems of communication made us commercially present around the world. As a result of our open-market economic system, our food was plentiful and cheap, our housing modern and elaborate—if not as abundant for all our people as it could be—and our hospitals well equipped. Labor-saving devices had become commonplace possessions of American families, and as though to culminate our knowledge,

235

enterprise, and power, we exclusively had produced atomic energy.

Should not the world's strongest and wealthiest nation be suited to take world leadership? We had no empire to trouble us. We had all the land we desired. We espoused the equality and dignity of man. Despite the hatreds left by war, which dimmed with time, we felt good will toward all peoples of the earth, and wanted to help them emulate our wonderful ways of life. If it was our turn to carry on, then our American democratic-scientific-Christian idealism was ready to accept the challenge. We sprang forward with limitless ideas for the welfare of mankind, packed with righteousness, prosperity, and peace. Under our leadership the United Nations organization was established. Into war-torn, underdeveloped, and poverty-stricken countries we would discharge a flood of our advice, education, commerce, and tourism, thereby improving foreign economies and raising foreign standards. We would set up enterprises, staff schools, build highways and hotels, and laboratories and shops, and demonstrate the productive qualities of Christianity and the practical principles of equality and freedom. We would display our American system openly, as the outstanding example of twentieth-century progress. Right progress, unprecedented progress, would avoid the major conflicts and tragedies of previous generations.

NINE

Plastic Discs and Marble Bones

The hand and finger of God in the Sistine Chapel are the symbol of creation, God as man with life emanating from his fingertip. A spark leaps to earth from heaven on the frescoed vault. The mystic power of a finger points to futures beyond rationality.

But I am not in Rome. I look down to a table, not up to a vault. I must stop dreaming and listen to the lecture. The hand and finger are living flesh instead of paint. They belong to an Air Force general who points to a conceptualization of destruction, not creation. My mind snaps back from Vatican walls, over an ocean and past stretches of two continents. Snow-dusted plains of Nebraska replace Rome's seven hills. My river is the Missouri, not the Tiber. I stand in a briefing room of the Strategic Air Command at Offutt Air Force Base, near Omaha. Uniformed officers of varying ranks group with me about the table. It is the early 1950's.

This finger, too, seems to be pointing with superhuman knowledge, as though modern man had taken the place that God held in Michelangelo's vision. My eyes follow to a black-and-white large-scale map of a foreign city, to streets, avenues, and river bends.

"This represents an area of ninety percent destruction." The general's left hand puts down a transparent plastic disc, tinting red the city blocks beneath it. "It would take three atomic bombs of such a kiloton type . . . to inactivate . . . to cause a casualty rate . . ." His voice continues to instruct. Words and paper, stratagems and plans, with only the faint drone of engines warming up to connect them with reality. The plastic disc, the city beneath it, in a few more minutes will be filed away in a briefing-room drawer. But memory leaps westward across six thousand miles of land and sea to circle black-haloed ashes in Japan, to the thought and the reality and the explosion of Hiroshima—sparked from the hand of man, not God, an act released through Adam's knowledge.

Another map is placed on the table. This time it is the American city Chicago, a perfect radar target, with its river and lake shore-lines. The general speaks again: "Soviet bombers would come in across the Pole. . . ." Again my mind contorts through space and time.

Across the Pole! That vague area of drifting ice and frozen tundra, never open to man's transit until my own generation took to airplanes. The top of the world. My wife and I made one of the early flights across its arctic edges in our black-and-orange monoplane in 1931. Ice cakes jammed against endless miles of frost-gray coastline as the slanted sun of August rode close to its horizon. A few Eskimos emerged from the landscape, their huts separated by days of "mushing" along bleak and barren shores. We refueled by means of cans and funnels at Canadian Air Force caches; we squeezed under clouds, skirted mist banks, frightened caribou herds by our passing over, landed our seaplane on bays, lakes, and lagoons, from Moose Factory through Aklavik to Nome.

The airplane brought a touch of magic to a land of dog-sled travel. My wife was the first white woman to arrive at the trading post of Baker Lake, in Canada's Northwest Territories, and she carried the first orange to reach that northernmost Alaskan settlement, Point Barrow.

Across the Pole! Twenty years later, riding the flight deck of a four-engine Air Force reconnaissance plane, I circled the North Pole. We took off in the day-long night and sub-zero cold at Fairbanks, and followed our line of longitude through northern lights, which flashed and faded, lifted and fell like a mammoth curtain across the sky. I could imagine that we were actors practicing a drama to be enacted on a gigantic and fantastically illuminated stage. We had banked around an imaginary extension of the earth's

axis, eighteen thousand feet above the ice field, and reset our course
—back through northern lights to the south, toward the bleak
Alaskan shore.

It seemed impossible that such a wilderness might be turned into
a highway for assaulting forces of the future. Even though Air
Force visits to the North Pole were frequent by the 1950's, arctic
navigation was still uncertain. We depended on the averaging of
gyroscopes, and on picking up Point Barrow's beacon when we
were closer to the coast. As long as the sky was clear, we could
check our position with star sights. Only a few months before, a
plane lost its way and crash-landed on the Greenland icecap, more
than a thousand miles off course.

Across the Pole! I return to charts, maps, and pointing fingers in
Nebraska. Aeronautical science has by now developed so that opposing bombers can fly north, then south to strike targets in distant
hemispheres with accuracy. A few words of command, issued from
the building where I stand, can send dozens of squadrons swarming
up through polar skies. Wings of atomic bombers based in California and Maine, in Florida and Washington, in Texas, New
Mexico, Massachusetts, and Montana flying nonstop, refueling in
air, each plane with more striking power than a whole army of the
past, are ready to hit targets in Europe or Asia within hours. Every
moment of the day and night aircraft fly on practice missions,
covering projected distances and using projected targets similar to
those already assigned in case of war. And for the crew in their
pressurized fuselages, cruising high above the earth, reality is as
lacking to the senses as it is in the neon-lighted briefing room where
I watch a finger obliterate a city on a map.

Map and finger fade. A luminous arm swings around the radarscope's green dial. A vibrating roar inside the fuselage shakes into
my ears and body. Parachute straps press flesh to bone, while eyes
smart from lack of sleep. I am flying with the 509th Atomic Bomb
Group out of Walker Air Force Base, New Mexico. We have
crossed the United States and Canada in our B-29s, staged at Goose
Bay, Labrador, and circled the magnetic pole. We have flown missions sixteen, eighteen, sometimes twenty hours long as part of the
rigorous training in preparation for attack. We operate day after

day, miles above the earth, above and through storms, independent of the weather. Gyroscopes, chronometers, radars, and dozens of other instruments hold our planes to schedule and course.

I sit on a stool in the fuselage where no window opens to earth or sky. A flight engineer at my shoulder glances along crowded rows of dials and switches. An automatic pilot holds altitude and heading. The air-speed-indicator needle says we are cruising at more than three hundred miles an hour. Fluctuating shades on our radarscope define a broken coastline underneath us.

There's a tap on my shoulder. I snap open my safety belt and crawl forward to the cockpit. The sky is blue. The storm's edge has passed. Other bombers of the squadron ride our wings while below us, reflecting the sun's blinding rays, are Greenland's snows and glaciers. A sprinkle of black specks on white, dime size, between icecap and sea, is the Air Force base at Thule. But we will not land. To simulate the wartime mission assigned to us, we are to swing westward and cross the bleak arctic wilderness of Ellesmere Island. I return to my stool in the fuselage. When I go forward again we will probably be close to the Beaufort Sea, but my sense of direction would have been the same had we set our course for Russia, on the other side of the Pole. Russia is that enigmatic country where airmen in bombers similar to ours are kept in training to attack us.

When my wife and I flew to Russia in 1938 to study its aviation, we had waited for days in London before the American Embassy obtained final clearance for the trip. Then, with typical Russian hospitality, after the typical and unexplained delays, we were offered our choice of landing at either Minsk or Mogilev in the expanses of White Russia to refuel. At the same time, we were informed that almost all pilots refueled at Minsk because facilities there were better and it was not as long a flight from Warsaw.

We were flying the Mohawk, the single-engine, tandem-cockpit monoplane with a black fuselage and orange wings that had been built to our specifications by the Phillips & Powis Aircraft Company at Reading, in England. When we arrived over Minsk there was no airdrome at the location given us by the Russian Embassy in London, and no sign of flying activity at an airdrome we saw much closer to the city. Since our tanks still held plenty of fuel, we decided to continue eastward.

When we reached Mogilev, we looked down on what appeared to be a training field for fighter pilots. Blunt-nosed single-seaters, in various stages of maintenance, were staked down along the field's edge. Cowlings and parts of engines lay scattered about on the ground. Our Mohawk had barely rolled to a stop on the grass surface when we were surrounded by officers and soldiers. Obviously our arrival was both unexpected and unusual. Shouts and scowls made it only too clear that the Russians were not pleased at seeing us. They motioned us to follow their cars to a place beside a line of red flags and signaled that we should cut our engine. I jumped down onto the ground and handed over the documents and letters given us by the Russian Embassy in London.

No one there understood English, but we did not have to understand Russian to realize that from that moment our actions would be subject to our hosts' approval. While our papers were being examined, a squadron of fighters came in to land, apparently back from some mission. They were of the low-wing type, with air-cooled engines, retracting landing gears, and fabric-covered wings. It took but a glance to see that they were inferior in design to England's Spitfires and Germany's Messerschmitts. Everything on the airdrome seemed deficient, I realized as I looked around: the hangars, the automobiles, the haphazard handling of planes, the signs of pilot laxity.

Soon the commander of the base arrived, and smiles began to replace scowls. We shook hands. A young officer was produced who could speak a little English, with great effort. What did we want? Gasoline? What kind? How much? I was concerned about the grade of fuel used at Mogilev, and decided to take on only enough to leave a safe reserve in our tanks for the flight to Moscow. My wife and I wanted to start as soon as the fueling was completed, for we knew people would be waiting for us on the airdrome at Moscow. But the interpreter smiled and said: "The commander wishes you to take something to eat at his house."

We bumped over the field to a building near one of the hangars. The commander went inside, and came back about five minutes later. We drove to another building, a large wooden one, which was the restaurant. Inside were a number of long wooden tables surrounded by heavy wooden chairs. Pictures of Lenin and Stalin hung on one wall. A dozen or so men in coats or shirt sleeves and women in cotton dresses who were eating looked curiously at us. We sat down at one of the tables with the commander, several flying officers, and our interpreter. A plump woman in an apron and bandanna began placing hot dishes in front of us: soup, fish, steak, eggs, onions, tomatoes—the platters kept on coming, well filled.

While we were eating, bars of formality dropped, one after another. What kind of weather had we flown through from Warsaw? Would we not like to see the city of Mogilev? Was my wrist watch made of gold? The food was good, the hospitality was genuine though cautious. Soon, everyone at our table was happy and laughing. But hours of the afternoon were passing, and I kept looking at my watch. At the end of each course we tried to leave, with no success.

Finally, we took off from the Mogilev airdrome at 5:52 P.M., local time. I set the throttle fifty revolutions above our normal cruising. Moscow was still a long way ahead and we were not well equipped for night flying. But the weather was good, and the northern twilight long. We landed at 8:34. Soviet officials welcomed us. Greetings were exchanged, photographs taken. Members of the American Embassy—Alexander Kirk, the acting ambassador; Lieutenant Colonel Philip R. Faymonville, military attaché, and others—were waiting to take us into the city. They had driven out to the airdrome several times that day because reports came in saying we would arrive at noon, at three o'clock, at six. Finally, a message from Mogilev announced that we had landed and were staying there for supper. In the limousine, driving to the embassy, we saw that the city of Moscow had changed noticeably since our last visit, five years before, in 1933. It had better streets, more cars and traffic lights. Fewer people were queued up in front of stores.

Within the hour following our landing, we were initiated into the tension and divergence of opinion that existed among foreigners in Russia. Our own people at the embassy grouped into "antis" and "pros." The one talked of secret police and fear and liquidations; the other of five-year plans and improvements and the terrible state of Russia before the Revolution. "We cover our telephones here," a member of the staff said, lifting a sort of quilted parrot cage from a parlor table to show the phone beneath it. "We never know when they're rigged up as recorders. These people like to listen in on conversations. We search our automobiles, too, each day." You felt every move you made was being watched, and that everyone was hesitant to talk for fear of getting into trouble. In the end you found yourself growing cautious in speech and action.

One object of our trip was to attend the annual air show, an event of great political importance. For this we received special tickets to the roof of a building where members of the Supreme Soviet were seated. The airdrome held a crowd of eight hundred thousand people. The show began with a parade of balloons, each with a huge picture of a political leader hanging below it. A formation of training biplanes followed, piloted by students, "who work in a factory during the day and learn to fly after work," our interpreter volunteered. Next came a formation of training monoplanes. Then strings of gliders appeared under tow—as many as nine gliders brought up behind one multiengine transport. There was mass parachute-jumping, individual aerobatics, and precision flying, which ended in sham combat by the Red Five, a set of star military pilots. The flying was good, though not generally of the best, and the planes were in varying degrees inferior to their counterparts in the major Western countries.

My wife and I remained fourteen days in the Soviet Union on that trip. We were guided through the museum of the Red Army and saw Lenin's body in his tomb. We were shown Moscow's subway, a marvelous ballet, and were driven past buildings that had been constructed since the proletariat took control. I visited aircraft factories, experimental laboratories, the Aviation Academy, the War College. We flew under Soviet escort to Kharkov, Rostov, Kiev, and Odessa. We inspected a flying school, visited a collective farm, watched a gas-mask parade, met scientists, officers, politicians, and aviators. Everywhere the tables were stacked high with carafes of vodka, bowls of caviar, and plates of elaborately garnished food. Men laughed and drank but spoke with caution. We talked of the weather, the vodka, the subway, about what a wonderful country Russia was. There was an obvious embarrassment whenever technical subjects were approached, and it kept our conversation away from industry and science. When I inquired about Russians we met in Moscow in 1933, our hosts of 1938 could remember only one—a bearded polar scientist, who for some reason, of which they were uncertain, had been in jail. "You get used to that when you live here," an American said later. "You see them for a year or two, and then they disappear."

The route we followed out of Russia passed over rolling fields of the Ukraine, mile after mile of furrows and stubble, with houses, barns, and sheds huddled together in thatch-roofed villages instead of being scattered like ours back in the United States. Under clear skies and with the relaxation that always comes from being homeward bound, I began to filter my impressions of the Soviet Union. Hospitality, propaganda, and a carefully escorted tour combined could not mask the primitiveness of Russia's strength or the struggle occurring within her civilization. I had seen nothing that rivaled America's scientific progress. The military and industrial development in Stalin's Russia could hardly be compared with that in Hitler's Germany. The Communist government was trying desperately to catch up with the accomplishments of the other Western countries. Designs were inferior, production methods less efficient, maintenance poor, and operation unreliable. The number of worker hours required to complete a project was extraordinarily high.

The word "mediocre" seems to me best able to describe Soviet existence in 1938. There was little that clearly excelled: the ballet, possibly a short stretch of Moscow subway—I could think of nothing else. But there was more: the magnitude of the country, its tremendous natural resources, the mass of its population, the determined ruthlessness of its government, the courage and endurance and genius of its men and women. How were such elements to be valued on our modern scientific scales? What did the future hold for the nation that had produced a Peter, a Dostoevsky, a Lenin?

My next contact with Russians came seven years later, in June

1945. World War II had ended. I was standing in the destroyed city of Dessau, near the western entrance to a pontoon bridge across the Mulde. It was at this point that American and Soviet troops had met. Now, several GIs stood guard on the riverbank while a single Russian soldier, with submachine gun slung from his shoulder, paced back and forth on the opposite shore. A long line of refugees plodded westward across the short bridge, ragged, dirty, a human stream in flood. A thinner line of freed prisoners and refugees moved eastward into territory now occupied by Soviet troops. I had traveled freely through western zones of Germany, which were controlled by American, French, and British armies, but where East met West, I stopped. I did not cross the Mulde. Papers that opened gates and brought salutes in the Western zones were of doubtful value in the East in spite of the alliance forced by war. Under Soviet occupation both men and women disappeared. Every refugee you talked to had a story of loss to tell.

But now I am no longer standing at the Mulde. I stand before a chart showing a proposed line of radar stations. "We must have enough warning to get in the air with bombs before our bases are destroyed," the general's voice continues. "Of course, from a purely military standpoint, the ideal situation would be for us to strike them first. In war, the aggressor often has a huge advantage. Take, for instance, the Japanese attack on Pearl Harbor, in 1941. . . ."

Memory takes me out of the briefing room again, to look down through the window of a Marine R4D after a twenty-six-hundred-mile flight to Hawaii from San Diego. Hulls, masts, and smokestacks of American naval vessels stick out at crazy angles from the water, wrecks of ships caught off guard by Japanese aircraft, the battleships *Arizona* and *West Virginia*. In 1941, bombers came in over Diamond Head to strike our fleet at anchor in Pearl Harbor. Now, they would "come in across the Pole." And if they come, we must have effective warning of attack.

We had warning of attack at Pearl Harbor, but it was not effective. A radar operator early in the morning of December 7 reported blips as the enemy planes approached, but they were thought to mark a friendly squadron flying in from the mainland. If American crews had been alerted, our fighters could have intercepted the

Japanese warplanes at sea, while our bombers counterattacked their fleet. Our ground guns would have inflicted heavy losses within the target areas. In fact, had Japanese Intelligence determined that American forces were well prepared, it is unlikely that Pearl Harbor would have been attacked.

"Of course, the Russians are constructing lines of radar stations, too. Their fighters are getting better, and their defense network is improving every year. We'd get through, but not without some losses. . . ."

Any pilot who has undergone interception, or heavy antiaircraft fire, has great respect for modern weapons of defense. He recalls black bursts in nearby space, deadly streaks of incandescence curving through the sky. Fighters and ground guns of World War II took a heavy toll of attacking aircraft. Bomber crews struggled back with wounded men in crippled planes to tell of entire formations lost, of miles of air strewn with plummeting bodies, swinging parachutes, torn wings and fuselages, of tracers and ack-ack.

Tracers and ack-ack! Fragments of steel fly like pollen through the air. Ack-ack! Those stemless flowers of the sky, so black and full of poison. Ack-ack! No one who has met it doubts the ability of defense to dull attacking power.

"When the Russians get their homing missiles in operation, they can make it pretty rough in the vicinity of our targets. But by that time, we'll have wings and guidance for our bombs. We can launch them a hundred miles or more away. And of course we are developing countermeasures. . . ."

Defense versus offense: how that problem has woven through my military life ever since cadet school. I had chosen "Pursuit" for my career. I loved small fast planes and combat aerobatics. Our mission was to hunt and destroy "enemy" aircraft. In sham combat, we would come in high, come in low, attack from every quarter for our theoretical kills and losses. To confuse defensive fire, we dove so close together that on one of the missions we flew, a wingmate and I once collided and had to bail out with our parachutes. That was in 1925, at Kelly Field in Texas.

The pilot of the DH we dove on was Lieutenant Russell Maughan, of "dawn-to-dusk-flight" fame. In the sham battle, he claimed two enemy fighters destroyed, and, of course, we said we shot him down before the collision took place. The argument continued in barracks and hangar, but since all of us were using imaginary ammunition there was little we could prove.

"You know those turret guns can't hit anything! Did you ever try them on a tow target?"

"By God, you fellows lost two planes! They crashed and burned, didn't they? Have we got to show you a photo of the wreckage to prove it?"

With "Pursuiters" determined to attack, how could "Bombers" live, once intercepted? But with prototype bombers almost equaling the speed of pursuit planes, how could "Pursuiters" in the future climb fast enough to intercept?

"We want fewer guns and faster climb."

"No, more guns and surer kill."

"Put in armor plate and leakproof tanks so that shellfire can be absorbed."

"Leave out armor plate and turrets to gain maneuverability and speed. Then you won't be hit."

In 1939, a colonel, I sat as a member of the Kilner Board, in Washington, to discuss advanced designs for Air Force warplanes. We considered carefully the proposals that a class of bomber be built to carry a single five-hundred-pound bomb, with the design emphasis on speed and range, and that a class of fighter be built to carry a single machine gun, its design emphasis on speed and climb. Three years later, when I was working as wartime adviser to the Ford Motor Company in Michigan, the Liberator produced at Willow Run had racks for eight thousand pounds of bombs, and the Thunderbolt (P-47) fighter on which I was running high-altitude ignition-breakdown tests was equipped with eight fifty-caliber machine guns. Defenses were still being penetrated. Attacking forces were still suffering losses.

In the Pacific, I piloted a Lightning (P-38) in a four-plane raid on the island of Palau. The Japanese, with dozens of fighters at their disposal, failed to intercept us, even though we shot down three of their planes and damaged a coastal vessel. Less than a week afterward, I watched one of our radar-equipped Black Widow

(P-61) fighters make a successful interception. I saw tracers stream through the darkness until a terrible howl pierced the night to signal the death plunge of an enemy bomber. Radar guidance of fighters in World War II stimulated the construction of jet bombers to fly at higher speeds and altitudes. To counter these, in turn, target-seeking missiles were later developed.

In every branch of combat, stimulus produces response. On the ground, trench fighting resulted in the tank, and the tank led to the bazooka. The surface fleet brought submarines, and submarines brought depth charges. Each development in offense spawns its defense. Each defensive countermeasure starts research in offensive counter-countermeasures. No matter how brilliant its developments, however, defense lags behind offensive warfare. Even when the aggressor is thrown back, it is usually after great loss of property and life to the defenders.

After World War II ended, I drove a Renault Quatre Chevaux nearly sixty thousand kilometers through the devastated countries of Europe. On an afternoon in northern France, while I was en route from Frankfurt to Paris, I noticed two low domes barely visible from the grass on a hilltop half a kilometer to the side of the road. I recognized them as positions of the Maginot Line. Only a few years before, details of the great Maginot Line had been highly classified military secrets. Barbed-wire entanglements had surrounded the forts, and in prewar flying between France and Germany, I had been careful to stay within the corridors between prohibited zones of the Maginot Line—crosshatched in purple on my map.

I parked my little car on the roadside and climbed the hill. Cow paths wound through rusting barbed-wire and weed-cluttered approaches, heedless of faded "Dangereux-Militaire" signs. There were no animals or men about. The first dome I saw sheltered an observation post. Its thick steel-alloy armor was torn like a sheet of paper where an explosive charge had been laid upon it. I pushed some brambles out of the way and looked down between jagged edges into an unlit recess of the abandoned "modern" fort.

The danger of relying on defensive warfare was attested by the abandoned and briar-covered domes of steel that stretched from the border of Belgium to the border of Switzerland. "Hardly had we declared war when, being in no state to take the offensive, we began to look forward to our annihilation," wrote the French airman Antoine de Saint-Exupéry. "We set up our haycocks against their tanks; and the haycocks turned out to be useless for defence."

Military briefings kept me in close contact with the dual modes of warfare. It was the soldier's role of survival through a scientific age. One day, I might be sitting on a committee whose mission related to getting nuclear warheads onto enemy targets regardless of methods of defense. Another day, I would be sitting on a committee charged with evaluating projects for intercepting and destroying nuclear warheads approaching at meteoric speeds. Some officers and scientists believed that nuclear weapons of aggression would make all defenses obsolete. Others had concluded that atomic explosives coupled with advancing electronics could make defenses more effective than they had ever been before.

Working with the Strategic Air Command initiated me into the fantastic complication of national survival in the environment of modern science. Following World War II, Secretary of the Air Force Stuart Symington and Generals Hoyt Vandenberg and Lauris Norstad had asked me, as a consultant to the Air Force, to study ways of increasing the combat efficiency of SAC. I found myself entering the extremely sensitive issues of interservice rivalry. Clearly, our Strategic Air Force could not attain maximum efficiency without maximum dispersion of its bases, and since seven-tenths of the earth's surface is water, maximum dispersion cannot be achieved without the co-operation of the Navy. As things were, however, the Air Force and the Navy were not co-operating in strategic bombing. High command had assigned this exclusively to the Air Force, whose bombers had been designed to operate exclusively from land.

I believed the Navy had lost an opportunity in the field of strategic bombing through its infatuation with combining the speed of wings and the size of ships in building aircraft carriers. As a result, the tremendous potential of flying boats for dispersal and strategic strike had been neglected. Admirals of the aircraft carriers were as blind to developments that were antiquating their vessels as had been admirals of the battleships a generation earlier. Few recognized the potentialities of flying-boat strategic bombers and submarines carrying missiles.

The services were trying to continue that custom of warfare that had developed under an environment of generations past—when fifty yards dispersed the field guns, and armies walked, and navies really sailed—before barriers between land and sea had been reduced by the more universal element of air. What possible difference did it make to our nation whether wheels, wings, or hulls were used to achieve victory in battle? It seemed to me that the fighting services should be assigned to missions rather than to the elements. I found many Air Force officers who agreed in this respect, but they usually advocated a "one-uniform" solution to the problem. To this solution the Navy was opposed, not without good reasons.

This argument was not going to be resolved by debates on strategy. It was inevitably a civil issue: the Congress would decide, if at all. At Pentagon conferences I realized that military power is rooted in civil power. To appreciate civil power one must first realize the lack of it. I had that experience in China in 1931, when the Yangtze River was in flood.

My wife and I had flown our Lockheed Sirius seaplane from New York to Tokyo over the great-circle route through Canada, Alaska, Siberia, and the northern islands of Japan. Then we bent toward China, and landed on Lotus Lake, outside the old walled city of Nanking.

The lake showed clearly enough on our map, rather small, with a sharply inked shoreline. But when we looked down from the sky above Nanking, it had lost its identity completely in the boundless yellow waters of the flood. Lotus Lake and the Yangtze River were indistinguishable as a huge inland sea. Nanking looked more like a diked island than the capital city of a nation comprising more than four hundred million people.

After landing, we taxied toward a point of dry ground that extended out some distance from the city wall, and dropped anchor about fifty yards offshore. Several Americans from the legation and a group of Chinese officials arrived to welcome us. Of course Lotus Lake had no facilities for seaplanes. The anchor we carried in one of our pontoons was too small for safety if a storm arose. I asked, through an interpreter, for a larger one. An hour later four slender Chinese coolies appeared carrying a huge iron anchor. It was unlike any I had seen before, but it was heavy and cleverly shaped, with spaded hooks. It would hold our plane, I felt assured on first glance, through any weather short of a typhoon. The coolies brought the anchor out in a rowboat, heaved it overboard, and handed me the free end of a rusting big-link chain, which I fastened to the plane's pontoon halter.

As a routine precaution, I inspected the chain, link by link. It was strong enough to have tied a barge to a tugboat—until I came to the anchor end. There, holding the last link to the anchor ring, were three rusted strands of bail wire! I could have jerked them apart with my hands. That anchor and chain came to symbolize China for me. The country was basically so great, yet so much of its life seemed to be tied together with a few rusted strands of bail wire.

After arranging for guards to watch our plane both day and night, we drove with members of the legation staff to a nearby gate in the Great Wall of Nanking. Bunched up against the outside wall wherever earth still rose from water were groups of refugees, packing into whatever shelters of matting, boards, and ragged canvas they could improvise. Unknown millions of Chinese had been driven from their homes. Cholera, dysentery, and typhus were spreading like the flood itself. Communications were broken. Land travel was impossible, and boat travel both difficult and slow. Hundreds died each hour. To organize relief it was important to know what parts of the valley were flooded and where refugees had gathered. Planes from the British aircraft carrier *Hermes* were helping to chart areas under water, but their limited fuel capacity prevented them from covering the periphery of the flood.

We soon realized that ours was the only plane in China with the necessary range. So we canceled the scheduled plan for our visit and replaced ceremonies of welcome by surveys of the disaster. Day after day we flew over flooded villages and cities, charting the weird inland shore on our maps—the sharp line of water against a hillside, its marshy vagueness in a field, a village half in lake and half on land, with streets ending as canals.

Scattered about the entire area, like seaweed tossed by storm, were the refugees. They were huddled on dikes, on ancestral grave mounds, on sampans floating above the fields they used to hoe— dozens on an eroding bank of the Grand Canal, thousands crowding an isolated hilltop that rose above the tide. In the security of our cockpits, well fed and warm and dry, it was impossible for us to realize the despair and tragedy below. Most of those people would get no outside help. Relief organizations did not have enough food to take care of them, and even if there had been food, there was no way to distribute it in time. Starvation would continue. Diseases would increase. Tens of thousands more were doomed to die. The Chinese system of flood control was typically tied together with bail wire. The strands had snapped in the storms.

The people's ignorance multiplied the difficulty of helping them. When I tried to carry a load of serums and medicines from Nanking to a plague-ridden city, I almost lost my plane. That was in late September. I had two doctors, one American, the other Chinese, on board in addition to the cargo. We landed above fields outside the walls of Hinghwa, near the center of a huge flooded district. The nearest dry land was twenty-five miles to the south. My mind eased as the anchor rope slipped through my hands to mark several feet of water. Before landing I could not be sure there was enough depth for the pontoons, or that a grave mound did not form a shoal just beneath the surface.

A sampan had sculled up to us. The Chinese doctor hired it to take him and the packages of serums to a city gate. Of course I did not understand what was being said, but a good deal of arguing took place and several minutes passed before the bargaining was completed. By that time dozens of sampans had surrounded us and dozens more were converging from all directions. The people in them were starving. You could see hunger in eyes and faces. They made cups of their hands and pretended to be eating with chopsticks. They thought the packages we brought contained food— they would not believe the denials of the Chinese doctor.

Before long the sampans were jammed beam to beam. Together they must have formed an acre or two. Thin ragged figures began moving toward us, jumping and crawling from boat to boat. A sampan with an open fire burning on its deck pushed under our left wing, and thick smoke curled up around the entering edge. Men were yelling and shouting. I had started to climb out onto the wing, to assess the danger of the fire beneath it, when I saw the Chinese doctor's sampan sinking under the pressure of too many feet. He had told me he could not swim. I watched him drop the package of serum he was carrying and jump into an adjoining boat as his went down. Water began pouring over the gunnel of the second boat. He jumped into a third. A fight started over the package of serum. I saw countless hands hanging on to the wings and tail of our plane. Our cries and gestures to keep off had no effect. The sterns of our pontoons were already pushed under water by the weight of human bodies. It reminded me of a frontier raid I read about in childhood—Indians in overwhelming numbers swarming over the fort's stockades.

Under my parachute I had wedged a thirty-three-caliber Smith & Wesson revolver. It was part of the emergency equipment we put on board in the United States. But to draw one gun against hundreds of sampans, crowded with desperate people, seemed a fool's move. At that moment the American doctor shouted, "Have you got a gun?"

"Yes, but some of the men in those boats must have rifles," I answered.

"You can be sure they don't," he shouted. "Every man with a gun has gone to the hills with the bandits." I knew the doctor had spent years in China. He had lived close to the people, but his statement did not convince. A single rifle would outmatch us and I was a perfect target, standing in my cockpit silhouetted against sky. Then a second sampan went down under the Chinese doctor. A man crawled onto the plane's left pontoon. Another followed on the right. Everywhere there were staring eyes, grim faces, gaunt bodies.

Our plane would sink. We might not get out alive. The man on the left started climbing onto a wing. I pulled out my revolver and pointed it at his belly. He stopped. I whipped my gun over to the right side. The surge forward ended, but people on the left closed in. I turned back quickly, firing into air, and aimed my gun at the nearest man. His expression changed. He raised his hands, stepped backward. Each side thought I had shot someone on the other. I covered always the nearest man, and he always moved backward. Hands let go the wings and tail. Sampans began to shove away. We pulled the Chinese doctor back on board, hoisted anchor, and took off.

We had modern serums in our plane. There were modern doctors in Hinghwa. But the "bail-wire" transportation available between our anchorage and the city gate was inadequate to hold the two together. How many people died as a result, I do not know. The waters of the Yangtze were still rising. The hungry would go on starving and the diseased dying until nature and China's primitive methods brought relief. How long would that take?

I had seen the hungry starving at Hinghwa. I saw the diseased dying at a refugee camp near Nanking. My wife and I circled over the camp in our Sirius, and then went to inspect it on the ground. I wanted to have a better idea of what we would report when we flew over similar camps in outlying areas. "How many people would you estimate the camp holds," I was asked as we started out with a car from the American Legation. I thought of the low hill, protruding from water, we had looked down to the day before. On it was a cluster of newly erected, mat-roof hovels. "Roughly five hundred," I replied.

"There are twenty thousand!"

Whole families squatted in dirt-floored pens less than eight feet square. Cholera was rampant. The stench was awful. If there were latrines about—I cannot know—they were apparently unused. As we walked by a family "pen," one of the children, a half-naked boy of eight or ten, collapsed and lay quietly in the filth. No member of the family moved; none seemed to notice him; each looked sick and dazed. "Cholera," the Chinese doctor beside me said. "He will die within twenty-four hours. It is too advanced to cure." And we walked on along one of the narrow alleys between pens.

The people in that camp were considered lucky. They were near the capital city of Nanking, close to the navigable Yangtze. China's resources and transportation system combined to allow them a dole of rice each day in addition to some medical attention. Most of them would live to return to their farms, rebuild their houses, and raise more crops and children. But hundreds of thousands were dying, tens of millions starving, in that great inland lake. The magnitude so dulled our senses that after a while compassion for the individual was lost. It was as though we were conscious of a pain so great and universal that it masked single sharp stabs. We walked around a half-dead body on the road, glanced at children wrung with cholera, flew over countless people whom we might have saved from death had we been able to drop sacks of rice.

Our job was to chart the borders of the flood on the earth's surface below us—pencil line on paper map, drawn across a railroad track, through a village, over a refugee camp, all of which were unimportant to the life in our Sirius, which existed within a framework of its own. Occidental aeronautical science had given us the magic power of flight. Occidental medical science had injected us with antigens that made us immune to plagues. Occidental economy, founded on incentive and technology, supplied us as plentifully with food as though we were living in an Iowa farmhouse instead of flying over the flooded Yangtze Valley. What happened underneath our wings had no permanent effect on us. After our survey was completed we would fly to other parts of China, into India, possibly westward through the Middle East, to Europe, around the world.

A sense of being overwhelmed pervaded us. China was overpopulated for its present resources. There was not enough food to go around in the best of times, yet the population was rising rapidly. More than ten million children were born each year.

Transcontinental flying makes you realize what tremendous civil power exists in the United States of America. I had made dozens of flights across the continent, but American power impressed me most keenly when my wife and I flew our reconditioned Sirius from California to New York after our experience of surveying the Chinese floods. For this flight, it was a landplane again. We sent the pontoons ahead by rail.

A strong wind blew on our day of take-off. San Fernando's fertile valley opened wide as we climbed, and the great city of Los Angeles spread flat to the south—miles upon miles of homes and stores, long avenues crowded with cars, huge pseudopods of suburbs. There was Hollywood, which supplied theaters of the world with films; Santa Monica, where Donald Douglas produced his famous aircraft; Long Beach, with its low hills and forest of oil derricks; Pasadena and Robert Millikan's California Institute of Technology. Farther east, orchards sloped up to mountains. Railroads and highways ran everywhere, guiding their traffic to Mexico, to Canada, to cities and villages all over the United States. In the tremendous strip of coastal country that stretched north and south below us, there was no sign of famine, poverty, or flood.

Of course, you would not expect to see a Yangtze flood in southern California. Heavy rains came at times but they were too soon drained off into the Pacific, leaving river beds gravelly dry. The problem was to get enough water, not an excess of it. As the population of Los Angeles increased, the water shortage became acute. And what had the citizens done? They called on engineers to bring water from the Sierra Nevada Mountains. A great aqueduct carried it over foothills and desert for more than two hundred miles.

The sky hazed quickly on our flight eastward. The wind carried us along at half again our normal cruising speed. It also picked up fine sand from the earth's surface, hoisting the particles to altitudes far above us. I worried about the effect such grit-laden air would have on our engine, and tried to climb over it. But when the altimeter needle marked fourteen thousand feet, the sky overhead was still yellow and the great ranches of Arizona had disappeared in dust. After that I kept nosing down to hold contact with the ground and landmarks with which to check our navigation. Clouds of sand billowed eastward like wind-ripped smoke. Wings flexed and our cockpits shook in turbulence.

When we reached the Panhandle of Texas we had descended to five hundred feet and dust was thickening. I decided to land. It was not an easy task, because I could not see far enough to pick out a strip of prairie to come down on. I watched hazy patches of earth rushing beneath us until one appeared to be reasonably smooth and level. Then I made a three-hundred-sixty-degree turn and set the Sirius's wheels on the downwind edge of the area I selected. I could not see ahead the length of our landing run. Fortunately there were no trees or clumps of brush and no prairie-dog holes where the wheels rolled.

I did not try to taxi after the plane came to a stop. I cut the switches. My wife and I climbed down from our cockpits and dug holes in the baked ground for wheels and tail skid. We had to leave our goggles on to keep the whipping sand out of our eyes, and we tied handkerchiefs over our faces. Grains of sand prickled against cheek and neck. The wind was gale force. It would have been dangerous for a biplane, with its lightly loaded wings, but our Sirius trembled only in sharper gusts.

We had flown over a wagon trail several seconds before landing, so we walked in the direction where I thought it lay until the plane behind us was almost blotted out by dust—that was less than a hundred yards, because blowing sand was thickest close to the ground. Then my wife stood still while I walked beyond her another hundred yards. She could see the plane. I could see her. But no wagon trail came in view, and while the storm continued we did not dare spread apart farther.

We returned to our cockpits, slid the hatches shut above us, made supper out of emergency rations, and prepared for the night. Combining the front cockpit with the baggage compartment gave plenty of room for a bed and we carried a big sleeping bag in our equipment for use in forced landings. We were tired enough to sleep soundly in spite of wind whistling through cowlings. By morning the storm had abated. When I looked out through the cargo-compartment hatch, soon after sunrise, I could see for a mile or more. The sky overhead was clear. We were in rolling plains country on which cattle grazed. A ranch house squatted next to its windmill less than a thousand yards away.

Flying eastward from Texas, our route took us over an area called the "Dust Bowl" because sandstorms had taken place there so frequently in recent years. Hundreds of thousands of tons of topsoil had been stripped from the fields. Prairies were washed with streaks of earth as though a gigantic paintbrush had been swept across them. Many ranch houses we saw below us were abandoned. Parched earth blowing away with wind—what a contrast this was to the mud and floods of China's Yangtze Valley! And what contrast it was for the human victims! When people in the United States lost homes through natural disaster, both government and private relief organizations sprang to their assistance. Trains, cars, and buses carried them to areas where housing and food could be obtained. New plans were laid to control a flood by dams and levees, to hold down topsoil by plowing alternate strips transverse to the wind. In America people did not starve by millions. Our civil power was too great.

As we approached the state of Missouri, oil fields and wheat ranches merged with farmlands of the Mississippi Valley. Below were dairy barns, silos, pastures, quarter sections of corn and hay. More than a dozen Yangtze-peasant huts would fit into a single barn. One American farmer owned enough land to cut across hundreds of Asia's rice paddies. Over China we had looked down on young and old hoeing the earth or hand-nursing blades of rice. Over the United States we saw machines pulled by tractors—gang plows, harrows, binders, combines. A Chinese peasant could work a lifetime without earning enough money to buy parts for an Illinois farmer's combine.

We flew for hours over the rich cornfields of Indiana and Ohio— taut lines of roads and fences marking out the sections and extending north, south, east, and west beyond the horizons we could see. There was a schoolhouse within reach of every child. Thriving towns and cities were connected by highways, wires, and railroads, maintained continuously.

Lying at the Appalachians was the city of Pittsburgh and its airport—laid out by cutting the top off a mountain. This airport was another example of the U.S.'s civil power. What other country had the means, at that time, to cut the top off a mountain so its airplanes could operate with greater efficiency and safety? Pittsburgh's engineers were renowned for their methods of handling earth. It could be argued that the economy of the city depended on it—on moving coal for the furnaces, iron ore for the smelters, dirt to make way for streets and buildings; on shaft mining and open-pit mining; on the transportation of millions of tons of material by truck, rail, and boat; on the design and construction of machinery to do all this at a cost that would bring expanding markets for steel everywhere. There were no bail-wire links in Pittsburgh's chain of activities. They stretched out in all directions to surround the world: steel rails enmeshing the products of a continent, plates for ships transporting commerce across oceans, pipes for gas lines carrying fuel between fields and refineries.

Cruising eastward over Pennsylvania, we saw the power that modern organization can give to man in the railroad entering a cliff, in the filling stations where concrete highways crossed, in the towers and electric lines that went slashing out through forests. The crude or subtle marks of modern science and engineering spread through valleys and spilled over ridges. New York was the eastern terminus of our transcontinental flight. At first, one saw a distant, off-colored patch of earth with the North Atlantic sweeping endlessly beyond. Then the scene hardened into streets and buildings and wharfs as we approached and descended.

Of all the world's cities, New York contained the greatest civil power, the center of about seven million people concentrated in areas of buildings that formed a single metropolis ahead of us. But New York, symbolizing power, always brought my mind and intuition into conflict. When I first flew eastward to the city in my *Spirit of St. Louis* in 1927, I had experienced both repulsion and fascination. I was repulsed by its bigness, luxury, and artificial life, fascinated by the stupendous forces it commanded and by its influence in the material accomplishments of man.

New York's influence had brought me from St. Louis to compete in the nonstop Paris flight. That influence had held me, as an adviser to C. M. Keys's Transcontinental Air Transport Corporation, to Juan Trippe's Pan American Airways, to Daniel Guggenheim's Fund for the Promotion of Aeronautics, and in other ways. To take part in the development of aviation, I had concluded, New York was the best headquarters I could choose. But on returning to the city from my frequent flights, I always felt I was leaving a better life behind me. Sometimes I circled to delay my landing. I would bank and let a wing blot out the expanse of buildings below while I looked westward to the mountains or eastward to the sea. New York, so important to aviation's future, then seemed unrelated to my existence in the cockpit. When I lifted my wing again, what difference did it make whether it had blanked out a forest or a city? The basic qualities of life would continue.

I became conscious of a relativity of time that escaped my mind and senses in ordinary moments. My airplane was my world to me: the world itself was quite unessential. I entered a core of timelessness in a turbulence of time, like the eye of a tornado. Permanence lay only in the instant. Outside, all was fleeting, my flight and my life, and when I raised the wing even the great city down below seemed impermanent. Riding the wings of power, I realized the fragility of power exposed to the dynamic elements of time.

How man is hypnotized by his surroundings! After I was back on the ground, driving my car in the traffic of Broadway, Madison, or Fifth, I felt surrounded by eternal permanence—the high brick walls, the massive steel of skyscrapers, the power of millions of men and women combined in economic organizations that channeled the stream of human life through their doors. The very tempo of the hurried city drummed off my awareness of the sky. Could anyone travel through New York without realizing that the great civil power of America gave firm roots to our military forces? Was it not wonderful to take part in the life of such a city? How could one do more to contribute to the progress, security, and survival of America?

It was close to twenty years later that I stood in the heart of another city and questioned the effect of power on survival. I had been walking along Pompeii's spade-excavated streets, stepping across wheel ruts worn inches deep in blocks of paving stone, and trying to recall school-day Latin as I studied painted signs on store fronts, faded but still clear.

The day before, in Rome, I had walked through crumbling arches where emperors' chariots had rolled, past the rostrum from which Cicero harangued his crowds, past the Vestal Virgins' temple, the Colosseum, and the cellars of Nero's "Golden House." Flying or driving, since World War II ended, from England to Austria, from Germany to Libya, from Spain to eastern Mediterranean coasts, I had passed ruins of the city of Leptis Magna on Africa's yellow shore, the stone baths at Baden Baden, the arched aqueduct across the Gard, watchtowers in Swiss Alpine passes, palaces that Hadrian and Augustus built. Faint signs of civil and military power remained in every Roman structure—in ships black-outlined in old Ostia's mosaics, in tombs lining Via Appia Antica for kilometers out from Rome, in conquests immortalized by carvings on broken blocks of stone.

At a street corner of Pompeii I halted to stare at the volcano in the background, resting tranquil as a human tomb. The belching horror of the Romans' day had become a landmark of beauty in our own. Those graceful slopes, with pastel purple curving and melding into pastel blue—how could they have spewn into the sky ash and molten lava? Was there a better symbol of the outcome of power? Vesuvius, Pompeii, the Roman Empire, all erupted through their crowning hours of celestial time. And for the life of Rome, as for the matter of Vesuvius, the very act of erupting seemed to have accelerated a predetermined end. Great monuments are thrown up, arches, temples, volcanic slopes, and always these manifestations of power are followed by decline—the lava slopes of Vesuvius and the marble bones of Rome.

What makes human power erupt like a volcano? What destroys it? The civilizations of Rome, Greece, Egypt, China were all eruptions from a human core. All left memorials of stone, of a bursting and exhaustion. Colosseums, temples, pyramids, great walls. Vesuvius, Popocatepetl, Fujiyama. Nature's volcanos and man's ruins alike show the catabolic tendency of power, the impermanence of magnitude.

TEN

The Primitive
Passing

Into the environment of wartime advances in aviation and out of the postwar dependence on aircraft as the primary means of defense was born the fast, nonstop intercontinental transport plane. It more than fulfilled the visions of my early aviation years, overcoming all geographical barriers, bringing peoples of the world together as never in the past, spreading the American way of life from pole to pole. Executives could fly overnight to Europe or the Orient for business conferences. Tourists could spend days of adventure on any continent with no more than a fortnight's holiday.

To move those passengers through their warp of time and space required the use of techniques attainable only through new mechanized environments. It required also a regimentation of body and mind that not all men were accepting without qualm. It was so different from my New York–to–Paris flight in the *Spirit of St. Louis,* when I never lost contact with the world and its weather, when the altitude was a part of my blood and breath, when I saw waves, touched rain, and sensed my connections to the trees and animals below. In those days engines failed and pilots made forced landings. Then, I was always conscious of the primitive elements of life, of the reasons for storing a rubber raft behind me in the fuselage, of the possibility that within seconds after my wheels struck water I would be submerged in the cockpit, pulling the sheath knife from my pocket and cutting through fabric skin to reach the emergency equipment. I knew in my bones that the water was icy, that I would have to pump up the raft by hand in a tossing sea, that my clothing could not be dried, that I would be short of food, and that rescue ships were unlikely to sail through that far-northern ocean. The feel of life was keen because the sense of death was near.

As civilization advances, man grows unconscious of the primitive elements of life; he is separated from them by his perfection of material techniques. He keeps insulating himself with a complication of devices that increase his security but also suppress his senses. He forgets that he is a naked animal subject to natural forces of earth and universe.

Measured on a time scale, in technology we got where we were going faster than most thinkers believed possible, and therefore had progressed. But had we advanced human satisfaction? During the years of my postwar traveling over Pan American routes, I saw how our American way of life was admired and criticized, desired and dreaded, copied and rejected by peoples of other countries. Men and women abroad tended to look on the United States as a fable become real, as a country having almost a planetary difference from their own, one of incredible richness, with a people wielding scientific magic that built skyscraping cities, automobiles by the millions, and homes filled with machinery, a land where work hours were short, where pockets were bulging with money and refrigerators with food, where such bountifulness existed that billions of dollars' worth of factory and farm products could be given away each year to needy governments.

At the same time that foreigners considered American life to be fabulous, they were likely to think of the United States as an adolescent nation with the strength, exuberance, and emotional immaturity to be found characteristically in early youth. They were amazed by accounts of our cities' gangsterism, disturbed that race riots occurred within our presumably equal and democratic system, baffled by our intrigue in the Bay of Pigs fiasco, which followed so closely on our righteous attitude toward the British-French invasion of the Suez. They had serious reservations about the tempo of life that accompanied political and business success in America. "I run a business to support my home," an Englishman said. "The American seems to run his home to support his business."

Wherever I traveled I encountered this mixture of admiration and rejection, and incredulity, regarding the United States. The Germans, while grateful for American aid in reconstruction, could not understand why we expected them to be ready to help us fight the very Russians who under our unconditional-surrender terms were allowed to take large parts of their country. Frenchmen found it difficult to rationalize our emphasis on law and justice with the long-drawn-out Chessman trial and the morbidity of delaying gas-chamber execution repeatedly. The South Africans perceived the utmost hypocrisy in our demands that they return their country to its native tribes while we smugly retained possession of a country we had ruthlessly plundered from its native tribes. Arabs felt our support of Israel to be an act of unrealistic and diplomatic immaturity in view of their own strategic influence in the controversial Middle East. Nationalist Chinese were astounded by American blindness to the towering Communist menace throughout Asia. Orientals could not reconcile our immigration quotas with our professed ideals of equality. Peoples of all countries were troubled by the contrast between our sermons on international morality and the facility with which we had dropped our first two atomic bombs.

The welcome extended by foreign governments to American assistance had in part thrown us off guard. But, in hindsight, why should our assistance not have been welcomed at the same time our wisdom and leadership were questioned? American dollars could be converted into countless political and economic benefits, from rebuilding France's war-torn cities to buying rice for India's population. American commercial investments and military bases increased prosperity as well as security in many countries during an extremely critical period. American slogans of freedom, nonagression, equality, and mutual trust were acceptable to idealist and demagogue alike. Our leadership would have been easier and more successful had the concepts of freedom, nonaggression, and equality been easier to define. But we soon found ourselves involved politically and militarily in countries whose divided peoples were so antagonistic to each other that many of them accused us of being "enemies of freedom," "supporters of tyranny," "suppressors of the common people," of opposing the very qualities to which we felt passionately committed. To give aid, one must inevitably favor one action over another. A foreigner bearing gifts is at once welcome and suspect. We were shocked by the underground resistance, by the student demonstrations, by the cry "Yankee go home!" Russia encouraged this hostility and the political schisms that produced it.

It is true that governments we supported sometimes were not democratic, their peoples not free by American standards. Much as we disliked doing so, we were at times forced to choose between aiding a government distasteful to us and letting Russian influence take hold. To our dismay, our attempt to lead the way into a peaceful and prosperous era for mankind had involved us, step by step, in a "cold war" against Russia. It was a war in which ideals easily lost their grounding as each side strove to gain advantage through competing propaganda.

The human intellect's impact on the instincts and means of biological survival has brought into competition subtleties of propaganda, rationality, idealism, psychology, theology, science, and of memory and compassion. The selected effect of all this information—some of it so recent in evolutionary time—remains to us obscure, its future beyond the reach of extrapolative probabilities. Man's predominance over all other forms of life shows that physical prowess, however inherently essential, is no longer the determining factor of human competition and survival. This may explain in large degree America's schizophrenic policies following World War II. On the one hand, our instinct, forged through experience, convinced us that to survive it was necessary to be militarily strong. On the other, our intellect warned us of what Lao Tse said of armies— that where they stand, briars and thorns grow. After an atomic war the "thorn" field would be far more terrible than any to which mankind had had to adapt before. We realized, at least vaguely, that the enemy we faced was a member of our own civilization, and that internecine struggle accelerates the breakdown of civilization.

In the early years of aviation, after my own barnstorming, carrying airmail, and flying to Europe and South America in my *Spirit of St. Louis,* I felt sure airplanes would bring peoples of the world together in peace and understanding. Possibly more than anyone else I had had an opportunity to envision the aeronautical relationship of peoples to each other and to world geography—a relationship that would be vastly different from any of the past. I had known youth's fascination with man's conquest of the skies. I had experienced the freedom of course-setting on an airplane's compass. I had helped to quicken the intercourse of cities. I had flown nonstop between hemispheres and between continents.

I realized that to a flyer's senses the earth's size is inversely proportional to speed. With a swoop of my wings I could land at a town or on a farm below me. With a glance from my cockpit I could encompass a desert, a valley, or a mountain range. Flying put me in closer contact with the earth through distance, a comprehension devolved from a spatial viewpoint. I could experience the ocean's squalls and the hill's air currents as well as altitude's distant contours and horizons. For me, the airplane shaped the near and the far into a single form of gigantic intimacy.

The tremendous economic success of Americans tends to separate them from whatever foreign environment they enter. Our tourists and businessmen abroad are treated as commodities, and in conditioning them to this the first-class hotel is especially adept. For this reason, a serious problem encountered during the growth of international airlines was the lack or shortage of first-class hotel accommodations. This problem was made pressing along Pan American routes by the high standards demanded by North Americans. I once flew into Pará, Brazil, on a Pan American Clipper, and spent the night at what seemed to me a much better than average hotel. The dinner was good, the water free from chlorine. "You ate *native* food and drank *that* water?" a stewardess exclaimed the next morning. "We eat only food that is specially prepared; and we bring bottles of soda pop from the plane to brush our teeth with."

As air passengers multiplied from dozens to hundreds, then to thousands and hundreds of thousands, and finally became more numerous than passengers traveling by great ocean-going ships, every city's best hotels competed for their patronage and catered to North American desires. Since the American's desires were created and satisfied by his home environment, he encouraged the reconstruction of that environment wherever he went abroad. Tourist-frequented shops, resorts, villages, and even areas of cities re-

Working in a Rockefeller Institute laboratory with Alexis Carrel
(seated left), John Zwick, and William Haratonik, 1935

rocket test in New Mexico
th Harry Guggenheim (left)
d Robert Goddard, 1935

Visiting Igor Sikorsky to observe
helicopter demonstration, October 1940

In Germany with U.S. Military Attaché for
Air Truman Smith (right), *c.* 1936

Testing effects of altitude in altitude
chamber at the Mayo Clinic, September 1942

After going
on active duty
as a colonel
on return to the U.S.,
1939

With Colonel Charles MacDonald and Major Thomas McGuire
in the South Pacific, 1944

On round-the-world inspection trip for the Air Force, 1948-49

Conferring with Boeing staff and Air Force personnel,
Wichita, Kansas, 1948

Receiving
the Guggenheim Medal
in 1954
from Harry Guggenheim

At Glenn L. Martin Company, Baltimore, in 1954

With Juan Salcedo, Jr., on a wildlife conservation trip
to the Philippines, *c.* 1969

With Juan Trippe and Harold Gray on
Pan American directors round-the-world inspection trip, 1967

Agta huts on northeast coast of Luzon

With Manuel Elizalde (striped shirt), Dr. Robert Fox (dark shirt), and Panamin troopers, in mountains of Mindanao, Philippines

At Yale Medical School, with drawing of his perfusion pump, *c.* 1965

In a Taboli hut in the Philippines, *c.* 1970

vamped their character to increase their profit from the increasing airline traffic. The resulting standards, prices, and customs isolated airline travelers more and more from the basic character of the countries and peoples they visited.

I never feel more keenly the separation of tourist from native life than when I stay in an "American hotel" abroad. All one finds is sterile food, sterile rooms, sterile buildings, sterile life; and it is offered to those travelers "who demand the best" for twenty or fifty or one hundred dollars a day. I would rather sleep in a flophouse with a flea. I once did that when I drove my Renault Quatre Chevaux, late at night, into an isolated village of northern Spain. Lights were on in the only hotel—men talking, drinking, singing. I was assigned a bed in an upstairs alcove, open to a hallway, at a cost equivalent to less than fifty U.S. cents. Supper, still available, was good—tough, simple, and anything but clean. The smell of a leaking old toilet permeated the entire hotel, and the blankets had gone so long unwashed that I unrolled my sleeping bag on top of them. A flea shared my sleeping bag that night, and thereafter accompanied me for several days on my trip. But there were no porters, bellboys, uniforms, air conditioners, electric-motor-circulated fountains, or artificial plants. I saw Spain, heard Spain, smelled Spain, and tasted Spanish food.

When I was a combat pilot, it seemed clear to me that competition and survival in the modern age were bound to science, industry, and organization. The possibility of primitive peoples actually competing with civilized nations never entered my mind. Modern war blinded me for a time to the primitive's strength and importance. I had assumed that the primitive was retreating. It retreated in my father's stories of his boyhood on the Minnesota frontier, where Indians fled from Army rifles and forests fell to pioneers' axes. It retreated in my own boyhood, westward across North American plains, as motor roads webbed the country and as grazing lands gave way to fields and fences. I saw it retreating in Panama when the canal cut through the isthmus, and later in the Antilles as transport planes brought tourists in by thousands. I saw it retreating in Canada and Alaska, where trading posts sold factory products to Eskimos; in the Marshalls, where Marines bought war clubs with cast-off cotton clothing; in the Solomons, where bull-dozers slashed bush and timber to make way for military camps.

In the interior of New Guinea, the natives of isolated lake vil-lages I looked down on, from the cockpit of my P-38 fighter, seemed apart from the main human stream. I knew they were mem-bers of my own species, and they interested me, as do all forms of life, but, like the animals around them, they existed by either the oversight or the toleration of the civilization of which I was a part.

But if you approach the primitive with a viewpoint unrestricted by modern civilization's time scale, you find that over and over again it has followed the principle of Lao Tse's "good general" in taking nine steps backward before taking one forward—steps back-ward toward its earth-penetrating roots. Even so, how great that step can be! Think of the marble bones of ancient cities scattered over the world.

Many years after the war, on Africa's continent, I came to ap-preciate the primitive framed by its own environment. Kenya was soon to confirm its independence, and the British government had well-advanced plans to relinquish colonial control. What would happen to the tribal relationships once the British forces left? Many Europeans thought Kenya would "blow up like the Congo." An unstable mixture was present. The agricultural Kikuyu had bred rapidly during decades of colonial control, while the nomadic Masai had not; Kikuyus numbered over a million, the Masai about a tenth that number. The Kikuyu needed land. The Masai had more than they needed.

The great lands of the Masai comprise plains, valleys, and moun-tains in southern Kenya and northern Tanzania, and hold ele-phant and lion, giraffe and buffalo, zebra, wildebeest, rhinoceros, hippopotamus, wild dog, and hyena, and an almost unbelievable variety of other animals and birds. They are lands where tribal conflicts still take place, fought with spears and shields, bows and poisoned arrows.

I had asked a Masai friend, an elder who had been educated both by tribal custom and in a mission school, would not the Kikuyu, after British law and order left, simply take what land they needed from the Masai?

"We believe," he said solemnly, "that when men are brave enough they do not have to fear greater numbers. Masai have often fought against greater numbers, even one to five."

"But you fight with spears," I said. "After the British go, the Kikuyu may buy rifles."

"The Masai are very highly trained spearmen," he said. "There are very many trees and bushes in our country. A rifle is not a great advantage. We are not afraid of rifles."

I did not question his statement about Masai bravery. It was traditional. But he had not convinced me. Certainly the primitive is no challenge to the civilized in fields of arms. The challenge exists in competition at deeper levels, which I recognize most clearly when I change quickly from civilized to primitive environments. I experienced such a change in the winter of 1964–65, when I took my wife through Masai country. It was my third trip to East Africa.

Just before we left, I had been immersed in briefings and conferences on future jet-powered civil aircraft. Speeds up to two thousand miles an hour had been projected. Costs up to thirty million dollars per plane had been discussed, in New York and later in Paris. During the Paris conferences Anne and I attended a formal dinner, with elaborate foods and wines. Its service and table settings and the gold-walled, tapestried salon were like those of Louis XVI's Versailles.

Then we had flown to Nairobi, in the heart of East African game country, where we rented a four-wheel-drive Land-Rover, bought a small tent, food, water containers, kerosene lantern, and other essential equipment, and set off for Masai lands to the south. We took no guide or servant.

Our first night out we selected a campsite on the right bank of the dry Selengai, about two-thirds of the way between Nairobi and the Tanzania border. Twilight had fallen when we arrived at the river bed and shifted into four-wheel drive to cross it. Animal marks were everywhere—tracks in sand, dung piles, water holes. A quarter of a mile upriver, elephants were standing.

We decided to pitch our tent between spreading acacia trees near the edge of a ten-foot earth cliff, from which the river bed stretched clear both ways. It seemed a perfect location, a few paces downriver from a well-worn game trail, and sheltered by a jut of bank so that we were not likely to be in the way of night-cruising elephants. The remaining minutes of twilight gave us time to bring in fire-wood—long-dead branches and tree trunks, enough to make embers that would last the night. Two giraffes watched us, their heads rising high above bushes some fifty yards away. Elephants plodded up and down the river bed. Two bulls stopped, faced our camp, and stood watching, like the giraffes inland. Their tusks grew whiter as their gray bodies merged with the night. We pitched tent by the light of our campfire and a rising full moon. Nearby, hyenas yelled, and a herd of zebra galloped upriver as we cooked supper.

The tent's cloth walls let through all the jungle noises—lions roaring, elephants wallowing in a water hole across the river bed, a rhinoceros clumping on the game trail. That night we became a part of the jungle, living as primitive man lived in ages past. I felt as separate from my civilization as I had felt from East African animals at that formal Paris dinner a few days before. My sense of immersion was deepened because the only weapon I carried was a Masai spear, which I used as a post on which to hang our kerosene lantern.

When we woke the next morning, elephant, giraffe, and zebra were gone—replaced by a herd of cattle at the water hole. Several Masai elders, naked except for the dark-red folded blankets slung across their shoulders, stood in an acacia tree's shade. Their spears, stuck upright in the ground around them, were within easy reach. Other Masai were repairing damage done to the water hole by elephants during the night. Spear-carrying boys herded the cattle. Thin clouds of dust marked the approach of other herds of cattle coming for water.

Three women, close-shaved bronze heads above wide bead necklaces and long red cotton dresses, came to stare at our tent and Land-Rover. An elder approached, spear shouldered above swing-ing blanket, unaware of his nakedness. He pointed to his left eye, swollen and bloodshot. I sponged it with a bit of cotton my wife had dipped in saline solution, and he appeared satisfied. Before leaving he pointed upriver, straightened seven fingers, and said: *"Simba."* Seven lions were nearby.

The Masai were ready to protect their cattle from all carnivores.

Even herdboys were expected to chase away marauding lions. I remembered listening to a Masai describing how to kill a lion with a spear. "The impact of a charging lion is very great," he said. "You must hold your shield high enough so its claws cannot get above the top." As he took his stance and grasped his spear, the implement became transformed from a harmless pole to a quivering arm of power. It was the same difference as between seeing a rifle in its case and holding one, loaded, at your shoulder.

The Masai were spearmen and seldom carried bows and arrows. Elephant, lion, rhinoceros, buffalo—there was no animal of the jungle they had not been known to attack. The spear was their primary weapon, too, for the tribal battles that were fought, usually over stolen cattle. An intra-Masai war had been fought only three days before, and less than a half hour's drive from the road we had followed to our camp. Four thousand warriors were said to have formed one side; twenty-five hundred, the other. Eighteen men were killed. The "weaker" side had won. Europeans in the area were concerned lest fighting break out again after women of the defeated tribe chided their men, as was apparently usual, about losing both cattle and the battle.

Our sense of being part of the environment passed once the Masai arrived. We could not talk to them at the water hole. None of them spoke English, and of their language I knew but a few words. Aside from the visit of the women and the elder, they carried on their work as though my wife and I did not exist. I was reminded of the South Pacific natives whose villages and campsites I visited during the war. I once watched a line of naked spear bearers walk along a Biak coast past our military camp. Three or four miles away, American and Japanese forces were engaged in combat, just as Masai forces had been engaged not far from our camp. In the South Pacific, American troops barely noticed natives walking by. I may have been the only man who stared at those spear bearers. Unless they were struck accidentally by a shell or bomb fragment, Biak natives had been as safe as my wife and I were in the midst of Masai tribal conflicts. A minority, in each instance foreigners, was separate from the immediate issues of life and death.

Among the tribes of East Africa I felt I had moved backward

thousands of years. There, man lived surrounded by other animals, many stronger than he; he was independent of machinery, even the wheel. Many Masai think "civilization" is not progress. They feel sorry for the white man because he has lost the contact with nature. They question our basic values. "You speak of freedom in your country," a Masai elder told me, "but we have known freedom far greater than yours."

Is civilization progress? Living among the primitive always makes me wonder. On what yardstick does one measure? In the environment of America or Europe, progress usually seemed to me as obvious as civilization itself. It was in the airplanes I flew, in the cities where I landed, in the factories I visited and the motor vehicles that carried me to them, in the machinery inside. There was progress in food processing, childbearing, nursery nipples, diapers, shoelaces, and razor blades. In fact, anything thought to be unprogressive was antisocial. But progress can be conceived, I think, only within an accepted framework.

In Africa I felt surrounded by the framework of living events, rather than of works, and there civilization lost much of its importance. In building a campfire and pitching a tent, I realized how little planning—checking and rechecking—basic life demands. A quarter hour gathering wood, another quarter hour setting up poles and cord-tautening cloth sheets, a few minutes to draw buckets of water from spring or stream, to light a lantern, to spade a hole—simple acts, simply learned, repeated.

Contrast this to the elaborate organization that supports apartment houses, electric appliances, oil furnaces: the pipelines, the dynamos, and the high-tension cables that supply them; the electricians, well drillers, agents, postmen, accountants, executives, and other specialists who make them work; the architects, builders, bankers, masons, carpenters, plumbers, truck drivers, trainmen, miners, lathe operators, insurance salesmen. Camped in its jungles, I feel that Africa's contribution to the progress of mankind will stem from its primitive and sensate qualities, and that through these qualities a wisdom is imparted to the intellect essential to the very existence of human life.

Yet, simple as it seemed to us, our camp became elaborate compared with a Masai's hut of poles and cow dung. The cans of food we opened belied our sense of independence of civilization's ways: meat from Argentina, peas from California, peaches from Japan, English marmalade and biscuits. The Masai could live indefinitely on blood and milk from his cattle, and occasionally a little beef. Ships, warehouses, and canning factories were not life lines to his diet.

Only from the framework of the primitive can one realize what fantastic complication our civilization depends on and imposes, what intricate organization the status of a "modern" requires. Africa brings to the intellect's awareness the sensate qualities of life. These are recognizably simple, found in the dances of the Masai, in the prolificacy of the Kikuyu, in the nakedness of boys and girls. You feel these qualities in the sun on your face and the dust on your feet, in the prick of thorns and from the heat of embers, in the yelling of hyenas and the bark of zebras.

The primitive teaches that life itself, unforced life, is progress, a fact our civilization tends more and more to overlook. In Africa you sense basic qualities of evolution that made life what it is today, made the variety of animals around you, made yourself. In wild animals you see the biological perfection of life that preceded the human mind's impact, a perfection resulting from nature's "ruthless" evolution, in which some hereditary assets are encouraged to multiply and some hereditary defects are either destroyed or suppressed. Thus the giraffe developed its reach, the gazelle its fleetness, the hyena its bone-crunching jaws. Africa's jungle does not seek equality, forgive error, or recognize compassion.

In the Masai you see the human mind's effect on instinctive evolution. Though toughened and muscle-hardened, they have defects of both form and function that show the lack of selection that becomes obvious whenever one compares man to wild animals. For generations they have suffered their own and more advanced civilization's diseases, and for a shorter time they have used civilization's medicines. Tribal taboos and privileges have long interfered with nature's biological selection. By American standards, the nomadic Masai represent a primitive life. By standards of biological evolution, they have already left the primitive far behind.

The spear-bearing Masai, who are superior to Kikuyu in battle, have been thinned in numbers by civilization's diseases, while the agricultural Kikuyu, previously suppressed by Masai raiding, have proliferated under British colonial rule. East Africa's environment as created by the white man's domination leaves the Masai's future insecure. Strangely, it is the withdrawal of the dominating white man that does so.

During early days of British occupation, Masai leaders signed a treaty that guaranteed them possession of huge areas of grazing land "as long as trees grow and rivers flow." When Great Britain's government withdrew from Kenya, in 1963, it seemed doubtful that the new African government would support the old British treaty. The Masai, holding vast tribal areas, but in numbers a minority ridden by disease, and bordered by the numerous and land-hungry Kikuyu, faced uncertain times.

My first impression of Africa, after arriving from New York, was the backwardness of almost everything I saw—stores, dwellings, costumes, customs, schools, roads. My second impression, which was inevitable but nonetheless overwhelming, was of the biological vitality of Africa's sensate life. I became aware of the lack of this vitality in the civilization I left behind in America and Europe. Soon I wanted to renounce the ways of civilization. Why had I conformed so long? The flames of a campfire holding back darkness, the hunger-taste of food after setting up camp, the call of animals and the nearness of stars, the rejuvenation of outdoor sleep that ends as the dawn silhouettes the trees made me feel that if I left the primitive again, I would be turning my back on God's greatest gift to man.

But I must say that I never live long in contact with primitive conditions before I recognize defects that for me counter their qualities—a lack of medical knowledge and facilities, taboos, ritualized magic, and excruciating torture. Ignorance imprisons the awareness essential to appreciation of the primitive itself. It is one thing to view the primitive from a four-wheel-drive safari car. It is quite another to view it when you are crucially dependent on it, without Land-Rover, bugproof tent, medicine kit, cans of food, a ticket home, and traveler's checks.

What is it like to live the life of a Masai? Driving along a one-track dirt road in southern Kenya once, I overtook two spearmen and offered them a ride. They accepted solemnly and started to climb into my small Volkswagen, but their sharp-bladed weapons were too long to take inside. Seeing their confusion, I switched off the engine, walked around to their open door, and held out my hand. Each man handed me his spear. I motioned one to the back seat and the other to the front, then placed the spears, point forward, against the side of the car. The man in front held them there, through the open window. My Volkswagen must have looked like an armed knight as it rolled on through dust and sand.

The spearmen sat completely naked, with bronze bodies and shaved heads and ornamented ear lobes. We did not attempt conversation. The meager road wound through thorny, sparse jungle growth. Splintered branches of acacia trees marked the passage of elephants. After several miles, the Masai beside me gestured toward jungle to our right. I turned in, straddling a wide footpath and bumping over grass clumps. Two hundred yards ahead, the roofs of their huts rounded up behind a *manyatta*'s dry-thorn fence.

Naked children and women in red cotton dresses stood outside the entrance where I stopped. Flies covered their shaved heads and speckled their faces. They stared while I helped the two spearmen dismount and rearmed them. I pointed to my eye, then to the gap in the thorn fence. The older spearman nodded. Yes, I could enter his *manyatta*. He followed as escort.

The flies outside were but a vanguard of those within the *manyatta*. A naked boy of about eight scraped a handful from his face as he looked up at me, then paid no attention as they alighted again. His eyelids were swollen from bites. Both of my hands were busy, unsuccessfully, trying to keep flies from my own face. Open-doored huts formed an oval ring around the *boma,* enclosing a trodden mash of dirt and manure. Cattle had been brought in the previous evening for security and blood-letting. I returned to my car, expecting to continue alone; but two more men appeared, one carrying a large gourd, the other, a rusted five-gallon can. Both vessels had been used for cow milk; both were unwashed.

Would I take them and the containers to the next village? Of course. It is astonishing how readily one converses through gestures in a primitive environment. Life's basic needs can be indicated without using words. The two men climbed into my Volkswagen easily. But no sooner had the elder in the front seat pulled the big gourd in between his legs than I realized it housed literally thousands of flies. I never saw so many in a small area before, not even on a farm manure pile in summer. They emerged from the gourd's neck like a swarm of bees, and kept on coming.

I pushed the shift lever into low gear, bumped back out over the grass hummocks, and drove as fast as the road conditions permitted. I hoped the flies would leave through the open windows. Some did, but it made no apparent difference in the interior population. It was as though the flies inside the gourd bred as fast as they lost numbers. Even the Masai beside me brushed his face occasionally. Fortunately, the nearest *manyatta* lay only two or three miles away. I unloaded my two passengers at the roadside, and did not wait for more travelers. Hundreds of the fly population stayed with me, flying out the windows a few at a time; but after half an hour more of driving, so many remained that I stopped and shooed more out. Nearly another hour passed before the Volkswagen fly population dropped to a midday normal for southern Kenya jungle.

"We believe God is in everything," a Masai once told me. "We believe he is in the trees, in the sky, the mountains, the grasses. We sing songs to the mountains and the trees because God is in them." But in the savage, as in the totalitarian who believes in concentration camps, there is an indifference to suffering, a morbidity and ruthlessness, and a cruelty unacceptable to the civilized body and shocking to the civilized mind.

During a trip to Ethiopia's border with the chief game warden of Kenya, Ian Grimwood, I learned more about customs of tribal fighting. A trail we followed near Lake Rudolph passed the scene of a recent massacre in which twenty-seven people had lost their lives. The massacre was one of a series that had taken place between feuding tribes—a feud started many years before over an assassination. Raiders, in killing, cut testicles off the men and teats off the women to be dried for souvenirs and luck charms. Sometimes they were cut off still-living bodies.

A few miles south of the massacre site, close to Lake Rudolph's eastern shore, I watched two buck topi fighting. Topi are hoofed, herbivorous creatures the size of elk. It appeared to be a fight to the death. Heads down, long curved horns butted together, leg muscles tensed, and brown bodies heaving, the animals attempted to wear each other out. Frequently one or the other would break loose from the horn-lock, wheel sidewise, and jab at chest or belly. Just as frequently the attacked topi dodged the thrust, and locked horns again with its attacker. Not far away, vultures plucked at a flap of skin still clinging to a topi skeleton.

I watched the duel for about a quarter of an hour before one topi, slightly more exhausted than the other, wheeled and retreated. The victorious buck followed close behind. Gaping mouths and labored galloping showed how little physical energy remained in the two animals, yet the chase continued, over sun-dried grass, between scattered lava rocks, up slope and down. When the fleeing buck's pace lagged, his pursuer would manage to gather enough venom to spurt a few yards, lower his head, and give a murderous horn jab upward at the buttocks. And at that moment the defeated topi would squeeze out just enough additional energy to avoid impalement. Fear and anger vied for the outcome.

It seemed impossible for either topi to continue that galloping sporadic pace. How could the toughest lungs and flesh maintain it? I watched them, through field glasses, shrinking in size as they approached desert hills a mile away. At any moment, I expected to see the pursued animal drop with exhaustion, or the pursuer give way to his fatigue. But after reaching the hills and starting to climb one, they turned back toward the lake still galloping. Finally, the victor halted near a clump of bushes on the shore and turned back.

I shall always think of that vanquished topi as a symbol of defeat—head hanging, mouth open, walking away from his herd as though his legs had lost ability to stop, terribly alone in wilderness. Life's dignity was gone. He had merely survived, no more. He was vulnerable to any enemy.

At a later time, in Tanzania, overlooking Lake Manyara, my family and I pitched tents in an area where scouts told us that a two-day-old elephant had been abandoned by its mother and was standing in a clump of brush only a hundred and fifty yards away. The mother might return, they thought, but such abandonment happened seldom in the jungle. We walked with them to look at the infant elephant. It was not much over knee high, gray and wrinkled, standing awkwardly, as very young animals do, with its head pushed between thorny branches in an effort to hide. It showed no sign of noticing our pats and stroking.

That night we heard lions roaring nearby. At sunrise, as my wife and daughters cooked breakfast over the open fire, an elephant herd plodded between our three small tents and the mountain range close westward. Now and then one of them stopped to stare at us, or to strip the leaves from a tree branch. In the other direction, in a marsh at the lake's edge, several buffalo were wallowing. While we were still eating, a Land-Rover bumped up the roadless hillside and stopped. A young park scientist jumped out and asked if we could guide him to the spot where the infant elephant had last been seen. He was making a special study of elephants, he explained. If the mother had not returned to claim her baby, he wanted to raise it himself.

My oldest son and I escorted him to the bushes where we had left the little elephant standing the evening before, but we found only trampled grass. In our Land-Rover, we turned first toward the lake, then south along its edge, then westward toward the mountains. In about ten minutes we encountered a herd of elephants moving slowly in the direction of our campsite. There were several young, but no infants. Some of the adults tossed their heads, trumpeted, and charged as we drove among them.

The charge of an angry elephant is a disturbing sight when you are his target, even when you are protected by a Land-Rover. But the charge always stopped when I drove slowly on through the brush, or else it broke off at least fifteen yards away when I held ground. It was clear that the animals had no intention of letting their ivory test metal.

On returning to camp we found three African game-scout visitors. One of the scouts, a Masai, seemed to me especially adept at tracking. I followed close behind him, down the dry, stony hillside, over a vague and often indiscernible trail of earth scuffs and crushed-down clumps of grass. We had pushed aside thorny branches and stepped easily across small clearings for only a short distance when he peered around a bush, stopped suddenly, and pointed to a mash of gray skin and red flesh less than three strides ahead of us—all that remained of the baby elephant. It lay partially hidden by dense tangled brush. At almost the same instant, the brush moved. There was a deep-throated growl, and I caught glimpses of a lion leaping away. It must have been lying within inches of its kill.

"Simba!" The terse word of warning was shouted by one of the Africans. Every man tensed—serious, alert. A scout readied the single rifle in our party. But it would have been too late had the lion charged. All had taken place too suddenly. When we recognized the danger, it had passed. The Masai I had been following threw his head back and laughed—the laugh of a man who has just escaped a danger he knows well, and enjoys the life he retains.

One does not walk up on a lion at his kill. That is a law of the jungle obeyed by beast and man. A few days later, on a Serengeti plain, parked in my Land-Rover on the far side of a water hole, I watched a lioness protect her kill—a zebra, so lean and flexible of limb that it must have lost its life in recent hours. The lioness was tugging the zebra's body toward a low bank of the water hole, about fifty feet away. Her teeth were sunk deeply into the black-and-white-striped neck. Her face was smeared with blood. Her muscles were bulging with the effort. The task was accomplished slowly, for the body weighed much more than the lioness herself and had to be angled back and forth over humps of earth that lay in her path.

A hyena, a score of vultures, and several maribou storks stood in cautious postures around the scene of action, forming an irregular circle. Obviously the distance they kept related to their estimate of the lioness's speed of charge, and at intervals their estimate was tested. The big cat would let go her grip on the zebra's neck, apparently to rest. She would glance in another direction, sometimes take a step or two that way; then, with astonishing agility, turn and spring at the hyena or at a group of birds. The circle would widen momentarily, then close slowly in again.

Why were the Masai scout and I not charged by the lion we

walked up on? Through this question some of survival's infinite subtleties take form. It was partly by chance, partly because of the instinctive fear wild animals have of man. Under the same circumstances, another lion might have charged and killed us, but it may have been killed in turn by the scout who had the rifle, certainly by the posse that was always organized to kill a lion who had killed a man.

"How cruel it was!" my youngest daughter exclaimed when we got back to camp with our story. But is the law of the jungle basically cruel? Is cruelty a moral judgment if it is fundamental to forms of life? Who is man to say that the workings of nature, and therefore of the divine plan of which he himself is part, are cruel? Are we ourselves not a result of that plan? Does not our well-being, our present existence stem from countless instances of such "cruelty" eons past?

Nature rewards abilities and penalizes defects too subtle for the human eye to note. The abandonment of the baby elephant seemed to be an abnormal event, infringing on the rules of survival. Had nature become suspicious that genes of the offspring would transmit a hereditary tendency toward such abandonment to future generations? Death could prevent this, and death was ordained. Was that more cruel than it would have been to condemn many successive infant elephants to similar abandonment through the hereditary spreading of defective genes? Is morality in nature a matter of numbers? Survival depends on numbers. Cruelty and compassion can transpose with time, and cruelty to the individual might be regarded as compassion to still other individuals emerging later from the immortal genetic stream.

Here one encounters again the juxtaposition of apparently opposed principles of nature—the importance and unimportance of the individual. He is the ultimate goal of life's evolution, yet his life is of such trivial value that it is snuffed out for the slightest cause. He is at once the ocean of mortality and a molecule within it. His presence is essential; his absence unmissed. He is timed and timeless, formed and formless, earthbound and universal. Within him life and death hold hands. His very extinction recognizes his importance. It is a concept difficult to recognize through rationalist philosophy or through civil law. It is beyond the encompassment of science.

Prolificacy. Competition. Selection. In the topi, the principles of nature were clearly manifest. Strength, skill, endurance had won for the buck who would return, victorious, to breed the herd and pass on to future generations those genetic characteristics that tend to support survival. The result was seen in the animals themselves. Among hundreds we passed, no blemish was visible. Life, moving with an age-dialed tempo, adapted to its environment. Principles of biological evolution seem simple, or at least definable, for lower animals, but how do they apply to man? The killing of humans by African tribesmen was more ruthless than the killing by animals in combat, as predators and as prey, yet a similar selection of qualities had not resulted for humans. Most of the human bodies I saw showed obvious defects—defects of form, of energy, or alertness, of muscle, tooth, and eye. Even in tribal organization—considered extremely primitive by civilized man today—competition has become separated from selection on biological standards of life.

It becomes obvious that, in spite of his genetic sciences, the impact of evolution on man's intellect is resulting in the perfection of his weapons rather than of himself. Given the human mind, man has more and more adapted his environment to his condition, rather than his condition to his environment. The developing human intellect impinges on biological evolution through infinitely intricate and devious channels—through arms, ideology, and religion, superstition and science, economics and law, custom and taboo.

A few years before his death, my wife and I visited Carl Jung at his tower home on the Zürichsee's north bank. An old wizard of a man, surrounded by books, mandalas, and collected charms, he sat and talked to us and to his friends Kurt and Helen Wolff, who had published his works in conjunction with the Bollingen Foundation. He spoke of his fascination with the lake's depths, likening them to the subconscious workings of the human mind.

Conversation turned to "flying saucers." Jung had written a book about them, *Flying Saucers: A Modern Myth of Things Seen in the Skies,* published by Harcourt Brace Jovanovich, Inc. I had expected him to discuss the psychological and psychiatric aspects of people's fantasizing "flying-saucer" sightings. I was amazed to find that he believed in their reality. I started to tell him about the negative results of U.S. Air Force investigations of hundreds of reported sightings, but he showed no interest. He asked how I accounted for a series of sightings reported by a line of observers in Europe, and for others described in the United States.

When I mentioned a discussion I had had with General Carl Spaatz, the chief of staff of the Air Force, in regard to reported flying-saucer sightings, Jung said: "There are many things taking place upon the earth that you and General Spaatz do not know about." He then cited the disintegration of a BOAC Comet, which he said had been reported hit by "an unidentified flying object," or, as they keep being called, a flying saucer. He appeared to be completely uninterested in the fact that in this instance, as in two other accidents with Comet jet transports, official investigations disclosed that the disintegration was caused by fuselage rupture resulting from fatigue.

Here was one of the most eminent psychiatrists of modern times believing and repeating myths less probable that those evolved by cave men. And when one reads present-day books describing "factual observations" of "supernatural phenomena," it is difficult to avoid the conclusion that myths, superstitions, and beliefs now held by many educated persons are as fantastic, intuitive, improbable— and perceptive—as those held by primitive men for ages.

Western civilization is not like others. Earlier and concurrent civilizations embraced relatively small areas of the world. Our Western culture spreads everywhere. If it is destroyed in one place, it grows and flowers elsewhere like the roots of wisteria. A feeling of certainty, no doubt fed by the extraordinary pervasiveness of Western society and its ways, looms in my mind whenever I question our civilization's future. I think of the benefits that science has brought. I am always confronted by these benefits when I question civilization's progress. I have friends who are alive only because of pharmaceutical discoveries and the scientific skill of physicians and surgeons. Diseases have been conquered, suffering minimized, infant mortality reduced, longevity extended.

Science has worked wonders with the obvious, but it seems baffled by the subtle. Unlike the nature it attempts to subdue, science delights in prolonging life but, with the naïveté of an adolescent child, shirks responsibility for recognizing the qualities of age and death. It preserves hopelessly unconscious people in a state of animation by elaborate techniques. Science saves individual life with infinite and possibly overelaborate care, but it also makes it possible to kill life in enormous numbers. Even when science is put to the work of sustaining life in great numbers, it seems to turn us away from our own planet.

For the bursting populations of an already overpopulated world, science offers developments in agricultural machinery, hybrid crops, synthetic foods, artificial fertilizers, oceanic products—a lengthening list of techniques for increasing the world's tempo and productivity. But a balance like that achieved by nature appears to lie beyond both its desires and its understanding. Suppose science finds a way of expanding our world in space rather than of contracting it in time. Our ancestors spent centuries expanding in space the known world. Then, when mankind had spread well over its sphere's dimensions, they began devoting their efforts toward contracting world distances in time. In this generation, our ballistic missiles have brought Russia closer to the United States than a commuter in the suburbs to his office.

As a college youth, I thought civilization could never be destroyed again, that in this respect our civilization was different from all others of the past. It had spread completely around the world; it was too powerful, too universal. A quarter-century later, after I had seen the destruction of high-explosive bombs and flown over the atomic-bombed cities of Hiroshima and Nagasaki, I realized how vulnerable my profession—aviation—had made all peoples. The centers of civilization were the centers of targets.

Once, in East Africa, I accepted the invitation of a Masai friend and member of Kenya's parliament, John Ole Kinchellah, to attend a political meeting near the Tanzania border, fifteen miles north of Mount Kilimanjaro. At the meeting place, in a clearing on the village outskirts, I felt the underlying power of primitive man as I never had before. By the time we arrived, several hundred Masai had gathered under the clear sky and hot sun. There was not another white man among them. Around us, stuck upright in the ground, like a leafless forest, were dozens of spears. Their owners sat or squatted, faces painted, solemn, folded blankets slung over shoulders. The dresses of more than a hundred women reddened the group's periphery. Ronald Ngala, a leader of the Kenya African Democratic Union, told me he had never before seen so many Masai women at a political meeting. Addresses were in Masai or Swahili, but now and then the speakers used English, obviously for my benefit, to castigate the British colonial system.

How could I, who had flown in atomic bombers and watched ballistic missiles leave their pads, recognize power in a Masai's slender spear? The spearmen around me controlled the area of earth I occupied. I existed there by their tolerance. How could I, who knew political audiences in America and Europe, suppose that these men squatting on the ground could compete with civilization? But in the sperm and ova of such Africans were genes capable of advancing life as it had been advanced through bygone ages. What reason had I to infer that tribal bodies contained lesser potentialities than mine? Who could say with certainty that black men are not the future carriers of human evolution, and that we whites are not so overspecialized a branch that we will rot away with time, nuclear warfare, and the trunk-of-life's extension?

Regardless of civilization's subtleties and despite the buffers it lays against competition, primitive biological life continues. Ideological and materialistic considerations do not extinguish it, however much they camouflage it. It manifests itself with extraordinary clarity in the environment of East Africa, where technological civilization struck in the nineteenth century, and where the primitive is now retaliating, not only by striking back directly, but also by being always ready to inhabit the earth's spaces.

To intellectuals living in highly developed areas, the extinction of civilization may seem synonymous with the end of man himself, but primitive peoples feel differently. Millions of men and women even today require nothing from civilization, and look on its encroachment with suspicion or fear.

Is civilization progress? How often I have asked myself that question! I believe that civilization is an emanation and a phase of human progress, but not necessary to it in a basic sense. We have no proof whatever that the five or six thousand years of civilization, here and there on earth, have improved man's fundamental qualities, or that in his essence civilized man is a being superior to primitive man.

Arguing on evolutionary standards, one might say that whatever does not survive is not progressive, that every civilization except our own has fallen, that the crisis our present civilization faces is only too obvious, and that a nuclear war between civilized nations will have the effect of cycling primitive peoples forward again.

Can it be that civilization is detrimental to human progress? Perhaps it reaches a point beyond which it is detrimental. Is it a severed head? Does civilization eventually become such an over-specialized development of the intellect, so organized and artificial, so separated from the senses that it will be incapable of continued functioning?

Year after year, more effort, more efficiency, more organization are demanded of civilized Americans to keep their lead economically and militarily, to raise our standards, to support the doctrines of compassion and democracy. Workers have to be kept employed and stockholders have to receive their dividends. Successful competition involves cheaper or more attractive products. Cheaper or more attractive products require more intricate research and organization. You awake to find that the pinnacle of achievement you struggled toward yesterday was no more than today's step toward tomorrow's necessity, and you begin to realize there is relief in less progressive ways of life.

Civilized life requires people to specialize and co-ordinate, with a resulting loss in individuality and freedom. On the one hand, man desires civilization and progress. On the other, he suffers its impositions. Man is born with the God-given privilege of living on earth and water, under sun and sky. He has flesh and senses, emotions and spirit, as well as mind, with which to share his life. What does the quality of living consist of if not a fluctuating balance between these elements? Must we sacrifice the full appreciation of living for a narrowing culture of the mind?

To a perceptive eye, the primitive always exists in juxtaposition with the civilized to raise this challenge, to claim that progress is marked by naked life, by a genetic core in comparison to which appurtenances of civilization are no more than clothing to a body. Like clothing, civilization separates man from his natural environment. It protects him, but it also insulates him from elements and qualities with which millions of years of evolution have maintained his conformation. It misleads him by its customs, styles, and popularity into believing that the work, not the hewer and mender, marks progress. But if the body beneath loses vitality, clothing will not preserve it.

Within every man, less disguised by skin than by clothing, is the spear-bearing savage. Our relationship to our ancestral past is inescapable. Often, it seems to me, the external conflict between the civilized and primitive is the counterpart of a conflict within man himself, a conflict between modern intellect and ancient sensate recollections, between systematic rationality and instinct. The extraordinary fact is that the intellect in the relatively short period of its existence has been able to gain such domination over the eon-developed and generation-proven senses retained by civilized man, and that the intellect is unappreciative of the value of these senses to its own astuteness, not consciously aware of the terrific powers they retain.

I believe there is wisdom in the primitive lying at greater depths than the intellect has plumbed, a wisdom from which civilized man can learn and without whose application his survival time is limited. It is wisdom born of instinct, intuition, and genetic memory, held by the subconscious rather than the conscious mind, too subtle and elusive to be more than partially comprised within limits of rationality.

The primitive remains internally in man as it remains externally in nature, challenging the intellectual constructs, forming its rebellions and revolutions. Whether they take place in civilization, in nations, or in a single individual, rebellions and revolutions touch on the primitive and subconscious.

"The wise are not learned; the learned are not wise," Lao Tse wrote. "Let your learned mind take leaven from the wisdom of your heart." How often the mind sweeps brashly past the heart's promptings, though dependent on its rhythm! The primitive is the heart of the civilized, but modern civilization takes little leaven from it—as though mind and heart were in mortal competition and one must prevail.

At first glance, conflicts between the civilized and primitive seem hopelessly one-sided, in view of civilization's overwhelming power—its guns, explosives, poisons, bulldozers, dredges, vehicles, and saws. But on deeper consideration, it seems impossible for the primitive to lose, because of its fundament, because of its laws of competition, selection, and survival that have governed life from the beginning.

Life instinctively attempts to avoid death, which is essential to it. Without death there would be no awareness of life, and the recurring selection and renewal that has caused life's progress would be ended. Maybe man's instinct here is too irrational. Maybe we should welcome death as we welcome birth, both as achievements in a spiral, supporting and completing one another. When man's intellect has gained wisdom through further and many more evolutionary ages, we will do so.

But in this still-early era of human progress, I want to prolong life, my own, that of my family and friends, of mankind, of my organized civilization. I enjoy living on this earth. I feel there is plenty of time beyond death, however long it is postponed, to explore and appreciate the qualities speculation may attribute to disembodied spirit. And there is more. I do not want to experience, or have my children and grandchildren experience, the long throes of having to pass from one civilization to another. I want to find responses to the challenges.

What responses can we make in our time that men have not made before, in previous crises of civilizations, without preventing breakdown? What creative acts are required? What new elements can we bring to our assistance? As life's progress is founded on the individual, the progress of life's organizations is inevitably founded on him. The best way to insure our civilization's survival is to concentrate our attention on the survival values of the individual himself. If we are to use our new tool of science effectively in meeting challenges to modern civilization, it must be to benefit the individual rather than to raise by additional complication the already intricate standards of the group. For survival, man must look to himself, only secondarily to his material creations.

Is this not the simple answer to which our unprecedented knowledge leads us?

ELEVEN

The Man on
the Beach

I think of a long sand beach on the Japanese-held island of New Ireland, in the summer of 1944. Great waves of war had surged first east, then west, over the Pacific Ocean, destroying and killing as they passed. I was an element of the return surge westward by angry American forces. I was flying Corsairs with Marine Fighter Squadron 223, based on Green Island, northwest of the Solomons. One of its missions was to patrol New Ireland coasts.

"There are no targets limited on New Ireland," the Intelligence officer had told us in ending his morning briefing. That meant we were to shoot at anything that moved, at anything that might contain life. It was a military euphemism: we would give no quarter and expect none. Stories about flyers captured on New Ireland stacked high in every combat pilot's mind: "They hammered slivers under his finger nails," "gagged him and poured water down his nose," "tied him to a tree and cut his guts out," "impaled his head on a pole in that clearing." . . . But if you were shot down, it was sometimes possible to escape.

I was assigned to an afternoon reconnaissance mission along the northern coast—four fighters. We were to observe new enemy activities and to attack "targets of opportunity." Heavy weather was moving in, and ceilings might be too low for combat flying, but we decided to take off and then to push on or turn back according to the conditions we encountered.

New Ireland's coast was almost clear when we arrived. The few low clouds would have no effect upon our mission. We nosed down to two thousand feet, looking for fresh scars on earth as signs of Japanese activity. But the enemy's camouflage was good; every track and mark looked old. We dropped down to two hundred feet above the jungle, zoomed up a mountainside, cleared the ridge by a wingspan, dove into the valley beyond, skimming treetops, watching for targets ahead or telltale streaks of tracers arising from the ground.

We stayed close to palm tops, mile after mile, zooming up to take our bearings, diving down before any hidden gunner had time to train his sights. We banked right to the coastline, left along the shore—four fighters now in line abreast, racing over water, myself closest to the land. Foaming surf raveled out in front of me. Trees whipped by, a streak of green running, the beach a band of yellow.

Was that a post in the water, a mile ahead? Or a man, standing? It moved toward shore. It was a man! Everyone was an enemy, everything a target, on New Ireland, for here there were only Japanese and unfriendly natives. Our orders were: "Shoot whatever you see." I banked slightly left and lined up my sight. At a thousand yards, my fifty-calibers were deadly—four thousand rounds a minute. I knew exactly where they would strike. I could not miss.

He was in knee-deep water. The beach was wide, and he could never make the jungle's cover. Now he was out of the water, centered in my sight, the naked and bronzed enemy.

My finger tightened on the trigger. A touch, and he would crumple on the sand. But he disdained to run. He strode across the beach. Each step carried dignity and courage in its timing. He was too human, too vulnerable; the shot was too easy. I released the trigger and gave him back his life. He reached the jungle and merged into the cover of green.

We went on to hit antiaircraft-gun emplacements and even plantation buildings. How many people did I kill that day? "You should have killed one more," a Marine officer asserted when I described the naked figure I left living on the beach. "He was probably a general. A native wouldn't walk like that. If you'd shot him, you might have saved the lives of Americans."

You could not afford to be sentimental in war. Every Japanese you did not kill would try to kill Americans. But then my mind drifted back thirteen years, to August 1931, to a harborless volcanic island named Ketoi and to a small seaplane lying off it in the dead of night, lashed by waves from the edge of a typhoon. My young wife and I lay braced against the fuselage walls while waves broke across our pontoons and wind howled through the cowlings. Each hour since sunset had charged the violence of the sea. We felt every tug on our anchor rope and knew that a surf was pounding on viciously sharp rocks less than a hundred yards away. For the first two or three hours of darkness, we had gained a fitful sleep. Then we lay awake and waited for the dawn.

A shout! Was it possible? Light flickered on the canopy above us. Wood banged on wood, outside. Human voices mixed with a screeching wind. I squirmed up into the pilot's seat and slid open the hood above. An open boat rode awkwardly beside my cockpit, outlined by the dim light of a storm lantern that was clutched by a member of the crew. It was manned by sailors from the Japanese ship *Shinshiru Maru.* Spray-lashed and glistening in black sou'-westers, the sailors clung desperately to wing and pontoon, trying to keep contact between tossing boat and rocking plane without letting either one bash the other. Their ship was anchored in open ocean, sixty yards farther from the shore, and they had brought the end of a hawser to secure our plane to the ship's stern in case our anchor dragged. The *Shinshiru Maru* had been sent to guard us, and it was standing by with deck watches through the night.

The *Shinshiru Maru* symbolized the Japanese to me, with their courtesy, their skill, their courage. On board, my wife and I had our first meeting with the people of a beautiful, compact, and extraordinary country. We had not planned on landing in the Chishima Islands. We had taken off from Russia's harbor at Petropavlovsk, on the Kamchatka peninsula, for a flight we hoped would be nonstop to Hokkaido. But we encountered fog and a low cloud layer covering most of the Chishimas—those mountain peaks that pierce the ocean's surface north of the main islands of Japan. Our fuel reserve for the flight was low. A storm rose high ahead. I dove down the curving slope of Ketoi's volcano through a thin layer of clear air between mountainside and mist.

I had hoped to wedge under the storm and continue our flight to

Hokkaido, but as we approached the ocean's surface, I saw that mist and water touched. So I cut the throttle and spanked across big rollers to a landing. Then, after taxiing to the doubtful shelter of the leeward shore, we had dropped anchor.

It was a wild coast—no mark of man. We spent the first night in a sleeping bag rolled out on top of equipment in the baggage compartment of our plane. The fuselage was barely wide enough for the two of us to lie side by side, and our bed rocked constantly. Expecting the weather to clear, we had radioed that we were in no need of assistance; but the next morning the *Shinshiru Maru* appeared suddenly through mists, sent by the Japanese Bureau of Fisheries.

The men on board shared with us their rice and fish at the captain's table. They saved our seaplane when sharp rocks cut through its anchor rope and wind shoved us toward the breakers on the coast. They worried with us about the height of sea and the path of the typhoon. And when our spray-soaked engine would not start, they towed us carefully through miles of open water to the neighboring island of Paramushiru and its calm bay, where we were sheltered by the steep walls of another volcano.

All Japan was like the *Shinshiru Maru*. Wherever we landed, whether it was near a lonely fisherman's hut on Kunashir, on a lake at Nemuro, or beside a wharf at Fukuoka, we were greeted as friends and honored guests. I remember Japan as a country of welcoming bows and smiling people, of space-washed paintings hung in teahouses, of rice paddies where each blade was nursed by meticulously thrifty peasants.

Yes, the man on the beach might have been a general. Why had I not killed him? I had killed others. Chivalry was not practiced in the South Pacific war. Both sides fought under the primitive law, and by that law, he was my prey. What momentary sense made him my brother? What spiritual bond had formed between us across chasms of war and power, time and space? Some quirk of the human mind and senses had evaded basic principles of competition and survival.

There are elements in man that escape rational description, that lie beyond the measurements of science. They may exist at distances beyond the body, yet still exert an influence within. They curve outward through Newtonian dimensions, past areas of our comprehension. They cause sensory reactions that impinge only indirectly on the conscious mind. Instead of just looking down on that naked enemy figure, it was as though I had left the cockpit of my fighter and its Vulcan power to merge with his existence in the surf, to leave the trappings and the cruel duties of war and momentarily return like Antaeus to the strengthening touch of primitive earth.

Within the major framework of an organized society, individuals are like the atoms making up the matter that our senses see and touch. Theirs is a framework within a framework, and while reactions of individuals are relevant to magnitudes above and below, they are also independent of them. Under some conditions individuals disintegrate, as under the fire of a neutron or a machine gun. For a time that cannot be clocked, that man on the beach and I had escaped from our organizations and the enmity of war. We met within the brotherhood of individuals, as fighting men may meet when their interest in the present severs the extension of their responsibilities in time. We were neither American nor Japanese, but two atoms of the human species, touching briefly, strangely, or maybe just randomly, through our fields of force.

It is the lot of civilized man to exist simultaneously in individual and organizational frameworks, and to accept in the world of life, as in the world of matter, certain standards of behavior in one framework that often are not valid in the other. The existence of an organization is bound to the co-operation of a group of individuals who act together through desire or compulsion. But the individual can break away from an organization, and as he moves away he can revert to the primitive. The combination of numerous individuals working in the organizational framework creates a quality of living that could not be attained by each independently. But it is from the individual framework that the organization's value must be judged; for here, in the end, the decision is made to support, to revolt, to abandon.

The man on the beach was a human atom, isolated from his Oriental organization by the circumstances and effects of war. I had startled him in the nakedness of his contemplation.

The tempo of modern civilization has a centrifugal force that carries us outward from the core of life toward ever-expanding peripheries. One should return frequently to the core, and to basic values of the individual—to natural surroundings, to simplicity and contemplation. Long ago, I resolved to so arrange my life that I could move back and forth between periphery and core.

The man on that New Ireland coast was at the core, while I, hurtling past above him, was at the periphery. And as he had found his strip of jungle beach, I found a clearing among the palms on Green Island to which I returned after the rattling guns, exploding shells, and long hours of a combat mission. Everywhere I went, I hunted for places in which one could in isolation contemplate. There was a cleft at Emirau I remember: the waves dashed spray into this little haven. I shared a coral shelf with gooney birds at Midway. Above all other places, a pool in the mountain jungle of Hollandia gave me the solitude I sought. It was a hollow in a stream bed with a yellow-sand bottom of such clear texture that it was water-magnified.

I would put my pistol, holster open, on a smooth stone that rose above the surface, strip, and lie beside it in the water. Remains of Japanese palm-leaf shelters were not far away, and enemy soldiers were sometimes encountered wandering through the jungle. They were usually hungry and unarmed, but my eyes watched for any movement and my ears remained alert for any sound. I had reverted to the status of primitive life, gaining confidence with time and the silence of the jungle, hoping to remain unseen, ready if need arose to hide, or fight, or flee.

Boughs above my head held back to show a ragged patch of sky. Vapor from thick-matted leaves wavered through sunbeams wedging down. Bubbles trapped below the falls eddied up around my feet, while the sand scrubbed pleasantly on my skin. I would roll over, push my head below the surface, swallow mouthfuls of the cool liquid, smell a mossy dampness as I emerged to breathe again.

No dream could have been stranger than the reality of finding myself alone in a New Guinea jungle pool. There, suddenly sensitized, was the presence of "I." I was flesh, sensation, awareness, the culmination of worldly life to date after billions of years of evolution, the result of design, of chance, of mating, and of selection through epochs. I existed at that hourglass constriction of time where past and future touch to form the individual.

I was suddenly stripped of civilization as I was stripped of clothes. I had uprooted myself from a tremendous military machine, and lay like a plant thrown into water, still virile with sap from the soil from which it had been torn, sensitive to each motion in a new and hazardous environment.

I, a plant, uprooted from a machine! What a ridiculous metaphor! And yet I did feel uprooted, as though I had left broken-off extremities growing back in the camp, back in America, at various places where I had been throughout my life. I looked down at my body, dug my toes into the sand, and realized that I could not very well take root with them in a pool, or anywhere else, for that matter. No, my body was mobile. It had traveled with the utmost freedom over the earth and through the sky. My body was a skin-enclosed, compact entity. It was my mind that took root, and then tore itself away and felt scars where it had left behind extremities. It had no trouble burrowing into a machine, or a concept, or a jungle pool.

The mind roots and the body moves, pulling the mind along with it. What a paradox of existences man is! I commanded my mind to return to my home in America, to exist for moments with my wife and children. I opened my eyes and merged with a cirrus cloud, skipped over branches of the jungle, rode on a bubble dancing near the bottom of the falls. I turned a wet stone between my thumb and fingers. Those fingers were also part of my existence, as much a part of my identity as was my mind. As I felt the stone, I sensed their movement and realized I had a body that was integral with mind.

"Realized." What did I mean by "realized"? Realization was a different thing from "thought." How often I had realized something that the thinking process of my mind denied! For instance, when I was quite young, my mind believed it was free to think independently of the limitations of the elements that made up my personality. I had found it difficult to understand why I often opposed the "will" of my mind, and sometimes actually put a restriction on its thinking process. There was the "I" of my consciousness, the "I" of my senses, the "I" of my body, the "I" of my emotions, the "I" of my dreams. Sometimes there seemed to be a limitless number of "I"s within me. I was not the same person in a combat plane that I was with my children at home. I was a different person at the age of forty from the one I was at the age of thirty, and still different at the age of twenty, or ten, or five. Each outward "I" seemed to have an inward "I" corresponding to it, and it was the inward "I" that underlay unity or else caused fragmentation.

The most difficult, and possibly the most important, times were when I seemed to consist of a mixture of repulsions and desires, when reason said "yes" and intuition said "no," and emotion poured its influence upon the senses.

In the early years of flying, from cow-pasture fields and with fragile, underpowered planes, I always used reason and intuition as a double check on safety. Before a short-field take-off, for example, I would estimate the physical elements involved—the wind, the load on board, the length of run, the toughness of the sod. Then, if my mind decided I could clear obstructions at the farther end, I confronted it with intuition. If I sensed a lack of agreement between the two, I either looked for a better take-off direction or waited for a change in wind. Sometimes I cut an open throttle because estimate and intuition diverged after the take-off roll started.

Establishing an inner attitude toward courage and fear formed an excellent example of bringing the various elements of existence into correlation. As a child, I had been afraid of many things—of the dark at night, of lonely places, of little "toughs" who chased and threatened. My heart would beat at double speed through adventures in the stories my mother read to me.

Then, at the age of eleven I learned to drive an automobile, and later a motorcycle, and finally I decided to become an aviator. I soon realized I could not be successful in such occupations if I were governed either by instinctive fear or by intellectual courage. Domination by the instinct would restrict both achievement and adventure, while a prideful domination by the intellect could easily result in injury or death.

From the start, I knew that flying was dangerous. My desire to fly outran my rational acceptance of this, but I was not foolhardy. I was prepared to plan. I was also prepared to take risks. To complicate the situation, experience had already taught me that neither intellect nor instinct could subjugate the other.

I do not recall the exact date or circumstance, but an hour came when I faced the problem of fear squarely. I did not then realize the significance of setting a trend for myself, although it did continue through my life. It was ridiculous, I told myself, to be afraid of doing something in which little danger was involved only because the senses got excited. Why flinch in pulling a pistol's trigger when you knew the sound and recoil would not hurt you? Why let a sense of altitude affect your stomach when you looked down safely from a height? Why be afraid of loneliness when the presence of a companion would not detract from risk? But how could I transfer such logic to my senses?

I decided on a course of training, a direct approach at first. I started with altitude because of my interest in flying. There was a high water tower a few miles away from my house, a black-painted metal structure. I rode my motorcycle to it and began climbing the slender iron ladder attached to one of the supporting legs. I would climb a few rungs and stop and look down, trying to rationalize away the strangeness that grew in me with each foot of height. I convinced myself immediately that this training technique was at least partially successful.

From the narrow walkway around the tank itself, I could look down with more equanimity. But it was still like bending over and staring at a landscape with your head upside down between your legs—the senses require time to become adjusted, using time, trend, and desire. My senses had no desire to climb on that water tower, and yet they loved to sway about at the top of a tree. My mind kept telling them this was irrational. Lower branches were not likely to save you if you fell. That its argument had some effect was confirmed by my method of descent. I zigzagged down to the ground, hand over hand and hanging slothlike, along the cross-brace rods that trussed each section of the tower's steel supporting legs. After that, climbing back up the ladder seemed less hazardous and I felt a little ashamed of my previous hesitance. Clearly, the trend I set was getting a good start.

But an incident that took place near Lincoln, Nebraska, where I enrolled in flying school, emphasized the need for caution in accepting courage of the mind. A farm boy of about twenty wanted to be a parachute jumper. Somehow he got a parachute that was made out of too-heavy cloth, and somehow he found a pilot who agreed to drop him. No one had jumped with that parachute before. It was much too small for the weight of a human body. Even if all had gone well, his impact with the ground would probably have caused broken bones. But he decided to make the jump without a harness. He simply hooked one arm around the shroud ring and clasped his wrists tightly together. The jerk of the parachute billowing out was too great for his strength. He fell free the rest of the way to his death. I felt sure his instincts must have objected to that jump, and that the courage of his mind had overruled them.

Possibly the flux of mind and instinct in relation to courage and fear was most pronounced for me when I started parachute-jumping myself as a flying student. It was before my first solo. A professional parachute jumper came to Lincoln, and as I watched his exhibition, fascinated, I decided to make a jump. It would be so wonderful to float down through air under a muslin umbrella, and it would be safe if I used the proper equipment and technique. The professional agreed to let me use two of his parachutes for my first jump—I had decided on a "double" one—although he said he did not know why anybody wanted to make a double jump the first time. But my mind had reasoned that since I believed parachutes were safe, I should be as willing to jump twice as once in a descent.

Logic kept reaffirming that a parachute jump would be less dangerous than "soloing" an airplane the first time. But my senses refused to support my mind's composure. They dreaded the moment when my body would force itself out of the cockpit and crawl through the tornado of the slipstream along a fragile wing slicing through air two thousand feet in height. They imagined realistically the slenderness of flying-wires grasped by hands, the final plunge into a nothingness of air. I was aware, though, of a certain difference. There was a difference between the dread I felt and the sickening fear, the kin to terror, I had sometimes known as a child. Now, my dread was countered by anticipation. I had no desire to escape.

Finally, when a timeless moment broke and I swung under the lower wing with my thumb and finger on the bowknot, a confidence had developed between my senses and my mind, and understanding that each depended on the other's wisdom, and that safety lay in their mutual support. The more the senses had considered reasons of the mind and the more the mind had respected instincts of the senses, the more fear was stripped of unreality.

Five years later, when I was preparing for my New York–to–Paris flight, the trend I had set influenced fundamentally both my instinct and my conscious thought. My mind and senses seemed to work as one in considering risks involved in the project. I felt no twinge of instinct when my intellect concluded that I would be safer with one engine than with three, that the weight of a parachute would more than counteract its value on a mostly overocean flight, and that the chances of success would be higher if I flew alone. My mind accepted almost too readily the judgment of my senses when they said that my overloaded plane could take off and clear the wires at the field's end, and that I could stay awake through two days and two nights of flying after twenty-three hours without sleep. High over the North Atlantic, in storm, at night, no sense of loneliness disturbed me.

Aviators in the early days seldom discussed fear however much people who gathered around our planes talked about it. But I doubt that any man can be trained to eliminate completely the element of fear. In any event, I wonder if such an accomplishment is desirable.

I know that fear still jumps up on occasion to catch me unaware, usually under the more trivial and unexpected circumstances. During my head-on combat in the Pacific, with enemy machine guns blazing at me, foiling death by inches and by seconds, I had not the slightest sense of fear. But riding with a skill-less driver in an automobile, either dodging traffic or weaving down a mountain road, I find myself suddenly afraid, when, statistically, the chance of an accident is not so very high. I always tense when I see a snake unexpectedly, even though a moment later I am ready to hold it in my hands and recall matter-of-factly that as a boy I let garter snakes crawl down my neck and out through my shirt sleeves.

Fear is conditional. For me, there is a kind of fear related to responsibility, and another kind related to inevitability. In the one case, I am apprehensive of disaster. In the other, I am just plain scared. In the former, there is usually some judgment I can exercise and some action I can take. In the latter, I exist under circumstances completely beyond my control.

I think fear is purest, and most difficult to combat, when circumstances make all action ineffective. Possibly the best example of this I experienced was when I was flying the night mail. I had been caught in a severe storm, had dropped my only flare in an unsuccessful attempt to land, run my fuel tanks dry to avoid a fire when the plane crashed, and jumped with my parachute. I was high in the storm cloud—close to fourteen thousand feet above the ground—for I had been climbing in an attempt to reach a clear sky.

After pulling the rip cord, there was, of course, nothing more I could do before my feet touched the ground. My mind and senses were free to anticipate, appreciate, imagine. Neither man nor bird could merge completely with a storm. Jerks on my harness told of the turbulence I entered. Sheet lightning showed stuff of mist and cloud around me, churning as though stirred by a giant. Between flashes, all was blackness, in which I swung, and jerked, and swung.

Soon I encountered rain, at first light, increasing, then drenching. I had not minded the swinging and the jerking so much. They were natural in a storm. But suddenly the silk canopy above me started cracking like a mule driver's whip, and I had a sense of falling between the swings and jerks. In flashes of lightning I could see what was taking place. The wet canopy collapsed and refilled with each gust of air, denting inward, snapping outward—threads of silk against the thunder. How could a worm's secretion withstand such blows of Thor?

Might the gusts blow my canopy inside out between its shroud lines? Had a man ever descended with so heavily a rain-soaked parachute before and lived? I might have faced death with courage that night, but I did not eliminate all fear.

Like all professional aviators in the early years of flying, I had made plenty of forced landings. There were pilots who said: "Select your spot for a forced landing, and stick to it. Don't change your decision on the way down." Even my mind disagreed with that philosophy. It had learned that success depends also on the judgment of the senses. At the first cough of trouble, my body jerked to attention, and my mind took immediate control. Rapid observations and decisions had to be made. What was the cause? Was there a chance of regaining power, by, for example, switching valves when a fuel tank ran dry? Was it best to cut the switches and concentrate on getting down without a crash?

As soon as I could divert attention from the cockpit's dials and levers, I would sweep my eyes over the earth to find the best area on which to land. How high was my plane? How far could it glide? What open spaces lay within that distance? My mind would estimate the wind's direction, the slope and quality of surface, the altitude and speed I should achieve to cross the leeward edge. My technique was to select a spot quickly, maneuver my plane toward it, and to hunt for a better one on the way down.

"A pilot who changes his mind is likely to lose control of his plane," my instructors had told me when I was a student. But my principle was to keep the plane always above stalling speed, and therefore under control, even if it would result in landing on a clump of trees. That left me free to change my mind as often as I liked, without danger of a stall or spin.

The role my senses played increased in inverse proportion to their altitude. While thousands of feet of air buffered them from physical impact with the ground, they held back to let the mind lay out its plans academically. But as material reality approached, my senses began to moderate the mind's instructions through a flashing communication which at moments seemed to block out the mind entirely. This happened when I made a forced landing with my mail plane while flying southward from Chicago in 1926. The Liberty engine was running smoothly, and my thoughts had strayed. Suddenly, earth, wings, and fuselage were shaking. My body seemed clamped in vicious jaws and my eyes jumped in their sockets. I expected the engine to leap from its mounts and hurtle earthward as I yanked the throttle shut and cut the switches. But the vibrating stopped. I found myself gliding fast and quietly, at an altitude of fifteen hundred feet, above plowed and stubbled fields of Illinois. The propeller had thrown its tip.

The plowing below me was wet and soft. Fences, ditches, and a winding stream bed spoiled a nearby pasture. Wind was light, from the west. I had not enough altitude to spiral. My mind picked out an oblong strip of stubble, and my DH airplane banked toward it. Thereafter, the movements of my plane did not require much direction. It was as though the wings, nose, and tail were a part of me. They followed my wishes just as did my arms and legs. It was no more necessary to think: Now move the stick so that the wing will drop, than to think: Now move the fingers so that a pencil will be picked up. As I neared the stubble strip, consciousness of mind and plan began to lose identity. Everything within me was merged, and this particular human existence seemed to merge with the mechanical existence of the plane.

Suddenly, I concluded I had made a wrong selection. There were wet spots in the stubble strip ahead. I might be a few feet too low to clear the fence. The wind, though light, was quartering. My mind jumped once, like a toothache, as I shifted plan, but I was too occupied to feel it keenly. Bank left. Reverse bank. Wing down. Left rudder and nose up. Straighten out. The senses had taken over. A fence flashed underneath. The tail skid plumped on ground. The wheels followed, rolling fast; a fence approached; then came a ground loop as wing skid touched and lifted. It was too fast for the mind to follow.

Too fast for the mind to follow! With practice, the handling of a plane becomes instinctive. You move without thinking because you have no time for thought. So long as you have to think to make your plane take action, you have not become its master and its complement.

I learned how quickly I could fragment or unify during the tests of a single-engine biplane at Lambert Field in the summer of 1925. It was a new design, locally built, the only one of its kind. Its plywood fuselage was a little on the short and stubby side. I had approached that plane while it was still under construction, through a planning of the mind: I would inspect it thoroughly; I would get a rough "feel" while taxiing, hold the wheels close to the ground while I tried out the controls, cut the throttle if anything went wrong— fortunately, Lambert Field was big and smooth. If I was well satis-

fied with take-off and response, I would climb slowly to two o
three thousand feet, which would give me plenty of altitude fo
using my parachute in an emergency, put the plane through som
wing-tip stalls, and then consider acrobatics.

At the end of that test flight, I experienced unity and fragmenta
tion pulsing back and forth in extraordinarily quick succession.
climbed to an altitude of twenty-five hundred feet, made severaι
wingovers and banks, tested the controls at increasing angles of
attack, power on, power off. Then I tried spinning; and on the
fourth attempt found myself trapped in a lunging left tailspin. Re-
versing the stick and rudder had no effect.

Mind, senses, body jerked to tension. I had never before flown a
plane that refused any response to its controls; and I had never
been in a spin so violent and lunging, and so flat. The ground
whirled erratically. Ideas inside my head were whirling, too. Maybe
the slipstream would bring more pressure on control surfaces. I
opened the throttle. My hand was not conscious of its movement,
but my ears heard the engine howling through other sensations.

The buck and plunge of the plane continued, carrying my body
through its wild convulsions. The ground twisted upward toward
my eyes. Muscles reported the rudder jammed full right and the
stick strained to the forward corner of the cockpit. I reversed ailer-
ons, closed the throttle, and tried another burst of power.

The lunging continued. Fields and houses grew tremendous and
the ground terribly close. Fingers snapped open the safety belt.
Hands grasped cowlings. Legs shoved and flexed in piston actions.
"I"—mind and senses and body as a unit—plunged out beyond the
confines of the cockpit. Tug on shoulders—turn of body—harness
hugging—canopy billowing, white on blue. I swung like the bob of
a pendulum, barely two hundred feet from the bottom of earth's air.
Body twists—feet hit ground—parachute drags me with the wind.

I reached for the shroud lines, but only one of my arms responded. I became conscious of dull pain. Several men ran up and
caught hold of my parachute. I found myself lying in a potato
patch. When I got onto my feet, I started to walk slowly in the
direction of the crashed plane. People from the village came crowding about. Pain began stabbing, cutting through my shoulder. I

realized that my left hand was holding my right arm, which stuck out in a rigid, unnatural position. I climbed slowly into the back seat of an automobile and started the trip to a hospital.

Pain makes you realize the juxtaposition of unity and diversity within the body, bringing out first one and then the other according to circumstance. Obviously, my shoulder was not my mind. My mind was not hurt. The shoulder joint had been injured while acting without the mind's knowledge or consent. It was responsible for its own troubles. My mind should arrange for its cure, and direct its care, and at the same time maintain an intellectual position above corruption by the flesh. But each jolt on the road decreased mental objectivity. My shoulder kept jabbing into thought and all the senses until it forced the elements of existence to unify again, to agree that, for the time being, the shoulder's pain was *me* and that little else mattered in my personal welfare.

In Missouri, at age twenty-three, I had not thought about elements of unity and fragmentation. My mind questioned my senses' wisdom, and attempted to maintain a tyranny which later it renounced. I was a disciple of the rising deity of Science, prepared to make daily sacrifices toward a mechanistic future that seemed to hold great benefits for men.

In New Guinea, at age forty-two, I realized that the senses often had contact with a wisdom deeper than the mind's. I had become skeptical about mechanistic ways of life. My mind welcomed occasional uprootings from routine procedures, and tried to translate into its own language the messages received from elements of body and subconscious thought.

Lying in that mountain pool, I let elements within me fragment or unify without restraint. There, I was unbound by law and custom. I felt no need for any article made by man. Physically, I had what I was born with, and there was nothing more I desired. No luxury could have added to the peace, the beauty, the contentment I experienced. There, in that pool, was the essential "I," escaped from the outer framework of my life as the Buddhist's soul must escape the body between its incarnations. Does the soul look back upon its body as I looked back upon my fighting plane, as an outer shell, as a convenient tool for material accomplishments?

Suppose I were actually cut off from my country and my civilization, like some of the Japanese soldiers within walking distance of the pool I lay in, like the man I had left alive on the beach of New Ireland, like the few who had escaped from the Biak caves—the encampment behind destroyed, the seas around controlled by enemies. I had with me little more than my clothes, my sheath knife. My automatic pistol, without oil, would rust to uselessness within a few days in the jungle dampness. I did not know much about the animals, fruits, and roots of New Guinea, but I did know something about the island's fish. With a wood spear, I could live indefinitely along the coast. Most natives of New Guinea were friendly to Americans. It would be best to reach one of their villages. I might be able to stay with them for years if I wanted to— even to mix with them.

How quickly, on a cosmic time scale, man can change his make-up! In three or four generations, my descendents could be brown islanders of the South Pacific seas. Scientists maintain that acquired characteristics do not affect the genes, and therefore are not inherited. But how meaningless that doctrine is to the practice of life. In reality, environmentally acquired characteristics enter heredity whenever a man chooses a mate or has a child, for environment affects both survival and selection.

On the one hand, man is an individual; on the other, he manifests a life stream that comprises the past of the human race and extends to its future. As an individual he creates changes in his life stream just as previous changes in the life stream created him. The individual and the life stream intersect on the endless web of time.

Theoretically, the individual can manipulate his life stream to revolutionize his race or temperament. He can shape successive incarnations as a sculptor shapes his clay. But practically, the excesses he might achieve are checked by his inability in one incarnation to control his actions in the next. Even so, as genetic custodian of the moment, the individual has tremendous choice in changing his nonmomentary form, for he can blend by half in the single generation over which he does exercise control. There in New Guinea, I could become in a child as much a brown man as a white, more tribal than national, more primitive than civilized. Many a soldier and sailor had thus transformed his make-up in the past.

On one of the smaller islands where I had landed when I first arrived in the Pacific area, I had noticed a strangeness in color of skin and texture of hair among the natives. "It's easily explained," a naval officer told me. "An Irish sailor was shipwrecked here a few generations back, and the natives welcomed him as an immigrant." Quite obviously that sailor, in his recent incarnations, had acquired characteristics of his South Seas environment and revolutionized the life stream he controlled.

What would be practical if a white man wanted to escape from the throes of his civilization? I could follow my grandfather's example, of course, and emigrate to New Guinea with my family as he had emigrated to the frontier of Minnesota. I could set up plantation life in a mountain paradise. Had my grandfather considered the effect on his life stream before he left Sweden for America? Probably not. Difficulties created by chance and intrigue had motivated him largely, if not entirely. But the effect of that move on the life stream he carried had been very great, not in the first generation—because he took my grandmother with him from the Old Country—but in the second, when my father mixed Swedish with English, Scottish, and Irish genes to form the individuality that was me. I was my grandfather's incarnation under American nationality. Now, in still another generation, I could mix and incarnate again.

The incarnation of my grandfather and father! A blending of ancestral streams! By what measure was I actually themselves, gene for gene, cell for cell? There had been moments when I could imagine myself being my father, when my reactions, sensory and mental, seemed to be identical with his reactions I had seen. In those moments I felt I was my father, and yet I knew my separate individuality. And I had the same relationships with my children that he had had with me. Often I could see my traits in them; now obvious, now not so obvious, impinged on by others that I could not recognize. Then, sensing identities with my father and at the same time with my children, I felt an immortality of life transfusing time.

Lying in that jungle pool encouraged fantasies of mind. Why should I be bound to background or convention? Why not start at zero and remake my life, setting course by whatever seemed worth-while, discarding the rest? Was I not an individual as able to follow my desires as was that man I had not shot on the beach? Suppose I had been killed in combat? All my worldly ties would have been broken as they had been broken for thousands of airmen in the war; why not take advantage in life of what happened inevitably in death? War has always shown, over and over again, that the possibilities are extreme: an individual can begin a new existence upon earth as well as die.

But suppose I did start at zero? How would I remake my life? What changes did I wish? There was a great difference between change forced by uncontrollable circumstance and change sought through combinations of your own revulsion and your own fragmentary desire. The jungle had stirred a desire within me that clarified the revulsion I had felt at many of my civilization's trends, but I was by no means ready to renounce my civilization. There were values of the mind I would be unwilling to give up—books, art, intellectual discussion, scientific skills that had led to man's conquest of the air and to modern medicine. Up to a point, I realized, civilization enhanced the qualities of human life. It increased the awareness of the senses through an understanding of the mind. Its science had cleansed religion of old superstitions, freed cities of their plagues, invented machinery to perform man's brute labor. Above all, civilization produced the organization and the arms that gave its citizens security. This was the barrier my mind always threw up against an onslaught of my senses' primitive desires.

The primitive was at the mercy of the civilized in our twentieth-century times, and nothing had made it more so than the airplane I had helped develop. I had helped to change the environment of our lives. Had it occurred by will? By accident? I made choices in my life that opened, or narrowed, choices for others and for myself. I was the child and father of the circumstances of my life.

TWELVE

A Match Lighting
a Bonfire

I think of my own life. As a young child I accepted my environment and heredity unquestioningly—the house, its food, its warmth, the attention that all adults showed me—the genetic composition that gave me life's birthright of individuality. Aside from routine incidents of boyhood, the first serious assertion of independence I remember was in going to church. That was when my father ran for Congress the first time. Apparently it was desirable for a candidate's family to be seen in church. At least my mother thought so. A Sunday came when I was dressed in scratchy new clothes; a felt hat was put on my head and tight-fitting leather gloves on my hands. Then I was taken to church in our home town of Little Falls. This seemed to me such an unpleasant and unnecessary experience that I marshaled all the forces at my command against it. I revolted so effectively that I was never taken to church again, but the incident left me a skeptic toward religion, questioning the beneficence of God.

My father's election to Congress soon involved other menacing developments besides religion and church—winters in Washington, and school. Both, I was told, were inescapable because I had become a Congressman's son and because all children had to go to school. The law did not make you go to church but it did make you go to school. The law seemed less tolerant than God in this respect —or more powerful. It was quite confusing. I conformed reluctantly, enduring city winters, finding the joy of life again during summers in the woods, fields, and rivers of our farm.

But there were two periods each year when education became compatible with the more important qualities of life. They spanned the visits to my grandparents' home in Detroit. My grandfather's dental chairs, his laboratories and reception parlor, in addition to a family dining room, study, and kitchen, were crowded onto the ground floor of a small gray-painted wooden house on Elizabeth Street, not far from the center of the city. There I could rob the icebox, melt lead, bake clay, draw wire, mix explosives, make electric batteries, turn out brass cannon on a lathe—carrying out the more dangerous activities under my grandfather's or my uncle's direction. Shelves and tables were piled with pamphlets, magazines, and books—*Scientific American, National Geographic, Illustrated London News,* a Webster's dictionary, a thick volume on pathology, all filled with pictures. There was no end to objects and articles of interest. I listened to discussions of the inventions of Edison and Marconi, about the theories of Darwin. I heard of the potentiality in the flights of Wilbur and Orville Wright.

My grandfather and uncle often talked about the great era of science then dawning and they explained the importance of education for any boy who wished to take a part in it. A scientist had to understand mathematics, chemistry, and physics, and a lot of other subjects, too. You had to graduate from college even to become an engineer. During those early visits to Detroit, I began to realize that someday I would have to choose the profession I wished to follow. There would come a time, at the rather arbitrary age of twenty-one, when I would be entirely responsible for what I did. I should think about that time and prepare for my profession, which should relate to my own interests and desires, for I was obviously a different person from my father, grandfather, or uncle.

My father's profession of law and his success in politics had no appeal to me. I thought the arguments of lawyers dull and a Congressman's life most tedious. Much as I was fascinated with my grandfather's laboratories, I had no wish to be a dentist and spend days drilling teeth. I decided I would become an engineer, like my uncle, but in connection with machinery, not mining. I was fascinated by machines, from my toy electric motors to the great steam locomotives that pulled the trains I rode on.

In choosing his occupation, the individual diverges or conforms with trends of his community and nation. In the early part of the twentieth century, the era of Ford, Edison, Rockefeller, and Bell, I was in fact conforming when I decided to become an engineer. All members of my family believed I had chosen wisely. But my conformity did not continue. I found the routine of grade and high school difficult: there were tedious hours sitting at desks and homework's drudgery. The far greater intensity of study required by my engineering college was too much. Nothing an engineer's degree would lead to seemed to me of enough value to justify the regime it forced me to put my body and my senses through. I did not want to spend my life walled in from earth and sky. So I decided to leave college and learn to fly—a desire I had felt since early boyhood. Being the pilot of an airplane would keep me in contact with both the machinery that fascinated my mind and the outdoor life toward which my intuition drew me.

When I began taking flying lessons at Lincoln, Nebraska, in the spring of 1922, I was diverging from the then apparent trends of my time. Most people thought "man was never made to fly," that airplanes, like balloons, would not have much effect on either war or commerce. In those days a pilot's life was likely to be short—averaging about eight hundred flying hours, I was told. A young man entering aviation was unlikely to have great influence on human evolution.

I had been attracted to aviation by its adventure, not its safety, by the love of wind and height and wings. It was the love of flying primarily, and secondarily the hope of advancing aviation's development, that caused me to make the New York–to–Paris flight with my *Spirit of St. Louis* in 1927.

I was astonished at the effect my successful landing in France had on the nations of the world. To me, it was like a match lighting a bonfire. I thought thereafter that people confused the light of the bonfire with the flame of the match, and that one individual was credited with doing what, in reality, many groups of individuals had done. Whatever the causes and interrelationships might be, the concepts of one individual, diverging from group trends, were effecting the evolution of group life.

The problems and hazards involved in my nonstop New York–to–Paris flight were so great that I had devoted little attention to plans beyond landing at Le Bourget. I took for granted that if I reached Europe, I would spend a few weeks touring her countries with my plane. It would be interesting to do so because I had never been outside the Western Hemisphere. Then I might return to America by way of Ireland and Newfoundland, or I might try continuing on eastward all the way around the world. After that I could break many records with the *Spirit of St. Louis*—records of endurance, of ranges with varying loads, of nonstop transcontinental flights. Possibly I would replace the wheels with pontoons and set records for seaplanes.

But soon after I woke in my American Embassy bedroom, the morning after I landed, it became obvious that my flight had taken on significance extending beyond fields of aviation, and that my plans must be accordingly adjusted. I had entered a new environment of life and found myself surrounded by unforeseen opportunities, responsibilities, and problems.

I had been deeply impressed by Ambassador Myron Herrick's invitation to spend the night at his home. I was amazed by developments that followed, although the reception I received on landing should have signaled them to me. They began when I opened my eyes and saw the Ambassador's valet, Blanchard, at my bedside, announcing that my bath had been drawn. He had a robe on his arm, obviously meant for me. And with the window curtains raised, I saw what I had been too sleepy to notice the night before, the immaculate white sheets and silky quilt that had been covering me. The room was like one of those I had seen in motion pictures back home.

To me, the attentions of a valet seemed as fantastic as my ocean flight had been, more appropriate to dreams than to wakefulness. And the bathrobe—I had always considered such things superfluous equipment. He held it open while I got up and slipped my arms in the sleeves. On a chair in the bathroom, beside a tub half full of warm water, was a pair of somebody's black socks, turned halfway inside out for easier donning. Breakfast would be brought, the valet said, as soon as my bath was finished. How would I like my eggs? Then he left me to step into the water and use, with hesitation, a big store-new scented cake of yellow soap.

The Ambassador's son, Parmely, and Parmely's wife, Agnes, with kindness and efficiency, took over the social scheduling of my Paris hours. There was a crowd on the street outside the embassy, Parmely told me when I had finished eating. Some of the people had been standing there for hours. It was not far from noon, for I had slept late. First of all, I should step out onto a balcony so the people in the street could see me.

The idea of exhibiting myself embarrassed and disturbed me. I had never been asked to do that before. It was quite different from exhibitions of wing-walking or parachute-jumping. There, you demonstrated your skill and daring. It was the act people applauded. You were part of a team composed of the airplane, the parachute, the pilot who carried you aloft. In flying circuses, it was fun to be pointed out as a member of a team, as "the pilot" or "the daredevil." But to stand on a balcony without anything to do while hundreds of men and women looked up at you and applauded—I did not want to step out through that door at all, even though the Ambassador went along with me.

I would not have been embarrassed if I had had something important to say. It was not so hard to give a lecture. I had done that a number of times. But the people there on that Paris street would not understand my language. And what would I have talked about if they could? "Just say you're glad to be in France," someone suggested. But that seemed too obvious and trite, so I just stood there while my face got red, and said nothing. I realized it was a great honor, and I was deeply touched by the ovation, but I slipped off the balcony as soon as I could with tact.

It was very important for me to get out to Le Bourget to arrange for the repair and servicing of my plane. When I arrived at the police-guarded hangar, it was a shock to see my plane. Holes had been cut in the fabric all over the fuselage. Riggers were, however, repairing the damage done by souvenir hunters. Closer inspection showed nothing worse than missing patches of fabric, which could easily be replaced, and a broken fitting where some collector, apparently stronger than the rest, had pulled a grease cup off my engine. When I looked over the equipment in my cockpit, I discovered only one loss, but it was a great one—the log of my flight had been stolen.

I had the problem of my clothes. To avoid weight, I had carried no unnecessary items with me in the *Spirit of St. Louis,* not a razor or a toothbrush. I had even trimmed the margins from my maps to save a few ounces. I arrived at Paris with only my flying clothes— breeches, heavy shirt, tan shoes, and high wool socks. These, Parmely Herrick suggested, were hardly adequate for the official and unofficial ceremonies that were being arranged. But Blanchard had been able to borrow from one of his friends a business suit that came close to fitting me. It was a little baggy around the shoulders and a bit short in the pants, but it would do for the moment.

I would not have to wear that suit very long, though, because a tailor had been found who would take my measurements and make the clothes I needed immediately. He was an Englishman with a shop in Paris. He would put aside his other work, and he could finish my first suit by the next afternoon. But of course I would need several suits and a tail coat.

By that time I was becoming somewhat adjusted to the repeated shocks of my new social diplomatic life. Since I had decided to conform, it seemed better to conform entirely. The black and white bow ties, stiff-collared shirts, and patent-leather shoes that accompanied my suits were accepted in the life I had entered "through the looking-glass." But with a high collar poking up my chin and pearl studs glowing on my chest, I realized with some pangs of conscience the disdain with which my previous self would have viewed my new existence.

Most difficult of all for me were the speeches of reply. I envied those men sitting at the head table beside me, from whose tongues words flowed so easily, and to whose translated laudatory sentences I felt so unable to make answer. "I want to thank you for the honor . . ." "I am glad to be in France . . ." What else was one to say? It was not so bad the first time or two, but after that I felt I was repeating myself like a phonograph record that kept jumping back each two or three rounds of the disc. I needed time to prepare a speech, hours to think about it, more hours to write it. With enough time, I felt I could say something worth listening to. But as it was, I did not like to take up the time of those important men who had come to honor me with the unimportant words I forced together. It was an inadequate return for the tremendous honors given. And their kindness in listening intently increased the embarrassment I felt. Talking about aviation helped a little. Everyone seemed interested in flight. "The *Spirit of St. Louis* is a first connection of America and France by air. Someday passengers will travel in airplanes back and forth across the ocean with regularity."

From the moment I woke in the morning to that when I fell asleep late at night, every hour was scheduled. Once when I thought I had a few minutes to myself, a hundred pictures were brought to me to autograph. There was no time for the things I wanted most to do: walk through the streets of Paris and eat at the sidewalk restaurants, talk to French pilots and maybe fly some French airplanes. I did not have time to be with my *Spirit of St. Louis,* even though I speculated over its condition. But mechanics and riggers were going over it with meticulous care, I was told, and reported both plane and engine to be in excellent condition. After the holes in the fuselage fabric had been patched and silver-painted, the French government was still not satisfied; the fuselage had been stripped of all its fabric, and had been recovered as perfectly as it had been covered originally at the San Diego factory.

Time was not the only quality I found lacking in my new life. I missed my previous freedom of action—the touch of earth and the brush of its weather when I stepped out a door onto a flying field or onto a city street. In Paris, even if there had been time, I could not have used it freely. I was a prisoner of the ceremonial life that had been arranged for me, with uniformed officers always outside the door of the building I was in and, always, newspaper reporters and photographers. If I had gone for a walk around the block, I would have been leading a parade. The great city of Paris lay around me, yet was as unreachable as if I were passing above it in my plane. Sitting, riding, standing, talking all day long, I began to have the slightly numbing sensation that comes from remaining indoors too long.

At first it seemed that a tour of Europe was developing for me, and of course that was what I wanted most. I accepted invitations to visit Belgium with my plane, then England. King Albert and Queen Elisabeth came to the Brussels airport to see the *Spirit of St. Louis.* At Buckingham Palace in London, King George asked me to tell him about some of the details of my transatlantic flight. I would have liked to land at Dublin, at Stockholm, at Berlin, in fact in every country. But at London, the American Ambassador, Alanson B. Houghton, informed me that the President of the United States had offered to send a warship to carry me and the *Spirit of St. Louis* back to America. Such an offer was practically an order.

I felt there was something improper about putting my *Spirit of St. Louis* on board a boat. It seemed like imprisoning the future within the past to bind my silver wings into a box that would be rocked and tossed back to America by the very ocean they had conquered in their flight. I suggested that, instead, I fly back by way of Ireland, but Ambassador Houghton was not at all impressed. A destroyer would be sent to get me, he continued. The time spent on the voyage back by ship would be needed in Washington and New York to arrange for my reception.

The idea of spending a week on a destroyer somewhat compensated for my disappointment. I had wanted to ride on a destroyer since I was a schoolboy and had seen one in the Washington Navy Yard. It would be a wonderful trip. I would get to know the officers and crew and learn a lot about the surface of the ocean. Thus I was impressed, but not really overjoyed, when the Ambassador informed me, a day later, that plans had been changed and that Admiral G. H. Burrage's flagship, the cruiser *Memphis,* had been assigned to carry me back to America from England: there would be more space on deck for the crates holding my plane; also a number of newspapermen wanted to make the voyage with me.

The nine-day voyage on that massive cruiser, with its turbines and its ten-inch guns, showed again the rise of America within a single lifetime. It was hard for me to realize that our Navy had achieved equal recognition with Great Britain's famous fleet of the war just nine years concluded. The histories I read always pictured the courage it took for American sailors to attack the vastly superior power of the Union Jack. Now, Admiral Burrage and Henry

Ellis Lackey, captain of the *Memphis,* told me proudly that the United States Navy was the best equipped and strongest in the world.

The *Memphis* was never out of radio communication with stations on land, and its navigating officers always knew their position on the ocean within a radius of ten miles at most. Someday, I felt, airplanes would achieve such communication and such accuracy of navigation. Maybe it would not take long. Had not my cousin Commander Emory S. Land crossed the Atlantic in a "square-rigger" when he was an Annapolis cadet? His ship had been becalmed in the Sargasso Sea, short of food and with no way of calling for assistance—and this was fewer than thirty years before.

On board the *Memphis* there were hours I could devote to another problem arising from my flight—money. Of the fifteen thousand dollars my partners and I had raised to finance the *Spirit of St. Louis* flight, only about fifteen hundred dollars remained when I landed at Paris. That fifteen hundred dollars, together with whatever money I had personally, would not carry me far in meeting the expenses awaiting me on my return. Before leaving Long Island, I had contracted to write the story of my flight for the *New York Times.* That would bring several thousand dollars into my bank account. But it was essential that I find ways of earning more money that would leave me as free as possible to pursue the development of aviation. I received many offers and suggestions; the most appropriate and practical one was that I write a book. Therefore I entered into an agreement with G. P. Putnam's Sons of New York. According to my understanding, the book was to be written in the third person, by means of interviews, and I would myself write a preface for it. An experienced *New York Times* correspondent was to be engaged to do the writing, and in fact he sailed on the *Memphis* with me. During the voyage he and I worked together while he made his preliminary notes.

When I arrived in New York, after disembarking and being welcomed in Washington, I was deluged with tens of thousands of letters, telegrams, and phone calls. These contained many business propositions, varying from a request that I become president of a manufacturing company to an offer of fifty thousand dollars for my signed endorsement of a cigarette. When I replied to the latter that I did not smoke, the company's representative said he would give me a package so I could speak truthfully and from experience. I could have had a hundred thousand dollars for making a lecture tour. And more. And more. When William Randolph Hearst offered me a motion-picture contract with a guarantee of at least one-half million dollars, I was not so quick to turn down the offer, as I had the others. The picture, he said, would be confined to aviation and filmed with dignity and taste. Of course the role of leading actor would be mine.

A half-million dollars was a fabulous sum of money, more than thirty times the cost of my plane and its flight to Paris, more than I would have made in a lifetime as a mail pilot. With it, I would be a man of independent wealth. The filming would require only a few months of my time and thought and the picture itself would contribute to public interest in flying. Thereafter I could do in aviation as I wished. But there were reasons against accepting. William Randolph Hearst controlled a chain of newspapers from New York to California that represented values far apart from mine. They seemed to me overly sensational, inexcusably inaccurate, and excessively occupied with the troubles and vices of mankind. I disliked most of the men I had met who represented him, and I did not want to become associated with the organization he had built.

Hearst suggested that I come and talk to him at his apartment in New York. I was as apprehensive as fascinated when I went there. It was a large and elaborately furnished place, full of paintings and antique articles, and dominated by a man of extraordinary character—tall, heavily built, with pale-blue eyes and a high-pitched voice.

He welcomed me warmly and informally and handed me a motion-picture contract ready for signature. A paper worth half a million dollars, possibly twice that much, was in my fingers. I felt embarrassed, for I had already practically concluded that I would not take part in a motion picture—that I did not want to become a Hollywood actor even temporarily. Also I realized that my flight to Paris had placed me in a position from which I could do a great deal to accelerate aviation's progress during the months ahead, and

I wanted to be free to devote my primary efforts to this end. Of course I had to make a living, and it seemed wise to set apart some extra money while the opportunity was there; but I believed I could do this without extending my activities beyond my own profession. To my astonishment, Hearst put me under no pressure to sign the contract after I started, hesitantly, to explain my attitude. He said, "Just tear it up and throw it in the fire." This embarrassed me more than I had been before. I started to hand it back to him with profuse thanks, but he said again, quietly and pleasantly, "No, if you don't want to make a picture, tear it up and throw it away." So I tore the document in half, and tossed it gently into the fireplace near which we were standing. Hearst watched with what I felt was amused astonishment.

We talked no more that evening about the subject of motion pictures. I put on a mask of aeronautical information, described a little of my Paris flight, and admired two antique silver globes, one celestial, one terrestrial, that were standing on a table. Finally, we shook hands and said good-by. The next day a messenger arrived at the apartment where I was staying with a present from William Randolph Hearst—the two antique silver globes. I was told later that they were valued at more than forty thousand dollars.*

I decided that regardless of the amounts of money I was offered in connection with other projects, I would devote most of my attention to the development of airplanes and air routes. Aviation was my profession. I had confidence in its future. I liked more than anything else to pilot aircraft, and I believed aircraft had a great mission in the modern world.

When, during the rest of 1927 and the first part of 1928, I flew through North, Central, and South America, lecturing on aviation and exhibiting my plane, I was again conforming with the trends of group and nation—new trends because more and more people were

* The Hearst globes are described on page 36 of the eighty-page inventory of the Lindbergh Exhibit in St. Louis (1942) as follows: "Pair of extremely rare silver Globes of Terrestrial and Celestial Spheres bearing Hanover Hall Mark. These globes were made about the year 1700. The surface of the globes is set in the graduate Meridian Circle which rests on a balustered support on circular repoussé base. The Globes are 14 inches high. There is no other known similar pair. Presented by Wm. Randolph Hearst, June 15, 1927. (Mr. Hearst paid $50,000.00 for this pair.)"

beginning to see a brilliant future in the medium of air. This was also true when I became a consultant for the Transcontinental Air Transport Corporation, for the Pennsylvania Railroad, for the Daniel Guggenheim Fund, and for the United States government's Bureau of Aeronautics. Then it was at the apparent zenith of success in my chosen field of aviation that I began to question the direction in which my life was pointing.

The first instance I remember clearly came at the end of a day spent flying westward in 1928. I had crossed the Rocky Mountain ranges of southern Wyoming and eastern Utah. Great Salt Lake and its desert flattened out ahead. The sun was lowering ahead of me, and night would soon overtake me from behind—night, with its disagreeable problems of finding a hotel and avoiding the demands of press-alerted crowds.

Newspaper syndicates had telegraphed station agents all along the railroad lines to be on the lookout for my plane, and to report immediately on sighting it. When I discovered this, I tried to fly at least fifteen miles to the side of railroads that paralleled my route— out of eye range of the agents. But I gained only a few extra minutes by doing so. Even when I arrived at an airfield unannounced, someone usually recognized my plane before its wheels touched the ground, and telephoned the newspapers. I was seldom out of my cockpit more than a quarter of an hour before a crowd began to assemble.

Reporters and photographers had crowded in at every airfield where I stopped since I left New York. Automobile-loads of people followed them. The hotels where I stayed at night were watched. I could not walk along a street without being followed, photographed, and shouted at. Not many days before, I had been recognized as I stepped out the door of a Wall Street office building, and before I could walk a block I was being followed by an enlarging flock of men and women. Fortunately, an empty taxi drove by and I jumped inside. I was tired of crowds and newspaper headlines, of telephone calls, telegrams, and interviews, of handshaking, back-slapping, and autographing. I knew that at any city where I landed for the night, the routine of welcome, picture-taking, and publicity would be repeated. I found it difficult to work and think in the spotlight of newspaper publicity. I began to realize that as one gains fame one loses life. Life meant more to me than fame.

I looked at the desert—mile upon mile of a heat-dried lake bed without a dwelling or sign of human life—and I realized how much I wanted a night of solitude. The high temperatures of afternoon were dropping fast. I saw hard and level strips of gravel. I circled one of them, throttled back, sideslipped in, and landed tail skid first.

The wheels banged heavily on hummocks before my plane stopped rolling. I climbed down from the cockpit and walked out among sparse clumps of brush and cactus. How wonderful it was to feel and be a part of the desert I had crossed so often in my plane yet never touched before, to know its heat, its dryness, the tough sharpness of its prickled growths! The sun was setting when I returned to my plane—such a strange and solitary creature resting in that wilderness, like an animal from some prehistoric past. It concentrated civilization's values, while all around me was a universal starkness. Evolved from one, evolving the other, I represented the vitality called "man."

Stars brightened and darkness gathered quickly as I made supper. The silver wing above me blended into dusk. Coolness came with night. What peace I found there, on that warm but cooling surface of our planet's sphere! Possessions and power seemed valueless. Existence was all that mattered, awareness and appreciation, the expanse, the mountain-cut horizon, the twig under my foot, the pebble in my hand.

During those hours, space and silence changed the beat of time. I grew aware of the juxtaposition of simplicity and complication in relationship to life—in the great sweep of a desert formed by countless grains of sand; in the smooth silver skin of an airplane; in the maze of instruments, tubing, pistons, ribs, and wires that it held; in the individual called "man" and in the elaborate environment he builds. Surely one of nature's miracles lies in the juxtaposition of simplicity and complication extending inward through the atom and outward through the star. Existence seems to require both.

I could not live long there on the desert alone, nor would I want to. But that night I felt the desert held values deeper than those of the civilization from which I came. Here was a paradox: I reached this place by means of transport created by civilization, yet the values of this place could not persist within that civilization's framework. Those values, I realized, were essential to me. They formed the core of life. I had experienced them as a boy on our Minnesota farm, in barnstorming, in flying the airmail. How was I to hold them in the kind of life I had led since my New York–to–Paris flight? Here was a personal, inner problem of bringing together qualities that were apparently incompatible—qualities of the primitive with qualities of the civilized.

I wanted neither to give up all contact with civilization nor to become overwhelmed by it. I wanted to keep close to the primitive core of life I had found there on the desert, yet also to orbit through the peripheries of intellectual accomplishment. Was this possible? The great freedom I felt was momentary, illusionary, an evening's dream. In reality I was bound both literally and figuratively to the mechanism of my plane, resting on the gravel beside me. Its magic had transported me to an austere wilderness and would return me to the luxurious city life of men.

How could I keep hold of both the primitive and the civilized—move back and forth between them as I had that one day? It required much more than the mechanical movement of a plane. It was not a case of just leaving civilization regularly and landing on some spot of solitude to contemplate. An inner receptivity was necessary and it could not be produced by mental power alone. The senses had to feel a spark. The body could not be lethargic. The mind must not be distracted by clutter or materialistic accounting.

Simplicity and complication juxtapose in man to form a unity of body on a diversity of structure, to contrast the awareness of his being with the abstractions of his mind. My civilized life did not encourage receptivity. There were too many details pressing for attention, too many problems, large and small, to occupy the mind. My time was a chattel of my obligations. My senses had less freedom than a slave's. But the juxtaposition that forms man also contains the capacity to change. In the future, I decided, I would devote more attention to the core without renouncing civilization. I would set a trend toward balancing the diverse elements of being, toward simplicity rather than more complications, toward appreciation rather than possessions, toward an objective I felt was before me but could not as yet define.

To select an objective and set a trend—how simple and routine that seems written in a sentence! And what momentous consequences can result in actual life! When I look back through my life, I realize that such selections and trends have had an extraordinary effect on its shaping. Usually I was conscious of their importance at the time.

The airplane, the desert, the civilized, the primitive, and on the surface of the planet the living "I" stood, able in some way to choose between the two. How easy it should be, how difficult it was, to combine my fascination with a complicated airplane and my love for the desert's natural simplicity! The machine had transported me as through time to a primeval bleakness, which itself enhanced the values of the machine that life's civilization had developed. Then to what extent were simplicity and complication in conflict? To what extent could they be justaposed?

I looked again at the plane—wing, fuselage, and tail within the taut silver cloth. It did not seem so complicated. And at the desert—eroded by stream beds, hemmed by mountains, strewn with cactus, brush, and pebbles. Surely it was natural, but should I call it "simple"? And I—man, spirit, thought, and life, inside a leather skin—was tranquillity and turbulence.

All is simple, all is complicated, depending on a viewpoint that emanates from life and shifts with time. From life comes the tangible element within one that in time names simplicity and complication, that at times senses tranquillity and distraction. One is surrounded by the complicated, made of its stuff, and yet one is aware of a resulting order, a simple beauty. Then one feels the stars and feels the seasons and sleeps as men who labor with earth upon their hands.

The trend I decided to set that night on the Salt Lake desert involved more subtle problems than merely setting a trend to combat fear. I had no clear-cut objective. I was trying to combine two seemingly contrary objectives, to be part of the civilization of my time but not to be bound by its conventional superfluity.

But setting a basic trend successfully was not like making a New Year's resolution, or promising oneself to do a better job in the future. An inner awareness was required, an acquiescence followed by a desire in which all the elements of existence took their part. It was a physical as well as a mental experience, a realization coursing through the body as though carried by the blood itself. I had passed through such experiences when I decided to leave college and enter aviation, when I decided to become a parachute jumper, when I decided to make the New York–to–Paris flight. And there were occasions involving less tangible action—a trend concerning my relationships with people, one affecting my inner attitude toward courage and toward fear. The final decision was always preceded by a growing awareness of desire, arising vaguely at first but becoming a crescendo within.

I felt intuitively that I needed time to contemplate and think, far more time than recent months had given me in the fast and complex life I had been leading. Something had always been pressing for attention—phone calls, letters, conferences, interviews, business lunches, parties, dinners, ceremonies, speeches, clubs, committees, friends of friends, and people I had never even heard of—dozens of items and personal demands every day, hundreds each week, many thousands in a year. There was seldom a moment when I was not conscious of something of importance left undone.

I would cut down on all of these activities. I would eliminate the superfluous, simplify my life, and let the trend develop. One thing seemed certain. The key to appreciation, to a balanced being, to joy and grace, lay in a basic simplicity beneath the elaborate garments of culture one chose or was forced to wear. I would reduce my obligations, give away some of my possessions, concentrate my business and social interests. I would take advantage of the civilization into which I had been born without losing the basic qualities of life from which all works of men must emanate.

The important thing was the core. But what was it: how much of it was physical, how much mental, how much spiritual? How could one reach one's core? To me the physical approach seemed most available and effective. From this approach, I felt ways for the spirit and the mind would certainly emerge. Often enough I had sensed the core as a child swimming naked in Pike Creek or lying in the sun on one of its yellow sandbanks. I had felt it when riding on my pony, when sitting on prairie grass under a fabric wing, when pacing back and forth beside a weather-grounded mailplane as I waited for dawn to break. The only times I had even come close to feeling the core since I landed the *Spirit of St. Louis* at Le Bourget were during long flights alone. Once, I had flown more than six hours to cover no more than the fifty-mile distance between Butte and Helena, Montana, just to have time to think without distraction— over lakes and forests, over Glacier National Park, across the Canadian border and back again.

I knew when I felt the sense of "core," when the balance of body, mind, and senses was reached, when there was no element of pressure, hurry, or distraction. I was related to my surroundings yet independent of them in an extraordinary way. The simple was always present. I found that it was only through simplicity I could immerse myself in time until I realized that time offers a release from tempo.

But there were other basic qualities of life that I could take advantage of immediately. Sleep was one of them. As I had stepped up into higher levels of civilized society after my Paris flight, I found that people stayed up smoking, drinking, and talking long after midnight. It was a contagious habit—not the drinking and smoking, for me, because I disliked both—but the staying awake. I always got up the next morning feeling dopey. I decided in the future to go to bed earlier whenever I could break away from a group of people.

On long flights when navigation was simple and no technical problems occupied my mind, or when I sat through dull addresses at formal dinner tables, or during the minutes before falling asleep at night and immediately after waking in the morning—at such times I would think of ways to implement the decision I had made there on the desert. I often used the simple fare of eggs and milk as a ritual to start the day. And on occasion, when I felt more than usually repulsed by the steam heat in my room, the sponge-rubber mattress on my bed, and the hotel's *nouveau-riche* style of furniture, I would throw my pillow down, take a blanket with me, and sleep on the floor.

The problem of simplifying my life was not even resolved once I had ended my ceremonial role following the New York–to–Paris flight. Commuting between Princeton and New York in 1931, I realized that the decision I had made on Salt Lake's desert three years before to simplify my life had not been implemented. I was involved in obligations and projects capable of absorbing many times the number of my days and hours. I was acting as a consultant to TAT, Pan American, the Pennsylvania Railroad, and the Daniel Guggenheim Fund. My side activities included membership on the National Advisory Committee for Aeronautics, consulting work for the United States government, and duties as a colonel in the Army Air Service Reserve. I had become a trustee of the Carnegie Institution of Washington. I was deeply interested in Dr. Robert Goddard's rocket projects. I had married, fathered a child, bought land for a home, contracted for a house, and found that my financial affairs required attention. In addition, I was planning a difficult flight through the Arctic to Japan, which necessitated equipping my landplane with specially built pontoons. I was having a more powerful engine installed, assembling emergency equipment, and studying the techniques of seaplane operation, inasmuch as almost all my previous flying had been with wheels. At the same time, I had become fascinated by fields of medicine, surgery, and biological science, with the result that I was spending many hours a month at the Rockefeller Institute for Medical Research in New York. Judged rationally, the trends I set had failed.

Yet in a deeper sense they had been effective. I no longer felt the pressure and suffered the distraction I experienced before. How could my life seem simpler when actually it had become more complex? What sequence of circumstances had preceded?

During the hours of commuting, while my eyes watched roads, signals, and traffic, my mind, consciously or subconsciously, reviewed incidents and conditions I had encountered following my flight to Paris three years before—the sudden mutation in my way of living, the adjustments I had made, one after another, to an amazingly changed environment.

A quality of "time" rides with travel which I have found under no other circumstance. It fertilizes subconscious apprehension until visions emerge like—but more rational than—the visions brought forth by the quality of time that lies in sleep. When my vehicle is not too complicated for the skill I have developed, when the roads are not too rough, the weather not too threatening, or my destination not too close, then memory and imagination act on a stage of thought improvising practical and fantastic roles. I daydream of impossibilities and lay plans of action to approach them, and, still further, plans to implement plans. I did this when I was walking to school from our farm in Minnesota, when I rode my pony along Morrison County roads, when I sailed a ship or cruised a plane. Under such circumstances I become more keenly aware of obstacles that limit my ambitions, and consider their pregnability.

At first, like a guest pleased and overwhelmed by the magnificence of his welcome, I had tried to comply with suggestions, requests, and invitations. I gave newspaper interviews by the dozens, posed for photographs by the hundreds, bought a tuxedo and a tail coat, attended lunches, cocktail parties, and dinners, made speeches, visited schools, dedicated airports, rode in parades, took part in apparently limitless activities, most of which were in most ways, if not all, distasteful to me.

In the twelve months following my landing at Paris, I made more than a hundred addresses, attended at least two hundred formal lunches and dinners, and took part in scores of parades. That was the background to the night on the desert when I decided again to change my environment, to start and gradually follow a trend toward simpler living. This trend had not in fact brought simplification, but it had resulted in my controlling my environment to a large extent. I had cut down drastically on the number of interviews, ceremonial speeches, and meals. I had declined to become an officer or director of any company. Typically, I had rejected a friend's suggestion that I enter Long Island social life and buy a stable of polo ponies. I gave to the public the thousands of gifts, medals, awards, and citations I received as a result of my flights, including William Randolph Hearst's celestial and terrestrial globes.

Two interesting phenomena emerged. One related to the effect of sleep on mental processes. I often found that the solutions to current problems in research came most effectively after thought during driving followed by a night's sleep. Obviously some rational process, of which my conscious mind was unaware, took place under such circumstances. Because the results were so consistent, I came to rely on this process. While driving I would consider a problem, then let my mind run free, then consider it again. Before going to sleep that night I would outline it in my mind. A solution did not always come the next morning, but invariably some clarification resulted.

The other phenomenon related to the effect of possessions on creativity. For me, concentration on ideas and research necessitated a tranquillity of mind, and I found few ways of gaining such tranquillity that were more effective than to reduce my possessions. My first serious attempt to reduce possessions resulted from my flights in the *Spirit of St. Louis*. It reversed the habits of my childhood.

As a boy I had collected about everything—stones, butterflies, coins, turtles, cigarette cards, cigar bands, stamps, tin cans, lead pipe, and burned-out electric-light bulbs, among other items. I kept the most valuable of these articles in locked boxes and I hid the keys. Material possessions then seemed to me as desirable as anything in life. One of my greatest fears was that God, being omnipotent, would take for his own use some of these possessions out of my locked boxes.

Following my successful flight to Paris, possessions accumulated literally by the thousands—decorations and gifts ranging from automobiles to watches, crocheted doilies, and diamond stickpins. I once had a room piled almost full of packages that had come by mail or express. My activities had not left me time to open or even think very much about them. Eventually I learned that a horned toad had been put in one, shipped unlabeled from a southwestern state. It had died long before I made arrangements for the packages to be unwrapped.

Fortunately, most people were too intelligent to send live presents, and a police dog which arrived unannounced by express was such a fine animal that one of my friends gave it a permanent home. A monkey delivered at Lambert Field, also by express and unannounced, created more of a problem. I was on a flying trip and so

I knew nothing about the incident at the time. The express-truck driver was faced with the problem that if no one on the field had a right to accept the monkey, then how was it to be fed and cared for? Finally, the lunch-stand owner agreed to feed the animal and keep it temporarily in his cookshack. The monkey turned out to be a big attraction. Lunch-stand business improved, and all went well until a man brought his daughter out from the city to watch flying activities. The girl tried to pet the monkey and was bitten, though not too seriously, it seems. The father threatened to sue for damages, but who was he to sue? The lunch-stand keeper said it was not his monkey. The express-truck driver said it certainly was not his. I was not there and would not have accepted it anyway. The incident ended by the father deciding that a lawsuit was not profitable under the circumstances, and the monkey was sent to the zoo. It had all become an elaborate joke by the time I heard the story.

What to do with the less volatile presentations caused more of a problem for me. It would take a museum to house them. The Missouri Historical Society opportunely requested the loan, for ten days, of all items I had received as a result of my flights in the *Spirit of St. Louis,* for exhibition in the society's museum in the Jefferson Memorial Building in St. Louis. The articles were laid out in cases on long strips of paper that covered prehistoric stone implements, arrowheads, beads, and documents and belongings of early Mississippi Valley settlers. So many people thronged through the building that the ten days were extended to weeks, months, and years, until I made a permanent gift of the entire collection to the society.*

Before my flight to Paris I had not had enough possessions to realize the distractions that mount with ownership. Most of those I had were easily tucked away in drawers and boxes, and in attic and basement corners. When I left home to take up a career in aviation, I knew my mother would take good care of anything she found belonging to me. But in the summer of 1927, with packages coming addressed to me in care of various friends, hotels, postmasters, and airfields, and hundreds of thousands of letters arriving, hundreds of which inquired about the receipt of letters and packages previously

---

* Among the thousands of items are some of Lindbergh's personal possessions, including the flying suit and his grandfather's watch which he wore on the flight.

sent, just the sorting of mail and disposition of unopened packages required more time than I had free. I began to regard possessions rather as debts than assets.

The smothering sense of possessions was intensified for me when I arranged for my mother to move from her small house in Detroit into a somewhat larger one several blocks away. I found that heirlooms of two families required many hours of attention—of considering, preserving, discarding, repacking. More possessions came with marriage, my wife's possessions, accumulated since early girlhood, and wedding presents, many of them so fragile and costly that they required special care. Before we had finished moving into our farmhouse at Princeton, I had concluded that numerous possessions became formidable obstacles to my awareness and accomplishment, and that every unneeded article was best gotten out of the way—like clearing the decks of a battleship for action.

Of course, the dynamic life I was leading could not be handled like a battleship, and even a battleship needed to put into port for reconditioning after an engagement—a port where the nearest wharves would have occasional litter. But I could set trends that would diminish my obligations to possessions rather than increase them. If I could not bring myself to give or throw something away, and if it did not have to be accessible, then I would pack it up in a box to be placed in storage.

This procedure started what I called my "brown-package policy." I bought a sixty-pound roll of heavy paper, together with some balls of twine, and began wrapping up articles I wanted to get out of the way—from photographs to special tools, guns, and flying equipment. It turned out to be highly effective. Closets, shelves, and drawers began to have extra room, and it was easy to find articles needed for current use, while the contents of the labeled and inventoried packages were well preserved and easy to get at.

Letters and papers came under a category of their own. Before my flight to Paris I had not thought of papers as articles or possessions. They were too intangible, too flimsy, too easily crumpled up or tucked away. But when my mail amounted to hundreds of pounds in a month, papers became as tangible as and heavier than the stones I once collected. Sorting out envelopes containing the most important items from a sack of mail became a formidable task, and attending to the items selected became a greater one.

It seemed to be a hopeless situation as far as my correspondence was concerned. Thousands of envelopes were never opened. Of the letters I read, I would stack those I hoped to answer in a pile, with the most pressing on top. I never reached those on the bottom. Every letter I answered seemed to bring another in return, sometimes several others. The top of the pile grew much faster than I could cut it down.

This gradually taught me several techniques. One was that papers were handled most efficiently when they were handled only once. When I picked up a letter or a document, I tried to complete the necessary action related to it and file it away. Another was that when I let letters go long enough, a lot of them did not seem to need answering any more. A third was that I could often control a correspondence or taper it off entirely by letting increased time elapse between letters. In general, the policy I adopted was just the opposite of an airmail pilot's. Instead of trying to speed the mail, I tried to slow it down.

To reduce the tempo and possessions of life was so contrary to modern trends that I began reconsidering the policies I was establishing. Airplanes were possessions. I owned an airplane and wanted very much to own it. Certainly aviation increased the tempo of life, and I wanted to develop aviation.

Yes, there were certain possessions that I wanted, that I needed to make my way in modern life. I also had to conform to many of the conventions of my time in providing for the needs of my family. How could I build and maintain a "core" under those inevitable pressures? Only by somehow finding time and place for contemplation regardless of the pressures. At the same time that I conformed, I would keep my mind and body aloof from civilization's increasingly synthetic environment. I found that I gained far more from such experiences than reason would expect. Their value seemed completely out of proportion to the time they took, for they entered into my existence thereafter in ways that baffle reason.

As years passed, I found time for solitude and contemplation with greater and greater frequency—on the coasts of Maine and

Charles Junior's first birthday, 1931

Illiec—the French island home purchased in 1938

Long Barn, the Nicolson home in England rented in 1936-38

Anne and Jon at Long Barn

Playing with his sons Land and Jon, 1941

Jon Lindbergh (born 1932)

Land Lindbergh
(born 1937)

Scott Lindbergh
(born 1942)

Anne Lindbergh (born 1940) and Reeve Lindbergh (born 1945)

Anne with her daughters, c. 1955

Mrs. Morrow with her Lindbergh, Morgan, and Morrow grandchildren, *c.* 1951

The Lindbergh family at Reeve's wedding, 1968

In St. Croix, 1959

With half-sister Eva Lindbergh Spaeth at the dedication of the Lindbergh Interpretive Center, 1973

The Lindbergh home on Maui

Lindbergh in 1973

Florida, on the rocks of Illiec lying under trees and stars, in a mountain pool in New Guinea. In the end I found it midway across the North Pacific where space, time, and life interlace the Hawaiian chain of islands, uniquely on the volcanic island of Maui. Seated there on some high bleak ledge, I would watch a foot trail angle down the crater rim and wind off into the desert, and sometimes, in the early morning, stand on one of Maui's beaches and watch day break in either east or west, judging by pinkness or cloud—the double sunrise of Pacific islands. Behind me was the constant roar of a white cascade; before me, the dark rippled blue of sea separated by a white raveling of surf.

Withdrawing to your core brings you closer to values of life and death. As a young man, when I began working on the design of a perfusion apparatus at the Rockefeller Institute, I was primarily interested in the mechanics of life. Could immortality be achieved through mechanics, surgery, and medicine? Forty years later, lying naked in the sun in a hollow in the rocks on the coast of Long Island Sound, I had little concern about death. In fact, it seemed a desirable phenomenon, part of a cosmic plan that lay above man's wisdom. The perfusion apparatus I developed was important only so far as it contributes to the welfare of the contemporary generation and does not add to genetic defects passed on to the future.

As I gained in age and experience, my interest shifted from the scientific toward the mystical. I found that any branch of science pursued to its peripheries ended in mystery. Man could neither explain the miracle of creation or the fact of his awareness, nor conceive the end of space and time. The miracles of science and technology become trivial in the face of the unknowable.

Studying science gave me greater insight to the myths and superstitions of theology and opened my mind to theological doctrine as it had never been open before. I concluded that the approach to the spirit, intuition, and myth of theology was through the factual knowledge of science, and that intuitive conclusions of theology assisted the progress of science. Man's intuition, erroneous though it may often be, always leads and stimulates his rationality. It was intuition that postulated God or gods—a factual concept beyond the values of rationality—with which the exactness of science has never been able to cope. God became a power, a being, an intangibility, a superhuman power, who could do inexplicable things. What could not otherwise be explained was attributed to God. The mysteries and superstition of religion challenged scientific thought, and at the same time created myths that have had tremendous effect on human life and even pointed the way for scientific thought to explore.

In Genesis, God tempted man with the apple of knowledge and banished him when he partook of it. Genesis leaves us in a mystery not unlike what lies beyond scientific rationality. Was man ruined in his knowledge because it is finite? Was mankind better off following dogmatic religious myths than the fearful future realities of science? Is the intellect man's tyranny over himself?

Critical and dangerous as the intellect's record has become, human survival still depends upon its wisdom. We must bring our intellects into balance with other elements of life or we shall perish as a species. We must overcome the hypnosis caused by our miraculous intellectual creations, and return to the essential life-stream values that evolved us through the epochs—merge the knowledge of our mind with the wisdom of wildness that produced us. This is our modern challenge. All others fade before it.

THIRTEEN

Banana River

The month is February. The year, nearly two thousand after Christ. My place is in New England. Scott Cove of Long Island Sound, outside my window, is ripped by wind and fringed by ice. I draw pencil and paper toward me, listen to a foghorn blow, let mind and memory leap freely through life, time, and space—revisit various areas of earth, relive experiences that reason proves are past although I still can sense them. I remember a ballistic-missile firing.

Sunlight strikes my face and chest, warm, glowing, blinding to desk-accustomed eyes. Waves tumble toward me, row on row, sending their scimitars of foam to cut against the beach. Pelicans and gulls, two or three hundred, stand eying me, concerned by my nearness. Beyond them, Cape Canaveral is a haze against the Atlantic Ocean.

Near the cape's end, striped black and white, and high, the old lighthouse tower stands, just as it stood five years ago when I camped here on this same coast with my wife and children—when the cape was a wilderness of myrtle bush, sea grape, and black-eyed yellow daisies. The wide, curving sand beach fits with memory's picture of the lighthouse. Time has caused no change. Thick-growing palmettos along the shore hide the inland acres. But I know what lies behind them, screened only by bladed leaves from view—houses and stores, newly built, springing up by hundreds, replacing the semitropical foliage almost as fast as bulldozers root it out of the way. The winding, rutted road I once followed northward, past a sign warning that it was IMPASSABLE TO TITUSVILLE, has been lost in a network of paved streets and highways.

From where I sit, a man's length above the tide's encroachment, only one mark is visible to signify this change: a second tower, pricking the sky like the lighthouse, and not so far away. Red and white against the mist-blue background, it is a stand of ascending platforms built to prepare our rocket missiles for launching into space.

Cape Canaveral has become a missile test base for the United States Air Force, and tonight a "shoot" is scheduled: a huge ballistic rocket is to be fired out over the instrumented range, southeastward. I have come to Florida to see that shoot. In another hour I will have to dress and start for the Control Center—out of my swimming trunks, away from the primitive beach, over the paved roads that so recently scarred the ground. I will drive past into an area protected by challenging guards and barbed-wire fences which contains some of the most secret, complicated, and advanced devices known to twentieth-century science.

A pelican leaps awkwardly into air, to flap across the surf, while a half-dozen boys come yelling down to play. For thousands of years men have dreamed of flying like that bird; yet my own generation is the first to bear children into the age of human flight. And already these youngsters take for granted travel through the air. In their dreams they shed atmospheric wings, build satellites, and comet out through space.

Missiles with atomic power—what does the future hold for rocket flight? The moon—the planets—stars—unknown galaxies and voids? At Cape Canaveral, time and space are contorted through forms I had never known. "Now" and "then," "here" and "there," refuse to recognize their boundaries. What does the future hold for rocket flight? A quarter-century had passed since I first asked that question, in 1928. Civilization did not seem to depend on the answer then. I was alone in my Ryan monoplane over an eastern reach of the Mississippi Valley, daydreaming as I flew toward the city of St. Louis. Clear weather and a cruising speed of eighty-five miles an hour, on a nonstop trip from New York, had given me plenty of time to think.

That year was momentous in the history of aviation, for we were organizing the first passenger airline between New York and California. I had spent many weeks surveying the route. Transcontinental Air Transport was our corporation's name. Anyone who could pay the price would soon be able to purchase the remarkable achievement of crossing the entire continent in two nights by train and two days by air in a big twelve-passenger, all-metal, trimotor transport. Twenty-five hundred miles in less than forty-eight hours—it was to mark a new era in human progress. We aviators were keenly aware of the importance, newness, and vitality of the profession we followed. We had accomplished miracles. We expected more.

I had been flying since early morning, with a light wind quartering my tail. Allegheny ridges were behind me. Comfortable clouds, puffed white, were ahead. Lambert Field still lay two states and some odd miles away. I was thinking about the tremendous advance aviation had made since the Wright brothers' Kitty Hawk flight. How impossible it had been for Wilbur and Orville, on those sand dunes of North Carolina in 1903, to envisage the changes even a single generation ahead. Orville Wright once told me that foresight, in the beginning days of flight, had been blinded by the element of power. He said he and his brother never imagined getting an entire horsepower from a single pound of engine weight.

Only twenty-six years would separate that Kitty Hawk flight—less than a minute long—and the passenger schedules that were about to link Atlantic and Pacific coasts. What would the next quarter-century bring forth, I wondered. What elements were now limiting our vision? With enough imagination, could one prove the relativity of time and bend the future closer? Earth, sea, and air had all been conquered. Only space, that emptiness between the planets and the stars, remained. Would someone, someday, organize an expedition to the moon? And later to Mars and Venus? What speeds might man attain when unbound by air's resistance? Was it possible that he could free himself of the world entirely, and become a universal creature piercing through space like a beam of light?

Of course wings and propellers were restricted to the atmosphere of earth. But what of rockets—the kind children shot up at stars, after supper, on Independence Day? They did not depend on air for either sustenance or power. How fast could a rocket go into space? What kind of powder could it burn? How much could it carry? Suppose you attached wings to a big rocket and flew it like a plane to start with—such a device ought to break world records for altitude and speed.

On that survey trip in my monoplane I decided to investigate the possibilities of rocket flight. But how to do so was a problem. Nobody I had met knew anything about rockets. Working in fields of aviation, you did not think about them. For many months, wherever opportunity arose, I inquired about rockets, but was unsuccessful in obtaining information. Finally I decided to ask the Du Pont Company people at Wilmington, Delaware. In that great organization, with its century and more of experience in making chemicals and explosives, I would surely be able to find answers to the questions in my mind.

I realized that a pragmatic approach was necessary if the proposal was not to end with negative results. I began casting around for some project that would involve only a preliminary step, some obviously practical venture that could precede piloted rocket flight as man-carrying kites had preceded man-carrying airplanes. I wanted to start those trained and brilliant minds thinking in terms of jet-rocket propulsion. The whole record of aviation showed that in the light of concentrated thought strange and fascinating fruits ripen.

How difficult would it be, I asked, to build a rocket that could replace a Wasp engine's thrust for one minute, and to attach it to the fuselage of a single-engine airplane for use in emergency? Then when a pilot's engine cut on take-off, he could press a button, ignite the rocket, bank around, and land. He would not have to worry about crashing into trees and houses at the runway's end. The problem was accepted, somewhat dubiously, as one that could be solved with existing materials and knowledge. The Du Pont executives were both considerate and interested. They arranged for a conference with about twenty of their scientists and engineers. On November 1, 1929, I flew to Delaware to attend it. A general shaking of heads took place. Rockets were too inefficient to be used as power plants for aircraft. The weight of fuel consumed would be immense, incomparably more per mile than that of gasoline run through reciprocating engines. It was all very well to shoot a few ounces of Fourth of July fireworks several hundred feet skyward; but for pushing the weight of a pilot through miles of air, rocket propulsion seemed too impractical to warrant further study.

A Wasp engine, at that time, developed four hundred horsepower. Based on the efficiency of black powder, about four hundred pounds of fuel would be needed, according to the report Du Pont sent me. The heat generated by burning this amount of fuel in one minute would require a combustion chamber lined with firebrick, which, of course, would be too heavy and too large for use on an airplane. Under any circumstances it would be difficult to handle the type of fuel that would have to be used; the danger of explosion would be high, and there was uncertainty about how even a firebrick-lined chamber should be constructed to withstand the pressure, time, and temperature involved.

That report certainly limited man to his earth and to speeds attainable with airplanes and propellers. I dropped further investigation into rocket propulsion for the moment; but my dream of jet flight remained.

Then, one of those unpredictable incidents happened that so often bend the trends of life and history. One morning later in the month, I was in Falaise, the Long Island home of my friends Harry and Carol Guggenheim. I was standing beside a window in the oak-beamed living room, looking out over the sound, comparing an airplane's speed with the slothlike progress of a string of gravel barges under tow.

"Listen to this!" Carol was on a sofa near the great stone fireplace, reading *Popular Science Monthly*. She had heard me talk about my interest in rockets. Her voice continued, reading:

AIMS ROCKET AT ROOF OF SKY

Goddard Tests New Missile to Explore the
Upper Air for Science

. . . First reports from the astonished city of Worcester [were] that a huge meteor had exploded. Witnesses informed the Worcester police station that an airplane in flames had shot across the sky and blown up. Two police ambulances dashed through the streets looking for the supposed victims, while an airplane took off to aid in the search.

The cause of all the excitement proved to be a test, by Professor R. H. Goddard, head of the physics department of Clark University, of a sky projectile that he invented to explore the upper air. A liquid propellant never before used in any rocket drove the latest model, which is the climax of experiments costing $12,000. With the new explosive Professor Goddard expects to shoot a rocket to heights never before attained. If one could reach a height of 200 miles above the earth it might obtain data of great value to science. Even a twenty-mile rocket would be an invaluable aid in answering the mystery of what is at the top of the sky.

. . . In the course of his experiments there have been persistent reports that Goddard planned to shoot a rocket to the moon, where its arrival was to be marked by the explosion of a heavy charge of flashlight powder visible through powerful telescopes. Professor Goddard never has denied that his invention might prove practicable. It is said, however, that, with a sufficient charge of explosive, one of his projectiles might even escape from the earth's restraining gravity and become a man-made meteor in outer space.

I inquired about Goddard's reputation. On finding that he was indeed not a showman but a respected university physicist, I telephoned to arrange for a meeting at Worcester, Massachusetts. It took place on Saturday, November 23, 1929.

He had been studying rocket propulsion for close to a quarter-century, Dr. Goddard told me. Progress had been slow because most of his time had to be devoted to duties as an instructor of physics at the university. Both the Smithsonian Institution and Clark University had helped him with small grants of money; but funds for development work had been difficult to obtain.

As to his rockets, yes, the fuel consumed was great, but the speed theoretically attainable was tremendous. In the beginning he used a solid fuel, but in his later designs he had replaced this with a mixture of liquid oxygen and gasoline. A firebrick combustion chamber? Ridiculous! His combustion chamber was made of Duralumin, only one thirty-second of an inch thick. Rocket propulsion for airplanes? A long way off. The Du Pont engineers were right: rocket efficiency was too low compared with speeds a wing seemed able to attain through air.

We sat and talked in the Goddard home, at No. 1 Tallawanda Drive, the professor, his young, blond wife, and I. I had driven to Worcester from New York in my Franklin car over traffic-crowded highways. It was late afternoon. Goddard had already spent considerable time showing me his university workroom and laboratory. Were his experiments leading to any practical objective, I asked. He said there were many uses to which rockets could be put, but that his greatest interest lay in developing one to carry scientific instruments into the upper atmosphere. What height could a rocket attain with known fuels? Theoretically, a multistage rocket could reach the moon; but the cost of building it was probably far beyond the value of foreseeable results. A rocket flight to an altitude of, say, one hundred miles seemed practical, however, and at that height much important data could be recorded.

I am sure Professor Goddard had no idea how his words set my mind to spinning. A flight to the moon theoretically possible! An altitude of one hundred miles predictable within a few more years! Then space was to be an extension of, not a limit to, the works of man. The rocket, like the wheel, the hull, and the wing, would throw back old horizons. What did it matter that the cautious Professor mentioned restrictions of practicability and cost? My imagination was not bounded by the thoroughness of his knowledge of physics. I had no learned reputation to uphold. A few weeks before, I had been told that a rocket was not suitable for an airplane to add a single minute's emergency power. Now, I had discovered a scientist who said one could be built capable of passing entirely out of the earth's gravitational field.

Maybe a more concentrated form of energy would be discovered. Maybe it would let us land on other planets and explore space around distant stars. Earlier, I had read an article claiming that if the atom could be harnessed, a water glass would hold enough energy to propel a battleship across an ocean. Maybe the pilot of the future would accelerate his rocket halfway to his destination, and decelerate the other half. Maybe man would learn how to travel faster than the speed of light. Impossible? Who dared, now, to say anything was impossible!

When I asked Goddard what he needed most in carrying on his experiments, he replied that he wanted to be free of the classroom duties that took so much of his time. Then he would look for a place, probably in the southwestern part of the United States, where he could set up a laboratory and launching tower and test rockets without worrying his neighbors or being restricted by the police. How much money would be required? Well, if he could obtain a grant of twenty-five thousand dollars a year for four years, he thought that would cover all expenses—his own salary, one or two assistants, transportation, material, rental, and equipment. Under such circumstances he felt he could accomplish within forty-eight months what might otherwise take a lifetime. He spoke as though such an amount was beyond practical realization.

Driving back to New York that evening, I considered ways in which I might help Goddard obtain the one hundred thousand dollars. It was almost seven times as much as I had raised to finance, just three years earlier, the *Spirit of St. Louis* and the flight to Paris.

I decided to approach the Du Pont executives again. If rockets had the future I envisioned, it would be a minute investment in proportion to eventual results and profits. On the other hand, if the Goddard project proved unsuccessful, the Du Pont Company was large enough to write the investment off against research costs. Whether or not the risk was worth taking, company executives would have to decide. At least they should be interested in the fact that Goddard was using a thin sheet of Duralumin to withstand temperatures their engineers had said necessitated firebrick. Professor Goddard was with me in Wilmington at the next conference, again promptly and considerately arranged by officers of the Du Pont Company. Engineers and executives listened intently and asked many questions, but they made no offer of financial assistance. Apparently, rocket propulsion was thought to have insufficient commercial value to warrant the investment of company funds.

My next approach was to the Carnegie Institution of Washington. It was a well-endowed scientific organization which did not have to relate the investment of its funds to eventual financial profits. In scientific fields, the statement was often made that knowledge itself justified expense. I felt sure Carnegie executives and scientists would realize what great possibilities lay in the development of rockets. On December 10, 1929, Goddard and I met with a group of scientists at the Washington home of Dr. John C. Merriam, President of the Carnegie Institution. Present were Dr. W. S. Adams and Dr. Harold D. Babcock, of the Mount Wilson Observatory, Dr. Charles G. Abbot, of the Smithsonian Institution, Dr. C. F. Marvin, of the U.S. Weather Bureau, and Dr. John A. Fleming, another Carnegie Institution executive.

I called attention to the fact that the airplane and its propeller were limited to the environment of air, and that if man was ever to reach beyond the atmosphere, or even to its higher levels, rockets seemed to be the only vehicles with which he could do so. Goddard then discussed his investigations and the lines of development he thought it advisable to follow. The scientists present were enthusiastic in discussing knowledge that could be obtained through instruments carried to great altitudes—knowledge about the sun's corona, about cosmic rays, about the Kennelly-Heaviside layer. Dr. Merriam said he would recommend a grant of five thousand dollars for Goddard's research, but that funds free of the Institution's existing commitments were too limited to give the Professor support of the magnitude he needed. For such support it would be advisable to look elsewhere.

None of the financiers I talked to in New York, and on my trips westward to California, showed more than passing interest in rockets and their future. For them, airplanes involved sufficient fantasy. I had met only one man who combined wealth, vision, and courage to the extent I felt necessary to provide the adequate financing of Professor Goddard—Daniel Guggenheim.

Daniel Guggenheim had accumulated a great fortune in the copper business. Like myself, although he was much older, he was a first-generation American. His father, Meyer Guggenheim, in 1847, at the age of twenty, had left a ghetto in Switzerland for the city of Philadelphia in the New World, a city where ghettos had never existed. At first Meyer made his living by peddling pins, needles, lace, shoestrings, spices, and such items, carried in a backpack. As years passed, he became a shop owner, a commission merchant, an importer, a mine owner, and in the course of his work a millionaire and a multimillionaire. His sons multiplied his fortune and became themselves multimillionaires.

With a basic sense of philanthropy, and in gratitude to the country that had given them such freedom, the Guggenheims began establishing great foundations for the benefit of mankind. Four years earlier, Daniel Guggenheim had created a fund of two and a half million dollars to be spent over a short period for the promotion of aeronautics. I met him through his son, Harry, who had been a Navy aviator in World War I. Harry and I met on Curtiss Field, Long Island, in 1927, while I was preparing the *Spirit of St. Louis* for the flight to Paris. Thereafter we became close friends. Harry was President of the Daniel Guggenheim Fund for the Promotion of Aeronautics, and appointed me an adviser to it.

I was hesitant to approach Daniel Guggenheim to ask him to finance the Goddard project partly because I did not want to impose on his friendship, and partly because I felt he had done so much to help the development of aviation that he should not be asked to contribute additional money to finance the still more visionary field of rocketry. But I felt the Goddard project offered an opportunity for the United States to take leadership in a field of such importance that I was justified in bringing it to the attention of anyone who might help. By 1929 Germany was taking the lead in rocket research, with little competition from other countries. In particular, the experiments of Fritz von Opel, with rocket cars and planes, had been widely reported. Germany's major position had already been attacked by Goddard's development of liquid fuel and his definition of the need for a lightweight, thin-skinned metal projectile. If Daniel Guggenheim did not wish to finance it himself, he could certainly give me excellent advice. Harry Guggenheim had recently been appointed ambassador to Cuba by President Hoover. I wrote to Harry in Havana, asking if he had any objection to my talking to his father about the Goddard project. His approval was immediate.

Daniel Guggenheim's Hempstead House, near Falaise on the North Shore of Long Island, was a castle of gray stone. We met inside the doorway through which a butler had admitted me. Guggenheim characteristically greeted me at the door, rather than expect his servant to usher me in. He was a man in his early seventies, short in stature, quick of eye, sharp in thought, intuitive, patriotic, and farsighted. I outlined my interest in rockets and my discussions with Professor Goddard.

"Then you believe rockets have an important future?" he asked.

"Probably. Of course one is never certain."

"But you think so. And this professor, he looks like a pretty capable man?"

"As far as I can find out, he knows more about rockets than anybody else in the country."

"How much money does he need?"

"He'd like to have twenty-five thousand dollars a year for a four-year project."

"Do you think he can accomplish enough to make it worth a hundred-thousand-dollar investment?"

"Well, it's taking a chance. But if we're ever going to get beyond the limits of airplanes and propellers, we'll probably have to go to rockets. It's taking a chance, but—yes, I think it's worth taking."

"All right, I'll give him the money. We'll want an advisory committee. Of course you'll be on that."

It was a short conversation, ten minutes perhaps, and most of it took place as we stood and walked in the hallway, yet it sent Robert and Esther Goddard to the little city of Roswell on New Mexico's desolate southwestern plains. On twenty-five thousand dollars a year (an extraordinarily generous grant according to the standards of the time), Goddard moved his family, his assistants, household furnishings, and laboratory equipment two thousand miles to Roswell. From the same grant he paid his own salary and his assistants', the cost of setting up his laboratory, and the purchase of Duralumin, steel tubing, liquid oxygen, and other components, and, some twenty miles away, built a test stand and rocket-launching tower. That tower, made out of the galvanized-iron framework of a windmill and pointing skyward from its concrete corner blocks, seemed to me like a huge cannon aimed at an unwary moon. Someday, I felt, a rocket launched from earth would strike the distant satellite.

I used to land my plane at Roswell to visit the Goddards, but I was never lucky enough to see a successful rocket ascent. Something always went wrong in spite of detailed preparations. The fifteen-foot-long, nine-inch-diameter rocket, nicknamed "Little Nell," would be hauled carefully over the prairie on its specially constructed trailer and installed upright in the tower with meticulous care. We would evacuate tarantulas and orange-spotted black widows from the nearby dugout observation post. An assistant would pour sub-zero liquid oxygen from a big Thermos bottle into one of the rocket's tanks. Stations would be taken—one man in the dugout, the rest of us at the control post about a thousand feet away. At a word from the Professor there would be a flame, a roar, and—on other occasions, when I was not there—a slender object streaking skyward. But for me, there was only a puff of smoke and a fire. I always left with an invitation to return to Roswell to watch the next attempt, for which more reliable techniques would be developed.

What did the future hold for rocket flight? It was in 1945 that I had my next close contact with rockets—at the underground factory of Nordhausen, in the devastated countryside of Germany. There I began to realize the terrible effect that the missiles and explosives of science could have on our civilization. What a contrast it was to the scientific dreams I had listened to at the Goddard home in Worcester sixteen years before. Professor Goddard was dead. World War II had placed a nightmare of time between me and the hours we spent together while he was carrying on his pioneering work.

Acting as a consultant to the United Aircraft Corporation, I had gone to Europe with a Navy mission in May 1945, immediately after the surrender of Hitler's forces. The purpose of my trip was to study the enemy's developments in high-speed aircraft. From the beginning it was a fantastic trip through countries dazed and wasted by six years of modern war.

At Paris, at the headquarters of Navy Technical Mission Europe, we had loaded a jeep and trailer into an Army transport plane and set out for the heavily bombed city of Munich. We were all dressed in GI uniforms and armed with pistols, for "werewolf" (resistance) activity had been reported in most of the areas we were to enter. Two members of our mission sat or slouched in the lashed-down jeep, trying to make up for sleep lost the night before. The rest of us found what comfortable spots we could in the crowded Dakota (C-47) fuselage. I wedged myself between a dust-covered window and one of the trailer's wheels, using my sleeping bag for a cushion.

Our route was plotted via Mannheim. The plane flew low against a headwind, and I could read the history of three great wars from marks on the ground—the mass graves of 1870, rectangular, brick-edged, bush-grown; the faint zigzag trenches of our fathers' generation; the fresh tank tracks and foxholes of the past six years. There were the shell-shattered villages of Lorraine and the blown-up concrete bastions of the Siegfried Line.

Landing in Germany, we divided into teams to question enemy personnel and to search for key material and documents. Taking turns at the wheel, several of us drove the jeep and trailer through bomb-leveled cities and along roads lined with hundreds of wrecked vehicles and thousands of plodding refugees. White cloths hung out of windows in the villages we passed.

Sometimes our route took us through areas still occupied by the German Army itself—an army surrendered, but with its guns and its discipline intact. I remember approaching a crossroad that held an entire Wehrmacht regiment on the march—trucks, cannon, and thousands of rifled infantrymen strung out at right angles to our line of travel. A seemingly endless column of green-clad German soldiers moving in one direction; a single American jeep rolling up against it, like a fly buzzing at the body of a serpent. A few days before, any one of those soldiers, whose mission for years was to kill Americans in uniform, would have brought gun to shoulder at the sight of us. Words of surrender, transmitted from a distant source, seemed intangible protection at that moment. But the green body severed as if by magic when we reached it, and enemy officers saluted stiffly while we cut across.

We stopped at demobilization centers; we confiscated documents, interrogated engineers and scientists, and picked our way through litter in looted laboratories. We flew back and forth between Germany and France, until one day, with Navy Lieutenant E. H. Uellendahl, I reached the underground tunnels of Nord-hausen. There, the Nazi government had established a production line for V-2 rockets—those supersonic missiles of which more than a thousand exploded unannounced on England during the last months of the war. These were "Hitler's miracle weapons." In its setting, with its scientific efficiency and its horror, that Nordhausen establishment seemed far from the earth I knew, as though I had ridden one of the missiles it produced and stepped out on a strange and terrible planet.

We approached through the barbed-wire enclosures of Camp Dora, a branch of the infamous concentration camp of Belsen. Labor for the factory had been furnished in large part by prisoners. Confusion, brought by the surrender, was immediately apparent. Gates were open, prisoners were gone, and displaced persons (DPs) of a number of Eastern European nationalities had taken over the squalid wooden barracks. There was the stench one always encounters where human beings live with inadequate sanitation—a mixture arising from stale urine, feces, sweat, and rotting garbage.

Hundreds of subassemblies for the V-2s were lying on flatcars or were scattered over the ground: nose cones, cylindrical bodies, and big Duralumin fuel tanks for liquid oxygen or alcohol. A number of tail sections, shining and finned, were standing on end like a village of Indian teepees. Other sections had been pushed over to form dwellings for the refugees who could not find shelter in the crowded barracks.

The tunnels of Nordhausen had been blasted out of solid rock, straight through a spur of the Harz Mountains. We drove our jeep into one of them, following a railroad track along a wall. Parallel to the track, pressed against the opposite side of the tunnel, a long row of lathes, millers, jigs, and other machines was strung out to form a production line for V-1 buzz bombs. Side tunnels ran off at intervals, each given to a specific production. One produced parts for Junkers engines; another, turbosuperchargers. It was tremendous, a gigantic human burrow. We saw no person in it, yet all the corridors were lit, as though waiting only for a change in shift. It seemed that no more than the hoot of a whistle would be necessary to man the lathes and start the wheels turning.

When we encountered a boxcar blocking the steel tracks we were following, we left our jeep and walked into a side tunnel, which contained a production line for V-2 rocket engines. In another tunnel we saw an entire rocket assembled. It had been hacked roughly into cross section by Allied experts anxious to learn the details of construction. Who would have imagined finding this demon of sheer space mutilated and hiding in the heart of a mountain, like a giant grub?

We walked back and forth through cross tunnels. There were miles of them, lighted, deserted, silent. Here, wood-planked rooms of a small hospital, with medicines and bandages strewn across the floor. Here, a row of offices, furniture upset and drawers turned upside down in the search for loot. We shoved a door open to find the floor piled with thousands of identification cards. Each card had a small photograph glued above a typed description of one of the factory workers, a man or a woman. What happened to those thousands of workers, I wondered, glancing over a handful of cards I had picked up. Where were they at that moment? I remembered the words of a DP on the roadside who had directed us to the tunnels. "When they sent a man there," he said, "they told him the only way he'd escape would be in smoke."

When we returned the next day to complete our inspection, the meaning of the DP's statement was impressed clearly upon us. On the mountainside above Camp Dora was a low-lying factorylike building, with a brick smokestack of extraordinarily large diameter for its height. We threw our jeep into four-wheel drive and climbed the steep slope, weaving in and out among the tree trunks. As we neared the building, we saw piles of stretchers at one end—twenty or thirty of them, with dirty, bloodstained canvas. One of the stretchers showed the dark-red outline of a human body that had lain upon it.

The place appeared as deserted as the tunnels we had gone through the day before; but a door was open. We stepped inside to a small darkish room. On our left was a coffin—black, simple, with a cross painted on its top. Beside the coffin, on the concrete floor and covered carelessly with canvas, lay what was obviously a human body. And beside that was another coffin. We hesitated a moment and then moved into the main room of the building.

There we realized what kind of "factory" we had entered, for we were looking straight at a pair of cremating furnaces, side by side. Steel stretchers for holding bodies stuck out like tongues from open mouths. The size of the furnaces, and the fact that two were needed for mass production, multiplied the horror of the place. As we were staring at the steel stretchers, a shadow brushed across the floor. We turned to see, standing quietly behind us, a man in prison costume—no, not a man, a boy; he was not old enough to be called a man. The striped suit bagged around him, pulled in at the waist, hanging loosely from the shoulders. He moved into a better light, and I found myself looking at what appeared to be a hide-covered skeleton. The padding of flesh between bone and skin that one expects to see in life was gone. The figure pointed toward the furnaces. "Twenty-five thousand in a year and a half," he said.

He was seventeen years old, Polish, the boy told us. Then he beckoned us to follow and walked back into the room we first entered. He lifted the canvas from the form between the coffins. It had covered another prisoner, thinner, lying half curled up on a bloodstained stretcher. I could hardly realize that the one was dead and the other living, they were so much alike: close-cropped bristling black hair, hunger-chiseled faces, burning dark eyes—for the eyes of the dead man were open. The most striking contrast between them lay in the expression on the dead man's face. Never, I thought, had I seen such tranquillity; as though after passing through hell on earth he had found peace, as though the spirit had at last triumphed over the human inferno. Even a Nazi prison camp could not remove the inner dignity of man.

"It was terrible—three years of it," the young Pole went on, his face screwed up in grief and the anguish of his memories. He pointed to the body. "He was my friend—and he was fat." Then he replaced the canvas. We walked outside after that, and stopped near another corner of the building. I had not noticed where the boy was leading us. I was looking off into the distance, my mind still dwelling on those furnaces, on that body, on the system that caused such atrocities.

Suddenly I heard his words again: "Twenty-five thousand in a year and a half. And from each there is only so much." The boy cupped his hands together to show the measure. I followed his glance downward. We were standing at the edge of what had once been a large pit, about eight feet long, six feet wide, and I guessed at six feet deep. It was filled to overflowing with ashes from the furnaces—small chips of human bone—nothing else. A trail of ashes ran over the edge of the pit toward the door of the furnace room. Apparently bucketsful had been thrown from a distance, as one might get rid of the ashes in a coal scuttle on a rainy day. And the pit had been dug as a man would dig a pit for coal ashes if he cared nothing for the appearance of the yard—it was within a few steps of the furnaces, and in an area so free of roots and sod that a spade would slip easily into earth. Nearby were two oblong mounds of clay, which apparently topped off older pits of the same size. The boy picked up a knee joint that had not been left in the furnace long enough, and held it up for our inspection.

I thought of the faces in the identification-card photographs I had looked at the day before, dumped on the floor as the ashes had been dumped in their pit. How many of those men and women had become part of the gray mass in front of me, as though their very bodies were burned for the factory's fuel? The height of human accomplishment and the depth of human degradation were there at the underground tunnels of Nordhausen; the two had somehow joined together to show the catabolic tendency of our civilization's science, which had produced Hitler's hellish V-2 rockets.

We drove back down between the trees of the mountainside, past empty guard posts, into the stench of Camp Dora. Pieces of the great rockets lay all around us—the fins, the fuel tanks, the piping, the immaculate white glass-wool insulation—ripped and scattered, like parts of human bodies, by the holocaust of war. All in pieces, useless, harmless now.

How those Nazi rockets reminded me of Professor Goddard's, blown up in size, and how deadly efficient they had grown! The Professor's record altitude was between eight and nine thousand feet, but he never tried for distance across ground. At the top of its trajectory a V-2 hurtled about sixty miles above the earth, and it carried a one-ton warhead from the Continent to England. How had the Germans jumped so quickly and so far ahead of Goddard's pioneering work? Partly because America built rockets for scientific knowledge, at a tempo set for peace, while Germany developed them for war. Hitler foresaw the gigantic force that would lie in his hands once he perfected rocket weapons, and he ordered a tremendous effort to produce it. The V-2s were the last symbol of the mystical drive and dictatorial power of the Nazi Führer, used to advance "Nordic civilization" and his political doctrines.

Adolf Hitler! Such a strange mixture of blindness and vision, patriotism and hatred, ignorance and knowledge. I remember him walking over the grass of the Olympic Stadium at Berlin in 1936, when his government was entering the heyday of its strength, a small, black-mustached, brown-suited man, stooping to take the bouquet of flowers from a little girl who was prompted out to meet him while a hundred thousand people clapped and shouted, *"Der Führer! Der Führer!"*

Some irrational quality of the man, his actions, and his oratory enticed the entire German nation to support his ideas. Hitler had built a war machine geared to land, sea, air, and space, the most powerful the world had ever seen. But the very power of his independence led to the dictator's destruction. His orders were issued without the need to listen to or persuade freely elected representatives of the people. He pitted intuition recklessly against experienced advice, turned his fighters into bombers that had little value for their mission, pushed V-2 rockets into production before they were accurate enough to be effective, thrust his forces eastward unprepared for Russian winters. He began with brilliant victory; he ended in staggering defeat.

What extraordinary pictures flash in memory: the adoring roar of the Olympic crowd, the little flower girl, the living skeleton and ash-filled pits of Camp Dora, the entrails of the rockets that had failed to start their mission. In Hitler himself was the contrast, the lack of balance, the abortive relationship between human values and mechanical perfection that one saw in the tunnels of Nordhausen.

"Human values and mechanical perfection"—at Cape Canaveral I was in touch with them both. My vision shifts back again through time and space. I glance at the missile tower; at the birds and ocean and at the children playing in the surf. How easy it is to think of human values on the beach when one is well fed, tanning, comfortable, and how separated from them my mind becomes under that tower, ten minutes' drive away! On the beach I think within a framework of peace and life. The tower is a framework of war and death. Man moves constantly back and forth between the two. How can one combine human values with mechanical perfection; the appreciation of life with the military strength that seems always to have been essential to survival and to civilization; the scientific vision of Robert Goddard and the philanthropic patriotism of Daniel Guggenheim with the fanatical drive of Adolf Hitler; the children in the surf—the rocket tower—?

"X minus ten minutes!" The bald signal, repeated over different phone systems, echoes through the blockhouse. A voice on the local loudspeaker keeps snapping out directions. In ten more minutes the command to fire will be given. Through a thick glass window framed by concrete I look at the erect and pointed missile. Oxygen vapor steams leeward with a light wind. Sheets of ice flake off from shell-thin walls, fluttering down to crack against the pavement. Will it be a successful firing? Or will it abort somewhere along the trajectory, fall back, and explode? I think of motion-picture films of failures: the slow rise—the hesitation—the drop—fins crushing against concrete—blast of flame—cloud of smoke—spurting fragments. In fact, I was once in the blockhouse when a fall-back took place.

"X minus five minutes!" The fire truck has left. The last workmen hurry toward the blockhouse. At goggle-dialed benches behind me, men check needles, lights, buttons. I am conscious of a German accent to English words. Wernher von Braun hands me his copy of the checkoff list. Young, heavy-set Braun, the man who did so much to produce V-2s for Germany and Hitler, the deadly enemy of a decade past—now a leading American scientist and friend.

It is a moment emphasizing the relativity of life and time. A quarter-century ago Goddard, financed by Guggenheim, was pioneering the liquid-fuel rocket that was developed for use against us a decade later, by Braun, financed by Hitler. At Cape Canaveral, Braun, now financed by America, is using his experience gained under Hitler to help in our plan to advance a system of government by making our country the leading missile power of the world.

Man feels he must conquer space. He works sometimes in the

interests of pure science, sometimes for the practical needs of war. His reason may be convenient to his motive, but the spirit of adventure is beyond his power to control. Our earliest records tell of biting the apple and baiting the dragon, regardless of hardship or of danger, and from this inner drive, perhaps, progress and civilization developed. We moved from land to sea, to air, to space, era on era, our aspirations rising with our confidence and knowledge. Wheels and hulls and wings changed our present environment. Where will missiles fit in the human scale of values as they may be recorded ten centuries from now?

I look at the faces around me: the civilians at instrument benches, the general at a window, the colonel and the captain with their check lists, the guards and workmen who have come inside for shelter, all intent on a missile and its mission—years of dreaming, designing, building brought to this moment, about to be tested by a firing. Their minds are concentrated on mechanical perfection. Who has time to think of what that rocket signifies in human values of the future? My eyes rest on an identification tag clamped to a workman's pocket. Suddenly I think of the tunnels of Nordhausen, the ash pits of Camp Dora. But I am here in a blockhouse on Cape Canaveral. The fantastic lives of modern men—

"*X minus two minutes!*" One feels the tenseness in the blockhouse although every man is trying to show an attitude of calm. A cigar tip accentuates the trembling of lips and a paper's flutter tattles on a hand.

"*X minus sixty seconds!*" Words of command grow sharp, terse. Multiple recorders click in the background.

"*X minus ten seconds! Nine! Eight! Seven! . . . Zero! Rocket away!*"

A muffled roar, then flame, and great clouds of smoke burst outward from the tailpipe. The rocket thunders, rising slowly, as though uncertain of its strength, yet firm and erect with no sign of instability. It moves faster, leaps suddenly upward, streaks out of sight beyond the range of blockhouse windows. Steel doors are thrown open. Men shout, joke, laugh with success. The tension is broken, the responsibility has passed to other hands. The Control Center has taken over, and instruments will from now on tell the missile's story.

I think of the long, sleek vehicle streaking out through space, far above our atmosphere's layer of interference. It is the prototype of man-made meteors that can be directed to atomize any spot on earth: Moscow, London, Tokyo, Rome, cities that can become a series of figures. Select your missile's destination, read the digits, set the dials. A cannon shell is sluggish, moving at a medieval pace, compared to this projectile in flight.

Millions of lives, centuries of labor, can be wiped out by words of command spoken more than an ocean-width away! It is theoretical; so, separate from the senses. Enclosed within a concrete blockhouse, your mind tells you the significance of what has taken place; but your flesh and bone do not feel it. There is no deafening scream, no hurricane of wind against the cheek, no sight of blood to assault the eye. You deal in contrivances, in ideas and imagination: a button pressed, a lever pulled, a city will disappear. I watched a cup of cold coffee tossed into a sink.

A ballistic missile orbits dozens of miles outside our world: the dream of science and dread of man; the culmination of military power and ultimate in civilized destruction. I step through the open doorway and look up to a tranquil sky. How can a modern airman comprehend the devastation he causes? And how often that question has churned my mind before—at Wotje and Tarawa; at Jefman and Samate; at Rabaul and Kavieng. And yes, at Kavieng.

Eyes of memory still see it clearly, the bombed city of Kavieng on New Ireland's northern coast. My vision shifts from Florida to South Pacific seas. Kavieng looked like an ant hill when I approached in my fighter-bomber on May 29, 1944. I was flying in a three-plane patrol from Major Joseph Foss's Marine Corsair Squadron VMF-115, Major Marion Carl and Lieutenant Rolfe F. Blanchard flanking me. My mind slips back easily through the stream of time, into that Corsair's cockpit. I feel the stick's vibration in my hand, and the pedals against my feet. My thumb has the power of TNT and my finger controls six machine guns.

A few miles ahead, fifteen thousand feet below my altitude, a scorched-brown texture between blue of sea and green of jungle is our target—so minute, so apparently trivial compared to the limitless expanse of land and water that rolls to the horizons. Careful scanning of the earth informs me that Kavieng, situated on the tip of a peninsula, is sheltered from the sea by two islands and their reefs, and that the hulks of several sunken ships obstruct the harbor. Minute circles on the ground warn of enemy antiaircraft cannon. Group Intelligence officers told us to be wary of those gunners: "The 'Nips' have none better in the South Pacific."

My exact target is an area of city in which Japanese troops are stationed. I want to kill some of those troops. In fact, I want to kill as many as possible. But when I tell myself I am going to kill, the idea somehow does not take hold inside me. I never have the feel of killing as I move the controls of my plane. Whenever I fly in my fighter-bomber, I seem to lose relationship to earth's community of men.

Everything is quiet on the ground and in the sky. It is hard to realize that we can strike with deadly force across such a magnitude of space, that we have come to toss five-hundred-pound bombs at humans down below, and that at any moment black blooms in air around us will symbolize the hostility of our reception.

An airman separates himself from the earth and its people when he follows a warplane's orbit. There are moments when the planet he is bound to seems as unrelated to his actions as does the moon, moments when he is completely isolated from the world's problems, its happiness and its sufferings, when the calculations of his mission appear as bloodless as the digits of astronomy. He guides his plane along independent courses through a space of air, watching dials, moving levers, caring no more about the lives he crushes than he would if the city below were an ant hill. How well I know the irresponsibility of the bomb's red button, and how often I have pressed it: in the Marshalls, over Noemfoor, in the Bismarcks, above Kavieng. . . .

The wings of Corsair 1 are rocking. We drop our dive brakes, purge our wing tanks, brighten gun sights. Corsair 1 peels off; it is Carl. Corsair 2 follows; it is Blanchard. I pull into a wingover, putting the sun behind my back, and nose steeply to the dive. I see the two Corsairs well below me, screaming toward the ground. My controls tighten, the altimeter needle touches ten thousand feet, air howls, wings tremble. At seven thousand feet I make a final adjustment to the trim tabs; six thousand feet, steady on the rudder;

pipper beyond the target. Fifty-five hundred feet. NOW. My thumb presses, my arm pulls back, I kick right rudder toward the sea, reverse bank to throw off enemy ack-ack, reverse again, and look down to check my marksmanship.

There was no sense of combat on that mission; it was like an exercise in aerial calisthenics. I saw no flashes on the ground to challenge my attack. I did not feel the bomb drop. One moment it was held firmly in its rack, completely under my control. Then my thumb moved ever so slightly against a small red button on the stick and death went hurtling earthward. I caught one glimpse of the bomb falling after I dropped my wing—cylindrical, inert, awkward, irretrievably launched on its mission; certain to destroy itself and the first object that it touched. In another second it was lost to sight. No power of man could countermand my action. If there was life where that bomb would hit, I had taken it; yet that life was still thinking, breathing when the bomb was still falling: there were still eternal seconds. Nothing had changed in my cockpit; nothing in my sky.

The little puff of smoke—the pebble-splash of debris—was centered in a row of buildings near the beach, an area where anti-aircraft guns had been reported. What a slight scar it left! I could not even find it with my eyes after the smoke drifted away. So far as I could tell, Kavieng was no worse off for our visit. But in reality were there torn and writhing bodies in that pinprick I had made in the ground? Were they already out of sight behind me? Was a machine-gun nest wiped out? Had I eliminated a score of soldiers from the war? Was some child without a mother, a mother without a child? I felt no responsibility for what I had done. It was too far away, too disconnected.

How can an airman comprehend the devastation he causes? He must stand on the rubble of a destroyed city to sense the power of the bomb's red button. He must see flashing concussion waves tear across the ground, debris vomiting through air, and great columns of smoke billowing. He must take the hammer blows on his chest, the thunder against his ears, hear the cries of terror. When you look down at two human heads above a single body, at bones protruding from a mass of flesh a dozen feet away; when you stand at some cross street on a pile of brick and let your eyes travel its four directions over block after block of fire-blacked, shattered walls; when you watch clouds redden with the flames beneath them, and feel after a bombardment the white dust of death that settles over everything—then your thumb's contact with the bomb button transmits significance.

Hiroshima lies flat and peaceful between plum-tinted mountain ranges and the island-studded beauty of Japan's Inland Sea. It is December 1947. I am in an Air Force transport plane, circling at three thousand feet. Two years have passed since the bomb was dropped. The aged mountains, the nestling city, the calm sea, all the crystal tranquillity beneath me—it seems impossible that the people here witnessed the horror of that August day when an airplane soared overhead, barely specking the sky, yet leaving behind it excruciating pain and devastation. There is no sign to mark the gigantic mushroom cloud that once towered in the sky, no sign except, when I look more carefully, the shades on earth below.

To see the terror of past war, an airman's eye must translate shadings. A city, like a human face, can show the pallor of death. A gray-ash saucer, a mile or so in width, marks the blasted, radiated, and heat-shriveled earth of Hiroshima. Surrounding it is a black halo of undamaged roots on the outskirts. The straw-colored stippling which glints now and then in sunlight, as we bank, is caused by the unpainted lumber of the newly built dwellings that have sprung up like fungi. Inside that gray saucer more than seventy thousand men, women, and children were killed, and that many more were burned and mangled. Over one hundred and forty thousand casualties from a single bomb—from words of command— from the pressure of buttons.

Since I flew over Hiroshima we have developed bombs of more than a thousand times the power. The kilotons and hours we used in our calculations at the end of World War II have been replaced by figures representing megatons and minutes. In planning for the possibility of an all-out nuclear conflict we discuss casualties running into tens of millions, huge uninhabitable areas caused by fall-out. Will half or three-quarters of a continent's population be wiped out?

Years have passed. I sit looking at a beach and ocean: any beach, any ocean, at any time and any place—on a dolmened shore of Brittany, or Roman Ostia's black sands; on a Cyrenian shore, a Mayan shore, on a beachhead of World War II. I could be on Florida's Captiva, on Arabia's hot coast, or on a shore that forms after glaciers melt and freeze.

There is a cosmic rhythm, a grace and magnitude. Waves curl and foam. Clouds tint with setting sun. Life mellows through an hour that rides the first meridian of night. I tilt eastward with our planet, toward a darkened universe, aware of both earthly and celestial tides, of the miracle of man, of a gravity that makes "up" and "down" irrelevant to orbiting dimensions.

On shorelines land, sea, air, and space converge to hold intercourse with life; and to shorelines life has pilgrimaged since it began—the Plesiosaurus evolving toward a lizard; the man drawn back to the environment in which his ancestry began.

A changed environment has sprung from scientific knowledge, transforming simplicity into complication. More than four billion human beings, all similar yet no two alike, communicate for peace or war with the speed of light and rockets, appearing, reproducing, disintegrating, in fields of energy and time, evolved from flaming gases, evolving toward a solar system's end.

Now again, I try to penetrate the future. What travel may, someday, take place beyond our solar-system space? What vehicles can we devise to extend the range of rocket ships as they have extended the range of aircraft?

As wings and propellers once limited man to earth's thicker atmosphere, scientifically established principles now seem to limit him to the space territory of the minor star he orbits.

Following the paths of science, we become constantly more aware of mysteries beyond scientific research. In these vaguely apprehended azimuths, I think the great adventures of the future lie—in voyages inconceivable by our twentieth-century rationality—beyond the solar system, through distant galaxies, possibly through peripheries untouched by time and space.

I believe early entrance to this era can be attained by the application of our scientific knowledge, not to life's mechanical vehicles, but to the essence of life itself: to the infinite and infinitely evolving qualities that have resulted in the awareness, shape, and character of man. I believe this application is necessary to the very survival of mankind.

That is why I have turned my attention from technological progress to life, from the civilized to the wild.

We will then find life to be only a stage, though an essential one, in a cosmic evolution of which our developing consciousness is beginning to become aware. Will we discover that only *without* spaceships can we reach the galaxies; that only *without* cyclotrons can we know the interior of atoms? To venture beyond the fantastic accomplishments of this physically fantastic age, sensory perception must combine with the extrasensory, and I suspect that the two will prove to be different faces of each other. I believe it is through sensing and thinking about such concepts that the great adventures of the future will be found.

FOURTEEN

Beyond Survival

Stinking caves and rotting bodies of the South Pacific war gave me no sense of emanations beyond death. I felt tightly bound to flesh and matter, subject to a hopeless fatality of earth. Death hovered all about one in the South Pacific—in the bombs exploding on the ground, in the bullets streaking down from the sky, in steel helmets and "red alerts," in trenches crammed with bodies. It was in the skulls decorating tents, the mold of the jungle, the shells on the beaches, the old and hardened coral on which your tent was pitched. You packed the belongings of companions who were killed the day before, realized that tomorrow someone might be packing yours.

But all life ends with rotting bodies, not just those killed in war. Every bone and every fossil marks a struggle and a death. In the Pacific I picked up a chunk of coral from a shelter floor. How trivial was the life it held, existing for an instant, building calcium walls, dying, disappearing. With billions of humans on the earth, and untold trillions of lives of lower form, why should any one have importance? Fingering that bone of coral in a dugout of the war, I was struck by the cheapness of the quality called "life." Life is limited in time. It exists in such tremendous quantities that it cannot have much value. How could anyone who studied rocks or fought in battle consider it precious? How could man expect God to watch over him individually and believe that every hair is numbered?

Where was life when the earth itself was still a mass of energy and incandescent matter? An exploding bomb reminds me of nuclear physicist C. F. von Weizsäker's description of creation. Inconceivably far away in time and space, he said, a tremendous explosion may have taken place; and from it all our universe of galaxies, stars, planets has formed, from random atoms fissioning and fusing, from energy and matter spewing outward through eternity.

Why is an explosion needed to explain the universe? Because man's spectrographs and telescopes tell him that his universe expands, that every galaxy recedes from every other. That is what happens when a bomb explodes. You can imagine yourself on any fragment, and watch the fragments all about you expanding into space. At the same moment, in your actual position securely far away, you can observe the relativity of movement. The highest fragments move the fastest; the lowest, slowest. All diverge in speed and angle, like the distant stars. You watch energy and gravity contend in clouds of gas.

What happened to the life, the awareness, that existed before speck and horizon touched? The eyes tell you it has passed away. Certainly life is no longer sensible within that moiling mass of rock, gas, and metal. Yet the mind knows that life and awareness both evolved from a still more titanic chaos—from energy infinitely greater than that released by a high-explosive bomb—from matter hotter, wilder, more contorted than I watched spurting from the ground.

Then can matter and energy breed awareness through time that extends beyond the sense of senses? How else explain existence? Maybe spirit, space, and matter are the same? Maybe awareness is never lost but only transmuted to another form, into an all-pervading quality. Maybe awareness, like life itself, passes through a cycle of continuing events beyond man's present understanding—a cycle in which life on earth is but a gamete, momentarily contracted to individual existence before expanding beyond the reach of gametic thought. How much change takes place with the physical phenomenon of death? Myth pre-empts certainty. Man feels intuitively that something beyond life exists for him—a continuance, a direction, surpassing the descriptions of his mind.

Visiting the caves of Biak made me feel half man, half ghost. I seemed to be experiencing a form of afterlife. The Marine squadrons in which I once lived so vividly had vanished like soldiers who had been bombed. The squadrons were dead, but I, an element, existed.

Organizations are conceived like men—we will form a squadron; we will have a child—and they live and die as men do. Like men, they have an individuality. When you were a member of a squadron, under the intensity of war, you could merge your existence with it the way an organ merges with its body to function as a whole. Headquarters became your brain; Intelligence, your eyes; Communications, the nerves co-ordinating action. You realized that the squadron's welfare had to come before your own. You flew bomber cover as a member of a fighting body and felt an airman's loss as a body feels a wound.

It was as part of a group that I felt I could function effectively in war. It led me to solve a problem that our flyers encountered in the Pacific. After one of the first missions I flew with the 475th Fighter Group at Hollandia, New Guinea, the commander, Colonel Charles H. MacDonald, told me the crew chief for my P-38 reported it landing with more fuel on board than had been found in the tanks of any other plane. How was that possible, he asked.

A simple investigation brought it out. I had not studied the 475th's operational procedures. On my own, I had adjusted my engine settings during the mission in accord with techniques I had adopted years before—manifold pressure high and propeller revolutions low. That increased the brake-mean-effective pressure in the cylinders, and decreased fuel consumption. It was an old procedure, well known to long-range flyers. I had used it in less elaborate form when I crossed the Atlantic Ocean in my *Spirit of St. Louis*. But the young fighter pilots of the 475th had, quite properly, been trained for combat, not for practicing fuel economy. During earlier stages of the war, combat was usually encountered within easy range of the home airstrip and fuel conservation was unnecessary. It was, of course, better to keep your speed up and your revolutions high so you could maneuver quickly on an instant's warning of enemy attack.

In the New Guinea area during the summer of 1944, a year

before the war's end, fighter squadrons often cruised for hours getting to and from areas where enemy attack could be expected, and the "juiciest" Japanese positions lay usually just beyond a squadron's range. A decrease in fuel consumption would let the fighters reach more distant targets, thereby increasing opportunity for combat and the achievement of more victories.

By raising manifold pressure and lowering revolutions per minute, the 475th could, I calculated, add well over a hundred miles to its effective combat radius. This seemed simple enough to Mac-Donald and to me, but we had the problem of getting a new technique accepted by group mentality, and then implemented by group action. Of course the commander could issue an order that all engines must be adjusted to the settings I suggested. But that would be like the brain telling the body to breathe slower and run farther. Without training, the result could hardly be satisfactory—especially if only part of the brain believed the idea was a good one. To be successful, we had to get the cruise-control procedures into their bones.

I gave lectures to officers and airmen, compiled simple engine-setting tables for pasting on instrument boards, flew extra combat missions. The fuel economy resulting from methods I advocated had to be accepted. My flights with the squadrons demonstrated that. My P-38 always had, among the others, the most gasoline remaining in its tanks. But were not mechanical parts in my engines being strained? Would breakages result at critical moments of combat when war-emergency power was in use? I sensed behind the pilots' questions a suspicion that I had access to some magic to be distrusted, that mine was a procedure that the squadron should not adopt for itself as a whole. It meant a radical change in technique for long-range, combat-zone cruise.

Pilots cautiously tried out the new procedures. It was an awkward and unco-ordinated effort at first—a little higher manifold pressure, a little lower rpm, rather than the exact settings I advocated. Then, when no breakages occurred and crew chiefs reported the engines to be still in good condition, laggers overcame their timidness and the group as a whole began to sense increasing power gained from range.

I was an individual pilot when I came in contact with the 475th. I had flown unescorted from Nadzab to Hollandia in a P-38 assigned to me for ferry. When I began flying with the group, I was sharply conscious of my individuality and strangeness. By the time we had advanced westward to Mokmer Drome on Biak, I was functioning as an organ of the body whole. I had contributed to group effectiveness, shared in group awareness, sensed a group reaction to whatever incident took place.

With the end of the war came the end of the group. Now its squadrons are but phantoms of the past—metal bones corroding at the edge of jungle airstrips, memories remaining in the minds of men scattered over the surface of the earth. Group awareness broke up into individual awareness, and individuals became parts of other groups.

Does this give any insight to what happens when a bomb explodes? Does individual awareness survive the greater body? One senses no awareness in shattered bones and shredded flesh. Has its essential quality then transferred to spirit or to atoms? Science cannot rationalize the phantoms I once sensed on Wake. But intuition doubts that awareness is contained in the minuteness of an atom. I have watched atomic vapor trails appear in laboratory cloud chambers as I have watched vapor trails appear behind airplanes in the sky, and I have tried to imagine the vehicle that passed. Airplane or atom departs, leaving behind a ghost. Does every existence leave some form, whether visible or not—a spoor often too subtle for perception by the normal senses? Are dreams, apprehensions, visions the remains of past but unseen reality?

How can one sense phantoms if no phantoms are there to sense, any more than a vapor trail can be seen without causation? And why judge their reality through the bigoted witnesses of eye, ear, and fingertip? When one dreams of long-dead parents or conceives terrors in the dark, what material phenomenon is lacking? What human sense cannot be stimulated by contact with a vision? Maybe the sensory and the visionary are simply different aspects of existence.

Shall I think of my father, now dead all these years? I see him walking toward me down the old farm road, hear his whistle, watch my dog jump high to lick his hand. It takes but a wish to bring the dead to life, to exist in the company of phantoms. And are not these phantoms as substantial as a rock, since they consist of the elements of atoms?

How is reality to be defined? Is it less in a proton than a gamma ray? More in flesh than vision? I look at my punctuation point again, made of the stuff of atoms—protons, neutrons, rays, and mesons come together to form the substance "carbon." How impossible it is for the mind to grasp the detailed character of atoms! What a miraculous existence the atom leads—now star, now man, now blade of grass; a brook, a flame, a mountain. It becomes eye, nerve, and memory, the awareness that perceives them, creates in the present, plans for the future, records the past.

In June of 1938, my wife and I moved to the French islands of Illiec, and occupied a house on the island next to Saint-Gildas Island, the home of Dr. and Mme Carrel. I had first heard of these north-coast islands several years before, from Dr. Albert Ebeling, a member of Carrel's staff at the Rockefeller Institute. "They are beyond description," he had said.

A visit to Saint-Gildas confirmed his impression. On my first flight there, in 1937, I had crossed the channel in a low-wing monoplane near Calais, used Mont-Saint-Michel as a checkpoint, and timed my arrival to coincide with an afternoon's ebb tide so I could walk across sea bottom between the mainland and the islands. The tides move more than thirty feet of ocean on Brittany's Côtes-du-Nord, and life upon the islands must be timed to them.

I was flying at about two thousand feet when I sighted Saint-Gildas—a rocky, wind-swept island slightly larger than the rest, an outpost of land heavily battered by the sea. At one edge, nested among stunted pines, were the buildings, a half dozen of them close together, with slate roofs on walls of stone—a house, a barn, a chapel, a garden high walled against the wind. Chickens scattered as I circled. The Carrels came out to wave. Two horses galloped across a marshy pasture.

I wrote on a slip of paper that I would land nearby and be back as soon as I could arrange for the care of my plane and for ground transportation to the coast. Then I tied the message to a cloth streamer, weighted with a stone I had brought from Long Barn, and dropped it over the side of my cockpit. It struck ground a few yards east of the house, in a small woods that Mme Carrel had named "Le Bois du Coeur."

But I could find no landing field on the mainland nearby. Like the islands offshore, those stony Breton hills allowed no areas smooth and large enough for airplanes. After more than an hour's search, I glided down onto an airdrome near the city of Dinan, about seventy miles southeast of Saint-Gildas.

It would be close to midnight, with the tide high, before I could get back to the coast; and I could not communicate with the Carrels, because they had no telephone. I tossed the plane's emergency rubber raft along with my personal bag into the car I hired; let the driver worry about navigating over winding roads northwestward. The north coast of Brittany was black with night when we arrived, and the tide was near its high point. I could see the island of Saint-Gildas, vaguely outlined, beneath some weak stars. I unloaded my equipment near the top of a concrete ramp, a man's length from the weedy sea edge. I pumped the oblong raft to plumpness, jointed its oars together, and stowed my gear.

A legend of Brittany tells that Saint Gildas arrived sailing over the ocean on his cloak. How like a cloak that raft was! My toes pressed on water through a single sheet of cloth. No more than a bubble of air supported me. Each dip of oar left phosphorescence swirling in its wake, and shiny jellyfish floated at different depths around me. I might have rowed backward through a million years without a mark to show it. My hands were wet. I tasted salt. I smelled the scum of sea.

Saint-Gildas had a steeply slanted beach of round and storm-ground stones. Since the Carrels had no idea that I would cross the water alone at night, no one was there to meet me. The phosphorescence of the sea, the silence of the night, the vague forms of rocks formed a primordial weirdness.

The next morning, in the Carrels' house, I saw through the open window and between pine branches the mainland and the concrete ramp from which I had launched my raft at midnight. The ocean I rowed across had vanished. No water was in sight except a few tidal pools where the tide was trapped. Three fishermen were making their way among scattered brown reefs, across sand bars and rocks, toward another island. Several fishing boats, beside a coastal village, lay keeled over on dry land.

On the way to breakfast, I stopped in the stone-floored hallway downstairs to look at a wood carving of Saint Gildas sailing—done by a Breton furniture maker named Savina. The message I dropped the day before climaxed four thousand years of human progress on Saint-Gildas, Carrel said, the stone age at one end, the air age at the other. On the beach, a few yards from where my raft had touched —that rubber raft both fascinated and amused him—were the remains of a dolmen. Its big flat rock was still propped up on pillars when the Carrels first came to the island, and there were traces of several other dolmens then. But waves had encroached inland until now only one remained. He mourned the passing of this last landmark of man's early life.

The ninth-century chapel of Saint-Gildas was also a vestige. Mme Carrel had seen to its reconditioning—a longish, low stone building, roofed by moss and slate. Nearer the center of the island, hidden by pine needles and fern, were the foundations of huts said to have been occupied by monks in the late Middle Ages. And beyond them, close to heaps of stones that edged the ocean, was a straight line of boulders that was attributed to Roman engineers, although no one could give a reason for it being there. The house and farm buildings were of Napoleonic times, mortared up out of the island's rock. Now, said Carrel, in the Bois du Coeur a stone monument would be erected on the spot where the first message from the air had dropped on Saint-Gildas.

As I climbed the rolling, storm-ground stones of its eastern sillon and looked down on the strip of empty sea bottom beyond, I forgot about Saint-Gildas. It was no ordinary tideland I saw. Here was the actual bed of the Atlantic—deep and wild, with big limpet-spotted rocks forming mysterious crevices and caves. A decade before, when I was flying from America to Europe in my *Spirit of St. Louis,* I had looked down on the Atlantic Ocean and wondered what shapes and contours were masked by the sameness of its surface. Certainly there were valleys and mountains of the ocean's bed by which a pilot could navigate if he could see them—landmarks by which I could have established my exact position after a night in drifting winds above the clouds. But the sea maintained its dignified aloofness. We met and passed formally, distantly.

At the edge of Saint-Gildas, each fastly ebbing tide opened the ocean's threshold, let you step into a strange and foreign realm. Fish, camouflaged by weeds, hung motionless in crystal pools. Green, protoplasmic masses lay inertly on the stones. A tentacle from a small squid flashed out. As I looked upward at brown flood lines, I imagined the sea beings that twice daily swam about each place I paused, appearing and vanishing like ghosts. Here was an eons-old conflict between the fort of stone and the siege of water— the frailty of rock in time—the strength of the intangible. I saw dolmen boulders crumble under the force of molecules that a feather's touch could scatter. I felt the moon's tug on my earth as it held forty feet of ocean back, or was it the reverse—did the ocean help to keep the moon from falling into space?

Living on Saint-Gildas, you felt the forces of earth and cosmos as though God himself exposed his hand. You sensed the beauty and danger of existence, the rhythms of the planet, the relationships of space. The entire island seemed a strip of tideland between a continent of science and a mystic sea outside, a threshold where ghosts and men could alternate and even meet in time, where past and future surged across the present fantastically.

With Dr. Carrel, on Saint-Gildas, conversation shifted from scientific subjects to phenomena as yet unexplained by mind, to accounts of a Breton peasant hypnotizing animals, and to miraculous cures that had been credited at Lourdes. Was there any reality to ghosts? What circumstances were most stimulating to supernatural perception?

Carrel believed a supernatural realm existed, and he was always searching for bridges between the physical and the mystical. He studied developments in the new field of psychosomatic medicine, listened intently to accounts of mental telepathy and clairvoyance, and was convinced of the efficacy of prayer and monastic discipline. He had written a manuscript about his experiences when he was a young doctor accompanying one of the pilgrimages to Lourdes.

While still living in England, I had talked to a number of people who were interested in the "supersensory" phenomena attributed to India, and I had spent many hours in the library of the College of Physicians, in London, reading reports about rhythmic breathing, controlling pulse rate, and walking on live coals in Asia. Between the trickery of the fakir and the asceticism of the saint, it seemed obvious that a wide border zone existed. The names of Christ and Buddha related both to solitude and to fasting.

I talked with Sir Francis Younghusband, the famed explorer and mystic, who did not believe the mechanics of life were of prime importance. I had gone to visit him at his home in England in the summer of 1936. He was a quiet man of striking features—beneath his white lashes, deep-set eyes held you. He was born in India and knew the Himalayan mountains well. He was deeply interested in religion and in mysticism.

Had Yogic masters found ways of sharpening perception until it could pass through walls enclosing the normal mind and senses, I had asked. Was it true that mystics sometimes sat in mountain snows for hours without any sense of being cold? Did their body temperature decrease? What benefit could be obtained by such procedures? I outlined my interest in physical bridges across which man might pass between the continents of science and mysticism, flesh and spirit.

Younghusband showed little interest in physical techniques. He could not tell me whether anyone had managed to insert a thermometer into the body of a contemplating yogi. Talking to him, I realized that his own approach to God had passed beyond the need for bridges. Sir Francis was traveling to Calcutta in the spring to attend the Parliament of Religions, which was being organized in honor of the eastern saint and mystic Ramakrishna. When I told him that my wife and I were planning to leave England in February on a flight to India, he offered to introduce us to some of his friends if we could arrange our schedule to meet him there. In return, I invited him to fly in our Mohawk from Bombay to Calcutta. He was delighted.

Our flight to India was beset with troubles. Yet we were still able to meet Younghusband when his ship docked at Bombay. Our plans for an expedition to the Himalayas had to be abandoned, however, and the time I had hoped to spend inquiring into accomplishments of yogis and fakirs was largely taken up by the social and mechanical requirements of a long cross-country flight. None of the people I talked to had heard of scientific measurements being made in relation to Yogic contemplation.

Back in England that spring of 1937, I decided to run a series of simple experiments in my home at Long Barn. It seemed obvious that the yogi's rhythmic breathing must exert a large part of its effect through changing the composition of gases in the lungs. Slow breathing, for instance, would decrease the percentage of oxygen and increase that of carbon dioxide. Working with circulating tissue-culture flasks at the Rockefeller Institute had shown me the great effect a change in oxygen percentage could have on living cells. Suppose I reduced the partial pressure of oxygen in air, and varied the partial pressure of carbon dioxide. What respiration rates and body temperatures might result? This could easily be tried out on animals.

I bought a vacuum pump and a glass bell jar in London, built some cages in the back yard, and presented my five-year-old son with some white mice and guinea pigs—enough so he would not notice the absence of several of them when my experiments were running. I found that reducing atmospheric pressure was followed by a lowering of body temperature in both mice and guinea pigs. A rectal temperature would drop from a normal 37° centigrade to 23° within several hours. On removal from the bell jar, an animal would gradually return to its habitual activities, showing no effect of the strange experience it had undergone.

Was this what happened to the yogi who sat contemplating in high mountain snows? Was the altitude a help to the techniques of rhythmic breathing? What happened to the mind and spirit as body temperature went down? It would be interesting to try out the bell-jar experiment myself.

I did not then have access to a tank large enough to hold me in which pressures could be controlled as in a bell jar, but I returned to the United States for several weeks that winter and, at the Rockefeller Institute, I made similar experiments with a rhesus monkey. For the first two or three degrees, the monkey's temperature dropped as did that of mice and guinea pigs. Then a reaction took place that brought the temperature up to a degree or two above normal. It was obvious that the body of a monkey contained a heat-regulating mechanism different from that of the animals I had experimented with at Long Barn, and that the reaction of a man would probably be similar to that of a monkey. Was it possible that the yogi's rhythmic breathing was used for the purpose of controlling the heat-regulating mechanism of his body? During the time I was in New York, I tried various techniques to control a monkey's body temperature. All were unsuccessful.

On Saint-Gildas there was no opportunity to experiment in this vein, although Dr. Carrel and I discussed the possibilities, but there were other phenomena to observe, I soon discovered. Among the features of Saint-Gildas was a haunted well. Its wide, stone curbing rose waist-high above the ground at the far end of a bridge over which the cattle lolled from barn to pasture. Local peasants had reported seeing ghosts around this well. I sometimes had an eerie feeling as I passed it, as though its phantoms had receded to make way for my approach but would then close in behind me. Mysticism would not stand long in second place to logic, especially when Mme Carrel was present. She was convinced that supersensory phenomena existed. She believed in telepathy and clairvoyance.

One afternoon, when I was walking through a garden, I saw a round, metallic object lying half-hidden in freshly spaded earth. It turned out to be a copper coin with the Napoleonic date of minting still visible. When I showed it to Mme Carrel, she suggested that we hunt for another one with her pendulum—a black, star-shaped piece of plastic that she suspended from her fingers on a thread. As we moved about, the pendulum refused to swing as it was carried back and forth across the garden. Nor would it swing in the court outside the entrance door, or in the barnyard. But when Mme Carrel stepped into the chapel of Saint-Gildas, the bob began to oscillate in widening circles over a point about a foot inside the threshold.

I examined the floor carefully. It was of hard-packed, long-trampled earth, no different in shade and texture from the rest of the chapel floor. Then I got a pick and shovel and began to dig. At a depth of about eight inches, I found another copper coin, the same size but more blurred than the first.

Surely this was proof that man had unexplained powers that a pendulum could tap. But as I looked at the two coins held together in my hand, reason argued in favor of coincidence. People had worshiped in that chapel for a thousand years and brought offerings to its altar. At that very moment, on a pottery dish were scattered a dozen franc and centime pieces. Maybe every cubic foot of earth contained a long-lost coin. We tried the pendulum again, but it refused to swing. Then I dug a trench one foot deep by one foot wide straight across the chapel, and found no other coin. Even with all the care I took in replacing the earthen floor, a clearly noticeable scar remained to mark its desecration.

I never accomplished anything using the pendulum technique. But with a forked stick in my hand, I thought at first that I might become an expert well diviner. The stick would twist and dip, and I felt it pulled toward the ground at times as though a current were passing through me. My greatest trouble lay in the fact that the stick would not dip repeatedly in the same localities as I walked back and forth across the island. Obviously, a good well diviner had to find a stable source of water. I had become as skeptical of the divining rod as I was of the pendulum, when a boy arrived at Illiec one morning with a message saying that a professional well diviner was working at the island of Saint-Gildas. The boy told us he would have come sooner if the tide had not been too high to let him pass.

My wife and I left our chores immediately and picked our way along sea-bottom ridges that rose above the water as mountain ranges rise above clouds. The well diviner had completed his exploration of Saint-Gildas by the time we got there. Dr. Carrel, his face showing an amusement that only his closest friends could detect, told us that the best source of water had been found to lie under the center of the biggest rock on the island—a tremendous hunk of stone, several times as large as the cow barn. That meant, unfortunately, he continued, that this wonderful source of water would not be available. I was so disappointed at missing the demonstration on Saint-Gildas that I asked the diviner to look for a water source on Illiec, where we were completely dependent on a rain-water cistern because our only well had gone dry.

The well diviner, it turned out, was the captain of a Breton ship somewhat larger than an ordinary fishing boat. He knew the northern coast of France in detail, although he had never before set foot on our islands. At Illiec, I was astonished to see that instead of a forked stick, he used his large, nickel-plated watch. The watch was attached to a nickel-plated chain which he held between his fingers as Mme Carrel had held her black thread. Any swinging showed that water was below, and the number of swings marked, in meters, how far the water was beneath the surface.

It turned out that the previous owners of our island had been wise. Or maybe they, too, had engaged an expert well diviner. By far the best source of water, the captain said, was right where our well was placed. There the pendulum swung most, although uncertainly. He suggested that we try removing any sediment that might have collected at the bottom of our well and dig it a few feet deeper.

The tide was beginning to come in when we escorted the captain back to Saint-Gildas. When the sea had risen sufficiently to let a small boat pass, he, my wife, Dr. Carrel, and I walked slowly toward the steep stone beach that faced the mainland. The captain was still holding his watch-pendulum in hand; suddenly, it began swinging. He halted for a moment, and then continued walking toward the beach and the waiting boat.

"Did he think there was water at that spot?" I asked Carrel.

"No. He thought there might be a hollow place in the rock," Carrel replied.

We said good-by and took different routes after the captain left. I had barely time to reach Illiec before the tide would cut me off. By chance, the way I started took me over the spot where the pendulum had swung. I stomped the ground without hearing any indication of a hollow underneath. There was only lumpy sod that almost covered a flatish stone—a stone unusually flat, it seemed. I looked more closely—kicked the edges of the sod away. It was almost certainly a dolmen! Maybe there was a hollow place beneath it.

Either the captain had clairvoyant powers or he must have

recognized a dolmen rock. Would scientists, someday, accept phenomena of clairvoyance as they had been forced to accept some of the miracles of Lourdes, eliminating the stigma attached to the word by substituting psycho-scholastic terms? Had I just made an excursion through a tideland of mysticism? Were there always tidelands opening for the awareness and experience of men? Logic argued that it was impossible for a man to sense that which lay hidden beneath the surface of the ground. The use of a pendulum was magic. But in part modern science developed from the magic of times past. Maybe science was like an adolescent child smiling too surely at its uneducated parents. Men still foretell the weather by the twisting of a piece of gut, or by the bend of grass tufts in a wind. Was not this once considered magic?

Along with the maritime tides of Saint-Gildas, there was rising a world-wide tide of war. I had wanted to bring the captain back to look for other dolmens, to study Breton folklore and its mystic superstitions, to make another flight to India, with more time for exploration. There were other places like Saint-Gildas that helped one to sense beyond the reason of the mind—the Himalayan mountains, the Tréguier cloisters, Mont-Saint-Michel, Chartres.

But letters came in over the tidelands, from Paris, London, Berlin, filled with concern about impending war. Problems of civilization and survival towered above my fascination with phenomena that sometimes lay exposed in the tidelands of rationality and life. Why spend time on biological experiments when our very civilization was at stake, when one of history's great cataclysms impended?

In December of 1938, my wife and I locked the doors to our house on Illiec and moved our family to a Paris apartment for the winter. In the spring of 1939, I sailed for the United States and began a tour of active duty as a colonel in the Army Air Corps. World War II was over when I next returned to France. Dr. Carrel was dead, and Mme Carrel had moved to her home in Argentina.

In May of 1945, I took a lonely drive in my little Renault from Paris to the Côtes-du-Nord, along roads lined by shell-pocked walls, past the undamaged cathedrals of Chartres and Mont-Saint-Michel, through the stone-walled, black-figured villages of Brittany, to the coast where I had launched my rubber raft nearly a decade before.

Walking out over the tidelands, I saw not a sign of change. Their reefs and bars collapsed my sense of time. But many of the trees of Illiec were gone. They had been cut down to make firewood for warmth and cooking. Illiec had been occupied by German soldiers—a lonely outpost, the local peasants said they called it. The house was looted but itself undamaged.

Saint-Gildas had now been taken over by a Catholic order of monks—Les Petits Frères du Père Foucauld. The monks kept the chapel, worked the fields, and lived in the old farm buildings. Their order was using Saint-Gildas as a school for apprentices.

Mme Carrel had reserved the house under the Carrel Foundation as a retreat for scholars and scientists who might come to contemplate and study. It was being kept exactly as it was when she and Dr. Carrel were living in it. Antoinette, the maid, had been retained to make sure of that. Alexis Carrel had been buried in Saint Ives, the small vine-covered chapel on Saint-Gildas, which was surrounded by a stone-walled yard. It was barely large enough to hold the length of his grave in front of the altar. As I looked down on the neat-edged, oblong patch of sand on which Antoinette had placed her daily offering of flowers, I felt that not a week had passed since Carrel and I had stood together before the chapel's door, or since he had said half humorously to his wife, "When we are dead, we will return to this island as ghosts."

Carrel's body lay a few feet beneath the surface—the dead body of the man whose lifetime work had been concerned with living bodies, the man who had preserved life in isolated organs and given "immortality" to isolated cells. His simple grave contrasted with the grandeur of his life.

My awareness surged outward from the island, to Lyons, where Carrel received his education and where he began his medical research; to Chicago and New York, where his innovations in surgery brought him fame throughout the world; to Sweden, where he was awarded the Nobel Prize; to Rome, where he received a citation from the Pope; to the Ile-de-France, on which he made so many crossings between the Old World and the New, and back to a library shelf on Saint-Gildas crammed with foreign translations of his books, which had been sold and studied on every continent. "The world of matter is too narrow for [man]," he had once said. "In time, as in space, the individual stretches out beyond the frontiers of his body."

Why did Carrel want to be buried on the island? To return as a ghost? Did he consider it a tideland between domains of life and spirit in which men and ghosts could mix with surging time? Monks were walking through the churchyard as monks had walked for a thousand years. They worshiped God and prayed to saints and believed in revelations. Was their framework, though intangible, less real than that of modern science?

I sensed Carrel existing as more than a memory or a vision of my mind—he was still pacing in his garden, his windbreaker buttoned tightly, his beret canted down, walking along the island's paths, the sea in front, the rocks behind, the tides of eternity around. At Saint-Gildas, my awareness rayed out beyond the heavy walls of knowledge, around the earth and through the sky, bending into past and future, Once you lived with ghosts, you raged with storms, you cycled with the planets, and you knew a wisdom deeper than the mind, a reality beyond the touch of substance.

I remembered our last meeting, in New York, soon after the start of war. It was a solemn meeting. We, like other men, felt channeled into destinies beyond our understanding. Carrel, at the age of sixty-six, more than a quarter-century after he started work at the University of Chicago, had decided to give up his research in America and return to his native France. "My country is in trouble," he told me. He thought he knew ways to improve the nutrition of French children amid the inevitable shortages of war. It was to be Carrel's last voyage across the Atlantic. I received no letters from him during the German occupation of his country, but word came through, in roundabout ways, that he was organizing a scientific institute under Pétain and Vichy's collaborationist regime. He died on November 5, 1944, "from a broken heart," his wife said, under harsh and bitter charges.

As soon as I reached Paris after Germany's surrender—it was in May of 1945—I began inquiring about my friend. In doing so, I met a woman who had seen him often during the strict and austere years of war. "He was innocent," she kept insisting. "We must clear his name of all the charges that were made." She handed me three typewritten sheets of paper. "Here they are, translated into English," she said. I had expected to read a list of serious accusations levied against Carrel, accusations that would be extremely damaging if they could not be disproven. Instead, I was amazed by the triviality of the charges. What appeared to be the most serious of them claimed that he had committed an indiscretion at the German Embassy in Paris. He had been requested to go to the embassy to discuss matters pertaining to his institute. To do so was accepted as a necessary act carried out under the authority of the German occupation. The charge was that at a party being held at the embassy, and after his business was completed, Carrel had lingered longer than was necessary, taking part in conversation and drinking a glass of wine.

Carrel was ill when Allied armies finally liberated Paris. "It was a bad winter for us," his wife recounted some months later. "The apartment was very cold, and we had little food. The Germans offered us wood to burn, but Alexi would not take it. They offered us food, too, but he would have nothing from them—nothing! It is bad enough to be cold when you are ill. It is bad enough to be hungry. But to be cold *and* hungry . . . Ah, that is difficult." He could never understand why the people he had tried to help turned against him. The British and Russian governments sent official representatives to the funeral of Alexis Carrel. The French and American governments did not. Such was the fantasy existing at the end of the war. Hatreds of conflict so overpowered the past that the man who had devoted his life to preserving life received scant gratitude from the living.

For me, the war brought changing values in relation to the preciousness of life and its transition into death. Those pulsing organs in my perfusion pumps back at the Rockefeller Institute, those minute cells moving under the lenses of my microscope, all that effort expended on biological research, seemed trivial compared to the war's titanic movements, to the caves of Biak, the ash pits of Camp Dora, to Hiroshima's great gray saucer, to the armies of Russia expanding westward into Europe.

Back at Saint-Gildas, all worldly experiences could have been a dream. I understood Carrel's desire to return there as a ghost, for he must have felt as I did, that the island was a tideland between the realms of spirit and of man. There were hours at the island when it seemed that one could escape from life's identity and, like a spatial phantom, speculate on the unpragmatical human world—a sphere where awareness converged with substance to form an entity called "life"; where a species was developed with a brain enslaved to logic, and with a mortality so self-centered that it called phantoms supernatural at the same time it hurtled through an atmosphere on artificial wings; where men worshiped God's creation, and atomized themselves by bombs.

To a spirit's superdimensional perspective, human life, racked between its bone-marked past and fearful future, must be as irrational as any apparition to the human mind. What lies beyond life's material accomplishments, beyond its competition and survival? How often I have wondered about just this question through the years! I did so at my friend's graveside on that Breton island; and when I was a boy and a catapulting plowshare barely missed hitting me; and when I stood in a Japanese crew shelter at Wake; and when I braced for the impact of a spinning plane after a test flight near St. Louis.

The rational mind of life seems unable to stretch past death. But its logic cannot screen the visions of dream and intuition. As a child I had dreamed of being killed after falling off high places, and the sensation immediately preceding death was like that when I thought the spinning plane would hit me. I tensed for death. I felt its impact, and then I remember my amazement when I found that a kind of consciousness continued, a consciousness that spread outside my life-abandoned body. It was a consciousness no longer bound to tissue. It was able to expand and to disseminate through space. It was like the awareness I felt in later years, at moments, as on the island of Saint-Gildas, or in a fighter's cockpit returning from a combat mission.

But this was a dream, my rational mind keeps saying. How far can fact combined with reason take me? And I return to the problem of early-childhood nights, in bed on my Minnesota porch. How much have I learned during the passage of more than fifty years—

from experience, from experiments, from war? Certainly life is not skin-enclosed individuality, as it seemed in early childhood; nor is it a simple combination of body, mind, and soul. Man is an organization that breaks up every lifetime. Individuality is a temporary concept, like the concept of a group or nation.

In considering problems that enclose my viewpoint, like the trees of a forest, by their proximity in space and time, I have often imagined myself on a dust cloud out between the stars, in a different framework of existence and objectivity. Suppose a million years were a minute; and a million miles a foot. Could I then look on human life with more understanding and perception? In three days I would see the world condense from flaming gas to earth and cooling oceans. For about half a day, I would watch life emerge from matter and evolve from a minute cell to man. Individuals would not be apparent because a lifetime would pass too fast to leave an impression on my eye—much faster than the individual photographs of a motion-picture film pass the lens of a projector. Only the stream of life as a whole would be visible to me, one generation merging into the next so rapidly that my rational mind could easily think individuality nonexistent. If some trick of science, in my spatial framework, could lay the photograph of a specific man before me, he would probably seem as far removed, and as theoretical, as one of the thousands of my body's cells that live unobserved and die each day.

Then, just as I had watched life emerge from matter, and matter before it from chaos, a third miracle would appear—emanations from individual life—unmeasurable by instruments, foreign to the materialistic world. I would recognize them by their manifestations rather than by form. Instances of the life stream would begin to extend their individual influence through time and space—discovering the past, affecting the future, knowing God, universe, and stars—an influence that rooted into the past and branched into the future with an existence of its own. Chaos evolves to life.

FIFTEEN

Kimana

In and around its tall green grasses in the Kimana swamp near Mount Kilimanjaro live East Africa's fantastic animals. Within a day's drive westward from our camp we found huge herds on the Serengeti Plains—more than a million gnu, zebra, and gazelle. Within a day's drive eastward, an estimated thirty thousand elephants stood and plodded through the jungles. Within a few hundred yards, in all directions, we encountered lion, cheetah, giraffe, buffalo, rhinoceros, wart hog, and hyena.

We pitched our four tents at the edge of a small bay of level ground indenting the jungle, near a spring-fed water hole. Acacia branches gave shade from midday sun, and scattered deadwood offered fuel for evening fires. Stepping from a tent, one faced a tree-surrounded area of several grassy acres with Kilimanjaro in the background—titanic slopes curving upward to the glacial cap. Forty-four degrees in latitude south of our New England home, that glacier's ice was our only reminder of Christmas. All else was strange. No snow lightened ground around us. The air carried no nip of frost. No ornamented fir tree gauded our camp. There was not, in a conventional sense, "peace on earth" to be found in the constant killings of the jungle.

Yet Christ's homeland lay closer to Kenya than to New England, I realized, and the circumstances of his birth corresponded more to a jungle camp's simplicity than to Western civilization's elaborate

Christmas rites. Only my northern rearing connected December 25 with snow, reindeer, and colored electric bulbs. As with good and evil, true and false, familiar and foreign, we judged this within our framework of reference, not wholly, not without principle, but still in some part.

Basically, civilization's ornaments should be the strange. The jungle environment man has evolved in through millions of centuries should be the familiar. This held true for the naked, spear-bearing Masai who strode by our camp. For them, God was in the form of a river, a blade of grass, a cloud, a mountain. And looking out on Kilimanjaro during sunset or dawn, I, too, sensed its divinity in its mass and shifting lights. The mountain bulked upward into clouds to a mystical Olympus. The glacial cap floated above mists like the site of heaven. Now moonlight reflected from nineteen-thousand-foot-high ice to transpose the sky: below and above were barking zebras, orbiting satellites, the bounds of earth, the boundlessness of space, the hovering glacier between.

For me, in East Africa, more than any other place on earth, the strange and the familiar interweave. Nowhere else do I gain a comparable perspective on evolution, time, and space. I think of camping in the Kimana with its game warden, Denis Zaphiro, on a previous trip through Kenya. We had staked down our tents in exactly the same location. One day a Masai messenger arrived to report elephants advancing on shambas near a frontier village. "Shambas" are thorn-enclosed patches of corn that are essential to the native economy. If the animals were not turned back, damage to crops would result. Some might have to be shot.

Zaphiro and I took off in his small monoplane, carrying a box of thunder-flashes—Fourth-of-July-like explosive sticks that ignite when scratched at one end. We located about a hundred elephants among dry sparsely wooded hills not far from the Tanzanian border. It was a successful mission. He piloted and I bombed, with the westernmost animal always my target. The first three or four harmless bangs and flashes started the elephants lumbering eastward in lines merging and separating as they followed bush-squeezed trails.

What a contrast of frameworks for modern man and the largest of his fellow land creatures—the white-tusked, trunk-swinging elephants below us and the roaring mechanical bird, terrifying, beyond their mental comprehension, above them. How safe I felt in our airplane, unreachable by trunk or tusk. As we dove, zoomed, and circled, reality and dream confused time. I was both a modern civilized man in a common twentieth-century vehicle and a cave dweller indulging in extraordinary visions—swooping out of the sky at huge animals from which I previously had hidden, controlling them with a god's omnipotence. I was immune to earthbound fury, invulnerable to the risk of competition from fellow creatures.

The animals of Africa seemed even less unusual when my wife stepped out of our tent one morning and encountered a lion and a lioness out walking, and when zebras, gazelles, and wart hogs scattered through the field before us, or when hyenas yelled at night and glowing eyes returned our torch beams. Each day that we camped made the jungle more real and, at the same time, civilization stranger, until I understood the Masai questioning our values. There in Africa, the sensate, intuitive, and intellectual combined to create what seemed a supernatural awareness, until I took the form of my environment as my own.

I recall a night at Kimana when Kilimanjaro's glacier was the sky's only cloud. We had finished supper. Black-charred pots were washed and turned upside down to dry. I lay down in grass beyond our campfire's glow and focused my binoculars on the moon. As I did so, a rocket-sponsored satellite traced its path through stars. The contrast between primitive and civilized had never struck me with such force. Here were dream and reality juxtaposed, miracles of man and the mysteries of the cosmos revealed by impossibilities come true. Another decade would bring human landings on distant spheres of space.

In 1929, Goddard told me that theoretically rocketry had possibilities of success, but that the cost might exceed a million dollars. In 1929, a million dollars seemed an astronomical figure, far too much to invest in rocketry. Later, we were spending many times that amount each day, and the moon had become a steppingstone toward planets. I focused my binoculars on Mars, then on Jupiter's vague satellites—light pricks many million miles away, now within the physical reach of men.

I thought of years past when I had lived in the ambience of

satellites, planets, stars, and space, first with Goddard during the early liquid-rocket experiments and then with military committees developing long-range ballistic missiles. If I had not decided against specializing in fields of missiles and space, as I did, I might have been orbiting in a satellite instead of looking up at one from the framework of a jungle. Then the cramped and weightless interior of a rocket head would be the familiar to me, and the gravity-bound expanses of East Africa the strange.

The fascination was great when I sat in early conferences where scientists argued the practicability of intercontinental ballistic missiles. As a member of scientific ballistic-missile committees, serving first under the Air Force and then under the Department of Defense, I had been kept well aware of the potentialities of satellites, space probes, and interplanetary travel. Committee members had discussed such projects at frequent intervals. But military requirements had been so urgent, in view of the Soviet Union's antagonistic stance, and there had been such a shortage of trained scientists and engineers, we had decided to concentrate on the building of nuclear-warhead carriers until the danger of enemy attack was reduced.

As years passed and part of our scientific and industrial resources could be devoted to experiments in space, I found my interest lessening, as indeed it always lessened when theory screened me off too much from practice. Missile development had confined me to the Pentagon building, to factory floors and windowless briefing rooms. Hours spent on testing grounds were too few. Even when I witnessed a launching, it was usually on a television screen in a thick-walled concrete blockhouse; I could have been five hundred miles away, rather than five hundred feet.

I recall a Thor launching at Cape Canaveral during shakedown tests of that intermediate-range ballistic missile. The blockhouse did not have a single observation window. I stood watching a television screen while the countdown was completed. Since several of the Thors had failed, everyone was tense. X minus ten, nine, eight . . . three, two, one. At the command "Fire," smoke and flame spewed from the bottom of the vertically pointed missile. It rose slowly two or three feet, and faltered. The television screen kept moving skyward, but the Thor did not follow. I noticed a barely perceptible impact of concussion. When the startled operator realized he was showing nothing but sky, he dropped his camera's focus to the fiery, billowing chaos below.

Along with the other men around me, I was confined to the blockhouse until explosive materials had been consumed or sluiced away. When we walked out, a little steam hung over the debris on the launch pad—nothing more. It had been an intellectual experience, but not of the order of my being present when Goddard's early spacecraft failed. Instead of bringing me closer to the moon, rocket development had taken me farther from it. You have to be outside at night to know the moon, not in briefing rooms and blockhouses. Of course I would like to have been one of the first to land on that earthbound satellite, and to explore its pristine wilderness.

I served for seven years on military ballistic-missile committees, and thereafter I declined a position related to the civil space program. I wanted to regain close contact with the land and sea, and reestablish my view of values surmounting those I found in scientific fields. Watching satellites and staring at the stars, I seemed to lose contact with my earth and body and to spread out through the cosmos by means of an awareness that permeates both space and life—as though I were expanding from a condensation of awareness previously selected and restricted to the biological matter that was my self.

Life and awareness fade when the death of an individual takes place. But does life itself—love, memory, and reason—expand into the universe or withdraw into the atom with physical decay? Do qualities of spirit orbit on electrons? Are these qualities lured by molecular combinations from the emptiness of space? Decline presumes origination. We reach a point in observation and analysis where the human intellect stares past frontiers of its evolutionary achievement, toward unreached areas infinitely vast—the mystical realm of God.

The realm of God! God was real to our ancestors. He entered their lives as a tangible being, intangible though he was. He spoke to them, guided them, rewarded them, punished them in life, and in the end took them into his kingdom or rejected them. In his grace, they were promised joy. "Thus, while reprobate angels and men are left to endure everlasting punishment, the saints shall know more fully the benefits they have received by grace," Augustine wrote.

What child has not been disturbed by ideas of God, his form, rule, and power? Some of my earliest memories relate to God and death, the one inseparable from the other. Why did God want the men he made to die? Was it not an inexplicable defect in his character? Even for the good people he would take to heaven, death seemed a horrible entrance. During childhood, the long perspective and the anticipation of time pushed thoughts of death away. They were aided by my conviction that for me death was in the inconceivably distant future—at least a century, I decided; nearly twenty times as long as I had already lived.

Close members of my family were unbound by religious dogma. My mother read the Bible to me but explained that no one knew how much of it was true. Surely the story of Genesis was a fairy tale, because my scientific grandfather had hanging on his wall a drawing of a hairy man born long before Adam. Even given doubt, there was schism. One of my great-grandfathers was a Baptist minister who reviled the Catholics and the pope with theological fanaticism. He preached in a wooden country church on the shore of a Michigan lake, and confirmed new members of his congregation by immersing them in water. My mother told about watching him when she was a little girl. He wore hip-high boots, she said, and sometimes waded out through a scum of ice. It did not make any sense to me, getting pushed into cold water to obtain benefits from God. I knew nothing about psychological effects, and I was deeply impressed by the fact that my preacher great-grandfather had failed to convert his own granddaughter to his faith.

I grew up in a generation torn by the impact of new scientific knowledge on old religious dogma. For millions of men and women, the names Darwin and Satan were synonymous. Yet I could not understand why evolutionary theory should cause disillusionment. Was human life less wonderful if it developed slowly from the sea than if it started suddenly in a seven-day creation? The idea of evolution appealed to me.

In Gothenburg, not long after World War II had ended, I talked to the German nuclear physicist Carl von Weizsäcker about his exploding-universe theory. "If planets, stars, and galaxies originated in a titanic explosion billions of years ago," I asked, "then had there been previous titanic explosions throughout unlimited time?" An exploding universe! I was struck by the contrast in ideas between eras of theological and scientific man—from our earth being the center of creation to its becoming a minute fragment of matter flung outward into space. Think of riding one of the fragments of a detonated bomb!

I try to sense a cosmic evolution in which ages become seconds; and light-years, miles. Then, the earth starts orbiting at an electron's tempo. Planets streak; meteors crash. Tranquillity disappears. Stars spread and fade from view. I tense with velocity, brace in turmoil as generations come and go with cinematographic speed. I realize that all questions lead to the creation of energy.

All experience, all reason, all of our sciences have sprung from the mystical and miraculous, for how else can man be aware of existence itself? The shape of God we cannot measure, weigh, or clock, but we can conceive a reality without a form. The growing knowledge of science clarifies man's intuition of the mystical. The farther we penetrate the unknown, the vaster and more marvelous it becomes. Only in the twentieth century do we realize that space is not empty, that it is packed with energy; it may be existence's source. Then, if space has produced existence and the form of man, can we deduce from it a form for God?

I think of the forms of man, of myself. I am at once my past, my present, and my future. I am the concentration of millions of ancestors. I will diffuse through millions of descendants and the unforeseeable existences they lead. I have been quadrupeds of the Mesozoic era, creatures of Paleozoic seas. With every generation I cycle from adult to sperm and ovum to child. I am now male, now female; now knowledge, now innocence. At the same moment I am an individual, I am an organization of billions of living cells, of trillions of atoms— each one itself a cosmos of unknown features, memories, and abilities. I am energy and I am matter, transposed by incomprehensible time.

A lion's roar brought me back to earth and speculation about the lives our planet rotates. I had previously thought myself unrelated to jungle creatures by a chasm millions of years wide. But what of my continuing self in atomic form? Are not my atoms me? My experience and spirit and personality must exist somewhere within their fields. Suppose I had been killed that night and devoured by lions, hyenas, and vultures. Some of my atom universes would have become their bodies, as much a part of them as they had been a part of me. As I was incarnated atomically by countless bodies of the past, I would incarnate other bodies than my momentary own self. I would become part of Kimana, of its earth and its acacia trees, of its grass that hides and feeds the buffalo and therefore of the buffalo themselves. I would return, somewhat more quickly than from civilized life, to what I really am—to the infinite existence in which the unenlightened man thought himself a finite part.

Atoms stay in contact with the universe through radiation received and transmitted. They exchange electrons, exhibit policies of aggression and alliance, defense and neutrality. They discipline titanic forces within atomically corresponding space. In their relatively minute circumferences, events must take place that have more portent for man than he yet can apprehend.

Our restricted senses blind us to the atom's magnitude. Who can look at a stone and comprehend its spinning planetary systems? An iron needle aligns itself with poles a hemisphere away. In man's present stage, he can neither see the tempo of atoms nor feel the pulse of epochs, but his understanding can be enhanced through merging imagination with scientific knowledge to reduce the tempo and contract the pulse.

The short record of human existence has been marked by an increasing penetration of the minute and the immense, until we begin to apprehend the immenseness of the minute and the minuteness of the immense, the tremendous power of an atom, the tiny light prick of a billion stars.

Possibly in subatomic elements there is awareness, intelligence, and beauty still more wonderful than that we recognize on earth. Does not my memory of Kimana prove that Kimana has actually entered the atomic organization I once thought of as the "individuality" of "me"? The immenseness of the minute is portrayed in our knowledge of reproductive cells. These form-compressing forms of life were unknown before the discovery of magnifying lenses. Who would have thought it possible that man's history, identity, and character are transmitted from one generation to the next through particles invisible to the unaided eye? Was it not inconceivable that a single cell could absorb such massive data, and then transmit it so precisely to billions of others that each could instruct billions more, ad infinitum, and so maintain the intricate detail of a species?

Life indicates the communicating ability of atoms, for life survives both individually and genetically while the atoms that maintain it are constantly replaced. Communication requires knowledge, and knowledge involves memory resulting from sensation and reaction, and in memory is the mechanism of selection. Sensation and reaction lead to selection. Atomic combinations transmit the memory of selections made ancestrally in primordial seas.

What happens to the fund of knowledge that departing atoms somehow code for the instruction of those replacing them so accurately within the human body? Do they carry it with them, as do professors who leave a university—transmitting from it to any group they join? Since we observe no life without atomic substance, the phenomena of life must be attached to the structure of atoms, and with their movements a reincarnation must take place in both organic and inorganic form. The paradox is that we cannot be aware of what goes beyond us, nor can we be conscious of the genetic memory that carried us here.

Death is an entrance to experience rather than an exit from it; it is an intercourse of existence in which the quality of each participating element is enhanced. Is this an evolutionary principle, a part of the mystique one senses in East Africa's wilderness in the kills of lions, in the grazing of gnu, in the pecking of birds, in the nets of spiders—aware that death lurks wherever life maintains its apparition and that death can spring at once, bringing torture and release, end and beginning, a disintegration essential to the integration of evolving spirit?

Still rooted in our civilization's customs, I was shocked, in East Africa, to learn that Masai place their dead outside villages at night for wild beasts to devour. I thought of lions and hyenas I had seen tearing at their kills. How could men and women so treat the bodies of their loved ones? Then I remembered being similarly revolted by my own civilization's handling of its dead when a Midwestern funeral director escorted me through his salesroom.

It was a large room, darkly walled and filled with open coffins of diverse design. They were lined with puffy white cloth, contoured to the human body. The director took me to a massive bronze baroque affair costing about eight thousand dollars. One could rest assured, he said proudly, that in it a corpse would be well protected forever. Then he described the problems of protecting a corpse underground. Most cemeteries were not well drained, he explained, and conditions within a coffin could be unbelievably horrible—the body floating, bloating, and grounding with water-level changes, sometimes turning over in the process. Fortunately, relatives do not realize what takes place. That bronze coffin represented only part of the elaborate techniques developed for modern funerals. A big hearse with drooping black curtains and hydraulic lift had been constructed to transport it. From the morgue's refrigeration of corpses collected upon death through the embalmer's chemical injections to perpetual care of a "final resting place," civilized man tries to preserve the unpreservable.

Is the Masai system of burial more revolting than our own, less in keeping with life's true values? To my amazement, I found myself concluding that I would rather have my body eaten by wild beasts than have it subjected to the treatment of a modern undertaker. At first glance the Masai custom destroys the form of man, while ours protects it. But this is true only in the literal sense of the outward form of the human body, of the two-armed, two-legged, skin-enclosed, time-frozen concept of it. Actually, the form of life including man depends on freedom, not preservation. Evolution is based on the capacity of biological substance to reincarnate. The life cycle could not exist without death and decomposition. "Self" is fleeting. The breakdown of life's momentary form is essential to the momentary form of life and therefore to its progress. This is the wisdom of nature, the cycle that takes form to formless and again to form.

It is impossible to preserve the form of man, for no instant leaves his form unchanged. Our cells form and die, our molecules combine and recombine, our thoughts vary, our memories accumulate and fade like a kaleidoscopic interplay of tide, wind, and light. In form there is no distinction between reality and illusion. Is it reality or illusion that is superbly juxtaposed on nonexistent spatial curvatures?

My father told me that when he died he wanted his body cremated. He mentioned it casually one day while we were walking over our Minnesota farm several years before his death. He had not said so, but I think he had recently visited the graves of his own parents. Cemeteries were an obligation for those left behind, he continued. The graves had to be kept up from year to year, and of course there would be more of them with every generation. He wanted to disappear completely after he died, he said. His ashes should be "thrown to the winds."

I pushed my father's statement to the back of my mind, and thought little more about it until I had become a flying cadet in the Army Air Service. Then, less than a month after my enlistment at Brooks Field, Texas, as intensive training was just getting under way, a telegram from my sister in Minnesota exploded through my life. My father had been taken, critically ill, to the Mayo Clinic hospital. The officer in charge of flying cadets granted my application for leave immediately, but told me that if I was not back within ten days there would be no use coming back at all: the cadet courses progressed too rapidly; military requirements were too strict.

The doctors at Rochester said my father could live a few weeks at most. They had operated for a brain tumor, unsuccessfully. Their report was a terrific shock to me, for the last letter my father wrote contained no warning of illness. Apparently he did not realize it himself until a friend noticed a blank area in the usual acuteness of his mind and insisted that he undergo medical examination. Now, he could not even speak. But he recognized me at his bedside and took my hand.

I returned to Texas and cadet training within the ten days specified. My father died the next month, May 24, 1924. His ashes were placed in a cemetery urn. I planned to disperse them from an air-plane over the old family homestead near Melrose. The physical framework of that funeral flight could hardly have been simpler, and little variation in my professional routine as an aviator was required to carry out my father's wishes. I navigated my plane to acres of land I knew by sight, and strewed the urn's contents as I circled—puffs of white in the slipstream.

Time inverted while I flew. Ghosts of ancient happenings ap-peared. Past and present fused to flout my life's direction. When I took off, I sensed my father next to me, not his ashes, as he had flown next to me in campaigning not many years before. Then, the houses and clusters of country roads and villages I looked down on seemed to rise and surround us as I chauffeured him in early days of motorcars. We stopped our Model T Ford to talk to farmers, to address political meetings, to eat lunch at town hotels. We hunted ducks in marshes, partridges in forests, prairie chickens in stubble fields. The old homestead took us back to childhood, to brothers and sisters, and farm chores. Here, my father had arrived as a baby from Sweden when my grandparents settled on the frontier. To these existences, and to countless more, I returned my father, and myself, for was I not also he? Was he not I? It was as though I had drifted down with his ashes, as though I were in the wind that took his shape from the flames and carried it away, as though he in his boyhood and I now were one.

I know myself as mortal, but this raises the question "What is *I?*" Am I an individual, or am I an evolving life stream composed of countless selves? Am I a man whose age is measured in a few score years, or am I as ageless as evolving time? As one identity, I was born in A.D. 1902. But as A.D. twentieth-century man, I am billions of years old. The life I consider as myself has existed through past eons with unbroken continuity. Individuals are custodians of the life stream—temporal manifestations of far greater being, forming from and returning to their essence like so many dreams.

I recall standing on the edge of a deep valley in the Hawaiian island of Maui, thinking that a life stream is like a mountain river —springing from hidden sources, born out of the earth, touched by stars, merging, blending, evolving in the shape momentarily seen. It is molecules probing through time, found smooth-flowing, adjusted to shaped and shaping banks, roiled by rocks and tree trunks—composed again. Now it ends, apparently, at a lava brink, a precipitous fall.

Near the fall's brink, I saw death as death cannot be seen. I stared at the very end of life, and at life that forms beyond, at the fact of immortality. Dark water bent, broke, disintegrated, transformed to apparition—a tall, stately ghost soul emerged from body, and the finite individuality of the whole becomes the infinite individuality of particles. Mist drifted, disappeared in air, a vanishing of spirit. Far below in the valley, I saw another river, reincarnated from the first, its particles reorganized to form a second body. It carried the same name. It was similar in appearance. It also ended at a lava brink. Flow followed fall, and fall followed flow as I descended the mountainside. The river was mortal and immortal as life, as becoming.

After returning from Hawaii to my New England home, I found a different life stream in the gulls outside my window. For over twenty years I had watched them drop clams on a granite boulder at the sea edge. A bird would fly in holding a shellfish in its beak, hover above the boulder, drop its load, and dive to retrieve the cracked-out flesh just ahead of some thieving brother. Year after year the gulls never aged and appeared in like numbers. I had no way of telling when one replaced another. I watched the life stream rather than the individuals, and the same life stream would be there for my grandchildren and their grandchildren to watch, if they lived beside the rock. The individuals were mortal only in that they changed form, and this change I did not see. Mortality is no concern of rivers and gulls. Neither matter nor lower animals consider that life ends. Only man is aware; only he is disturbed by such a concept.

In generations past, when men thought less scientifically, they turned to religion and faith on meeting death. Then, God emerged more from intuition than from reason. As rationality became a dominant mode, it challenged intuition's concepts and entered the doldrums of spiritual atmosphere. Today, we have gained too much knowledge to rely on faith, and too little for understanding. We say that God in human form is a phantom of imagination and desire. We are only beginning to realize that tangibility of form is not crucial to our understanding.

Mortality is an illusion in the minds of men, a figment of reason. I am past as well as present. Actually, my father and I and our human clan are like the gulls, one life stream, aging and ageless—individualities which emerge and merge again—fields of force reacting on a central core. We are life and spirit fluxing to the pulse of time, the one as real as the other.

Each generation has added to its life stream force fields so that modern man is orbited by numberless forms of influence, forms becoming more discernible to his sharpening perception. Like gulls, we form a life stream, but unlike them, we grow aware of its relation to individuality, while our evolving intellect breaks down old barriers between flesh and spirit. At each new individual's conception, the transition between matter and spirit begins. The visible advances from the invisibility of a cell, while the adult body moves along its path toward universality. The concept becomes reality and with time reality fades to memory, dream, and fields of influence. In the emerging individual, unseen forces gather—phantoms, old superstition's ghosts.

Science clarifies man's vision beyond his birth and death and links him to universality. I think of watching my own sperm cells in a microscopic field—thousands of living beings, each one of them myself, my life stream, capable of spreading my existence throughout the human race, of reincarnating me in all eternity. My selves I stared at: my pasts, my presents, my potentialities. Yet how unlike myself they were—huge oval heads, thin lashing tails, no eyes, ears, arms, or legs. Swimming in their environmental ocean, struggling through channels and around reefs blocking their way, vibrant with energy, avoiding one another in their helter-skelter quests, they appeared not human but not quite fish.

Here I was reverted to life's earliest organic stage, once more a unicellular being—the "I" suddenly transported through time as though to a Pre-Cambrian sea. I would have thought those simple cells a primary emergence of vitality from matter had I not known they were man. What invisible and fantastic changes removed them from cells of early seas! What infinitely complex forms are condensed from their simple shape—male forms, female forms, face and eye and heart, formless forms of sensation and emotion, of instinct, intuition, love, and joy—so microscopically minute, so delicate are those cells that they contain in memory the capabilities achieved by human life since earth's life began.

Translucent, preconceptual ghosts, shades of ancestors, self, descendants, specks beyond the naked eye's perception, they must devolve from hallucination. Surely I was indulging in a dream. The wigglers I looked at could not mate, co-operate, organize, and produce, within an orbit of the sun, the complexity of man. I took my eyes from the microscope, looked down at the glass slide beneath the lenses, at the liquid smear fast drying on its surface. How could there be within it, precarious as it is, dried to dust or washed away in a moment, millions of swimming "I"s? And yet . . . this miracle was true. Just such a microscopic form within my father mated to a microscopic form of my mother's, and thereafter multiplied and organized through unimaginably diverse forms into the trillions of beings, motile and fixed, that form a group illusion of individuality, the momentary phantom form of myself.

Phantom? Yes, a phantom. I am spirit masquerading in matter's form. I am composed of infinitesimal force fields interacting with each other as still different force fields interact to form a river or a gull—assembling, communicating, co-operating, departing, during an existence to which men attach the names "individuality" and "life." I cherish the illusion of being substance, yet I am as much the spatial nothingness of atoms. I am as empty and as potent as the space between stars. Electromagnetic waves slice through me; I am a specter cleft by swords.

An hour later, I returned to the microscope. The area within its lens field was as desolate and lifeless as a plain upon the moon. In a century, all but a few of the youngest now living would have disappeared. I had actually seen a portion of life's prenatal domain, entering it through a scientific instrument available only to recent generations. Will some instrument now be developed to show part of life's post-mortem domain—some spectroscope or supercyclotron?

But how far can scientific aids penetrate mystery? Will not we find in awareness itself the deepest penetration of all wonder? Only in man, in recent times, has life become aware of its awareness, only after the selective intercourse of epochs. What further sensitivity will this awareness reach? With the evolution of awareness, man perceives. Senses cannot bind him. Intuition and rationality converge in a supersensate penetration, and we learn how reality forms phantoms and phantoms form realities.

I once experienced the transition between reality and phantom. This took place in the twenty-second hour of my transatlantic flight in the *Spirit of St. Louis*. I had been without sleep for nearly two days and two nights. My conscious mind had lost control of its body. My movements were made by instinct, not by will. The desire to sleep grew more agonizing and uncombatable than any pain I knew before. I could stay awake only because the alternative was death.

It was no use. I had passed limits of rationality. I remained only temporarily conscious of intellectual resolves. No will power I could exert stopped my eyelids dropping. I seemed to act without the act of acting, to see without the use of eyes, to lose the sense of senses functioning. I was staring blankly at the instruments as I grew aware of phantoms grouped in the fuselage behind me, where there was not room for even phantom forms to crowd. I saw them clearly, without turning, as though my entire head were one great eye. I heard them as though my entire being were an ear. They were transparent forms, devoid of substance; shapes human, yet intangible as air.

At first they were phantoms and I still a man of earth, but I felt I had known each of them before. At once they would ride silently through time; then one or two slipped forward to converse. They disappeared and appeared again from nothing, in the way substance must have originally formed from space. Gradually, the apparent difference between self and phantoms faded and I, too, existed independently of time and matter. I felt myself departing from my body as I imagine a spirit would depart—emanating into the cockpit, extending through the fuselage as though no frame or fabric walls were there, angling upward, outward, until I re-formed in an awareness far distant from the human form I left in a fast-flying transatlantic plane. But I remained connected to my body through a long-extended strand, a strand related to the form of man, a strand so tenuous that it could have been severed by a breath, an ethereal breath unrelated to the propeller's wash.

Then I re-formed slowly as a man again, returning from spatial distances to my plane and body, condensing and collapsing into earthly qualities.

That reincarnation of my body reminds me of boyhood returnings to my Minnesota home after winters spent at the capital, a thousand miles away. Riding the train westward in springtime, I seemed drawn by an elastic force, an attraction like gravity that grew stronger as I neared my home—drawing me over mountains, hills, and valleys, over great distances akin to those I had contracted through in space, drawing me back to central Minnesota, to our farm, and finally through the doorway of the house itself.

Entering the house was like reinhabiting my body in the *Spirit of St. Louis*. Incarnation was not completed by passing through the door. I still sensed the city I had left, the voyage I had taken, the extension and contraction that had occurred. It took time for me to get out of city clothes, to occupy the house, to merge with it until I became again what I departed from eight months before.

After returning to the farm home I loved so deeply, I sometimes imagined having been cut off from it forever. It was a depressing, almost terrifying concept. Of course I would have continued to exist in my same form, in the same way I had existed through the winter among children I studied with at school. I would simply have had to adapt myself to eastern city life—as I did to a large extent in later years. But suppose I had been cut off from the *Spirit of St. Louis* when I was an awareness far away in space. Suppose that tenuous strand I felt had snapped. Would I have remained a phantom among phantoms?

Our sciences offer easy answers. All I had observed existed within the confines of my skull. My sense of being an awareness at great distance was no more than a hallucination of exhausted mind. But intuition stays skeptical of the intellect's frail logic. When we exchange "phantom" for "hallucination," what more has been described? Did my sense of the phantoms have less tangibility than my sense of "material" forms? Had there not been moments when the plane, the flight, even the great continents of earth appeared as fantasy, while the phantoms and my spatial existence were the real? If phantoms are real, they must be everywhere around us, awaiting only to be discerned by an evolving sensitivity.

In memory, reality of flight and phantom merge, and what is memory but phantom without form? The definition of reality involves sensory experience, yet experience itself cannot be sensed. While we are aware of its existence, it can be as illusive as specters in the mind. Every concept forms its own reality, emerging, as matter does from space, to call itself "awareness." Progressing through evolutionary epochs, life in man has at last become aware that its individual awareness is without form in time.

My father had been converted to carbon, gases, and particles of calcium scattered over soil. Death transferred him from life back into matter. But are there such absolute states as life, death, and matter? These may be fleeting apparitions of intellect and sensation. Can we speak of a physical framework without recognizing that outside it ghosts await recognition by an evolving perceptivity?

In how many forms my father still exists, both physical and mystical—dynamic forms, static forms, forms transposing between the intangibility of awareness and the tangibility of matter! He is formed in me, in every cell of mine from brain to muscle. I sense himself in me. In fact he is half me. There are times when my reactions are identical with my memory of his—as though I actually were my father remembering the past, continuing in life beyond my death. I look down at my body and contemplate the reincarnation that takes place from one generation to another. My father took form in me, in my children, in my sisters and their children; he will take form in all of his descendants, without limit as to numbers. He will take literally trillions of forms in their ova, sperm, and genes, spreading out in the form of all humanity. I am an ancestor.

But form is transmitted by other carriers than genes. My father thought, spoke, and wrote, thereby multiplying his forms in the framework of idea. Nothing better demonstrates transposing form than idea and its transmission between peoples. An idea, weightless and dimensionless, is formed within an aggregation of energy called "matter," an aggregation that has evolved through generative cycles. It is re-formed by consideration of the multiple forms of brain, expounded by a co-ordinated movement of atoms forming mouth and tongue, transmitted by atoms of exhaling air, all apparently without depleting the source-form of idea.

Forms of idea may transpose to electromagnetic waves, and spread over the earth's surface in an instant. They may re-form in brains, attached to listening ears, and be re-formed again by them to the infinite. They can multiply themselves through centuries by lying dormant in static forms of print, yet taking new form in minds and eyes that scan them anew. The ability of idea to expand and propagate is limitless; yet, as in the human embryo, the form of origin persists.

I sense my father's form in books and articles he wrote, in biographies about him, in conversations with men and women he influenced. In East Africa, I find my father's form in combinations of memory and intuition—in his love of wildness transposed to me, in the mental images of him that the wilderness surrounding me brings out. I find it in the wind and all that the wind touches, whenever my perception enables me to see.

There are nights when I dream of my father. He appears to me still alive. I see and sense him as clearly as I did before his death. I talk to him from the vantage gained through intervening years, assist him as he once assisted me. I wonder why we have stayed so long apart when we have had such easy access to each other. No experiences of life appear more realistic than these experiences of dream. Waking the next morning, I think of something Chuang-tzu said, to the effect that "When I was asleep, I dreamed I was a butterfly. Now that I am awake, I do not know whether I am a man who dreamed he was a butterfly, or a butterfly dreaming he is a man."

How are we to distinguish the difference between reality and dream? Dreams result from a relationship of atoms. So do our bodies. Before the advent of scientific thought, man recognized the difference between vision and substance, at least in his waking state. Now, substance itself is an illusion—electric charges related through vast distance, like infinitesimal suns and planets in the universe. Reality becomes impression, while space and matter are both diverse and one.

During my lifetime, I have watched dream turn into reality and reality into dream until I am convinced they do transpose beyond our realization. Dreams of flying as a boy, of flying the Atlantic as a youth, of sending rockets to the moon as a young man—all these are impossibilities come true. Not long ago I dreamed of camping in East African jungles and now I have been transported here by the dream of human flight. I see satellites orbiting above me, wild animals roaming about me, and the snows of Kilimanjaro white in night, and in this reality of dream, again I am dreaming—reaching planets and stars—of unrestricted travel back and forth through time, of making the temporal human form persist, of impossibilities compounded. Dream, thought, and vision are not restricted by bonds of time and space. Our individuality is universality condensed in a cosmic moment. Death is no more than the stuff of substance transposing to the stuff of dream.

Robert Goddard dreamed of reaching distant galaxies and connected his dreams to earthly speculation. Suppose man could find a way of putting himself in a state of suspended animation, of reducing his metabolic rate to zero in ice-rigid hibernation. Suppose he could devise a time-adjustable apparatus that would set procedures in motion to bring him out of his frozen state and back to normal functioning at some other point in time and space? Might he not then navigate to a life-blessed planet of a sunlike star?

Not long after I met Robert Goddard, I came to know Alexis Carrel's interest in human longevity. How much could man's life be extended by the control of diet, by replacing the blood plasma at intervals, by reducing the body's metabolic rate? The difference between Carrel's and Goddard's speculations was that of years to ages, but Carrel's ideas about suspended animation could be partially tested through laboratory experiments. I designed and constructed for him a centrifuge in which blood corpuscles could be held in suspension while their plasma was replaced. We discussed ways in which other experiments should be conducted.

Biological studies and experiments had increased my basic interest in fields of mysticism. The experience of war intensified this interest. I came to the conclusion that life's greatest values did not lie in results to be obtained through biological mechanics. After Alexis Carrel died in 1944, his Department of Experimental Surgery was closed. I did not again take part in organ-perfusion experiments for almost twenty years. By that time, fantasies of space travel and human longevity had markedly converged.

Mme Carrel had placed all her husband's papers under the custody of the Jesuit Fathers at Georgetown University, in Washington, D.C. After the war ended, she and I had packed them into about fifty wooden boxes. These boxes were eventually opened and their contents filed under the direction of Father Joseph Durkin, Professor of Historical Philosophy. The university assigned a special room for the purpose. At Father Durkin's invitation, I went to Georgetown to see the "Carrel Room" and to discuss the Carrel biography he was planning to write.

Soon after my arrival, Father Durkin introduced me to Lieutenant Vernon Perry and Dr. Theodore Malinin, who were studying Carrel's records and were themselves engaged in organ-perfusion experiments. They were carrying on their work in a basement assigned to the Tissue Bank Department of the Clinical Investigation Division of the Naval Medical Research Institute, at Bethesda, Maryland, using glass perfusion pumps blown to the same design I had developed for Carrel. They drove me from Georgetown to the institute to see one of the pumps in operation. It had been constructed for them by a master blower of the Corning Glass Works as part of an order for a dozen units costing five hundred dollars each. Perry said they had made a general survey of perfusion apparatuses and concluded that the one I had designed and built, more than a quarter-century before, would best suit their research program, but that the small size and high cost of the flask placed serious limits on the experiments they planned. The use of larger organs would be desirable. Inasmuch as glass fractured easily at low temperatures, they could not afford many replacements. As a result of our discussions, I began working on the design of a new glass-and-plastic apparatus that was more versatile and far cheaper.

The Navy cryobiological-perfusion-research program had the objective of creating a storage bank of human organs for transplantation. It had already been demonstrated that tissue cells could be frozen, held at low temperatures for months or years, and warmed to apparently normal-functioning condition. This had been thought impossible a generation earlier. If cells could be frozen and still live, why could not a similar process be applied successfully to organs?

Thus at the Naval Medical Research Institute, where I worked after World War II, the dreams of Carrel and Goddard met. If organs could be preserved alive in frozen state, why not entire bodies? And if human bodies could be frozen, then man's individual scale of time and distance would be revolutionized! Think of ice-stiff human beings hurtling, like meteors, through space, unconscious yet alive—products of earthly evolutionary epochs emigrating to universal vastness, mechanically clocked to become aware once millions of generations have come and gone on earth. Goddard wrote about such voyages in the closely guarded pages of his imaginings.

As our sciences demonstrate their capabilities, they proscribe their limits. At the same time that lenses probe the universe, they portray a limiting speed of light; and in studying the relatively simple cell, they encounter the body's unending complication. Our increasing knowledge of distance and time confronts us with barriers far more formidable than those encountered by previous generations. It is one thing to send space probes out past our solar system's planets. It is another to power and navigate spaceships through the light-years of galaxies. The accomplishment of freezing single cells into a condition of latent life is simpler, by orders of magnitude, than achieving the same result with an entire human body.

Our accomplishments of the past are minor in comparison with the accomplishments we dream about today, whether they be in longevity or space travel. Yet when I see a rocket rising from its pad, I think of how the most fantastic dreams come true, of how dreams have formed into matter and matter into dreams. Then I sense Goddard standing at my side, his human physical substance now ethereal, his dreams substantive. When I watched the fantastic launching of Apollo 8, carrying its three astronauts on man's first voyage to the moon, I thought about how the launching of a dream can be more fantastic still, for the material products of dreams are limited in a way dreams themselves are not. What sunbound astronaut's experience can equal that of Robert Goddard, whose body stayed on earth while he voyaged through galaxies?

Now that Goddard is dead, what difference does it make that his earthly individuality never left the ground in rocket flight? He thought of the stars; he became part of the stars. What physical fantasy of man can compare with my living memory of him—to my time-escaping vision? There is better proof of immortality than this; dream is life and life is dream transposing.

The crawling of a tick across my stomach converged my consciousness to the dry grass of Kimana in Kenya. I had converged to that spot in the jungle from eras and spaces past. I looked down at my body—my arms, my legs, my hands and feet. I am this momentary figure, this skin-covered body named "man," yet actually I extend throughout all infinity! I am all of my imaginings, my hopes and memories, my dreams, real and unrealized. In how many ways will I continue to exist? In my children, in my life stream, in memories, on printed pages, in my impact on the environment.

Observing life from a distance removes the fetishes of individuality. Like God, you look down on your intangibility as before you looked up to the intangibility called "God." You consider life's relationship to cosmic being, and wonder why the apparition of individuality exists. When you re-enter that individuality, you bring a new awareness with you. In man, in all of us, an awareness has developed that re-encompasses the universe from which life came, an awareness of beauty and love, and a knowledge of sensation, intuition, and the reaches beyond knowledge.

We are aware of our being, our inheritance, our environment, and that they combine to give us that awareness. Awareness is the achievement of man, because he finds himself endowed with the power of selection. It is the gift of God, because it is formed beyond man's control or understanding. As the miracle of awareness has evolved in our existence, intuition tells us it will continue to evolve, that the miracle of human life contains potentialities still more miraculous, that the miraculous is unconfined. In some future incarnation from our life stream, we may even understand the reason for our existence in forms of earthly life.

The growing knowledge of science does not refute man's intuition of the mystical. Whether outwardly or inwardly, whether in space or in time, the farther we penetrate the unknown, the vaster and more marvelous it becomes. Since man's intellect seems bound to man, at least in earthly guise, the search for the form of God begins in the form of man. The form of man is everything. What else is the form of God?

That night at Kimana, I grow aware of various forms of man and of myself. I am form and I am formless. I am life and I am matter, mortal and immortal. I am one and many—myself and humanity in flux. I extend a multiplicity of ways in experience and space. I am myself now, lying on my back in jungle grass, passing through the ether between satellites and stars. My aging body transmits an ageless life stream. Molecular and atomic replacement change life's composition. Molecules take part in structure and in training, countless trillions of them. After my death, the molecules of my being will return to the earth and the sky. They came from the stars. I am of the stars.

Genealogy

Bibliography

Index

THE
Lindbergh-Land
FAMILY

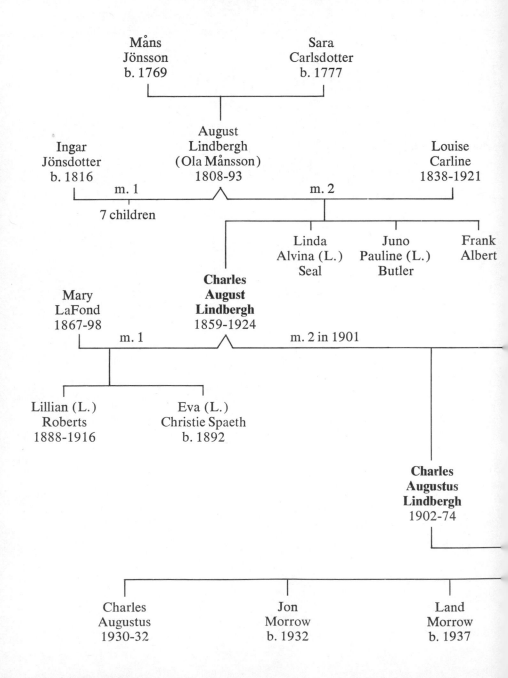

Måns
Jönsson
b. 1769

Sara
Carlsdotter
b. 1777

Ingar
Jönsdotter
b. 1816

August
Lindbergh
(Ola Månsson)
1808-93

Louise
Carline
1838-1921

m. 1

m. 2

7 children

Linda
Alvina (L.)
Seal

Juno
Pauline (L.)
Butler

Frank
Albert

Mary
LaFond
1867-98

**Charles
August
Lindbergh**
1859-1924

m. 1

m. 2 in 1901

Lillian (L.)
Roberts
1888-1916

Eva (L.)
Christie Spaeth
b. 1892

**Charles
Augustus
Lindbergh**
1902-74

Charles
Augustus
1930-32

Jon
Morrow
b. 1932

Land
Morrow
b. 1937

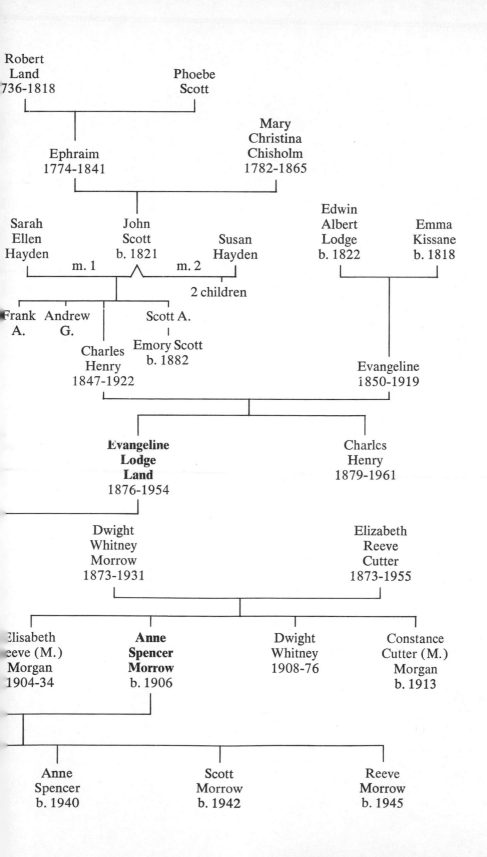

Robert
Land
1736-1818

Phoebe
Scott

Mary
Christina
Chisholm
1782-1865

Ephraim
1774-1841

Sarah
Ellen
Hayden

John
Scott
b. 1821

m. 1

Susan
Hayden

m. 2

Edwin
Albert
Lodge
b. 1822

Emma
Kissane
b. 1818

2 children

Frank
A.

Andrew
G.

Scott A.

Charles
Henry
1847-1922

Emory Scott
b. 1882

Evangeline
1850-1919

Evangeline
Lodge
Land
1876-1954

Charles
Henry
1879-1961

Dwight
Whitney
Morrow
1873-1931

Elizabeth
Reeve
Cutter
1873-1955

Elisabeth
Reeve (M.)
Morgan
1904-34

Anne
Spencer
Morrow
b. 1906

Dwight
Whitney
1908-76

Constance
Cutter (M.)
Morgan
b. 1913

Anne
Spencer
b. 1940

Scott
Morrow
b. 1942

Reeve
Morrow
b. 1945

Select Bibliography
of Charles A. Lindbergh's
Writings

Books

"We": The Famous Flier's Own Story of His Life and His Transatlantic Flight, Together with His Views on the Future of Aviation. With a Foreword by Myron T. Herrick. New York: G. P. Putnam's Sons, 1927.

The Culture of Organs. With Alexis Carrel. New York: P. B. Hoeber, 1938.

Of Flight and Life. New York: Charles Scribner's Sons, 1948.

The Spirit of St. Louis. New York: Charles Scribner's Sons, 1953.

The Wartime Journals of Charles A. Lindbergh. New York: Harcourt Brace Jovanovich, 1970.

Boyhood on the Upper Mississippi: A Reminiscent Letter. St. Paul: Minnesota Historical Society, 1972.

Articles

"Lindbergh's Own Story." *Current History* 26:513–22. July 1927.

"And Then I Jumped." *Saturday Evening Post* 200:6–7. July 23, 1927.

"Lindbergh Jumps Headfirst; Report of Northbound Mail Flight, November 3, 1926." *Review of Reviews* 76:202–4. August 1927.

"Making of an Air Mail Pilot." *World's Work* 54:472–81. September 1927.

"Lindbergh's Own Story of his New York–Paris Flight, as Published in the *New York Times,* May 23 and 24, 1927." New York, 1927. [Pamphlet]

"To Bogotá and Back by Air." *National Geographic Magazine* 53:529–601. May 1928.

"Address." National Education Association 1928:808–9.

"Air Transport." *Saturday Evening Post* 202:7. February 1, 1930.

"A Method for Washing Corpuscles in Suspension." *Science* 75:No. 1946:415–6. April 15, 1932.

"Collecting Micro-Organisms from the Arctic Atmosphere." By Fred C. Meier. "With Field Notes and Material" by Charles A. Lindbergh. *Scientific Monthly* 40:5–20. January 1935.

"The Culture of Whole Organs." With Alexis Carrel. *Science* 81:No. 2116:621–3. June 21, 1935.

"An Apparatus for the Culture of Whole Organs." *The Journal of Experimental Medicine* 62: No. 5:409–31. September 1, 1935.

"Aviation and War." Speech in Berlin, July 23, 1936. *Vital Speeches of the Day* 2:696. August 1, 1936.

"A Culture Flask for the Circulation of a Large Quantity of Fluid Medium." *The Journal of Experimental Medicine* 70:No. 3:231–8. September 1, 1939.

"Appeal for Isolation." Radio address, September 15, 1939. *Vital Speeches* 5:751–2. October 1, 1939. *Congressional Digest* 18:250–1. October 1939.

"What Our Decision Should Be." Radio address, October 13, 1939. *Vital Speeches* 6:57–9. November 1, 1939.

"Aviation, Geography and Race." *Reader's Digest* 35:64–7. November 1939.

"What Substitute for War?" *Atlantic Monthly* 165:305–8. March 1940. Abridged in *Reader's Digest* 36:43–7. May 1940.

"Our National Safety." Radio address, May 19, 1940. *Vital Speeches* 6:484–5. June 1, 1940.

"Appeal for Peace." Speech in Chicago, August 4, 1940. *Vital Speeches* 6:644–6. August 15, 1940.

"Strength and Peace." Radio address, October, 13, 1940. *Vital Speeches* 7:42–3. November 1, 1940.

"Plea for American Independence." Radio address, October 14, 1939. *Scribner's Commentator* 9:69–73. December 1940.

"The Radio Addresses of Colonel Charles A. Lindbergh." Pamphlet sold by *Scribner's Commentator* 1940.

"Impregnable America." Part of speech at Yale University, October 30, 1940. *Scribner's Commentator* 9:3–6. January 1941.

"Our Air Defense." Testimony before House Foreign Affairs Committee, January 23, 1941. *Vital Speeches* 7:241–2. February 1, 1941.

"We Are Not Prepared for War." Testimony before Senate Foreign Relations Committee, February 6, 1941. *Vital Speeches* 7:266–7. February 15, 1941.

"A Letter to Americans." *Collier's* 107:14–15+. March 29, 1941.

"We Cannot Win This War for England." Speech in New York City, April 23, 1941. *Vital Speeches* 7:424–6. May 1, 1941.

"Election Promises Should Be Kept." Speech at Madison Square Garden, New York City, May 23, 1941. *Vital Speeches* 7:482–3. June 1, 1941.

"For the Record." *Scribner's Commentator* 10:No. 5:7–13. August 1941.

"My Last Address." Excerpts from address at Fort Wayne, Indiana, October 3, 1941. *Time* 38:15. October 13, 1941.

"Time Lies With Us." Speech in Los Angeles, June 20, 1941. *Scribner's Commentator* 11:88–93. November 1941.

Address at Aero Club of Washington, December 17, 1949. Published as "A Lesson from the Wright Brothers." *Aviation Week* 51:42. December 26, 1949. "Man Cannot Thrive Indefinitely in the Hot-House Atmosphere We Are Creating." *U.S. Air Services* 35:No. 1:11–13. January 1950.

"Skeptics Ten Years Ago, Too." Excerpt from address, February 6, 1941. *U.S. News & World Report* 30:64. February 23, 1951.

Acceptance speech for Guggenheim Medal, New York City, January 25, 1954. Published as "Honors Night Dinner Address." *Aeronautical Engineering Review.* 13:48–51, 87. March 1954. "I Have Stated a Problem: You Have a Right to Ask Me for a Solution."

U.S. Air Services 39:No. 3:17–9. March 1954. "The Future Character of Man." *Vital Speeches* 20:293–5. March 1, 1954. Variant versions: "Fourth Dimension of Survival." *Saturday Review* 37:11–12+. February 27, 1954. "Survival Versus the Atom." *Science of Mind* 27: No. 7:1–5. July 1954. "But How About Man." *Reader's Digest* 64:1–2. May 1954.

"Our Best Chance to Survive." *Saturday Evening Post* 227:25. July 17, 1954.

"Thoughts of a Combat Pilot." *Saturday Evening Post* 227:20–1+. October 2, 1954. Also published as "Church in the Gun-Sight." *Reader's Digest* 65:11–14. December 1954.

"Is Civilization Progress?" *Reader's Digest* 85:67–74. July 1964.

"An Apparatus for the Pulsating Perfusion of Whole Organs." With V. P. Perry, T. I. Malinin, and G. H. Mouer. *Cryobiology* 3:No. 3:252–60. 1966.

"The Wisdom of Wildness." *Life* 63:8–10. December 22, 1967. Also published in *Reader's Digest* 92:83–7. April 1968.

"Letter from Lindbergh." *Life* 67:60A–1. July 4, 1969.

"The Way of Wildness." *Reader's Digest* 99:90–3. November 1971.

"Feel the Earth." *Reader's Digest* 101:62–5. July 1972.

"Lessons from the Primitive." *Reader's Digest* 101:147–51. November 1972.

"Organ Culture and Perfusion by the Carrel Method." With Theodore I. Malinin. Pp. 47–67.

Forewords and Prefaces to Books

Foreword to *Listen! The Wind,* by Anne Morrow Lindbergh. New York: Harcourt, Brace, 1938.

Preface to *The Voyage to Lourdes,* by Alexis Carrel. New York: Harper & Brothers, 1950.

Introduction to *Winning the War with Ships,* by Emory Scott Land. New York: Robert M. McBride, 1958.

Preface to *This High Man: The Life of Robert H. Goddard,* by Milton Lehman. New York: Farrar, Straus, 1963.

Foreword, plus two appendices, to *Challenge to the Poles: Highlights of Arctic and Antarctic Aviation,* by John Grierson. Hamden: Archon Books, 1964.

Introduction to *Maui: The Last Hawaiian Place.* San Francisco and New York: Friends of the Earth, 1970.

Foreword to *Vanguard: A History,* by Constance McLaughlin Green and Milton Lomask. Washington, D.C.: NASA, 1970.

Foreword to *Alexis Carrel: Visionary Surgeon,* by W. Stirling Edwards and Peter D. Edwards. Springfield, Ill.: Thomas, 1971.

Foreword to *Lindbergh of Minnesota,* by Bruce L. Larson. New York: Harcourt Brace Jovanovich, 1973.

Foreword to *Carrying the Fire: An Astronaut's Journeys,* by Michael Collins. New York: Farrar, Straus & Giroux, 1974.

Foreword to *The Gentle Tasaday: A Stone Age People in the Philippine Rain Forest,* by John Nance. New York: Harcourt Brace Jovanovich, 1975.

Index

417

Lindbergh, Charles A. (*continued*)
17–18, 38, 41, 88, 104, 108–16, 118,
121–22, 129, 130, 202, 263, 335; as
Army Air Corps officer, 19, 22–23,
117, 147, 188–91, 218, 247, 325, 373;
as Army Air Service cadet, 9–10, 63,
64–66, 117, 121, 147, 246–47, 389;
and aviation, commercial, 14–15,
16, 32, 66–72, 78, 80–88, 96–116,
141–42, 220, 259, 266–67, 269, 310,
316, 317–19, 325, 330, 335; and
aviation, early experiences with, 9,
55, 58, 63–64, 121, 154, 216, 262–63,
265–66, 296–304, 310, 321; background and childhood of, 3–9, 44–63,
120, 296, 308–10, 327, 384, 395;
biological research projects of, 16–
17, 18, 21, 24–25, 129–39, 325, 331,
369–70, 376, 398–400; in China,
250–55; in East Africa, 36–37, 38–
39, 268–81, 283–84, 379–82, 386–88,
397, 398, 401–02; environmental
activities of, 32, 35; European military aviation surveys of, 19 and *n.*,
20, 22, 146–48, 163–69, 170 and *n.*,
171, 178–85, 240–44; as farmer, 8,
35, 61–63; Illiec home of, 21, 161–
63, 178, 331, 364–67, 371–74; in
India, 20, 148–51, 368; kidnapping
of son of, 17, 18, 139–40, 142; marriage and family of, 16, 18, 123–28,
130, 132, 140, 143–45, 154, 158, 187,
220, 295, 306, 325, 329, 330, 333;
as military aviation consultant, 23–
31, 196, 215–30, 237–40, 245, 247,
249, 344–50, 382–83; move to
England, 18, 145; and navigation, 68,
77–78, 85–87, 93, 256; as Pacific
combat pilot, 26–27, 29–30, 40, 195–
202, 207–13, 247–48, 267, 268,
289–91, 292–93, 299, 305, 353–56,
359, 361; and parachute jumping,
298–99, 300–01, 303; in Philippines,
34–36; and press, 16, 17, 18, 74–75,
76–77, 118, 122, 123, 125–28, 139–
40, 142–46, 154, 158, 179, 187–88,
215, 319, 326; receipt of German
medal, 181 and *n.*; return to America, 187–88, 373; and rockets and
space travel, xvii, 15, 31, 38, 159,
325, 334–44, 350–53, 357, 381–83,
398, 400–01; *Spirit of St. Louis*

flight of, xviii, 11–14, 70–81, 84, 117,
154, 259, 262, 299, 310–18, 328, 340,
342, 361, 366, 394–96; on survey
flight for Atlantic air route, 18, 113–
15, 140; on survey flight to Latin
America and Caribbean, 14, 88–96,
107–08; on survey flight to Orient,
16, 109–10, 228, 238, 250, 291–92,
325; U.S. tour of, 14, 81–83, 117,
318–20, 327; world tour of, 226–30;
World War II activities and isola-
tionism of, xvii, 22–23, 159–61, 163–
94; writings of, xiii–xiv, xvi–xvii,
137 *n.*, 226, 316
Lindbergh, Charles A., values and
thoughts on: America, 156, 157–59,
176–78, 187, 214, 233–36, 255–60,
263–65; aviation, 20, 28, 129–30,
147–48, 158, 177–78, 283, 307, 336;
civilizations, 20, 30–43, 91–92, 129,
148–49, 151 and *n.*, 152, 159, 172,
177–78, 187, 220, 222, 261, 263, 265,
272–74, 282–88, 320–22, 330, 352,
379–81; communication, 40–41;
competition and survival, 154, 198,
201–02, 203, 206, 213, 225, 235, 265,
267, 269, 281, 292; conflict between
instinct and intellect, 5, 39–43, 217,
286–87, 292–307, 395–96, 401–02;
coral reefs, 195–98, 201; democracy,
194, 233; dreams, 397–401; environment, 31–36, 46, 120–21, 159, 213,
225, 228, 305–06; European and
Asian countries, 145, 147–48, 155–
58, 160–61, 164–68, 170, 172, 174,
175–78, 179, 186–87, 228–35, 244–
45, 291–92, 349–50; fame, 12–14,
79–80, 89–90, 122, 310–25, 326–30;
fear, 296–300; freedom, 39–41, 150,
285; heredity, 31, 32–33, 42–43,
118–20, 122, 150, 153, 159, 280, 281,
284, 305–06, 331; individual, the,
128, 157, 197–98, 280, 285, 287–88,
293–95, 305–07, 320–22, 361–63,
375, 378, 385, 386–87, 390–93, 396,
398, 401; isolation when flying, 85–
86, 324; life and death, 5–6, 26–27,
36, 134–35, 263, 280, 287, 331, 359,
376–78, 383–402; life stream, 36–43,
129–30, 157, 195, 305–07, 332, 378,
390–92, 396–97, 401–02; love, 128;
mail, 329–30; marriage, 16, 118–29;